Italy
Unpacked & Unwrapped

A foreigner in
Italy's Green Heart

. . . .

'*You may have the universe*
if I may have Italy.'

Giuseppe Verdi

To all who have made my life in Italy so special

Italy
Unpacked & Unwrapped

A foreigner in
Italy's Green Heart
. . . .

First published in the UK by Graham Hofmann in 2023

Copyright © Graham Hofmann 2023

Graham Hofmann has asserted his right to be identified as the author of this work in accordance with the Copyright, Designs & Patents Act 1988.

Cover design, page layout and typography by orangecircle
www.orangecc.co.uk

INTRODUCTION

About the Author

· ·

Graham Hofmann

· ·

As a working-class lad from South Yorkshire, England, Graham never imagined that one day he would own a house in Italy. A house in Italia! A house purchased with nothing more than a little Italian phrasebook in his back pocket. With the bewildering naivety and excitement of a small child; he took the plunge. He gambled that all would be fine, what could possibly go wrong?

His first book, Lorenzo's Vest, tells of his time having a place in Italy as a holiday home. The book reaching out of the region of Umbria, its exquisite joys and frustrations, to give the reader insights into Italy's recent history as a nation, its politics and fallibilities.

This second book, Italy Unpacked & Unwrapped, takes you beyond the experiences of a tourist and part time visitor. Now retired from a professional life in education, Graham enjoys a full life in the stunningly beautiful Green Heart of Italy – Umbria. The seductive power of Italy complete.

You can contact him by email: ghofmann732@btinternet.com

You can also follow him on Facebook.

Also on Facebook: Mystical Umbria

CONTENTS

....

The Italians

Sublime yet exasperating. Italy is a country of riddles.
How can a culture that gave us the Renaissance have
produced the mafia?
And what made a people so concerned with bella
figura - what others think of them - choose Silvio
Berlusconi as their leader?

. . . .

John Hooper

Voices in my Head

....

"Italy is fascinating, if perturbing. Brits, Yanks, Germans and Scandinavians gaze on it with rapt suspicion, as if they were staring at a woman who is too good-looking to be true.'

....

Beppe Severgnini – La Bella Figura

Italy is now my chosen place to live. Although, if I'm really going to fit in, I guess I should say that Umbria is my chosen place to live. Better still, Gubbio. No, not Gubbio, the village of Colpalombo.

Surely Graham, aren't you being just a little too pedantic?

No, listen, I'm not. This is important for you to know and understand. In the mind of an Italian, the region is more important than the state, your local town more important than the region. The village perhaps more important than the town. For an Italian, your loyalty rests with the bell tower, the main piazza. It's even given a term to describe it, that deep attachment to your community – campanilismo. Understand this and you've moved on from being a tourist. You are starting to know Italians; you're starting to understand Italia.

Yes, I know I'm not a true Italian and will never be. The Britishness in me will always be there. Although my Britishness has never been quite that straightforward; the son of a German father and an English mother. Just to add a little twist to my background, a German father who came to the UK as a POW in 1945.

So, I'm a foreigner living in Italy. British/German, but no longer just another tourist. I'm the inglese who lives in the little hamlet of Case Colle, close to the village of Colpalombo. Those who know me by name, I'm Ghrem, Ghreme or Carlo. You know who he is, the inglese that lives next to Aldo and Benedetta.

What I'd really like to be identified as is British European. Although the strong tide of Brexit may make swimming in European colours, blue and yellow, just a little more problematic.

I guess you could label me as a lifestyle immigrant. I'm in Italy purely by choice, no economic necessity and certainly no hint of political refugee. Expat: NO! I'm an immigrant, a foreigner living amongst Italians. From the moment of buying my house as a holiday home, the welcome from my Italian neighbours was warm, inviting and totally accepting. The neighbours who very soon became close friends. Without their generous help and support, the experience of having a holiday home in the hills of Umbria would have been completely different. The thought of moving here far more problematic, a much bigger risk.

The final decision to move to Italy came as I was making one of my long drives back to the UK. The drive gave me time to think. Having two homes was really a luxury. Why do I need two? Both houses cost money, surely it would be logical to just have one. With the decision made, all I had to do is tell my daughters that I intended to abandon them. Guilt, it's a heavy burden.

My daughters' response to the news of my decision to abandon them: 'Do it Dad, it makes perfect sense. You can enjoy the best of Italy and return at any time to enjoy the best of the UK – a perfect combination.' Very true, a combination with Germany sandwiched between. I'd already established myself with the local community of Colpalombo. I had Italian neighbours who had become close friends, who were more than willing to give help and support to their vicino inglese. In fact, for some time they'd been asking me when I would make the move.

So, the Arrivederci Inghilterra party took place, my house in the UK was sold, the van packed to bursting; I set up my life in Italy. And now I'm here, a British European living in the hills and mountains of Umbria.

What should I tell you about my Italian life, about the Italians, about the country? Should I simply focus on La Dolce Vita, Italy as Il Bel Paese? A country seasoned with a never-ending number of stereotypes. Do I simply feed misguided foreigners with even more dreamlike perceptions? Italy is more complex than that. People need to have a glimpse at the realities of life in Italy. Obviously let people know about the beauty of the country, but there's also the need to explore its antagonisms and frustrations. There's the need to try and let people know what makes Italy, Italia.

Some have described Italy as a living museum, and yet as a nation the country is young, only coming into being as one political entity in 1861. The birth of Italy traumatic, bloody, and resisted by many. The Catholic Church only officially recognising the state of Italy in 1929, the country then under the dictatorship of Benito Mussolini. A relationship of mutual convenience between Catholicism and Fascism that, in just a few short years, resulted in complete disaster for the Italian people.

Industrialisation came late to Italy, the sprawl of urbanisation really only a feature of a few Italian cities and towns. The late arrival of economic development resulted in many Italians leaving their country of birth, seeking what they hoped would be a better life in other parts of the world, especially the USA. I guess, as a result of the misfortunes of those who came before, each region of modern Italy has, by design or fate, been able to retain the distinctive character of its buildings and culture.

To really know Italy, I ask you to put to one side the easily fallen into trap of romanticized sentimentality, the glory that was Italy, an Italy of the 'Grand Tour'. The beauty of Italy, so delightful to explore and savour today, in many ways only remains because of the grinding poverty found in most areas of the country in the not-so-distant past. It's easy to forget that the relative economic prosperity of modern Italy, really only came about from the early 1960s onwards.

I remember when I first visited Rome, I walked open-mouthed. I found myself walking through an open-air, living museum. How could so much of the past still remain? A modern city in the 21st century, and yet I'm seeing and touching sites stretching back to the time of the Roman Empire. I was completely mesmerised. It was as though I was walking in slow motion, every single step I took transporting me to some ancient glory. The history lessons of my childhood and the films from Hollywood given life. I've returned to Rome many times since. I still find the 'Eternal City' awe-inspiring.

From the ashes of WW2, Italy made a surprisingly rapid economic recovery. The recovery bolstered by the fact that a good deal of Italy's industry remained intact. The country also had a cheap labour force, especially from the south.

But I guess the crucial factor was the support given to Italy via the Marshall Plan, economic aid coming from the USA. The aid not given out of some quality of benevolence on the part of America, it was one part of the plan to create a European bulwark against the growing power of the Soviet Union. It was a time when the west, the USA in particular, had an almost paranoid fear of the likely spread of Communism. The political shape of Italy would be very much influenced by what the USA was willing to tolerate.

The enticement of rapid economic growth from the 1960s through to the 1980s, did, for a time, threaten to destroy what attracts so many people to Il Bel Paese. The potential disfigurement of the country was especially felt in the south, where unregulated building threatened to completely sweep away much of what was beautiful. Recognition that all was in danger of being lost has now slowed down such 'development', but the risk has not completely gone. There's also a recognition that something has to be done about the migration of people from the land to the cities, from the old to the new. Attempts now being made at both a local and national level to redress the balance.

The desire to conserve the old while aspiring to the new, is a bit of a conundrum for Italy. Italians are well aware of the natural and architectural beauty of the country, they're incredibly proud of it, fully accepting that both have to be protected and nurtured. And yet, at the same time, there are thousands of houses across the whole of Italy left empty in the countryside and in villages, almost impossible to sell. Thousands of houses simply left to decay and eventually become derelict.

My closest Italian neighbour, Gina, died at the age of 93 several years ago, what was her home is still vacant. The property is for sale but with absolutely no interest shown. I have the impression that my Italian neighbours and friends still don't really understand why I would buy an older property, in a rural setting, some miles from the closest town. It's very rare for Italians to buy old houses, however grand and ornate they may appear to be. There are exceptions, obviously, but from my experience most Italians want to live in or near to a town with all the modern amenities that brings. Why would you buy something old? Something that, potentially, could cost a large amount of money to restore. Those who do have money are more likely to ignore the buildings that many foreigners eagerly fall in love with, instead choosing to build something from scratch, even if that takes an excessive number of years. Something modern and new, but with a style of the old to fit in with its rural landscape. All too often you will come across houses half completed and then apparently left. Others almost completely finished externally, with just internal fittings to install, again apparently abandoned, waiting for nature to move in and occupy.

So, Italy is a relatively new country in terms of nationhood. As you're well aware, a country with incredible beauty. A country in many ways unique. Italy, easy to spot on any world map, its booted shape dangling down from the Alps in the north, stretching steadily south towards Africa, the Mediterranean to one side, the Adriatic to the other. And just like any other nation, a country with contradictions and problems to resolve.

It's this country that I want to share with you. Italy, especially Umbria, as seen through the eyes of a straniero (foreigner). The sheer exuberance that Italians have for life, the welcome and friendship that makes this such a special place to live. What follows as you turn each page, is my particular view of life in Umbria, of Italy and Italians

I'll explore the many hilltop towns and villages of Umbria, each one just as delightful as the next. The stunning geography of the country that at times simply takes your breath away. But a geography that can be incredibly fragile, at times a geography that literally shakes the ground, delivering death and destruction.

The friends that I've made, both foreign and Italian. The adventures I've had both in Italy and elsewhere. Yes, at times I do leave Umbria – Italy.

And the politics. From moving here to live, what felt like rational certainties have been completely sent tumbling out of balance. I am, of course, talking about Brexit. But not just Brexit, the rise of nationalism generally, including its rise in Italy. And, I guess, no discussion about politics could leave out the impact of Trump. I remember in my first book making a statement about Italy as a country and its politics:

'It's a country that's not sure of where it was, not sure of where it is, and uncertain of where it's going. A body politic that is as fractured as Italian geology.'

I guess I'd fallen into the trap of regarding other countries, the UK for example, even with whatever faults you may want to identity, as being more rational and logical. It's certainly a perception that many of my Italian friends and neighbours had. How wrong we were. The quote above, almost in its entirety, could now so easily apply to either the UK or the USA. How quickly what we once took for granted can change. So, at times, the book will inevitably leave the borders of Italy, dissecting Brexit and Trump, then returning to look at the rise of nationalism in Italy itself.

Unfortunately, since last writing, death visited Italy again. In 2016, another earthquake, killing hundreds, destroying buildings and leaving many homeless. But more death was to come.

The year 2020 delivered something totally unexpected. Something that at first I totally discounted, it would soon 'blow over' – Covid-19. All of you will have your own stories and experiences to tell. By the time you read this book, we may have moved on, Covid-19 and its impact in the past. A future free from the virus. Perhaps, at best, a virus we have been able to accommodate and live with; vaccines enabling that to happen.

Phew, what a sombre interlude to introduce you to the book. Keep faith with me, the book is not loaded down with doom and gloom, far from it. This is Italy – ITALIA!

Italy, a sea of sunflowers from July into August. From snow covered Alpine peaks in the north, the mountains of the Apennines running almost its entire length, to the crystal-clear seas of the south. A country smothered in olive groves and grape vines, delicious foods to savour and refreshing wines to drink. Villages and towns that appear to have stood still in time, their history locked in and preserved. A country of architectural treasures, from Venice floating in its lagoon, to Pisa and it's leaning tower, Renaissance Florence, Siena and the Palio, the majesty that is Rome, chaotic Naples, the trulli of Puglia, the islands of Sardinia, Elba, and Sicily. The country is quite simply a treasure trove of delights. The Italian people adding to its colour and warmth. And the place where I live, Umbria – The Green Heart of Italy, the medieval splendour of Gubbio at its core. The frantic emotion that is the Ceri on the 15th of May, only second in fame to the Palio in Siena.

I always have voices in my head when I'm writing. What do I put in the book, what do I leave out? The little voices in my head prodding me to change this and to add that. This time you should go into more detail about the mafia Graham. The mafia are important to the story of Italy. But could it frighten people away? No, it's fine, the different mafia are only one part of Italy.

Luigi Barzini, when commenting on foreigners writing about Italy:

'The best books on Italy often contain brilliant flashes of intuition and some revealing truths, in a clutter of clichés, superficial appraisals, supine acceptance of preconceived notions, wrong information, and misspelled Italian words.'

If he were still around today he would certainly prove to be an exacting critic. Could I withstand the disembowelment? I'll do my best not to disappoint him.

I hope the book feeds your desire to know more about Italy. Despite its many frailties (the country having no less and no more than any other nation), Italy remains simply enchanting. There is something about Italy that gets under your skin, it seduces you. Italy becomes your lover. It entraps you, teases you, pleasures you; at times tormenting you. It's a lover that can totally frustrate you, at times even anger you. But still, you desire to be there. Italy breathes life into you. However, there are also times when you want to escape. I'm lucky enough to be able to do just that. Italy doesn't mind, she knows I can't resist her. She knows I will soon return.

By turning each page, I hope that the book allows you to unpack and unwrap Italy, looking at the country with knowing eyes. Hopefully, it will do more than simply feed your appetite for La Dolce Vita. Think of it as an invitation to slow down and step back, to have an understanding of Italy beyond that of a tourist. Perhaps asking questions about Italy that you had never thought to ask, opening doors that you'd never before thought to open. Marvel at its beauty, enjoy the history captured in its towns and villages, and be open-eyed to the Italy of today. I hope that the book is a realistic celebration of Italian life, especially life in Umbria. My rambling observations, as they often are, mixed in with a critical view on a world beyond the borders of Italy. A world that none of us can escape.

What you'll read in the pages that follow is all based on fact, real experiences, real places, real people and genuine emotions. At times it may feel that I've simply fed stereotypes. I can assure you that I've done the best I can not to fall into that trap. To have simply told you how wonderful life is here in Italy would be a disservice to you and wouldn't be honest to Italy and its people. Obviously,

I wouldn't have chosen to be here if I'd not fallen for the country and the Italian way of life. But I hope I've been as honest as I can be about the frustrations, antagonisms and annoyances of moving on from simply being a foreign tourist. Some of the words put down in print, the story of my life in Italy so far, are based on memory, hopefully recorded with some accuracy. Much of the book telling of my life here, its unexpected twists and turns as they happened. And, just as important, it tells of events in other parts of the world and their impact on my life in Umbria.

Do It!

It's a terrible thing, I think, in life to wait until you're
ready. I have this feeling now that actually no one is
ever ready to do anything. There's almost no such
thing as ready. There's only now. And you may as
well do it now. I mean, I say that confidently as if I'm
about to bungee jump or something – I'm not. I'm
not a crazed risk taker. But I think that, generally
speaking, now is as good a time as any.

. . . .

Hugh Laurie

CHAPTER ONE

Tanti Auguri!

....

'Few countries are as comprehensively associated with happiness as Italy. Just the mention of its name brings to mind sunny days, blue skies, glittering seas; delicious, comforting food; good-looking, well-dressed people; undulating hills topped with cypress trees and museums crammed with the best Western art.'

....

John Hooper – The Italians

Arms are put in, arms are taken out, people turn around, hands joined with others, a circle of friends and neighbours rush towards each other, hot bodies clashing in fits of laughter and song.

At almost 2.30 in the morning, another request rings out from my Italian neighbours and friends for all of us to go crazy, yet again, with the Hokey Cokey. By now I've lost count of how many times the dance, totally new to the Italians, has been requested since we took them through the steps several hours before.

Drink is still flowing. The dance floor is full. The moon is bright, the sky is full of stars. Early morning is warm. The three Giovanni sit side by side observing, commenting on those out on the terracotta tiled dance floor, the temporary area for dancing being just one part of my neighbour's garden: that neighbour being Aldo.

The garden can be found in the little hamlet of Case Colle, just over one kilometre from my local village, my borgo - Colpalombo. The community of Colpalombo just ten kilometres (six miles) from the medieval town of Gubbio, this historic gem standing proud in the north of Umbria - The Green Heart of Italy.

We're celebrating what some may regard as significant staging posts. For me it's – 'I can't believe I'm sixty already?' Kara, my elder daughter is 30. Along with Kara, it's the birthday of my brother-in-law, Peter, aged 70, and Sam, the partner of my younger daughter Lucy, he's also 30. A birthday party that demands a birthday cake big enough for a combined total of 190 years. Although we had an extraordinarily enormous cake, I'm not sure that we had quite that number of candles to blow out.

At its height some 80 people are at the party, a party that began at around 7.30 in the evening. Out of the 80 only 11 are foreign, the rest of the celebrating assembly from the little hamlet of Case Colle and the village of Colpalombo. This is a real community event. The planning only having taken place a few weeks before.

After lengthy debate with Aldo and his daughters the decision is made, probably more by them than by me, that the grand event will be held in Aldo's garden rather than my own. My garden only separated from that of Aldo by the now vacant garden and house that had once belonged to Gina.

Gina had been my closest Italian neighbour, always active until the very last year of her life at the age of 93. Each day she would be out early, tending her small vegetable plot, maintaining a precarious balance with the support of a walking stick. At times, as she shuffled over the ground, exchanging the walking stick for the low green fence that separated my garden from her own. Almost always with her head covered by a flowered scarf, large dark sunglasses, dark dress well below her knees, heavy, thick, dark chocolate brown stockings, a rather chunky cardigan, and, for want of a better description, sensible shoes. Always the possibility that there may be a stumble, but thankfully a fall never came.

Greetings and goodbyes were always a close and warm affair. My hands clasped between her own, Gina's hands aged by the years and roughened by working on the land. After kisses are exchanged to both cheeks, questions about how things are, and always comments are returned about health. Gina giving quite detailed accounts of ailments that have come with age, some of the Italian understood by me, most not. My leaving for the return journey back to the UK, always a rather melancholy happening. Gina asking when I would be back, my reply always followed by her releasing the gentle hold of my hands . With one hand pointing to the sky, she would tell me that she would no longer be here, God will have taken me. I responded by giving her another gentle hug, guessing that she would at least make the century.

All others knew Gina as Farfallina (Little Butterfly), the name apparently appointed to her because in her younger days she was always busy, never still, constantly flitting around. In the end, she was right. On my departure, always telling me that God would take her before I returned. I just couldn't imagine it happening. In my mind, she would always be my closest Italian neighbour.

So, back to il grande evento! The venue for the birthday celebrations is decided. Now we need to think about food, drink, and entertainment. Brief discussion takes place about paying someone to provide catering, but this is soon talked down by the middle daughter of Aldo, Paola. She is very keen that we should all work together, all of us preparing food. There will be any number of people only too happy to join in. So, in the end we are agreed. Paola, along with other Italian friends and neighbours, will prepare a variety of Italian food. We will prepare food with a more English slant. We, meaning myself and my sister. I'll be paying the bill, so all that's required now is to go on a massive food and drink shop.

Paola's partner, Stefano, knows a catering warehouse, close to Gubbio, where we can buy drink in volume. And so, the following day Stefano joins me in my search of all the drink we will need to quench the thirst of 80 plus people. We stand in a large open warehouse packed with everything required to satisfy your catering needs, from every size of pot and pan, from every type of alcohol to every type of soft drink. Every item you would need to set up a bar, to every item you would need to set up a mobile kitchen. This is an Aladdin's catering emporium. My Italian is now much improved, but I'm still grateful to have Stefano by my side. I really don't want things to get lost in translation and find that I need a heavy goods licence to transport my misunderstood Italian home.

We walk up and down the aisles packed with hard and soft drinks, an employee from the emporium following along, keeping a note of what we want and quantity. Big five litre bottles of red and white wine are placed on the list, along with a variety of spirits and soft drinks, lots of water included, acqua frizzante e naturale. Although in general Italians are not big beer drinkers, Stefano assures me that once the party is in full flow and they have had their fill of wine, beer will be in demand. So, to ensure that we can satisfy the need for beer, we place five litre mini kegs on the list. Hundreds of paper plates are added, along with cups, knives, forks, and spoons. Done, the list is complete. Just one thing that we appear to have forgotten. The employee keeping a tally points out that we need the appropriate equipment to get the beer from the kegs. Apparently, we can hire the equipment from the emporium. The list is now definitely complete.

I can't remember how many kegs of beer, bottles of spirits, water and five litre bottles of wine we had, but apart from the passenger and driver's seat, the car is full. A print-out is handed to me with everything listed, prices per item and total, just as you would expect. I also expect that I will now have to pay. But to my total surprise, as I hand over my credit card, I'm told that I have no need to pay yet. No, a credit card is not required at this point. You can pay when you bring back unused beer and wine. I guess it works on a similar principle to sale or return, although here no money has been handed over upfront. With the car full, we drive away. Not one single euro has been exchanged. Nobody has asked for my address or contact details. The whole process has taken place based on trust. Trust in a total stranger, me the straniero, the uomo inglese. Trust that I will return with unused items, or not, and pay the final bill. Perhaps they know Stefano, so it's not quite a totally optimistic trust in the straniero. But Stefano is as surprised as me, he doesn't know anyone in the warehouse, and they don't know him. Italia, I love it!

Paola has already told me that we can hire trestle tables and benches from L'Associazione Pro Loco di Colpalombo, the local community organisation. The village of Colpalombo can be found to the back of my house, its centre medieval in character and just a ten-minute walk downhill from where I live. It sits on its own hill, but then surrounded by other hills covered in oak forests. In the near distance, the mountains of the Apennines. A region rich in tartufo (truffle), cervo (deer) and cinghiale (wild boar). It really is a wonderful place to be, to find yourself and simply escape.

The winter months bring deep snow on the higher mountains, with the possibility of cross-country skiing on Monte Cucco, the mountain rising to a height of 1,566m (5,138ft), making it the highest point in Northern Umbria. The Apennine Mountains, including Monte Cucco, clear to see as you step out of my house and into the garden.

Just out of interest, the Apennine Mountains stretch over 1,200 kilometres (746 miles) along almost the whole length of Italy. Corno Grande (Great Horn) is the highest point, outside the Italian Alps, found in the Abruzzo region to the south of Umbria. Part of the Gran Sasso massif, Corno Grande reaches up to a height of 2,912m (9,554ft). A fantastic place for walking and a great place to find small, uncrowded, ski resorts.

The months of April through to June bring the colourful plenty of spring flowers. Thick, white, mystical mists hang over the land; valleys and villages hidden in the early morning. But by the time of preparations for Easter, the cold of winter has long gone. Although snow may still be found on the higher mountains, crisp and clean against a deep blue sky, Umbria is already pleasantly warm. It feels like the countryside and the people have quickly come out of hibernation. Oak forests are alive again, carpeting hillsides in green. In every town the streets are decorated with millions of flower petals, part of religious celebrations. The elaborate and painstakingly put together pieces of flower artwork spread out over the ground, waiting to be visited and judged, but gone in a matter of days. A time to be out and active, a time for long walks before the heat of summer arrives.

The 15th of May brings people from all over Italy to join with foreign tourists and the Eugubini of Gubbio for the colourful and frenetic race of the Ceri. The Ceri being the most important event of the whole year for Umbria, perhaps only coming second to the Palio in Siena as a national event. The Ceri being so significant that the symbol for Umbria comes from the race. The symbol made up from a representation of the three ceri, the three columns, carried at speed, on heavy wooden platforms, through the streets of Gubbio before the frantic climb up to the resting place of Sant' Ubaldo, a Bishop of Gubbio from the 12th century.

June passes into the hot summer months of July and August when life is forced to be lived at a slower pace. The summer a time of endless festivals of food, live music, song and, obviously, wine; drinking for the Italians never done to excess. Umbria Jazz Festival, an extravaganza of live music in the medieval heart of Perugia. The music in Perugia followed by the Trasimeno Blues Festival, its backdrop being the beautiful Lago Trasimeno. A time of slow meals in the garden with neighbours and friends, the food and drink set out on long tables sheltered from the heat of the sun by the shade of olive trees. A time of promenading in the local town, every age group partaking, my local town of Gubbio being a medieval charm, a total delight.

August is the month when Italians take their annual holiday. For most, a two-week holiday with the 15th, Ferragosto, in the middle, a national Italian holiday. The 15th is also known as Assumption Day. This is an important holy day in the Catholic calendar, celebrating the Assumption of the Virgin Mary into Heaven. But the national holiday has its origins long lost in the distance of time, long before the birth of the Catholic faith. Some suggest that it's associated with Emperor Augustus in 18 B.C, Ferragosto taking its name from the Latin Fariae Augusti or the festivals of Augustus. In truth, its origins are probably more related to the need to have a break from hard agricultural work. As a tourist, be prepared for the main resorts and cities to be crowded and hot. Also be aware that many smaller shops, restaurants and bars could be closed. Well, this is holiday time, what would you expect? And do not be surprised to find a note taped to the door: Chiuso per ferie (Closed for holidays).

The start of September finds most Italians returning to work, the days still warm, even hot. The weeks of mid-September are busy with la vendemmia (the grape harvest). The main areas of wine production in Umbria are found around Orvieto and Montefalco, with Montefalco producing the most famous wine of the region, Sagrantino. The hills and mountains surrounding Gubbio not really that ideal for large scale wine making. September moves into autumn, different shades of green begin to be exchanged for crisp varieties of red, gold, orange and brown. October brings the first smell of wood burning stoves, oak logs having been gathered throughout the summer months, stored, neatly stacked, and then left to dry. The first few weeks can still be quite warm, more rain than before, but still pleasant enough for long walks, promenading in Gubbio and days sat in the garden.

The last weeks of the month have a definite autumn feel, the days are shorter, and the evening air carries the slightest hint of burning oak. Gubbio prepares for the Truffle Festival, the festival turning the medieval centre of the town into an open-air street market. The tartufo is obviously the main celebrity, alongside stands offering not only a wide range of local produce, but also delights from as far distant as Sicilia (Sicily). It's an occasion to allow your senses to be tempted by the sight, smell and taste of wild boar salami, the many varieties of pecorino cheese made from the milk of sheep, parmigiano that's better than anything you have tasted before, olives of green and black, wine, local and national liqueurs, hand-made chocolates, fresh pasta, roasted chestnuts, Italian pastries – the temptations are endless.

During the last weeks of October, moving into November, it feels like everyone is involved in the harvesting of olives. For a few weeks, the ground is covered in green netting, spread out beneath olive trees, some trees perhaps hundreds of years old. The nets are there to catch the olives, green and black, as they fall to the ground, disturbed and shaken from thousands of trees by those who are picking. This is one of my many favourite times of the year in the Italian calendar. Although, if you really pushed me to give you my absolute, most favourite time of the year, I would not be able to come up with a definitive answer. In Italy there are just so many to choose from. But, for me, the olive harvest is one of them. Everyone comes together, neighbours come to help you, and in return you go to help your neighbours. The days can be long, the work not easy, but for me this is one of the most Italian things you can do. And at its end you have the thick, dark, lime green elixir of olio extravergine d'oliva (extra virgin olive oil). The oil, slightly peppery to the taste, exquisite with fresh, crusty, white bread.

In Umbria, the last week of October, going into November, also brings the Chocolate Festival (Eurochocolate) in Perugia, my closest city. For one whole week the medieval centre of Perugia is lined with stands offering chocolate in every form imaginable. I would guess that it is perhaps the biggest festival of its kind in the whole of Europe, attracting an estimated one million visitors each year. And not to forget the Wine Festival in Montefalco (Enologica Montefalco). This beautiful little medieval town sits on its hill, surrounded by wine producers, field after field taken by vines. Close to the end of autumn, the town full to bursting with people celebrating the grape harvest.

The month of December brings preparations for Christmas. It's unlikely, but there could be the first flurries of snow. If there is to be any significant snow, it tends to fall in January and February. Yes, it does get cold in Italy. On at least one occasion, I've known the temperature to drop as low as minus 15°C! Although, it must be said, a temperature as low as this is rare. The higher mountains of the

Apennines will have snow through from late December into March, with strong winds well below freezing.

Even before November has had a chance to move into December, the people of Gubbio are preparing for Christmas. Work has been ongoing for some time building figures and stalls that will become part of the biblical scenes set out along the stone streets of Via Del Camignano and Via Del Fiume.

On the 6th of December, Italian families celebrate St Nicholas Day (San Nicola), with children traditionally receiving small gifts of sweets and toys. In effect Christmas in Italy lasts for over a month, as with many other countries, Christmas Day being of most special significance.

On the 7th of December, the lights on the world's tallest Christmas tree (Albero di Natale di Gubbio) are turned on, the event bringing crowds into the town from across Umbria and beyond. The same date is also the Eve of the Immaculate Conception. The tree is visible from miles around, climbing over 650 metres up the slopes of Monte Ingino. Although some distance away, on a cold winter evening, the very top of the tree, with its hundreds of lights, can be seen from the back of my house. The tree is looked after by a group of volunteers known as the Alberaioli; the tree so big that you can find it in the Guinness Book of World Records.

January brings La Befana, a witch who arrives on a broomstick with presents for children. Part fairy tale and part religious, Befana mixed with the arrival of the three wise men. The wise men and Befana said to be searching for the baby Jesus, hence the reason for carrying gifts. As with the rest of Italy, she arrives in Umbria on the evening of the 5th of January. Good children receive gifts, 'bad' children receiving a lump of coal. The 6th of January is another national holiday, a time for families to come together. For children, the evening before almost as important as the arrival of Babbo Natale on Christmas Eve.

What was I talking about before I got distracted? Back to the trestle tables and benches. As I said, Paola informs me that I can hire these from L'Associazione Pro Loco di Colpalombo. Paola negotiates the hire and arranges for them to be transported to Aldo's garden on the morning of the grande evento. Two days before, I've gone food shopping with Paola and Stefano, bringing back enough to feed a small army.

The father of Aldo's son-in-law, Davide, has said that he will buy everything required to make porchetta, this Italian speciality being his birthday present to me. Porchetta, not quite a hog roast, but along the same theme. Traditionally the body of a young pig is deboned and then ever so slowly roasted on a spit, the meat so succulent that when bitten simply breaks apart in your mouth. The skin is deeply scored, massaged with a range of herbs, and then slowly turned on the spit until a rich, crispy, golden brown. The meat itself is flavoured with sage, rosemary, garlic, pepper and salt. But the real secret to the wonderful flavour in Umbria is a hefty dose of finocchio (fennel). The meat is set out flat as one large piece and the mixture of ingredients are rubbed in. The meat is then rolled, tied and skewered. Although you can find porchetta wherever you travel in Italy, often sold from small kiosks and vans as a panino, the boast is that this very Italian delight has its origins in Umbria. Davide prepares it in his much-practiced, traditional way, on the evening of the grande evento roasting it over an open pit until perfect. Apparently, porchetta is listed by the Italian Ministry of Agricultural, Food and Forestry Policy as a food of Italian cultural significance. This delight is recognised as a prodotto agroalimentare tradizionale (a traditional agricultural product). I would guess that if you have ever been to Italy, you will have tasted porchetta. If not, this is a definite must on your next visit. Just be a little careful with your teeth when you bite into the crispy golden-brown skin, I do not want anyone holding me responsible for a broken tooth.

Marcello, the son of Davide and married to the youngest daughter of Aldo, Alicia, has volunteered to provide the music. On the morning of the party, he's busy setting up the sound system. Marcello has a full-time job, but he's also an accomplished part-time musician, playing the guitar and ukulele, performing at different venues around Gubbio. Usually, Marcello is part of a duo (Florida Keys), Angelina being the voice, always singing in almost perfect English, although she understands hardly any. However, today Angelina is unavailable, her friend's wedding, understandably, having first call. Marcello is going to be joined by another friend, Manetto, he can often be found performing as the lead singer with his own successful band.

The trestle tables and benches need to be transported the short distance from the community centre in Colpalombo. One of the three Giovanni's has said that he can provide the means. This Giovanni lives about 100 metres from my house in Case Colle. Tall and slim in stature, with a slightly dark moustache and dark, slightly greying hair, swept back. He walks past most days with a large, but surprisingly placid, Rottweiler. I would guess that he must be in his early 50s, Giovanni that is, not the dog. Another Giovanni lives just across the road that bends and climbs past Case Colle up to the village of Carbonesca. This Giovanni is slightly shorter in stature, again probably in his early 50s, a dark head of hair and spectacles. He also has a dog, a very pale Labrador, about the same size as the Rottweiler, but a dog that insists on barking at everything that passes. The third Giovanni lives down the road towards Colpalombo, but no more than 200 metres from Case Colle. I would guess that he is just a little bit older than the other two, his obvious distinguishing feature being that he only has one arm. How he lost his arm, I have yet to discover. Not really a question that you can casually throw into a conversation. Just a coincidence I guess, but there are at least two others living locally who have lost an arm. This is a rural area, with agriculture being one of the main employers, so I suppose unfortunate accidents do happen.

One common practice, when a trailer load of overly large logs is delivered, is to hire/borrow for the day, a tractor, the tractor stationary but used to power a large upright type of bandsaw. Health and safety don't appear to be a great priority. The tractor noisily powers away as large logs are fed towards the limb severing blade. I've no idea if that's how arms have been lost, but it could be a possibility. You'll be pleased to know that I have my tractor load of oak logs delivered already cut and small enough to easily fit inside my stufa (wood burner).

So, Giovanni, owner of the Rottweiler, arrives with his vehicle to transport the tables and benches from Colpalombo. There are times when it's impossibly difficult to accurately describe something, this is one of those times. Giovanni's vehicle is bright red, that's the easy bit of the description. It has one seat, with long high handles rather like a chopper bicycle, but the handles are bigger and slightly leaning backwards towards the driver. In front of the chopper handles is the motor, with no real cover to speak of. How can I describe the motor? The best I can say is that it's like the motor you could find on a large, sit on, grass mower. You could perhaps describe the whole thing as a large motozappa (soil rotavator), but with the blades, which would usually churn up the soil, removed. The vehicle only has two wheels, rather large for its size, set on an axle that places them either side of the motor, but just slightly back. I hope from my description you will realise that it is impossible for the vehicle to balance without something added. The balance is provided by a small, red, shallow sided trailer. Once la macchina (the machine) is hooked up to the trailer, balance is achieved.

Giovanni uses la macchina all the time, transporting anything from a mountain of cut olive branches or freshly cut green hay, to small live animals. I'm always amazed how the animals calmly sit in the little red trailer, looking like they enjoy the ride. I almost expect them to smile and wave as they pass my little bit of Umbria. Almost every other day Giovanni will pass my house on his macchina, sat, leaning slightly forward, brown legged, brown arms held high on the chopper handles to control the rather noisy contraption. On his head a colourful bandana, and, after all he is Italian, dark sunglasses. As he picks up pace rather than any genuine speed, Giovanni bends forward, head down, I guess to cut down on any wind drag, thus making the macchina more 'aerodynamic'. I imagine him sat with the motor noisily idling, he's leaning forward, hands gripping the high chopper handles, pensive and intent. He has the best qualifying time, this obviously placing him in pole position on the starting grid at Monza. The light is red, it changes to green, Giovanni is away, head now lower than the top of the chopper handles, leaving those behind in his dust. The truth is, I could probably run faster than this chopper-handled macchina. But the other truth is that this is a handy machine to have, cheap to use, and ideal for all those little transporting jobs. I think we will have to have make quite a few journeys down and back up from Colpalombo, the trailer not able to carry that many tables and benches.

La macchina arrives in Aldo's garden, Giovanni in all his racing gear, as always a big grin on his face and a sparkle in his eye. It's a hot summer morning, the temperature already creeping towards 30°C. Greetings are exchanged, hands are shaken. We agree that I'll drive down with Andy, the husband of my elder daughter Kara, and start to gather tables and benches together, Giovanni will follow on with la macchina. After what feels like an age he arrives, I guess he must have been chatting with Aldo. One trestle table is lifted into the trailer and placed top down. This is followed by one bench, again top down and squeezed in by the side of the table. The trailer is just big enough for one table and one bench to be slotted in. Another table and another bench are lifted in. Then another table and another bench, until we must have about five of each, precariously balanced on top of those below. The folding metal legs of the tables and benches make it difficult to stack them with any trustworthy stability.

We stand back and assess the situation. I agree with Andy that it would be a bit of a gamble to stack any more on top. Giovanni clearly has other ideas and encourages us to continue stacking. We have serious doubts, but he insists that there is no problem, all will be fine. So, we continue, with Giovanni's help, to stack more on top of the others. Including the height of the trailer, our 'Jenga' of stacked tables and benches must now be at least 12ft from the ground. Without any movement from la macchina, our stacking is already defying the laws of gravity. But Giovanni appears to be supremely confident as he throws ropes over the wobbling 'Jenga' from one side to the other. We catch the ropes, but then leave it to Giovanni to make sure that they are tight and secure. All roped up, he's happy, not the slightest hint of concern on his face. We are just as happy not to be with him when gravity does take control and the whole load tumbles to the ground.

Giovanni gives a strong pull on the rope that's partly wound round the flywheel. La macchina chugs into life, our 'Jenga' gives a little jiggle and Giovanni jumps on board, a confident smile on his face and a cheery wave. What could possibly go wrong?

We've decided to give him a good head start before we follow in the car, certain that our short drive will soon be blocked by tables and benches scattered all over the road as it climbs up to Case Colle. The path of vehicles coming down in the other direction blocked, heated exchanges taking place in speedy Italian, arms and hands frantically gesticulating for greater emphasis. The hot morning air infused with any number of vaffanculos, interspersed with a whole range of other expletives, shooting backwards and forwards between our racing driver, Giovanni, and those who have just a scintilla of annoyance.

We soon find that we're creeping along behind the racing motozappa, Giovanni bent forward, head down, brown arms held high gripping the chopper handles. There are no wing mirrors on la macchina, Giovanni therefore oblivious to the fact that we are now almost pushing him up the hill. Come to think of it there are no licence plates, front or back. No brake lights. Is it even legal to have this thing on the road? I'm guessing these minor details have never even crossed Giovanni's mind. I'm also guessing that if I asked the question, he would simply smile with a twinkle in his eye, a shrug of the shoulders, responding with, 'questo non é un problema' (this is not a problem). In terms of being caught, he's most probably right, the Carabinieri hardly ever venture up to Colpalombo. Even if they did, I doubt that they would take any notice of Giovanni on his racing motozappa. Minor law enforcement in Italy appears to be a rather arbitrary affair.

As we climb, we decide that it could perhaps be wiser to keep a little more distance between us and Giovanni. Progress is slow, but there is enough motion for the tower of tables and benches to sway from side to side. The next bend has the whole load tilting to the right, threatening to topple at any moment. My eyes are only open because I happen to be driving. On the next bend, the load leans to the opposite side of the trailer. We only have a short drive, but the drama is intense. The expectation that gravity will inevitably have its way and, the fact that the temperature of the day is now well past 30°C, has both myself and Andy dripping in sweat.

Giovanni takes the sharp right to Case Colle and then right again into Aldo's garden. The motozappa and trailer trundle to a stop, our 'Jenga' moves slightly forward, jiggles a little and is still. Miraculously all the tables and benches have remained secure. The odd table and bench slightly skewed and out of place, but the tower is still intact. We should have had greater confidence in Giovanni, or at least enjoyed his casual optimism. All we need to do now is unload the trailer and set the benches and tables up around the garden. What we expected to be a few journeys, has been done in one. Perhaps I should start to believe in miracles.

Now almost midday, most of the garden is set up and birthday decorated. Time for just a little break, to relax in the shade of one of two large persimmon trees. Space in a busy day to have a snack and a cool Peroni. This is the spot where you often find Aldo, at least for a short time, on most hot afternoons, half snoozing in a hammock strung between the two trees. The swing of the hammock controlled by a string hanging down from one tree, at intervals ever so gently tugged by Aldo. At this time of year, the trees have a full canopy of deep green, glossy, wax textured leaves. The fruit of the trees not ripe and edible until September at the earliest. You must pick them perfectly ripe, otherwise they tend to be rather bitter. It's a fruit, sweet and similar in taste to an apricot, but not one of my favourites, the flesh leaves a film lining the palate of your mouth.

By late afternoon, food preparation is at its peak, a mini army of people hard at work. The kegs of beer have been hooked up. Something not done by me, I have no idea how to do it. Marcello took on this task. Kegs are now stood in a relatively shaded area that has been set up as the bar. The job of bar design and creation, also done by Marcello. Two refrigerators have also been set up, extension cables trailing back into Aldo's house.

The food will be served from a string of small outbuildings that, I guess, were once used to house pigs. Be reassured, the pigs have long since gone, the outbuildings perfectly clean. The buildings and tables are decorated. Happy Birthday banners hang down, along with the names and printed photographs of those who make up the 190 years. A mobile kitchen of sorts is set up behind the tables, large gas bottles, gas rings, army size pans and all other paraphernalia that could possibly be required. All the equipment coming from L'Associazione Pro Loco di Colpalombo. We had to send Giovanni back down again to transport it with his motozappa and trailer. Almost forgot to tell you. The tables and benches, along with all the cooking paraphernalia, come free of any hire charge. I have to say it again. I love Italia!

As 7.30pm approaches, family, friends and neighbours are all at their respective stations, ready and eager to serve food and drink. Marcello and Manetto have gone through a brief sound check and are already playing as the first guests start to arrive. The evening sky is still a deep blue, the horizon just starting to sizzle as the sun begins to sink behind the hills to the back of the house. A warm Umbrian summer evening, the moon already bright, with just a glimpse of the odd star. More people arrive, greetings are exchanged, hugs, kisses, and smiles. Food is being served, wine and beer are flowing, friends, neighbours and family gather, some at tables, with others standing. The evening bubbles with laughter and conversation.

However, there is one person who finds it difficult to completely relax and let go of life's concerns. For just one evening he could have left the message he wants to spread at home. An English friend, Mark, finds himself reluctantly having to listen to dietary advice from someone else who just happens to be English. Mark lives close to Montefalco, he and his wife, Giselle, running a successful wine tour business (Gusto Wine Tours). Andrew, the other Englishman, lives about one kilometre from Case Colle in a beautifully renovated church. Until the very recent transformation, the church had been totally derelict, large trees growing where there had once been a roof.

I don't know Andrew that well, other than he is a totally dedicated vegan. At the time of the party, along with his wife, he offered the renovated church for holiday makers who want to experience a kind of vegan retreat. Nothing wrong with being a vegan. But Andrew definitely has an overzealous nature. He is evangelical about veganism, behaving as though he has come to Colpalombo to save heathen meat eaters from the eternal damnation of serious gastric illness and early death. He is a vegan missionary in a backward land of meat eaters. And, for a time, he has Mark cornered with his missionary zeal, informing him that if he does not change his heathen meat eating and alcohol drinking ways, his time on earth will be cut short. Leaving Mark somewhat disgruntled and annoyed by the lecture, Andrew then moves on to find another victim, and the next and the next. Andrew speaks almost no Italian, so I'm not sure how he intends to save the native heathens. This little tale has quite an ironic and sad ending, but I'll leave that to some other part of the book; don't want to be a party pooper. Remind me not to forget.

Anyway, as the evening moves on people begin to drift onto the dance floor, Marcello and Manetto belting out one song after another, Manetto is a good singer and all in English. However, unlike Angelina, who has an equally good voice, Manetto does understand every word. By 9pm, I've already left drinks all over the garden, the sort of thing you do when it's your party. As the host you feel obligated to constantly move around, mingling, making sure that you've spoken to every single person at least once. Checking that they have a drink in their hand and more food than they can possibly eat. Moving on to the next group of people, you realise that you're probably the only one without a drink. You did have a beer a minute ago, you've placed it somewhere, but can't really be bothered to try and seek it out. Another fresh bottle and you move on, but before taking your first sip, getting dragged onto the dance floor; probably never finding that exact bottle of beer again. Marcello has, temporarily, exchanged the live music for recorded. I think I must have been 'volunteered' to give 'dance lessons'.

You put your left arm in
your left arm out
in, out, in, out
you shake it all about

You do the hokey cokey
and you turn around
that's what it's all about

Woah, hokey cokey
Woah, hokey cokey
Woah, hokey cokey
knees bent
arms stretched
ra-ra-ra

My Italian students are quick learners, soon picking up the moves, putting everything in, taking everything out, grabbing the hands of others to form a circle and charging towards the centre. A clash of raucous laughter as perspiring party animals demand to go through the whole thing again. There's a tiny window of no dancing as people recover from a few minutes of temporary breathlessness. Marcello and Manetto are now back on stage playing the first line of Happy Birthday. People sing, some in English, most in Italian. This is the signal for me to get ready to make a speech, a speech that I obviously must make in Italian. Ask me if I'm nervous.

Tanti Auguri a te,
(Happy Birthday to you,)
Tanti Auguri a te,
(Happy Birthday to you,)
Tanti Auguri a Ghrem
(Happy Birthday Graham)
Tanti Auguri a te!
(Happy Birthday to you!)

As the voices ring out, I gather Peter, Kara, and Sam around me to form some type of security blanket. The singing comes to an end, the audience in silent expectation. Whilst most people gather round, moving closer to ensure that each word falling from the lips of the inglese can be clearly understood, there are others who appear to be leaving. It can't be something I've said, broken Italian has yet to leave my lips.

I won't go into any detail about what I said. And I'm certainly not going to transcribe my words here in Italian. Basically, I thank all my Italian neighbours and friends for making me feel so welcome and very much part of the community from the day I bought the house. I thank them for all the different ways they have given me help and support over the years. This celebration is as much for them as it is for those who make up the 190 years. And as a kind of thank you, I present the village of Colpalombo with three cast iron, old style, tractor seats, transported over from the UK. You can now find the tractor seats in the little piazza, the piazza close to the church in Colpalombo.

The speech appears to go down well, nothing is thrown, clapping and hugs following its end. It's only at this point that I become aware of a caravan of people carrying rather large objects past the front of my house and into the garden of Aldo. It's the same group who appeared to be leaving prior to my speech.

Whatever it is being carried, the items are decorated in large red ribbons and bows. As the caravan enters the garden, it's greeted by another chorus of 'Tanti Auguri a te'.

Whilst I'm distracted by the caravan, the most enormous birthday cake is placed on a table set before myself, Kara, Peter and Sam. I remember going with Paola to place an order for the cake at a gorgeous pasticceria, just outside the medieval centre of Gubbio. However, I had no idea of its potential size or how it would be decorated. It really is the biggest and most beautiful birthday cake I have ever seen, taking two people to carry it and set it down. On top there is bold lettering spelling out BUON COMPLEANNO and the names of all four birthday people. But before the candles can be set alight, the caravan comes to a halt.

It's now more than obvious what I'm being given as a birthday present, a full set of Rattan style garden furniture. A complete set for an outdoor garden lounge. Speeches in Italian follow, along with very generous presents for Kara, Peter and

Sam. Hugs, clapping, smiles and laughter, introduce another chorus of 'Tanti Auguri a te', the four of us blowing out the candles on the cake. The chorus followed with more clapping, more hugging, more laughter, more smiles.

Marcello and Manetto soon have almost everyone back on the dance floor, including some that had never ever been seen to dance before. Out of all present, there are just two who remain as spectators throughout the whole evening. No amount of cajoling from me gets two out of the Giovanni threesome to give even a little wiggle. Giovanni of the motozappa dances the night away until he can dance no more, the other two remaining stubbornly seated by the edge of the dance floor. They're quite happy to enjoy what's unfolding before them, joining others in chat, drinking and laughter.

I'm not sure, but I would guess it must have been around midnight when Manetto had to leave, Marcello now becoming the DJ for the next three hours. More drinking, more dancing, some eating and at least one, perhaps more, conga out of Aldo's garden, snaking into my garden, down the street and back again. Sam, if you remember the partner of Lucy, repeating each and every time I happen to bump into him, 'This has to be the best party I've ever known, it's unbelievable', before giving me and anyone who may want one, another hug. Although I've probably left as many drinks around the garden as I've swallowed, I'm in an incredibly happy party mood, dancing and singing with all around. Lucy has taken on the responsibility of leading a full dance floor through the Macarena yet again, then moving into another Hokey Cokey. By now I really have lost count.

Kara, my elder daughter, has grabbed hold of me again, both of us back on the dance floor, arms linked with others. Andy, Kara's husband, really is in a party mood, singing, dancing, hugging, laughing with all around. The numbers partying may have dwindled, but the sky sparkles with stars, the garden still bubbling with laughter, music and song. We soon arrive at 3am. Marcello must be at work by 5. Just one more dance. Clearing up can be left, bed and sleep are calling.

Sam feels the need to tell me yet again that it's the most unbelievable party. Andy, not sure where he is, Kara having to help him to their room. As I collapse onto my bed, I reflect on what has been a wonderful occasion. Un grande evento completely full of enjoyment, laughter and overwhelming generosity. Meanwhile, as I drift to sleep, the drink consumed by Andy has decided that it no longer wishes to remain inside his body. Apparently, his desperate scramble to the toilet is not successful. I won't go give any detail, other than to say that Kara was not best pleased when Andy decided to sleep on the floor between the bedroom and the bathroom, he having already slid through what had left his stomach. An autopsy to determine how he arrived at this state can wait until we have all partially recovered. There is one big clue as to the cause of his inebriation, this being that Andy did spend a good part of the evening in the company of one of my Italian neighbours drinking copious amounts of grappa.

By late afternoon of the same day, almost all trace of il grande evento has been removed. Trestle tables and benches, balanced and secured by Giovanni, have been returned. And again, amazingly, not one topples from the trailer pulled by the motozappa, as it trundles down the hill to Colaplombo. I make the short drive back to the catering emporium, the car now relatively empty. All that remains from the party is one keg of beer and the equipment used to extract the contents. The inglese has returned to pay il conto. Apart from Andy, all others feel relatively unscathed by drinking, eating, dancing, and singing, through to the early hours of the morning. Andy eventually emerges, somewhat embarrassed and pledging to never, ever, drink one drop of grappa again - not ever, never! Neighbours walk past. All talk is about the party. There's laughter about the music, and comment on those who had never been seen to dance before.

That evening we are all invited for dinner by Aldo. We all go, apart from Andy, still not feeling recovered and still a little embarrassed. Paola, if you remember, the middle daughter of Aldo comments, with a big smile on her face:

'He was a lion last night. Now he is a little pussy cat.'

Lorenzo, the neighbour to the right of my house, has from today taken to calling me by my middle name, Carl, now Carlo. I'm not sure how my middle name was revealed at the party, but the use of Carlo sticks, also being adopted by another neighbour, Federico. For all other Italian neighbours and friends, Ghrem or Ghreme is the closest they ever come to Graham. This is an improvement on Grent, the version of Graham used for quite a few years.

Kara, Lucy, and their partners are only here for one week, much of that taken up with party preparations. The few days left of their visit are taken by enjoying the hot Umbrian summer sun, meals with my Italian neighbours, visits to Gubbio and to the beautiful little hilltop town of Montone, yet another medieval delight. After my daughters have left for the UK, my sister and her husband stay for another week. Along with me, they no longer have the demands of paid employment. Relaxing in the shade, short walks down to the bar in Colpalombo, meals sat out at night under the stars and the sound of cicadas. A potential romance also calls for my attention.

For the past month, a friend has been encouraging me to meet her cousin in Florence, my friend assuring me with, 'You will be ideal for each other, you both have a lot in common.' We are both single, we have that in common, I guess that's a positive start. If you happen to be single, it's the sort of suggestion that happens now and again. Increasingly for me this is not very often. Should I go along with this, such meetings can be so awkward – what to do? I also have an inquisitive older sister staying with me. She will inevitably want to know where I'm going and expect a full and detailed report on my return. There is also the fact that Florence is more than a two-hour drive from Colpalombo. My sister and husband only have a few days left of their stay.

Thursday morning and I'm on the train from Perugia to Firenze Santa Maria Novella, the main railway station in Florence. The station located only a few minutes' walk from the historic centre of the city. It's been arranged that I should meet the cousin of my friend at around 11.30am in the station. Mobile numbers have been exchanged. We've had a brief chat via Facebook, but we haven't actually spoken to each other. My train arrives on time. I'm quite nervous about the meeting. I get a call from Martina, my friend's cousin, to say that she is going to be late. This looks like a good start. It will probably be 12.30 before she arrives, and she will have her teenage daughter with her. This should be an interesting rendezvous.

In our brief conversation, we agree that we should meet in front of the Salone Biglietti, the lettering indicating the hall where passengers can purchase tickets, easily big enough not to miss from any point in the station. She's an attractive woman, slim, a brunette with hazel brown Italian eyes. Smiles and polite greetings are exchanged, air kisses to each cheek, a brief explanation as to why they are a little late and introductions to Sophia, Martina's daughter. What feels like a stumbling discussion follows. What should we do and where should we go for the afternoon? I guess we both feel a little awkward and nervous. We quickly agree that we should first find a little place to eat, ideally some distance from the station. The temperature in Florence has risen well past 30°C. We walk along, engaging in rather guarded conversation, looking for a quiet piazza and a small osteria where we can sip on vino rosso, enjoy good food and sit shaded from the heat of the Tuscan sun.

As much as I try, I find it quite difficult to remember any detail of what we chatted about. We soon start to feel relaxed, very much more at ease, laughing and joking as we begin to expose a little about ourselves to the other person who, until very recently, had been a comparative stranger.

Whilst enjoying a meal together, the three of us exchange ideas about where we should go and what to see.

Most tourists new to the city will almost inevitably gravitate in the direction of Piazza del Duomo. Walking into the piazza for the first time is an amazing experience. The Duomo really is a spectacular architectural wonder, the colourful patterned exterior simply breath taking, the inside just as beautiful. I guess after photographing the Duomo from all sides and visiting the inside, the next thing you must do is go to the top of the campanile, the Duomo's bell tower. But you will have to be prepared to climb its 463 steps, the climb quite steep and narrow. Once at the top you are rewarded with impressive views of the city and the hills of Tuscany beyond. Be sure to book tickets in advance, once you have the tickets making sure that you are there at the allocated time. Also be aware that in the main tourist season the piazza and the Duomo will be crowded.

Another tourist hot spot is the Loggia della Signoria, found to one corner of Piazza della Signoria and close to the Uffizi Gallery. The building is made up of wide arches that are open to the piazza. I suppose you could describe it as an open-air sculpture gallery. Among the sculptures you'll find Perseus with the severed head of Medusa, the Rape of the Sabine Women, the fight between Hercules and the centaur Nessus, statuettes of Jupiter, Mercurius, Minerva and Danae, also the Rape of Polyxena. I don't know the story behind all of these, some telling gruesome tales, but they are well worth a visit. To one side of the main arches, you will also find the white sculpture of Michelangelo's David. Although the statue is magnificent, don't get too excited, the original is in the Galleria dell' Accademia. I forgot to mention, as you walk into or across the piazza you'll find yourself stood close to the impressive Fontana del Nettuno, the fountain situated in front of the Palazzo Vecchio. All of this is free, day and night. Just make sure that you do not sit down on the steps or decide to relax against the walls to the back of the arches, it is absolutely forbidden. After not being able to rest your feet here, you may wish to have a break before you visit the Uffizi, the home of so many masterpieces.

I'm not suggesting you do this immediately after visiting the Loggia della Signoria, but the Mercato Centrale is very much worth a few hours of your time in Florence. It's said to be Europe's largest covered food hall. It was first opened in 1874. It is a splendours place, with every type of Italian food you could wish to buy, places to eat and drink. It's whilst eating here with my sister and her husband that I came across my first real life Donald Trump enthusiasts. An elderly couple sat at our table, she born in the states, he originally from the UK, but both having lived together in the US for some time. They were hoping that Trump would be elected as President in order to make good what they regarded as the terrible presidency of Obama. The two are both apparently intelligent and from professional backgrounds. I'm not sure why, but this made their position on Trump and Obama even more bewildering. I guess I had a lot to learn about American politics and even more about Americans in general. We did our best to engage them in rational debate but failed miserably. The reasons behind their support for Trump, from our perspective, exaggerated and naively simplistic. But what did we know, this was 2015, we still had Brexit to come?

Anyway, putting our struggle at rational political debate behind, I'll get back to the delights of the market. The streets around the building contain perhaps the busiest of Florence's outdoor markets, with stalls selling clothing and all types of leather goods. But beware, the goods on offer may not necessarily be all they appear to be. Bit like Trump and Brexit, I guess.

At some point make sure that your walk takes you to the Ponte Vecchio, the old bridge that has crossed the Arno since 1345. Walking along its pedestrianised length really does feel like a journey back in time. Small shops squeezed together side by side, line both sides of the bridge; most of them partially hanging over the river below. For at least two hundred years the bridge provided a platform, first for butchers and fishmongers, and later for leather tanners. The waters of the Arno flowing below acting as a ready-made waste disposal system. It will come as no surprise to you that the 'waste disposal system', over many years of use, produced rather noxious smells around the whole area. Something had to be done, and it was Ferdinand 1st who did it in 1593. He decided that only goldsmiths and jewellers should be allowed to have shops on the bridge, and that's exactly what you find lining each side today. If you happen to be in the city for more than a day, go back again in the evening and enjoy a romantic stroll when all the shops are secured with wooden shutters. Both day and night the bridge offers you wonderful views over the river. Another little snippet of information is that this was the only bridge in Florence not to be destroyed by the retreating German army during World War Two.

Well, that's just some of the many places to see in Florence, trust me there's so much more.

Now back to our conversation about where to go. Given that the three of us are not first-time visitors to Florence, we decide to try and avoid the main tourist spots. I think it's my suggestion that we find our way up to Piazzale Michelangelo. I sell it to Martina and Sophia by explaining that we will have the most fantastic view over the whole of Florence, plus we can enjoy the view with another rest for vino. I'm not sure why I'm trying to sell it, there's no real need. Martina and Sophia have visited Florence before, Martina probably knowing the city far better than me. But I play the part of tour guide, Martina and Sophia apparently happy to go along with this. Their trust in me may have been a little premature. Perhaps it was politeness rather than trust.

We walk along, chatting as we go, the temperature now closing in on 40°C. I have a notion of the direction we need to take. Perhaps it would have been an idea to have brought a tourist map. Looking back, it would have been a good idea to ask for directions from Martina. But I'm the guide, I know where I'm going, I'll get us on the right path in the end. My two companions follow on, at other times walking by my side. We continue to chat, the two continuing to smile politely, but I think they may be starting to have less faith in the navigational instinct of the man they only met today. Inside I'm getting irritated with myself. I should know the direction to take. This is not a good first impression. In the end I admit that

I'm not sure which way we should be going. My companions are polite, agreeing that we should give up on our quest, find a shaded little bar and stop for a drink. I already know that they must be back at the station in a relatively short time. They're meeting friends at around 8pm, their train journey back being just under one hour.

Back at Firenze Santa Maria Novella, we say goodbye and warmly thank each other for a very pleasant afternoon. Air kisses to cheeks are exchanged and promises are made to keep in touch, but nothing is said about meeting again. We turn and walk away in opposite directions. I like her, she's attractive, her looks matching the chocolatey smooth voice. An intelligent, interesting woman. But I'm not so sure that I've made the best impression. Perhaps we could become friends, although I don't think the distance between where we live will really help.

Umbria

Il Cielo E La Terra: La Regione Dei Santi

Heaven And Earth: A Region Of Saints

Put plainly, Umbria is wonderful.

It contains dozens of significant medieval towns and incredibly beautiful città d'arte perched atop the hills that characterize the region. And Umbria has a never-ending supply of fields and woods. From high in the hills you see the mist in the valleys below. The winding rivers and sparkling Trasimeno.

As you wander the lanes of small towns, take in the wide-open landscapes and stand before the fresco-covered walls of churches. You'll be struck by how much beauty surrounds you, in art and nature.

. . . .

Stefano Zuffi

CHAPTER TWO

Arrivederci Inghilterra

....

'Travelling, it leaves you speechless, then transforming
you into a storyteller.'

....

Ibn Battuta

We're in Germany, heading south, just about to pass Karlsruhe; apparently the second largest city in the state of Baden-Württemberg. Our progress has been good so far, no major hold ups, but I'm feeling quite tired after driving for the past three hours. I think it's time for a change over, for Andy, my daughter's partner, to take the driver's seat and for me to get a little sleep. We've covered about 1150 km (700 miles). The Sprinter van is full to absolute bursting point with every single item from my house in the UK. Perhaps I should have been more hostile in my approach to saying goodbye to items that I no longer really need. It's not been necessary to strap items down, there's not a chance of anything being disturbed. With one last momentous effort we were able to force a reluctant mattress into a space that didn't have any legitimate right to exist. So tightly packed is the history of my adult life, that I think we may have managed to squeeze out every single drop of oxygen from the back of the van. Open the back doors and I think the van will spontaneously unload its cargo, each item scrambling out for a gulp of fresh air. My house in the UK is on the market, and I'm moving my life to Italy.

I indicate to turn into the next lay-by. Kara is sat in the middle, Andy by the passenger door. As the van comes to a halt, we can see stationary police vehicles about twenty metres ahead, officers apparently checking vans. The owners of the vans appear to be moving items from one van to another. Police officers filling in paperwork, others walking round the vans checking tyres and doing other things that police do. A television camera crew, large boom mike, and other assorted television type people follow the police around, all looking extremely busy.

'We could be on German television Dad!' Kara sounding quite excited.

Andy is now sat in the driver's seat, Kara still in the middle, me by the passenger door. Just as Andy begins to pull away, one of the busy police officers holds up his hand indicating that we should stop. The officer approaches the driver's side of the van mimicking for Andy to lower his window.

'Guten Morgan. Wurden Sie von einem anderen Polizisten angehalten?' ('Good morning. Were you stopped by another police officer?')

Andy simply sits looking bewildered, not comprehending a single word spilling from the officer's very polite lips. It's left to me to respond.

'Guten Morgen. Nein, wir haben angehalten damit wir den Fahrer wechseln können.' ('Good morning. No, we stopped to change drivers.')

To my surprise, the officer understands my faltering German, but it's also noticeably clear that he doesn't believe a word I'm saying.

During our brief conversation, another officer has been walking round the van. Her inspection complete, she speaks to our Guten Morgen officer, informing him that the van looks to be overweight. He then speaks to Andy, this time in English.

'You are overweight.'

Andy smiles back, saying yes, he is, patting his stomach at the same time. The officer smiles and agrees with Andy, yes, we are both a little overweight.

'Your van has too much weight.'

Out of all the places I could have stopped, why did I have to pull into this lay-by? We must have driven past hundreds. Now I'm sat watching other people unloading items from vehicles. I assume they were also overweight and having to move items into another van. This is going to be a bloody expensive lay-by. Andy attempts to make another joke out of the situation, but it's not going to work. He's instructed to drive the van onto some type of mobile contraption for weighing vehicles. At this point I get out of the van in some optimistic hope that the loss of my weight may make a difference. But the female police officer spots this, smiles, and instructs me to get back in the van. My less than cunning plan is foiled, not that it would have significantly reduced the weight of the van. No, really, I'm not that big.

The van, including the combined weight of two passengers and a driver, has its weight taken. All we can do now is sit and await the verdict. I just know that this is going to be expensive.

After a very brief time, our Guten Morgan officer approaches Andy's side of the van. I think you have probably already guessed. The verdict is not good, the officer looking a little more serious as he speaks.

'You are illegal. The van has a lot of weight. Do not move your vehicle.'

Having decided that we are illegal, the officer walks back to his colleagues and appears to be filling in paperwork.

Why did I decide to pull into this exact lay-by? The one before or the one after would have been more than fine. Filling in paperwork can only mean one thing, a fine. Not only a fine, but I'm also going to have to hire another van. I really don't think I'm going to be offered some preferential deal on the hire costs. I guess we could take out the things that I don't particularly need and leave them by side of the Autobahn. Problem is, it's the heaviest items that I need. I'm also more than certain that our Guten Morgan police officer won't take kindly to the Englander simply abandoning general household flotsam in the lay-by. There is absolutely no alternative, I will have to hire another van.

Here comes the final judgement, the same police officer walking back to the van, necessary paperwork in his hands. He smiles at Andy, but it's a serious smile. He looks down at his paperwork and looks across to me. I smile back. A very hopeful, but also a worried smile. Andy speaks first.

'Is everything good?'

The smile has now vanished from the officer's face.

'No, your van is zu schwer. Your weight is too much. Where are you going?'

'Italy', Andy replies.

'You will be stopped again at the Schweizer grenze, the Swiss border. But you can go.'

Andy asks again if everything is alright.

'No, you are illegal, but you can go.'

Me, through whispered lips - 'Quick Andy, start the engine before he has a change of mind.'

We thank the officer. Wish him a good day and away we go, fully loaded. I guess you could say that this was another 'Great Escape'. I have no idea why we are being allowed to escape and I don't want to stay around to ask. I just hope that Swiss border police are not quite so vigilant. Conversation flows between us, with suggestions being offered as to why the German police allowed us to go. I can only guess that they couldn't be bothered to go through the tiresome paperwork involved with a foreign vehicle - who knows?

Another 300 km (190 miles) and we're approaching the Schweizer Grenze with our illegal, overloaded, van. I'm driving, the border police directing us into the lane where payment is requested for the right to drive through Switzerland. In return for a payment of €40, I have a vignette in my hand. Why the term vignette is given to what is basically nothing more than a plastic sticker, I have no idea. Anyway, in exchange for €40 I have the vignette, a sticker with the number 15 in the centre (2015). If you have Swiss money, it's a payment of 40 francs, payment converting to a little less than 37 euro. I attempt to gently stick the vignette to the windscreen. Just enough pressure to hold it in place, but not firm enough that it can't be easily removed. I intend to drive back through Switzerland from the UK in just a few weeks, why would I want to have to pay for another? I'm from Yorkshire, thriftiness is embedded within my DNA. Proud of my gentle efforts, vignette in place, I edge forward, just about to drive away. However, I notice that the border officer has other ideas. He indicates that I should not move on. The German police officer was right, the Swiss have spotted that the van is overweight. The border officer walks to my side of the van. Without saying a single word, his hand reaches in through the open window. Is he trying to ensure that the illegal van can't be driven away by taking the ignition key? No, surely not.

The Swiss hand reaches in front of me and very firmly presses the vignette to the windscreen, I guess he knows all the tricks. He has no intention of removing the key. There is nothing I can do or say. After one last firm press, the Swiss hand reverses from the van, the same hand indicating that we can drive away. No words have been exchanged, I simply wave in thanks, start the engine again, and away we go. The illegal van is now in Switzerland.

I always marvel at the absolute beauty of Switzerland, it's high alpine peaks, lush pasture, crystal clear lakes and cuckoo clock villages. Spotlessly clean and tidy, with carpeted roads. Once through the Gotthard Tunnel, almost 17 kilometres (10.5 miles) in length, we have another 110 kilometres (68 miles) before we cross into Italy and pass Lake Como.

Although I'm very tempted to rest by Lake Como for the evening, Kara and Andy are determined to make the entire journey from the UK in one go, no overnight stops. I'm a little disappointed, not only will they find the journey exhausting, but they're also missing the opportunity to enjoy what I regard to be the most beautiful of the three large lakes of northern Italy, the others, as you're no doubt aware, being Lake Garda and Lake Maggiore.

After a journey of 2080 km (1293 miles), we at last arrive at the house in Case Colle, and yes, we are exhausted. The illegal van is left fully overloaded, all will be safe inside until the following morning. It's around 11.30 in the evening, the only movement around the little hamlet is the silent fluttering of bats as they feed on insects mesmerised by the bright light of the streetlamp at the end of my garden. The odd car passes on its climb up to Carbonesca, the only other sound is that of deer barking to each other in the darkness of fields, a short distance from the house. We collapse into hastily made beds and sleep.

Up early the following morning, we make the short drive down to Colpalombo for breakfast. I have an espresso and a sweet pastry. Kara and Andy have a cappuccino, with Andy declining a pastry, instead having a small panino of ham and tomato. It's a relatively warm early morning, so we sit outside the bar, the village starting its quiet, daily, routine. My life is still firmly packed into the back of the van, the contents not having been checked since we started the long journey from the UK. Cars pull up, some just with the driver, others containing passengers. All exchange cheerful greetings with the three of us, then disappearing inside for a morning fix of strong espresso. No sooner have they walked in, they are back out again, caffeine in their veins and ready for the day ahead. With pastries and a panino inside, we climb back in the van and make our way back to Case Colle.

The doors of the van are thrown open, a few small items struggling out, falling exhausted to the ground. Then our work begins, prising items apart that have been so tightly squeezed together they just don't want to leave each other. The rest of the day is taken by lifting and carrying from the van to the house. Nothing is sorted, items are simply haphazardly placed in rooms where they will probably live, some having to be carried up three flights of stairs. Although it's only April the heat of the day continues to rise. Our reward for all the carrying and lifting, an evening in Gubbio. On returning to the house, we do the same as the night before, simply collapsing into bed.

We have just one more full day before starting the return journey. I have the impression that Kara and Andy are having second thoughts about not breaking the drive by stopping in a hotel. The problem is that they have to be back at work in just over 24 hours, the drive has to be made with the only rest being stolen moments when not in the driving seat. I suggest that they should take back boxes of Prosecco, wine, and Italian beer. For some reason, they decide to buy just one box, the cardboard box holding just six bottles of Prosecco. Apart from the three of us at the front, the rest of the van is an empty void, just one solitary box tied firmly in place. Plenty of room should any illegal migrants decide to jump in when we reach the Channel Tunnel at Calais. That's if they manage to get past the fortress like barrier of high double fencing, topped with razor wire, continually under observation from video surveillance.

Early morning, just as the sun is starting to rise from behind the Apennines, we climb into the van. With Andy in the driving seat, Kara in the middle, myself by the passenger door, the long journey back to the UK begins. All three of us, still not yet fully recovered from the journey in the opposite direction.

Up through the village of Carbonesca, steadily climbing out, before dropping down into Casacastalda, on our left the high mountains of the Apennines, their tops keeping hold of soft white cloud. The road then twists and turns endlessly down to Valfabbrica, levelling out to take us through Pianello, before we pick up the road that takes us past the edge of Perugia. The city of Perugia left behind, we come through the final tunnel that opens to a panoramic view of Lago Trasimeno. It's a beautiful morning, low Umbrian hills to our right covered in olive groves, the wide expanse of the lake to our left, early sunlight shimmering on its surface. Our direction of travel is Florence. We pick up the A1 autostrada, with Andy driving, I snooze, my head trying to keep a jacket pressed up against the side window.

After several hours and a number of change overs, we're driving past Milan towards Lake Como and the border with Switzerland. It's only a few hours before we have left the country of endless chocolate box scenery, high snow topped mountains, manicured pasture, crystal clear lakes and cuckoo clock houses. We are in Germany, driving through the Black Forest, in the direction of Freiburg. We stop, have a longer break and eat.

Back in the van, out next target is Karlsruhe, passing Ludwigshafen, cutting across towards Trier, Liege, navigating round Brussels, passing Gent, then Bruges and eventually into France.

After what feels like an excessively long drive, we at last reach the fortress installation at Calais, this being the boarding point for the trains that transport you through the Channel Tunnel; I'm driving.

We pull up next to the cabin that acts as British passport control, the position staffed by UK officials. In a sense, the border with the UK starts here. I'm not sure how long this will be the case once Brexit becomes absolutely final. Will the French simply ask the UK to move its border to its proper place, on English soil, across la Manche?

Anyway, we pull up. As I said, I'm driving. Apart from the three of us, the van is almost completely empty. I pass three passports to the UK border official. A quick check. A quick glance at the three of us, he passes the passports back.

'Where have you been?'

'Italy', I reply.

'How long were the three of you in Italy?'

'Just three days.'

'What's the relationship between the three of you?'

I'm not sure why the relationship between the three of us should be of any real concern.

'My daughter and her partner.'

'What do you have in the back of the van and why were the three of you in Italy for only three days?'

Why does officialdom make the completely innocent feel and act so guilty? I'm hoping the van still only has one box containing six bottles of Prosecco, no human cargo having crept in without us knowing.

I explain that I've moved to live there. We've taken furniture over and now we're making the return journey.

'Pull the van over, we want to check inside. You're honestly telling me that the three of you have driven all the way to Italy, having spent no more than three days in the country, and you're driving back with an almost completely empty van?'

I'm not sure that I like his condescending attitude. We have no choice but to follow his demands.

With the nervousness of someone involved in human trafficking, I crunch the gears into reverse. I then move forward in first gear, but for some bewildering reason I manage to mount the concrete base on which the cabin stands, the border official having to move swiftly to one side. Luckily, I've not destroyed the cabin or killed the official. Kara and Andy not saying one word, look at me with genuine puzzlement. I look at myself in genuine puzzlement. Just to be sure for his own safety, the border official asks me to turn off the ignition before he and a colleague check the back of the van. I'm sure they are now totally convinced that the three of us are guilty of something. Perhaps it's their big day to find a van stuffed to the roof with illicit drugs or illegal migrants, front page news across the UK.

I open the doors to the back of the van. Surprise, apart from the single box, the van is completely empty. Perhaps a little disappointing for the border officials, not even one illegal migrant and not a sniff of some illicit substance. We're thanked for our cooperation and allowed to continue with the almost empty van to the train.

After just two weeks in the UK, I drive back to what will be my home in Umbria. A quick visit to see relatives in Germany, one compulsory stop to pay the fee to drive through Switzerland, and I'm back in Colpalombo. I'm here, my home for the foreseeable future. It's May, the weather already warm. The welcome from my Italian neighbours even warmer. By June, my house in the UK is sold. That's it, here I am, home. My home, Case Colle, Colpalombo, Gubbio, Umbria – Italia.

Umbria

Those who are looking for ancient towns would be
wise to head for Umbria

Sometimes it feels that every inch of Umbria has been
filled with a small gem of architecture and art

No one can say they know Italy without having visited.
Gubbio and Todi, Orvieto and Spoleto

And Umbria has still more treasures
tucked behind this curtain of green
In Umbria, history lives

It is felt and experienced daily, without excess and
without being forced, but tastefully and naturally

. . . .

Stefano Zuffi

ABRIDGED

CHAPTER THREE

Vivo in Umbria

······························

Some proclaim Umbria to be the Galilee of Italy

·····························

Gubbio, Assisi, Perugia, Orvieto, Spoleto, Montefalco, Spello, Trevi, Todi, Bevagna, Montone, Città di Castello, Foligno, Castiglione del Lago, Passignano sul Trasimeno, Panicale, San Feliciano, Città della Pieve, Norcia, Narni, Castelluccio, Deruta, Rasiglia & Collepino

The names of medieval cities, towns and villages spill endlessly from the tongue, each one unique, each one equally enchanting. Sitting on hilltops, some standing steadfast on volcanic outcrops, others climbing up mountain sides or resting in valleys.

Umbria, a totally landlocked region of Italy. A land of natural beauty. A mystical place to explore, with untouched landscapes right in the centre of il bel paese, at the very heart of the boot of Italy. A region dominated by the Apennine Mountains. The very mountains that I can see when I step out into my garden.

Monte Cucco, Monte Subasio, Monti Sibillini, Monte Tezio, Monte Vettore

Then there are Umbria's lakes and rivers.

Lago Trasimeno, Lago di Corbara, Lago di Piediluco, Cascate delle Marmore, Fiume Tevere (Tiber), Fiume Topino, Fiume Chiascio & Fiume Nera

In many ways Umbria, even now, remains an unknown treasure to foreign tourists in Italy. A region of warm summers, often hot. Usually mild winters, but sometimes freezing cold. Colourful spring months, preparing for the drier months of June, July and August. And sunny autumns, full of colour, still with warmth on your back.

Almost the end of May 2015. You find me with friends from the UK, sitting in the shade of olive trees, sipping on cool Umbrian white wine. I'm with Samantha and Alex. I was best man at their wedding, with Alex being that one special friend who feels to have been in your life forever. A friendship formed in the first year of high school, with something so special about it, that months or even years apart feel to simply disappear when you meet up again. Within seconds of coming together, everything simply falls into place. Conversation flows, humour cascades, shared memories come rushing back. You almost know what the other is thinking.

Samantha and Alex are holidaying at my place for the week, although their stay is almost abruptly interrupted, possibly even abandoned, by my driving on the very first morning at the house. As is almost always the case I rise early, well before any others have been disturbed by bird song, before even a hint of sunlight sneaks its way through shuttered windows. That's just me. I'm one of those lucky people who never needs to have that much sleep. I'm awake before my neighbour's cockerel begins his testosterone ritual, the shouting and crowing all part of some territorial display.

It's a beautiful morning, distant mountain tops coloured orange. Whilst Samantha and Alex sleep, I make the short drive up to the village of Carbonesca, literally no more than five minutes; I'm in search of milk. A quick espresso in the bar, brief chat, milk purchased, I make the briefest of journeys back to the house and breakfast. The distance is no more than two kilometres, the road twisting and turning under a thick canopy of trees. The branches of oak reaching across from each side to create a tunnel of green. I drift down the road in a dream-like state, my brain totally separated from the physical process of driving; the car driving itself. My mind simply marvelling at the joy of living in Umbria.

I drift round the next bend, my dream instantly interrupted by a car heading directly towards me – what the hell?! The two cars so close, each driver able to see the look of shock on the face of the other. What appears to be an inevitable collision is somehow avoided, my car swerving to the right side of the road, the other car passing to my left as it continues its climb to Carbonesca. You're absolutely right, I'm so distracted by the beautiful morning, completely lost in a world of my own, that I've been driving on the wrong side of the road. Phew, that was close. It will have certainly woken up the other driver. It's not very often that you will have a British car heading directly towards you between Colpalombo and Carbonesca. I admit my guilt to Samantha and Alex as we sit having breakfast in the garden.

The sipping of cool Umbrian white wine is taking place in the grounds of the Rocca del Leone, the castle that protects Castiglione del Lago, the town and castle looking out over Lago Trasimeno. This is the fifth day of my guests' stay in Umbria, each day Samantha and Alex commenting on the present day being even better than the last; this day being no exception.

In the grounds of the Rocca, surrounded by mature olive trees, is a small unassuming café/bar, the backdrop to the scene being the medieval walls of the castle. Samantha and Alex simply relax, enjoying the wine and the chance to be shaded from a hot sun. To them it's a Mediterranean idyll, the shade of olive trees, cool white wine, deep blue sky, hot sun, Lago Trasimeno sweeping round the town of Castiglione del Lago, built on a promontory pushing out into the lake. We do nothing more than sip, chat, laugh and relax.

The Rocca del Leone is totally intact, dominating the eastern part of Castiglione, and well worth taking up some of your time. In the 16th century it was considered to be one of the most impregnable castles in the whole of Italy. Inside the walls of the castle is a beautiful amphitheatre, where music and exhibitions are enjoyed. It's a favourite venue during the Trasimeno Blues Festival that takes place every summer. It really is a wonderful setting on a warm Umbrian evening, a place I've sat enjoying live music a number of times.

We've toured the Rocca, now browsing the many shops in Castiglione selling every type of pasta, cheese, salami, ham, olives, wine, and olive oil. All invite you in to sample what they have to offer, most also providing you with a table to eat and drink. Every place packed with foods to tempt your tastes and excite your sense of smell. Samantha has been inside one of the shops for what feels like ages. Eventually I go in and suggest that she buy the whole shop. The owner responding before Samantha, saying that if I'm really interested he would sell it for €110,000.

'Seriously, you want to sell the shop and everything in it?'

Whilst Samantha continues to look around, nibbling on this and nibbling that, the owner engages me in serious conversation about buying the business.

I've lost count of the number of times the same story has been told. The tale that the owner has to tell is by no means exceptional. Italy is not good. Italy has too many problems. You can't make a good living if you have a business in Italy. The owner has a dream of moving to London and setting up a similar business there. He has enough English to serve the needs of tourists, but very little beyond that. I try to explain that property in London is incredibly expensive. If he is really serious he should think about other places, perhaps in the north of England. But no, he's determined to set up a business in London. In the right place there would certainly be a good market for what he has to offer, but he would never be able to afford the costs of London. I'm unable to convince him. We wish him well, leaving his dream just a little dented, Samantha with her arms full of all types of tasty goods.

If you want to eat in Castiglione with good views of the lake, you have two main choices. Ristorante La Cantina offers excellent food and service, its beautiful garden area giving views of the lake. The other place is Ristorante Café Latino, really more a place to have a snack, enjoy a drink and a gelato. My favourite little place to eat is just outside the walls of the town, Ristorante Osteria Le Scalette, Via 25 Aprile. It's a little, unpretentious place, full of charm. A small, terraced area to the front gives you a partial view of the lake. I've eaten here a number of times, the food always excellent and reasonably priced. Everything is homemade and typical of the region. Its specialities are dishes that come from rare breed pigs and wild boar. The restaurant also offers fish, fresh from the lake and pasta flavoured with truffle. A husband-and-wife team run this small, exceptionally friendly place. It is a must visit.

Friday evening we're in Perugia at Bottega del Vino, the food, the service, the ambience of the place, absolutely perfect. It's a tiny bistro/wine bar on Via del Sole 1. You'll find this little gem by the side of the Duomo, having already walked past the Palazzo dei Priori, across Piazza 1V Novembre with the Fontana Maggiore. It's the same place that once absolutely refused to serve a cappuccino to my sister at 9.30 in the evening. Honestly, don't let that stop you booking a table or simply calling in the hope that they have one spare. It's a cosy place, sometimes having live jazz. Only a small menu, but everything exquisitely delicious. It's an inviting place wherever you sit, but if you can, try and get the table by the window overlooking Duomo San Lorenzo. Our dessert has just been placed on the table. We all have the same, tiramisu. Samantha and Alex simultaneously dip in a spoon, lift to their mouths, both in unison, gasping with delight. I do the same, dipping into my tiramisu. Beyond any doubt, it is the best I have ever tasted. It is the cocaine of the tiramisu world.

The following day, we're invited round to my neighbours for a coffee and a swift grappa. We tell the tale of having the best tiramisu ever to have touched our lips. Paola, the middle daughter of Aldo, offers to show Samantha how to make her version of tiramisu. We all jump into my car, taking the quick drive up to the store in Carbonesca to buy the ingredients (me driving on the right side of the road). The store is closed for lunch, another thirty minutes before it opens. Much to the surprise and delight of Samantha, Paola suggests that we have a glass of Prosecco whilst we're waiting. Samantha still comments about this being the best way to shop, sat outside in the warm sun, waiting for opening time. Soon back at the house, demonstration and instructions given, we have Paola's tiramisu. It is delicious.

We spend lazy days in the garden, slow walks down to the bar in Colpalombo, climb up Monte Cucco, and the absolute necessity of an evening at Martintempo in Gubbio. The week soon over, my guests depart from Perugia airport back to the UK.

I absolutely adore Lago Trasimeno, just over a sixty-minute drive from Colpalombo. A relatively shallow lake, the deepest part only being around 7 metres, its circumference 45 kilometres (28 miles), making it the fourth biggest lake in the whole of Italy. The lake, its surrounding hills of olive trees and vines, villages and towns, offer a quiet escape even at the very height of summer.

The lake has three islands, Isola Maggiore being the only one that's really inhabited, with a population of about 35. A visit to the island is well worth it. Just like the rest of the lake it has a slow, peaceful pace. As you step off the small ferry from Passignano sul Trasimeno, Tuoro sul Trasimeno or Castiglione del Lago, you immediately come to a few informal restaurants by the side of the lake. Walking past these, in no more than a few minutes, you come to a charming 15th century village, the people here once earning their living from fishing the lake. The islanders live in sand-coloured houses along Via Guglielmi, the homes just a short distance from the water's edge.

I was last on the island in the summer of 2019. A hot, dry, July day. The short ferry ride across from Tuoro offering a refreshing breeze. My first stop was for a small bite to eat in one of the restaurants by the lake and then a slow walk along the islands one main street. Here you find quaint little bars, cafes and gift shops. Leaving the tourists behind, I then explored footpaths that take you around the island and also to its highest point. It's easy walking, through olive groves; a chance to enjoy the islands tranquillity. The island's small size giving plenty of opportunity to have views of the lake.

After exploring all there is to offer, I made my way back to the village for an ice cold, delicious, gelato. If you're there at the right time, you may be lucky enough to see an amazing sunset, the heat of the sun sizzling into the lake. I understand that there's now the possibility of accommodation on the island. If you really want to escape, it would be a wonderful place to stay for the evening.

Isola Polvese is the largest of the three islands, though there's no village where you can sit to have a snack and people watch. For me, it's an island to do a little walking through ancient olive groves, a little swimming, and a little sunbathing on one of its small beaches. There's the chance to explore the ruins of a medieval castle and a few places, close to the stepping off point from the ferry, where you can get something to eat and drink. The few times I've been to the island, my day has been spent in the lake and on the beach. The first time I visited, walking along its footpaths.

Isola Minore is the smallest island and privately owned.

Passignano sul Trasimeno has perhaps the most resort feel out of all the places by the lake. Although it can get busy in the summer months, it still has a quiet charm. The main part of the resort stretches along the side of Trasimeno, with lots of small restaurants, cafes, and bars, all with views over the lake. It's not really a sunbathing, swimming sort of place. Whenever I visit, I take a slow walk along its promenade, relax in one of its bars, have a drink and simply watch the world pass by. Either before or after that, exploring the medieval little lanes that climb up towards the 14th century castle (La Rocca Passignano). Once at the castle, you have brilliant views out over the lake. Here again, there is the opportunity to sit and relax in a small café/bar. I'm here in early September, about 4.30 in the afternoon. A glass of red wine, stunning views of the lake, the music of Fleetwood Mac floating through the air. The sun still warm, I'm the only person on the small terrace outside the little bar. Swallows/swifts, I can never tell the difference, dart around at speed. Small craft skim over the lake, its water in rippling stillness. Olive-covered hills and tree-covered mountains form a basin to hold in Trasimeno. I sit and sample the wonder of it all. My contemplation interrupted by a small group of Italians. How dare they!

The busiest time to be in town is the third Sunday in July. This is the day of the Palio delle Barche (Race of the Boats). Teams in medieval costume carry boats, shoulder high, through the narrow streets, before launching them on the lake and the start of the race. It represents the medieval struggles between the Baglioni and Degli Oddi families of Perugia in the 15th century. The day ends with the 'burning of the castle', a spectacular firework display over the lake.

Passignano describes itself as, Uno dei Borghi più belli d'Italia (One of the most beautiful villages in Italy). It's a bit of a grand statement to make, but it is worth spending a few hours there.

San Feliciano really is the place where I simply come to relax. Again, it sits close to the lake, more a small village than a town.

It's the 25th of April. I'm sat at my favourite place, my little bar, just twenty meters from the edge of the lake, with a cappuccino and a small pastry. The sky is pale blue, the sun pleasantly hot. Late Umbrian spring, with the promise of long summer days waiting round the corner.

Drifting between the Italian conversation that surrounds me, I have 1950s American Rock & Roll. To be exact, at this very moment, Elvis - Blue Suede Shoes. Tiny sparrows flit between tables in the hope of a few crumbs. A large boat in full sail glides past, slicing through the mirror like surface of the lake. Wake Up Little Suzy, wake up ...... Italians stroll past, stopping for a photo opportunity. They stand and pose, taking advantage of a picture frame strung between two trees, the lake providing the canvas.

It's a public holiday in Italy, Liberation Day (Festa della Liberazione). Also known as La Festa della Resistenza (Celebration of the Resistance). The day commemorates those who died fighting against the Fascist regime and retreating Nazi forces. It's also a day to celebrate the end of what is now regarded as the Nazi occupation of Italy. The 25th of April was designated a national holiday in 1949. Across the country there are numerous official ceremonies. Most cities and towns having services of remembrance and parades. Italian flags and t-shirts remembering the partisans (partigiani/partigiane). Often with voices singing loud and clear, the song 'Bella Ciao', now known by most as the anthem of the Italian resistance to Fascism.

Peggy Sue, Peggy Sue, pretty, pretty ....

Quiet, relaxed calm. Tutti Frutti, the saxophone kicks in. I leave the speedy chatter of Italian, the sound of music fading, as I walk by the lake, hot sun on my back. The walk is not that far, coming to an end where you find small yachts and boats tied up; then returning to pass the little bar. My car is parked close to where the fishermen of the village dry and fix their nets, flat-bottomed boats bobbing around on the lake. This is the home of Trasimeno's fishing cooperative. If you happen to be a real fish eating person, then the restaurants around the lake are the places to eat. The Festa del Giacchio Sagra del Pesce del Lago Trasimeno, the festival lasting several days, takes place at the end of July. Each evening having food, music and drink.

The locals call San Feliciano, La perla del Trasimeno e il paese dei Tramonti (The pearl of Trasimeno and the town of sunsets). If I were you, I would listen to what they have to say, giving up a little of your time to sit with a glass of wine, watching the lake swallow the Umbrian sun.

Tuoro sul Trasimeno - I guess this is the place to go if you just want to spend the day on a very pleasant beach. There is little more to see, apart from the museum telling you the story of the area, especially the defeat of the Roman army at the hands of Hannibal. You can also take a ferry from here to the lake's islands.

Panicale is a small town resting a little distance from Trasimeno, but giving superb views of the lake, and gentle olive covered hills. It's a beautiful little town, with a few pretty piazzas, the main one being Piazza Umberto 1. Here you'll find a 15th century fountain and the 14th century Palazzo Pretorio. This is also where you'll find a good choice of restaurants, bars, and cafes. Take the time to wander around the cobbled streets that climb out from the piazza, once away from this main area you have a calmer feel to the place. And that is one of its downsides. I guess because it is so picturesque, the little town does attract lots of visitors, the vast majority being foreign. Most of the voices, as you walk around or sit in its bars, will generally be anything but Italian. Put it on your list of places to visit, you being one of many, but well worth it.

It's the middle of a hot July, I'm in Panicale to see a band performing in Piazza Umberto 1, part of the Trasimeno Blues Festival that takes place every year for a couple of weeks, with most music being free. I think everyone has had the same idea; the place is incredibly busy. But even with so many people, it is a beautiful setting to sit listening to live music. I eventually find a table outside one of the small restaurants, the owner trying to squeeze more tables onto his allotted part of the piazza. All voices are foreign, just the occasional Italian voice.

Along with the excellent music, the tables are squeezed so close together you can't but help picking up snippets of conversation from those around you. To my left I have an older American couple and an elderly Brit. From their conversation, the impression I have of them is that they are stereotypical 'expats'. They've clearly lived in the area for quite a number of years, the Brit knowing the owner of the restaurant by his first name, but all three speaking hardly any Italian. They give off an attitude suggesting that they see the local Italians as quaint and eccentric, different and comical. It almost feels inevitable that their conversation would include comparisons between Italy and the countries they come from, comparisons at no point favourable to Italians. The owner of the bar moves between tables, taking orders and clearing things away, the elderly Brit trying to engage him in conversation - in English, obviously. I order a beer and lasagne, trying my best to ignore the complete nonsense that's being spoken.

The music is good, the piazza full of people, the bars and restaurants overflowing. The elderly Brit asks me what I think of the lasagne. Before I have the chance to answer, he tells me, and others around, that the owner makes the best lasagne in the town. The food is reasonable, but certainly not the best I've ever had. The owner is squeezing past tables again, cheerful but also looking a little harassed.

'I'm just telling this chap here that your lasagne is the best in Panicale.'

The owner smiles, quickly moving to other tables, collecting used plates and empty glasses.

'I don't know how he gets it so good, in and out of the microwave in just a few minutes.'

I've finished my meal, responding that I'm sure the food hasn't come out of a microwave.

'No, it has. I don't know how he does it. I come here two or three times during the week to get a quick microwaved evening takeaway. I've ordered one this evening, haven't I Giacomo?'

The owner of the restaurant nodding, keeping his head down, as he carries food to another table. I'm wishing that the Brit would take himself away. People on other tables looking just a little quizzical about the possibility that their meal has been slid in and then out of a microwave.

The two Americans, sat at the same table as the lasagne expert, ask him if he has a bag to carry the takeaway home.

'No, I've left the old bag back in the UK.'

There's laughter from the three of them.

I've had enough. I pick up my beer and then walk to edge of the restaurant's tables that have spilled out onto the piazza.

'On your way then, you've not finished your beer. I'm not bothering you am I?'

'Seriously, is that a rhetorical question?'

As I squeeze past other tables, I leave him looking a little confused. Perhaps he'll choke on his takeaway.

Città della Pieve is about 24 kilometres (15 miles) to the south of Lago Trasimeno, a red brick town, making it very different in style to Gubbio. In some ways giving the town a slightly warmer feel. The guide books will almost always start descriptions of the towns and villages of Umbria with the phrase, 'well preserved' or 'largely preserved'. So, from this point I'm not going to use either. You can accept it as a given. Almost all towns and villages are at the very least medieval in character. It's one of the things that makes Umbria such a wonderful region. Città della Pieve is no exception.

I'm here in the middle of June for the Infiorata Di San Luigi Gonzaga, it's a traditional festival of medieval costume in honour of San Luigi Gonzaga, the patron saint of the Casalino neighbourhood.

The town sits inside ancient protective walls and is said to have the narrowest street in the whole of Italy – Via Baciadonna, just 80cm wide, others suggesting it's even less, only 50cm. Whatever its actual width, they say that it's so slim you could lean out of a window and kiss your lover on the other side of the street. I'll leave you to check the measurements, then travelling all over Italy, tape measure at hand, to check if this is fact or fiction. Perhaps, better still, test out if you are indeed able kiss your lover across the street.

It's another lovely Umbrian little town, to wander the streets, sit outside its cafes and bars, soaking up the atmosphere.

The main piazza is the Piazza del Plebiscito. Here you'll find the Palazzo della Corgna and the Duomo Santi Gervasio e Protasio.

As I said, I'm here for the festival, Via Pietro Vannucci covered by a brightly coloured carpet of flower petal art. Hours of delicate work having taken place the evening before. It's a beautiful warm day. Having explored the colourful displays, all I do is sit, order the next glass of Umbrian red wine and people watch.

We'll leave Lago Trasimeno behind; I know I will be there many more times.

A Sunday, early June, you find me in the dappled shade of an 80-year-old oak tree in the garden of Marcello and Alicia. From late spring through to early autumn this is the place where any outside eating takes place. A long heavy table, with benches of oak either side, sits here throughout the year. Eating is an extended family event, four generations, a few friends added, and Ghrem, l'inglese adottato (the adopted Englishman). I would say, in total there must be fifteen adults plus assorted children. If you're looking for a scene to fit the exact Italian family stereotype you've found it here. And the most exquisite thing is, I've been totally absorbed, not just by this one gathering but into the very heart of the Rosso and Balzarini families. Along with the beauty of Umbria, it's this connection that makes living here so special and beautiful.

Our meal begins with cured ham and wild boar sausage. Both have been nurtured, butchered, and then turned into the smoky, mouth-watering, sliced tastes that we have in front of us by Aldo. Along with this, one of my absolute favourites, zucchini flower fritters. Simple to cook, the courgette flowers dipped into a batter made from water, flour and salt. Once coated on all sides, the flowers are then deep fried and allowed to cool – absolutely delicious.

Almost forgot, as people gather, all are offered a glass of prosecco as an aperitivo. Well, when I say glass, it's actually a white plastic cup offered to you by Pietro, the husband of Francesca, Aldo's eldest daughter. But the cup is never full, that's just not the Italian way of doing things. The cool, sparkling drink is just enough to set the taste buds tingling in your mouth. Pietro always the joker, a beaming smile, a cheeky grin.

We're seated along both sides of a long heavy table, the children together at one end, Aldo at the other. Wine, water, a few bottles of beer and the obligatory bread. The bread still warm, having only just come out of the pizza oven built close to an outbuilding. For primo piatto we have mushroom risotto. Conversation and laughter flow easily across the table, calls from one end to the other, beer poured as if it were wine to simply sample. Children leave half eaten food, chase round the garden, run to parents and sit on adult knees, then returning to their food. The hot Umbrian Sunday afternoon, relaxed in happy contentment.

Roasted hare and chicken are placed at strategic points along the table, people free to pick the pieces they find to be the most appealing. A mixed salad accompanies the meat, tossed in nothing more than extra virgin olive oil, the green, peppery nectar, coming from sixty or more olive trees; harvested in the October of the previous year. Red wine, sparkling and still water are passed from one to another and along the table. Another drop of beer to sip.

Il dolce will have to wait. Some sit at the table, some having moved place to speak to others. Hammocks strung between trees and low canvas chairs taken by those who simply want to snooze in their fullness. Children are now changed and ready to jump into the large free-standing pool. And I'm being chased round the garden by a bucket of ice-cold water. After my inevitable drenching, I then return the favour to others; the children being the most obvious targets.

Bisnonna (Great Grandmother), Caterina, the mother of Davide, grandmother of Marcello, smiles as she observes the gathering. Caterina's diminutive form, gentle nods and knowing, slow shakes of her head, remind me a little of Gina. She still has a sparkle in her eyes, at times a playful, cheeky grin. Others arrive at the same time as il dolce - torta Nutella or crepes with ice cream are being offered. More wine, along with grappa and liqueurs. Hands are raised in answer to the question, who wants an espresso?

I'm now back at the table, my shirt and shorts almost dry. Just one more small, plastic, watering can of water poured down my back; giggling legs running away and scattering around the garden. Homemade spirits, of unknown strength, are grouped together on the table. I find myself having to try and explain why you're not able to buy almost pure alcohol in the UK. Those questioning me, explaining that it's readily available from supermarkets in Italy. A look of bemusement on the faces of those questioning.

The hot afternoon moves to early evening. Some sleep in the shade, others chat, a few leave, to be replaced by others who have just arrived. Even the children have now slowed down, changed from being in the pool, no longer any threats of a drenching in cold water. I'm sat at the table with another espresso, also being offered a taste of a spirit with unknown alcohol content. Most of the conversation I pick up, some I misunderstand, and some simply floats above my head. It's relaxed, it's funny, it's a warm evening, the odd lucciola (firefly) making an early appearance.

Marcello asks if I would like to try a small sugar cube that's been sitting in alcohol. The jar containing the cubes and liquid of unknown strength, looks innocent enough. It's a sugar cube, what concern could there be? He gives me no advanced warning. I pop the cube in my mouth. Almost instantly, the whole of my mouth and my lips are completely anesthetised, I'm hardly able to speak. I grimace, not even able to get out even one expletive in protest. Marcello pops a sugar cube in his mouth, smiling and suggesting it tastes fine. The initial oral shock lasts a little time, then reducing to numbness as you wait for the dentist's drill to begin its work. I never knew a simple sugar cube could be so demonic.

Once my mouth has fully recovered, I ask if anyone knows of a good physiotherapist who deals with sports injuries. No connection with my mouth, obviously. It takes some explaining, with me searching my brain for the correct Italian terms. For some months I've been experiencing pain at the back of my right foot when running. It's not the Achilles, more of an egg-shaped lump, tender to the touch. If you have any sports injury knowledge, you may have some idea of what it could be; I didn't. There are shrugs of shoulders, more questioning, some offering suggestions. Francesca saying that she has a friend who is a physio, his business near Fossato di Vico, the small medieval village being just a short drive from Colpalombo. The problem with the back of my heel has become increasingly painful. If I can't resolve it, I may have to give up running completely.

The conversation brings to mind the first race I took part in with Gubbio Runners. An evening race, through the medieval streets of Gubbio, 2014, the year before I came to live in Umbria. The route of 8 kilometres trailed through most parts of the town, the whole circuit having to be completed twice, eventually ending where it began. To officially take part in a race you have to be certified as physically fit and healthy, I guess they're trying to cut down the risk of someone suddenly collapsing with a heart attack. You also have to be registered with the Italian National Athletics Federation. Although I've not yet been certified as fit and I'm not registered, I can still take part, but only as a guest. The race organisers, Gubbio Runners, will accept no responsibility should I die.

The race starts at 9pm. I don't think I have taken part in any race like it. At least 100 runners, pounding through the old streets of Gubbio, running past tourists and people from the town sat outside restaurants enjoying an evening meal. We charge past, feet slapping down on stone, lungs breathing heavily, hot sweaty bodies at times almost touching those who are eating.

I've never been a fast runner. Even in my younger days I always finished in the middle of the pack, rather than anywhere near the front. Now, I tend to be somewhere in the back third. Anyway, having completed the circuit twice, having avoided stumbling into a dish of ravioli, I arrive at the finish. The reward for completing the race, a bottle of white wine and a packet of pasta – how Italian can you get? I have medals and t-shirts for completing a race, never have I had a bottle of wine.

I remember the following evening, Marcello telling me that he had asked his friend if he had seen the inglese at the race. Marcello's friend asking what the inglese looks like. You will have seen him, he has a red face and white hair, Marcello responded. Apparently, from that 'flattering' description, Marcello's friend did remember seeing me. Really, that's how I'm identified, the man with a red face and white hair. I think I have some serious work to do on building up a tan, perhaps dying my hair. I should probably go for both.

Back to the meal under the branches of the old oak tree. More food has arrived on the table, a selection of different cured meats, cheese, and cake. A few more bottles of wine, and the offer to sample yet another suspicious homemade spirit. The sun has now disappeared, the hills lit dark orange. Marcello has his guitar resting on one knee, fingers gently strumming on the strings. People gather round in anticipation of a song from his young daughter, Emma. Little more than six years old, with no understanding of English, she gives a brilliant rendition of New York – Alicia Keys. With a beaming smile on her face, she receives rapturous applause. The singing continues, the adults joining in, some songs in English, most in Italian. Bats flit above in silence, insects mesmerised by the soft glow of garden lights, a performance from lucciole floating above and between low bushes. The afternoon and evening coming to an end as people start to leave. Italians leaving, always at least a thirty-minute process. More hugs, more kisses to faces, more discussion and more light-hearted gossip, more laughter; then people leave.

Having left the garden behind, I walk in almost complete darkness. Surrounded by trees and low bushes, a gravel track takes me to the narrow tarmac road that climbs up, eventually bringing me to the road and Case Colle. It's only a walk of about one kilometre, but in the darkness it is completely magical. The sky is awash with stars, the moon having momentarily hidden itself behind a thin wisp of cloud. And absolutely everywhere – lucciole (fireflies). Unbelievably bright pinpoints of light, flash and float in front of me and behind. There are so many, it feels as though I could be lifted from the ground. The tiny lights so bright that they appear to have no body attached. Just hundreds of lights, hovering and floating, silent, close enough to touch; to gently capture for the briefest moment in your hand. Never before have I been completely surrounded by such a display. The only sound to break the silence, the barking of a deer, hidden behind a screen of trees. It is a dream-like world.

I walk home, mesmerised by the slow-motion ballet of lucciole.

The following week I have an appointment with the fisioterapista (physiotherapist), at the Centro Medico Fisiolog. After explaining my problem, and a brief examination, Roberto decides that possibly the best approach is to try laser treatment. I'm a little dubious but decide that I may as well give it a go. This will be the first of probably five sessions, with one week between each; no running in between. Roberto speaks very little English, and I've become Grent again.

Roberto asks me to turn face down on a low table, the sort of table you find in all medical facilities. He then explains that I will feel nothing more than slight heat, possibly a little burning sensation. He then gently glides the tip of what looks like an oversized pen over and around the egg-shaped swelling on the back of my heel. No burning, just the sense of gentle massage and warmth, lasting little more than five minutes. All done and we have a little chat about where I live, where I come from and why I decided on Italy; the questions I'm almost always asked. With that, the session is done, I leave with an appointment for the following week.

I'm still not convinced that laser treatment will resolve my problem. Perhaps a little bit of online investigation could throw some knowledge my way. Retrocalcaneal Bursitis is what I appear to have. Apparently the condition is common in ballet dancers and athletes. I'm definitely not a ballet dancer, so I must be an athlete. I can but dream.

Life continues around Case Colle, with me taking a rest from running. Steady walks result in little discomfort. The valleys, forests, hills and mountains, local to where I live, offer endless opportunities to explore. And there's always Lago Trasimeno.

But before any more walking and running up and down the hills of Umbria, I'm flying back to the UK from Ciampino Airport, Rome. I have a wedding to attend.

It's the wedding of Kara and Andy. I'm sure most fathers have gone through the same feelings. For me it's a feeling of immense pride in the tiny girl who has grown into a beautiful, intelligent, young woman. The wedding is a large gathering of family and friends. The moment comes for me to collect Kara from her hotel room, both of us ready to take the short walk to the banqueting room where guests are gathered, waiting in quiet anticipation for the marriage to take place. We stand looking at each other, both trying to keep swirling emotions under some level of control. My daughter has a serene beauty about her, still my daughter, but no longer my little girl. It's a moment of incredible sentiment. Our faces don't mean to look so serious as we pass those gathered, it's just that both of us are trying to keep any tears inside. It's strange how the body reacts in the same way to happiness and sadness.

Kara and Andy are now married, let the celebrations begin! Well, the celebrations can begin once all the photographs have been taken, food has been eaten, the cake has been cut, and speeches have been made. I attempt to make what I have to say convey the pride I have, at the same time trying to add a little wit. To the relief of Kara, I eventually sit down, leaving the best man to make by far the best and most entertaining speech. Formalities over, the dancing can begin. It's a wonderful occasion of fun, laughter, chatting and joking, drinking and catching up with those you may not have seen for some time. The occasional quiet moment for me to sneak to one side and give yet another emotional hug to both Kara and Lucy, my younger daughter. The enjoyment, happiness and laughter continue into the early hours of the morning, only then do we start to drift towards our rooms, most of the wedding guests having already left.

Within a few days, Kara and Andy are on their way to honeymoon in New York and then Mexico. I remain in the UK for several more days visiting friends, before my return flight back to Rome and then the drive to Colpalombo.

It's now July and I'm back for another laser treatment to the back of my heel. This is the third treatment; I think it may be working. Roberto asks about England and apologises if the laser feels too hot or is a little painful.

'Mi dispiace, fa troppo caldo e doloroso?'

The treatment certainly feels a little hotter, but not really painful.

'Un po 'caldo sì, ma non doloroso', I reply.

Third treatment soon over, I leave the coolness of Roberto's treatment room and venture back out into the heat of the Umbrian summer. I've decided to drive to Deruta, a small town just past Perugia, in the direction of Rome, about 50 kilometres (31 miles) from Colpalombo; the place famous for its ceramics.

Deruta is a tiny little town, its centre, as with all towns and villages in Umbria medieval in form and shape. Just about every shop in Deruta sells ceramics. The town, along with Gubbio, has provided Umbria with its workshops for the production of ceramics since the 13th century. Having passed Perugia, you leave the autostrada, finding even more outlets selling ceramics before you make the short climb up to the town.

Some suggest that the name of the town comes from its long history of being repeatedly destroyed, caught in the middle of competing armies (distrutta – destroyed). Even without its fame for ceramics, it's a pleasant little place to have a break, to sit at one of the bars in the main piazza, a glass of Umbrian wine, watching the slow pace of life. In the centre of this little town, you'll find the church of San Francesco, built in the 14th century and the Palazzetto Municipale dating from at least 1300. This building acts as the Town Hall and as the Museum of Ceramics. Even the street furniture is ceramic, beautifully crafted and ornate. Certainly, if you are looking to buy ceramics, Deruta is the place to visit. Most of the shops and outlets sell very similar traditional items.

For my tastes, Domiziani offers something spectacular and different. It's still, as with most of the other outlets, family owned, having a small showroom in Deruta and in Gubbio. I've also come across Domiziani in Montefalco and Orvieto. But if you really want to explore what Domiziani has to offer, I suggest you visit the main place of production and showroom outside Torgiano, just a few kilometres from Deruta. In the main showroom you can buy something as small as a pepper pot to something as large as a table, garden furniture, whole shower units, a whole staircase, basically almost anything your imagination comes up with can be made in ceramic by Domiziani. You could even combine the purchase of ceramics with visiting the wine producing Lungarotti family.

It's the hot month of August 2015. The rather unresponsive petrol mower transported from the UK has given up the ghost. I'm in need of something, bigger, stronger and tougher. I know just the man who can point me in the right direction: Aldo. After asking his advice, the very next day we are at the showroom and workshop of Argentina, on the edge of Gubbio. There is everything here to keep any mini farmer happy, from sit on mowers costing anything up to €4,000, your heavy-duty strimmer, your chunky big motozappa (rotavator), generators, water pumps, irrigation systems, anything you can possibly think of to cut things, from monster chainsaws to secateurs. Every form of protection, from visors, thick gauntlet-type gloves and bright orange overalls, to steel toe-cap boots. A whole range of other items that I have no idea what they would be used for. We have a saunter round, as men do in such places, speculating on the two of us clubbing together to buy one of the more expensive mowers.

After chatting with the owner, we eventually decide (notice the term we, not I) that an Emak K650, OHV 159cc, the maker being Oleo-Mac, is what I want. No, I'd never heard of the maker before and, probably like you, I had no real idea if I have a powerful machine or not. It's big, bright orange and black. And yes, it turns out to be very powerful, cutting through tall grass and giant weeds with disparaging ease. I also need a motozappa, no self-respecting rural Italian would be without one, an essential item for a real Italian man. But that can wait, I'll buy one in the autumn to churn over what will become my vegetable plot in the spring of next year.

I've had another confrontation with Benito. He's a neighbour who lives, some of the time, in Case Colle, about 100 meters from my place. Over the years we have had 'words' on a number of occasions. The relationship between the two of us became tainted when he built a concrete bunker, admittedly on his land, but directly to the rear of my house. He has plenty of land, most of it stretching along the back of my property and planted with at least fifty mature olive trees. The bunker, apparently a cantina, is completely illegal, but of more significance for me, it is completely brutto (ugly). He's been denounced to the authorities in Gubbio, but he appears to have little intention of removing it. Anyway, we've had another falling out.

Between the back of my house and the land that belongs to Benito is a right of way, just a few meters in width. And literally, within a few inches of this right of way, just inside Benito's land is a giant oak tree. From old photographs of my place prior to renovation, it's clear that the oak tree simply planted itself there sometime in the past. The tree is so big now that it is causing me problems with its long branches and roots. A number of branches have grown over so that they're actually touching the roof of my house. When there is a breeze or heavier wind, the branches scrape on the side of the house and the roof, especially annoying at night when you're trying to sleep. The tree is of absolutely no use to Benito. I've even suggested that I would share the cost of cutting it down, but he refuses to even talk about it. There is legal permission from the Corpo Forestale (basically the countryside police) to cut it down, but Benito has to give his consent, something he just will not give.

I'm sick of the branches scraping and brushing against my house. It's around September time when I climb out through the skylight that gives access to my roof. In less than ten minutes I've cut down the offending branches, leaving them to one side on Benito's land. Just a few branches, that's all.

The following morning, as I work in my garden, Benito approaches asking if I would come to his place for a chat. Perhaps he wants to come to some sort of compromise, even an apology for building the concrete bunker. Nothing is said as we walk to his house. I enter, it's cool and dark, shutters closed to keep out the morning heat. He gestures that I should take a seat. Is he going to suggest some peace agreement? Perhaps I've been too harsh in my judgement of him. His wife is also in the room. Usually, she at least offers a friendly hello, on this occasion not one word leaves her lips. No offer of an espresso, glass of water, nothing.

'Who cut down the branches on the tree?'

Benito blunt and accusative in his tone. He obviously knows who. I feel like a pupil in the office of the headteacher, being reprimanded. I almost expect him to ask me what my parents would think. That's an easy one, as they're no longer living I'm reasonably certain that they don't hold an opinion. He stands, headteacher face, arms folded.

'Well, you know who did. I cut the branches down, they were causing a problem. The whole tree is a problem.'

Not a hint comes from Benito that I have a reasonable point to make.

'You had no permission to cut any branches from the tree. I didn't give you permission. The Forestale will give me a fine for cutting down the branches.'

'They're not going to do that; they've already given permission for the whole tree to be cut down, but you won't do it. Anyway, just tell the Forestale that the inglese did it.'

Benito has every intention of continuing to harangue me, his wife having now left the room, I can only think out of embarrassment.

I've had enough. I'm annoyed and angry. Why does he have to be so uncompromisingly rude? I simply stand and walk out, leaving a passing comment that the tree needs to be cut down. Benito has not spoken to me since that morning. Not even a passing nod, no quick glance in my direction when he happens to be passing the back of my house. For a while I offered a gesture in his direction, a quick wave, but now I've given up.

For a number of years, I'd assumed that Benito was an incomer to the hamlet of Case Colle, always being rather separate from everyone who lives here. It turns out that he grew up in the house that, for a brief moment, transformed into the office of the headteacher. He grew up with others who have lived all their life in the little hamlet. The only difference being that he moved away to work in Perugia. He spent his adult life working in banking and living most of the time in the city. The sad thing now is that nobody engages with him; it's not just me. Even his sister has no relationship with him, they simply don't speak. Her house is attached to that of Benito. Clearly Benito is not his real name, but it sums up his character. Shorter in stature, but just as arrogant, secretive and stubborn as his namesake. He must be in his late seventies, why does he make life so difficult for himself? This is a tiny hamlet, where everyone knows if and when you sneeze. It's a place where everyone helps every other.

Although the concrete bunker remains, along with the oak tree, thankfully Benito is only here part-time, the rest of his time spent living in Perugia.

It's late September. My sister, Katherine, and her husband are staying with me for three weeks. They're more than happy to spend most of their time in and around the house and garden, walking down to Colpalombo and up to Carbonesca, the occasional visit to Gubbio, especially when it's market day.

They've become friends with all who live in Case Colle, apart from Benito. Often you'll find my sister sat with Benedetta and Aldo in their garden, other times invited for espresso by Federico and Elisabetta, the two of them living with their middle-aged sons; their house no more than 100 meters from my own.

That's where you find us one morning, in the house of Federcio and Elisabetta. We're sat in the dining room, a small kitchen area off to one side. As with almost all Italian homes, the outside shutters to the windows are closed, the actual windows opening to the inside. The room is protected from any curious flies and mosquitoes by a fine wire mesh frame, this able to be slid up and down. Even with the shutters closed, the heat of an Umbrian September is still finding a means of creeping its way into the relative darkness of the room. Elisabetta slides up the mesh screen, swinging the shutters open, then pulling the screen back into place. At least a little breeze flows into the room, I don't know of any Italian neighbours with air conditioning. I don't have air conditioning.

With the large camino (fireplace) and caldaia (boiler) taking up most of one wall, the opposite wall having the window, the rest of the room is relatively full. A round table sits in the middle with four chairs, a low couch against one wall, a dark wooden cupboard against the other. I think Federico is now 80, Elisabetta just a few years younger. Out of the two she's certainly the fittest, more sprightly and agile. It's been noticeable over the past few years how age has started to slow Federico down. He once went hunting with Aldo, but his sight and a slight shake makes that problematic; he no longer goes. He still drives, but always at the speed of a snail. I know, very different to the majority of Italian drivers.

Federico always sits on the couch, it being so low he finds it difficult to stand and greet us, so he remains seated. Elisabetta does most of the talking for the two of them, telling my sister that it's good to see her again and asking how long she will be staying. My sister points to a framed photograph of a young boy on the wall, asking in English who he is. Although Elisabetta understands not one word of English, she understands what my sister is asking. That's my grandson, a very clever boy, he speaks very good English. He lives with our daughter in Florence. My sister then shows Elisabetta photographs of her grandchildren saved to her mobile phone. Elisabetta disappears into the small kitchen, returning with espresso, biscuits and a range of spirits that look almost as old as her and Federico.

Elisabetta smiles and apologises for her lack of English, gesturing that we should take a biscuit. What would we like to drink?

Federico says that he will have a drop of brandy, so we do the same.

Silence sits in the room. The quiet being broken by Federico talking about his various ailments and his coming death. I find it difficult to understand what he's saying, the words spoken through closed lips. How do you respond, what can you say to someone speaking about their own death? I translate for my sister and her husband. The three of us give a half smile and shake of our heads. Elisabetta smiles and tells her husband to stop talking about death, to stop being so miserable. She smiles again, looking in our direction and slowly shaking her head.

Federico continues speaking, again about death, only to be stopped by Elisabetta. For some reason, he then goes on to say that he once worked in Germany and Luxembourg, I'm not sure why he's telling us this. I translate what's being said to my sister, she then asking me if they know that our father was German. Tell them our father was German, a German soldier. I respond by saying that they already know that we're half German, do you really want me to tell them that he was a German soldier? This is starting to feel like the Fawlty Towers sketch from the 1970s – 'Don't mention the war.' Given that German soldiers shot 40 civilians in Gubbio in 1944, do you really want me to tell them that he was a German soldier? As far as I'm aware our father was never in Italy, but still. My sister responds with, we have to talk about something. Elisabetta and Federico are now looking at us wondering what we're talking about.

'Are you sure you want me to tell them?'

'Nostro padre era un soldato Tedesco nella seconda guerra mondiale.'

My sister assumes to know what I've just said and smiles. Elisabetta smiles back. Then Federico mumbles something from the couch.

'Si, ero un ragazzo che viveva a Gubbio. Ricordo che I soldati tedeschi sparavano alle persone. Tuo padre era un soldato Tedesco in Italia?'

My sister still sits smiling, nodding as Federico speaks, then asking me what he's saying. Me telling her first not to nod, and to stop smiling. Her asking me why she can't nod?

He's saying that he was a young boy in Gubbio. He remembers when German soldiers shot people. Stop nodding, he just asked if our father was a German soldier in Italy. Oh bugger, she responds, and stops nodding.

'No, nostro padre era un soldato in Grecia e Russia.'

What are you saying? I'm just tell them that our father was never in Italy, he was in Greece and Russia.

'Yes, in Greece and Russia', my sister confirms to them in English.

Luckily Elisabetta intervenes, asking if we would like another drink. We have another sip of brandy.

Federico has settled back into his couch. No hint of agitation in his recollection of German soldiers shooting people. Just an elderly man recalling a childhood memory.

We're often invited round for coffee. We don't ever mention the war again.

Another week has gone by, as my sister and her husband Pete relax in the garden, I have a trailer full of logs delivered. The tractor reverses in, the driver asking where I would like the logs. As close as possible to the little stone shed, I reply. A few adjustments in the positioning of the trailer, the trailer is raised to an almost vertical position, and hundreds of logs come tumbling out. A little shake of the trailer, and the last few stubborn logs join the rest. With payment gratefully received, the deliverer of fuel for the winter months gives a cheery goodbye and trundles away on his tractor, empty trailer banging and rattling behind. All I have to do now is move the mountain of wood into the little stone log shed and stack other logs next to the wall of the house. I can't just let my sister and Pete watch me; they join in. It's quite hard work, taking a number of hours when added together with the breaks. In the end almost all of the logs are either in the stone shed or neatly stacked against the house, with a small pile still where they had originally tumbled out of the trailer. They will eventually be moved when there's space in the shed. Job done, time for a beer/glass of wine.

The following morning I'm out cutting the grass with my new, powerful, monster mower. It's another warm September day. Through the noise of the petrol mower, I can hear my sister calling me from the kitchen, something about a snake. With mower silenced, I can make out what she's saying.

'There's a snake in the kitchen, come and do something.'

From where I am, at the far end of the garden, I can see something just inside the kitchen, the door always left open when it's warm. I call, saying that it's probably just a large slow worm, nothing to worry about.

'It's a bloody snake, come and look. First scorpions and now bloody snakes, come and look.'

In my head, it's not a snake.

It is a snake, a little viper. A skinny thing, only about five inches long.

'Well do something!'

My sister is good at giving orders, perhaps it's the German in her.

That's exactly what I do, I do something. I take my mobile phone out of my back pocket to take a picture. I'm not sure that's what my sister had in mind. It also turns out that the little snake is camera shy. Before I have a chance to take a snap, the little viper has disappeared under one of the base units of the kitchen.

'Well trust you to think of doing that first. How are we going to relax knowing that we have a snake in the kitchen?'

It's not really a question. It's said as an accusative statement.

'You're going to have to find it.'

I'm now on my stomach, torch in hand, peering under the base unit. No snake, it's disappeared. This news brings no end of joy to my sister.

'You had to mess about taking a photograph. Well, we're going to have to find it, I won't be able to relax.'

Older sisters, what a dramatic fuss. Clearly I only think this, no words actually leave my lips. My sister's venom is far more worrying than that of a snake.

The kitchen has never been cleaner. Every single corner is spotlessly searched. No snake, it's simply vanished. I try to reassure my sister that it's only a small snake, it's not really a danger. I can't repeat what she had to say.

That evening we sit at the large oak table in the kitchen having a meal, my sister constantly imagining she can hear the snake moving around. With her next bite of food, suddenly asking what's that in the corner?

We go to bed that evening, the disappearing snake a bit of a mystery.

The following morning, I hear a call from Pete, he's spotted the snake in the kitchen. He being the one who first spotted it yesterday. By the time I arrive in the kitchen, he's seen a second snake at the bottom of the stairs. My sister is not a happy woman, giving me strict commands that I don't even think about trying to take a photograph. Which snake do I go for first? With a small pan and brush, I go for the one near the bottom of the stairs. As I'm doing this, my sister asking if a snake can climb stairs? I guess they can, is not the reply she was hoping for.

One small viper on one small dust pan, the next small viper brushed on to join the other already there. I ask my sister if she wants to have a look, the sort of thing little brothers do.

'No, I bloody don't want to have a look. Get rid of them.'

The little snakes are transported down the garden and given their freedom well away from the house. Job done, calm returns to my little home in Case Colle.

In all the years I have had the house, there has never been a snake of any size that has ventured inside. In fact, in all the time I've had the house, I've only come across a snake outside on less than half a dozen occasions. And the two given their freedom were very small.

What is it they say about not counting your chickens? In this case counting snakes that I've very rarely come across. Who is it that spots yet another snake in the kitchen the following day? Pete. He's just walked into the coolness of the kitchen to collect two bottles of beer and a white wine. We're enjoying a warm afternoon, sat in the shade of the walnut tree, the tree that grows over the corner of my garden from that of Lorenzo. Pete calls to us:

'Another snake, that's three now. How many more will I see?'

None hopefully, is the response from my sister.

Again, it's a very small viper. Pete sweeps it up, carries outside and allows it to escape at the far end of the garden.

I debate with my sister, should we call Pete the Snake Whisperer or should we give him the name of Snake Eye? It would appear that he is the Pied Piper of Snakes. We go for Snake Eye, the name now totally associated with Pete, even by my Italian neighbours. All now referring to him as Snake Eye rather than Pete. I think he quite likes the name; it adds a little mystery to his character. My sister pleads with him not to charm any more snakes into the kitchen. That, indeed, is the last one. Well, the last one we know of. As I think I've already said, when the weather is warm, the kitchen door is always left open. Don't say anything to my sister.

On telling Aldo and Paola about Snake Eye and his skill at spotting snakes, they both agree that there is probably a bigger, fully grown snake close by. Perhaps hidden away in the branches of the cherry tree close to the house. It's clearly a possibility, the little snakes came from somewhere, either the tree or in the delivery of logs. I can't tell you how pleased my sister is to have this news relayed to her. The shade of the cherry tree being one of her favourite places to sit and read.

Before Snake Eye and my sister return to the UK, their holiday almost over, It's decided that we should invite friends and neighbours for pranzo. Every day of their stay has been one of deep blue skies and incredibly warm sun. My sister appears to have got into the habit of not being happy just to invite a few people for a meal, it's her idea to invite 35, plus the three of us. She started writing names down, adding just another two, then another three, then another two, not wanting to leave anyone out. In the past, when I've been in the UK and she's been at the house on holiday with friends, through invitations lost in translation, she has ended up with totally unexpected numbers turning up either for pranzo or cena. On this occasion the numbers expected are correct, there will be no surprises.

Almost the end of September, a warm morning, bright sun and clear blue sky. We've asked people to arrive at about 1.30, all is good. The morning has been taken by preparing food, enough to feed forty. There is always the chance in Italy that others could turn up. I think my sister missed her true vocation in life, she should have had a catering business. However, she's not alone, she has her little brother and Snake Eye hard at work, following her instructions, perhaps a polite term to describe her commands.

By 1.15, all is ready. Tables and chairs have been borrowed from a number of neighbours, the tables set out in train formation from the veranda at the front of the house, trailing out in one long line down the garden. Tables decked with tablecloths, bottles of vino rosso and vino bianco, aqua and soft drinks, cutlery (some borrowed from neighbours) and forty places with antipasto. As is common, when eating at my neighbours, the food is served on plastic plates. It's perhaps not the most environmentally appropriate way to serve food, but it certainly saves on the washing up, and we would have had to ask to borrow plates from the whole of Colpalombo to feed people if we had gone for the real thing. Anyway, that's my attempt at an excuse for not being more environmentally friendly – sorry, you're going to have to accept it. Primo piatto, secondo and dolce already prepared, the dolce taking up just about every spare space in the kitchen. I'm not sure if I've already said, you step out directly from the kitchen to the patio/veranda and then the garden. With everything set out in the garden, it is the picture-perfect Italian scene. All we need is a live performance from Andrea Bocelli.

The invited guests all appear to arrive at the same time, most on foot, a few in cars. And just as they walk up the garden and decide where they going to sit, what had been a clear blue sky decides to darken. No, this can't be happening. No, it can't possibly decide to rain. Oh yes it can. Tiny drops at first, just to make people feel a little fidgety. It will pass, it's not going to really rain. Yes it is. Other dark clouds join the one already in position directly above the house, the tiny drops quickly increasing to a downpour; this was not the forecast. Still very warm, but now also very wet. People grab their antipasto, cutlery and drinks, making the short dash for the cover of the veranda.

The patio area covered by the terracotta tiles of the veranda, on a good day, could perhaps accommodate sixteen people. We now have almost forty huddled together trying to hold food, drinks, and remain dry. Several of us break cover, grabbing tables and chairs, then dashing back under the veranda. The huddled mass then sorts itself out, somehow managing to create enough space so that all can be seated at a table; this in space that theoretically is just not available. But all are seated, very much shoulder to shoulder, with very little possibility to easily move, knees touching other knees. People are squeezed together, a little hunched, with elbows drawn in. It's become a very 'cosy' and crowded pranzo.

Those close to the protection of the house are fine. Those in the middle of the veranda are fine. All a little squashed together, but at least dry. However, the downpour continues, a strong wind now deciding to join the rain. Those sitting at the edges of the cover offered by the veranda are getting increasingly wet. Marcello and a few others dash away, something is called out in speedy Italian that I don't manage to catch. Whilst they are gone, we have moved on from antipasto to primo piatto. Very few people can actually move, so myself, Katherine, Snake Eye, Paola, Francesca and Alicia have to pass food from the table in the kitchen to those sitting closest. Those sitting closest, pass the food to others, some food having to be reached over the heads of those seated. By the time Marcello returns, looking just a little wet, everyone has their primo piatto.

Marcello, with the help of others, then somehow manages to hang plastic sheeting around the veranda. The plastic sheeting offering at least some protection for those more exposed. Although a little damp, some a little wet, all tightly huddled together, conversation and laughter flow. Food is being eaten, some asking for more, wine is passed, and we eventually serve the secondo over the heads of the chattering neighbours and friends. Jokes about the weather, jokes about being squashed together. Eventually we arrive at dolce and espresso. Aldo offering to make the espresso at his house and bring it round. The rain is starting to ease a little and the wind has left. You just know that by the time we have finished the sun will have decided to return.

We were not able to enjoy pranzo relaxed in the garden, the iconic Italian scene almost literally washed away. But, without coming across as a little immodest, il pranzo turned out to be a great success. We're told that it's the first time in ages that all the people from Case Colle have come together like this. And just to top things off, with applause coming from those seated, Paola presents us with an enormous hamper containing wine, salami, cheese, pasta, olive oil, truffle oil, biscuits and other assorted goodies. The hamper having been put together by all who had been invited. I'll say it again, I love Italia!

The whole gathering has probably been here for a couple of hours before people start to leave. And sure enough, as people leave, the sun reappears in a blue sky. Aldo and Benedetta return to their house for a snooze. Paola, Alicia, Francesca, their husbands and a couple of other friends, Peter and Laura, remain. Between clearing things away, we have a few more drinks, moving on from wine to just a couple of spirits. As always, the homemade spirits of unknown strength.

I offer to make bacon and egg sandwiches. Some saying yes, others, including Marcello, saying no, they are just too full. I make enough for everyone anyway. The bacon is from the UK, something not easy to find in Umbria. Although having said he was full, Marcello takes one bite, bright yellow yolk dripping down his chin; he's hooked.

As September moves towards October, my sister returns to the UK. Autumn has definitely arrived. The days are shorter, the temperature of each day falling but still pleasantly warm. Oak valleys that have been covered in green now changing to crisp red, orange and yellow. Most mornings now starting with heavy mist hiding valley bottoms, the higher mountains appearing to rise up out of a white sea. Each morning Colpalombo, to the back of my house, waiting to be unveiled. Although there is not the heat of summer, the chance of rain being more likely, Umbria in the autumn remains enchanting.

With Aldo's help, I now have what all rural Italian men need. I have my motozappa, purchased from the same place that I bought the petrol mower, equally big and equally powerful.

I also have another confrontation with Benito. My garden is not fenced in, it's open for anyone to walk through. The same applies to Benito's land that runs along the back of my house. If you remember the land has quite a number of well-established olive trees and the annoying concrete bunker that is supposed to be a cantina. He also has a number of grape vines. At this time of year, the vines are heavy with juicy green grapes. No, I haven't tried them, honest, I'm just assuming they are juicy and sweet. Anyway, I'm on what is technically his land. The sun sets at the back of the house, sinking each evening into the hills and mountains. This evening the picture is spectacular, the sky on fire. I'm stood between the vines, trying to capture them in the foreground, silhouetted against a blazing sky. I really have not touched one single grape; they are totally unmolested.

I'm crouched down trying to get that one perfect image. I don't see Benito approaching.

'What are you doing on my land?! You have no permission to be on my land. Get off my land!'

I could respond with equal anguish, but it's such a serene evening. I stand, turn and smile.

'Benito, it's a beautiful evening. Just look at the sunset. I'm just taking a few photographs, that's all.'

There is no smile on the face of Benito. Absolutely no hint of friendly neighbourliness.

'It's my land! Get off!'

I simply smile. Leaving HIS LAND, without saying another word.

Aldo is absolutely right. Whenever you mention the name of Benito, he simply says that he is an imbecille, an idiota. I have to agree. In such a little community it's total nonsense not to get on with people. All help and support each other. In just a few weeks it will be time to harvest olives. Benito must have at least fifty mature trees. Who will help him?

Let's forget about Benito for now. Something more important, how's the back of my heel? If you remember, during the summer I'd been having laser treatment. Having had two more visits to see Roberto, the treatment appeared to have worked. Admittedly the last two times, the laser was particularly hot. The final treatment quite painful, the back of my heel feeling like it had a lighted match held against it. But it was only for a very short period, soon forgotten. And it worked, the swelling gone, no pain when running – success!

It's the last week in October and I have my niece, April, staying. A week that has incredibly good weather. By late morning, each day, the temperature climbs to at least 23°C. We do the usual tourist things, a day in beautiful Orvieto, an afternoon in Assisi. We visit Montone, where we have a meal in one of my favourite restaurants. An afternoon and evening in Gubbio, with the essential few drinks in Martintempo. A meal with my neighbours, in part to celebrate the purchase of my very first, totally new car. I'll tell you about the car in the next few pages. And a day of hard labour for April, I guess as 'payment' for her stay.

I plan to have chickens, so I need to fence the land just across the road from my house. With help, as ever, from Aldo I already have wooden posts and fencing. So that's what we do for the day. April holds a post in place, nodding her head when she wants me to hit it (some jokes last forever). By the end of the day, we have most of the posts solidly fixed. Now all I have to do is fence what will become the vegetable plot to keep the chickens out. Once April has left for her return flight to the UK, I complete the rest of the fence.

So, here I am, the straniero, l'inglese, living in his little bit of Umbria. Adopted and embraced by my Italian neighbours and friends. It is simply wonderful.

Your Italy & Our Italia

'First of all, let's get one thing straight. Your Italy and our Italia are not the same thing. Italy is a soft drug peddled in predictable packages such as hills in the sunset, olive groves and raven-haired girls. Italia, on the other hand, is a maze. In Italia you can go round and round in circles for years. Which, of course, is great fun.'

. . . .

Beppe Severgnini

La Bella Figura

CHAPTER FOUR

Being Italian

···

'For us to go to Italy and to penetrate into Italy, is like the most fascinating act of self-discovery.'

···

D.H. Lawrence

The straniero, the foreigner living in Italy. The British European. The inglese, with an English point of view. I may try not to do it, but I guess it is inevitable that I come to this with a whole bunch of stereotypes. So, what follows are my perceptions, my own particular take on things. Some will come close to reality, others perhaps distorted by my own peculiar way of seeing and listening. Keeping all of this in mind, here goes. My look, now that I live in Italy, at 'Being Italian'. Others write whole books on the topic. I intend to do it in one chapter. Wish me luck.

UN AUTO NUOVO

October 2015. If I intend to live in Italy, I need an Italian car. At present I have a Ford Focus, right-hand drive, UK registration. Not a new car, I've never been the owner of a totally new car. A car that comes with that new car smell, a smell that you can never capture again once you've driven the car away from the showroom.

Don't you find that car showrooms have become temples to the internal combustion engine (I guess in the near future, temples to the electric engine). Lavish opulence to entice you in, to feed your desire to have a new car. New car temples, cavernous in size for no practical reason. Brightly lit, everything glorious and glistening. Temples offering the very latest models, car doors open gesturing for you to sit inside, examine and imagine. They're giant rooms of peace and solemnity, soft music playing to ease you into the sale. Places where deals can be done, finance offered, your desire for a new car fulfilled. And that's where I am, in the Temple of Sunco Automotive SpA, Corciano, Perugia. The target of my desire, a Renault Kadjar. The temple is almost begging me to enter. How can I resist?

Prova – Nuova Renault Kadjar

I step inside air-conditioned coolness.

After casually examining other models on offer, some way too expensive, some far less, I approach someone who fits the look of a car salesperson. I'm not really sure what that look is, but he has it. I explain my interest in the Nuova Renault Kadjar, also asking if he speaks English. He smiles, shakes my hand, and responds by saying he does speak a little English, but only if I speak slowly. This is fine for both of us, with him agreeing to speak Italian slowly. In truth his English turns out to be quite good.

I crawl over a bright red Kadjar, both inside and out. We talk about technical details, some of this I understand, some I don't. The bits not understood by me, have nothing to do with my Italian, the same would apply if the whole of our conversation were in English. Eventually a deal is done, a deal, after a little pressure from me, that includes a free set of winter tyres. You always feel good when you come away thinking you have something extra.

Forms are completed, all details given, along with a hefty deposit. Here is where you come up against the Italian system. It's important that you're aware of this.

To do almost anything other than a grocery shop, paying for drinks in a bar or a meal in a restaurant, you must have a Codice Fiscale (a Tax Code). Even something as simple as paying veterinary bills requires a Codice Fiscale. I've had one since I first bought my house, all organised by my Italian estate agent. It's also helpful if you have a Carta d'identità (Identity Card). If you're not technically resident in Italy, you can't buy a new or used car. Anyway, there is no problem, I have both an identity card and a tax code. Andrea, the salesperson, will contact me when everything has gone through their technical and financial system, the car then being ready for me to collect.

I leave the showroom with the simple task of seeking out Italian insurance. Sorting out the insurance may sound like an easy task, but you may have already guessed, it's not. One thing you will soon find out when you live in Italy, nothing is straightforward. And I do mean absolutely nothing. This is the same for Italians, there would appear to be no procedure that you can possibly be involved in that would register as uncomplicated. At times those who are supposed to understand and make sense of systems and regulations, the 'experts', will give differing advice. If you easily get frustrated, then Italy may not be the place for you. And if you're just not able to resist comparing how things work in Italy with how they work in the country you're from, Italy may not be good for your blood pressure.

In the end, I have no doubt you will work your way through, or if not through, around Italian systems that feel impossible to understand. It will all come good – possibly. Non ti preoccupare (Don't worry). Stai calmo (Stay calm). Tranquille, be chilled, quiet and relaxed. Follow these simple mantras and enjoy all the positives that Italy has to offer, trying in your mind to dilute the frustrations. If you don't dilute, you won't survive living in Italy.

In little more than a week I get a call from Andrea, the car is ready to collect. Better still, he's willing to collect me from Colpalombo and drive me to Perugia to pick up my brand spanking new Renault Kadjar. You see, one of the positives about Italy is its people.

As we drive, conversation drifts around before eventually settling on our perceived differences between Italians and the British. Although, I have to say, most Italians will refer to the English rather than British. If you happen to be Scottish, Welsh, or Irish, let them know. Otherwise, you could for ever remain another inglese.

Andrea does most of the talking. How does he, and perhaps, many other Italians see the British? What he has to say may surprise you, then again, maybe not.

'The English are very much like the Germans; they could almost be the same.'

Now there are two important bits to this observation from Andrea. The first being, he, like many Italians, substitutes English for British. The second point, and this is one most Engländer/Brítisch will find hard to schlúcken and digest. According to the English they are, of course, nothing like the Germans. Two world wars, one world cup, sausage, sauerkraut, lederhosen, bierkellers and, not to forget, no sense of humour. How can anyone possibly think the English are like the Germans?

Andrea puts flesh on his comment.

'The English and Germans are organised; they get things done. Things are done on time, and they work. They are more rational then Italians, not as excitable. The Germans and the English plan things out, they don't have to come back to something and sort out mistakes that were made. Italians are creative and inventive, but never get it done right the first time.'

Andrea asks how the English see Italians? You can fill this bit in. Imagine it's you in conversation with Andrea. I know that Andrea will smile at what you have to say, he's well aware of the stereotypes and readily accepts the truth of some. He continues to patch together the English and Germans.

'They both like to drink lots of beer. Both are noisy and loud when they're drunk. English girls in particular are different to Italian girls. I've seen English girls out drinking when I've been to Manchester and London. They're even worse on holiday in Spain. You see them stagger around in groups, hardly wearing anything, some falling over and some being sick in the street. They also have a reputation for being 'easier' than Italian girls.'

Not exactly the most flattering image of English womanhood. Andrea goes on to say that he knows not all English girls are like that, but this is the image many Italians have.

'Also, the English and Germans - both are a little too formal and cold. Italians are more friendly, they like to hug, have fun. They're just not as serious.'

'Most Italians work to live. When we look at the English and Germans, we see people who are better at business, but also people who live to work. For most Italians, having enough money to have a reasonable life is enough, why would you just keep on working? Italians work hard, but they don't work for the sake of working.'

So, what do you think? Are there any truths in Andrea's observations?

Our drive continues, conversation moving on to my life in Italy and why I chose Umbria. We soon arrive at the car showroom, my first ever brand-new car waiting for me. The car sits in a special part of the temple, where excited new owners come to literally unveil their expensive purchase. In Italy, a new car is treated like a work of art. Unveiled, the glittering new Kadjar stands exhibited to be admired, not just by me, but also those employed to sell the dream. Exhibition and admiration continue when I arrive back at my house in Case Colle. My neighbours come to congratulate me on my new purchase, to celebrate the new arrival. It almost feels like I've given birth or accomplished some great deed. The only deed I've committed is being fortunate enough to be able to afford a new car.

RULES V SUGGESTIONS

In 2005, Italy became the fourth European country to make it illegal to smoke inside public places. The ban includes places of employment, bars, restaurants and shops, etc. Given the reputation Italians have for breaking the rules, a reputation justified or not, I'll leave it for you to guess how the ban has gone. However, if you know Italy well you will already have a good idea. Just out of interest, the smoking ban in the UK didn't come into force until July 2007. You see, the Italians can be ahead of the Brits.

From my time visiting and now living in Italy, I've found that Italians have an almost laissez-fair attitude to rules. When there is absolutely no alternative, they do follow some. But if there is an alternative, well, you would be a fool not to take it. Faced with a rule, you adopt a pragmatic approach, you balance out the costs and benefits. In the mind of an Italian rules are negotiable, breaking them can be justified for all sorts of reasons. You may see the sense of some rules, but not others. You can see how they apply to some people but less willing to accept that they equally apply to you. What I'm suggesting is that the mind of the average Italian sits between seeing how cunning you can be when it comes to getting away with rule breaking and how foolish you would be not to try. An Italian has the cunning of a fox (furbo come una volpe). Depending on what you have done or not done, admired by others.

And it's not just the everyday, average Italian citizen who adopts a balancing act when it comes to rules. Those paid for the responsibility of enforcing rules often take what you could describe as a 'very flexible approach'. I guess the police of any country are allowed a little elasticity in the actions they take when faced with a rule that has clearly been broken. It would be almost impossible to enforce every single rule and then prosecute every single misdemeanour. An intelligent officer is encouraged to use his/her judgement, acting with the appropriate discretion that the situation dictates.

Let me give you an example of the rule breaker and the law enforcer. Mobile phone use whilst driving, unless hands-free, is illegal in the whole of Italy. This has been the case since the 1990s, breaking the rule can bring very heavy penalties. I know I shouldn't be comparing the UK with Italy, but I'm going to do just that. As is the case in Italy, mobile phone use when driving is illegal in the UK. There are some who break this rule, but from my observations this tends to be an exception rather than the norm. In Italy not to have a mobile phone in your hand when driving is the exception. I once sat having a coffee with an English friend outside a bar close to Assisi; the bar looking out on a roundabout. At least every third driver that entered the roundabout had a mobile phone in his/her hand. Without exception, one of my Italian neighbours will make regular use of her mobile when driving. When challenged the reasoning given is:

'Ghrem, you are not in England. This is Italy.'

As in any country, Italy will at times have purges against all sorts of lawbreaking, mobile phone use included. And then it appears to be ignored or at least tolerated if the phone is not unashamedly used. Just a couple of years ago, a friend, an English friend who has lived in Italy for a good number of years, was caught by the police on his mobile whilst driving. As he should have been, he was pulled over and asked if there was any justified reason for him being on his phone. He didn't have a reason and quite rightly received a fine. Good, I can hear you thinking. The Carabinieri were doing their job - however.

A few weeks go by and my friend, who just happens to be an electrician, carries out some work on a house. That evening, the same police officer who caught him on his mobile phone walks into the kitchen, it's his house. He shakes hands with my friend, recognising him as the person on his mobile phone. He shakes his head and smiles.

'If I'd known it was you who was going to do this work, I wouldn't have given you a fine. Why did you make it so obvious that you were using your mobile phone? You should keep it out of sight, held it lower down. If only I'd only known...............'

The flexible approach to following the rules, is something that was promoted to me when I first bought my Umbrian house. The estate agent said that I should declare the house as my prime home, my first home. I pointed out that my prime home was in the UK, this is my second home. She then asked if I would rather pay 10% tax on the purchase or 3% tax? Declaring it as my prime home would save me money. All that would happen is that the Carabinieri would come and check on the house to see if I lived there. I pointed out the obvious fact that in all probability I would not be at the house. This apparently would not be a problem. She had a friend who was married to one of the Carabinieri, this friend would let her know when they were going to call, she would then tell me. Yes, I think you may have recognised the little problem in this cunning plan. It's more than likely that I will be in the UK when the estate agent lets me know that the Carabinieri are coming. I can't just ask my employer for a couple of days off and jump on a plane. It's all a little bit long winded but, in the end, I only paid the 3% tax. You'll also be interested to know that a couple of years went by, and I received a fine for not paying the full amount. Perhaps I just don't have the cunning fox instinct.

We may as well stay with the payment of tax. I'm guessing that you, like many foreigners, think the avoidance of paying tax, tax evasion, describe it as you wish, is a national pastime in Italy. I'm not going to disappoint you; in many ways it is. Then again, it may not be quite that straightforward.

You need to start by understanding a simple fact, this being that the Italian state appears to have a deep distrust of its people. In return, the Italian people have a deep distrust of the state. It's been like that since 1861. If you remember, that is the date when Italy became an almost unified nation. The mutual distrust applies to all sorts of things, but here we'll just look at tax.

The Italian state assumes that everyone will be doing their absolute best to be a cunning fox, finding any possible way not to pay the correct amount of tax. The people argue that the state is ripping them off, this belief therefore gives them a legitimate excuse to avoid contributing to state coffers.

Imagine that you're a self-employed Italian. We'll make it nice and simple. You declared to the state that your business made, say, €90,000. The state takes the appropriate amount of tax. All well and good, sort of. Next year your business is not quite as profitable, you declare a drop in income down to €75,000. The state automatically smells a rat, you must be hiding something. You can plead that you're telling the truth, business has just not been as good. You can even present your evidence. NO, you must be trying to avoid paying tax. I hope you can see the problem here. There's even an assumption on the part of the state that different types of business will generate a minimum level of income. Let's say that you're a self-employed builder, you have your own van and equipment. The state will tax you on an assumed income of say €30,000. It's no good telling the state that you don't make that much, that's what the state expects any self-respecting builder to earn, the state then demanding tax on €30,000 even if you only made €20,000.

The state is never going to believe you, so why tell the truth in the first place? Added to this is the fact that the Italian system of taxation is a whole fog of complexity. So, be honest. If you were Italian, what would you do?

Silvio Berlusconi, when Prime Minister of Italy, in effect gave his blessing to tax evasion. Basically, he said if the state demands a reasonable amount from you in tax, you have a moral duty to pay it, in return the state provides services. However, if the state demands an unreasonable amount of tax from you, it should come as no surprise if people employ inventive ways to avoid paying. He added even further justification for tax avoidance by saying that the seriousness of tax avoidance should be a matter of private morality, just choose methods that don't make you feel too guilty. If anyone knew anything about tax avoidance/ evasion, it was Berlusconi. Investigations into his tax affairs plagued the whole his business and political career. When in office, Berlusconi made sure that laws were changed in ways that would make it more difficult for courts to prosecute him. Some of these changes also made it more difficult to prosecute ordinary people involved in corruption and fraud. Berlusconi was certainly imbued with the cunning of a fox.

Again, imagine that you are an Italian. You're extremely hard working, you deserve to be able to keep more of your money, it's only reasonable. Why should I have to give it away and get nothing in return? They're all doing it at the very top of society. You have a Prime Minister saying people should be able to set their own moral compass when it comes to paying tax. What's wrong with me fiddling around a little with my moral compass, what I'm doing is small fish? You, what would you do?

You'll find that Silvio Berlusconi crops up again and again in my ramblings. I'm sure that if you were able to break the boot of Italy like a stick of rock, you would find the letters spelling out the name Berlusconi running through it. He sticks to the boot shape of Italy like dog crap sticks to the tread of your shoe.

Think back to the last time you paid for something in Italy. If you've not been to Italy yet, remember this when you go. As with most countries, when you pay for something you get a receipt, this providing evidence of what you've paid. That all makes sense. The person, the business, taking your money usually keeps a record of payment, that's how things work.

What? No, don't worry, it's the same in Italy. But in Italy the state doesn't trust you or the person/business you paid. Leaving a shop without a receipt is against the law. Did the shop give you a receipt? If the answer is no, the state automatically smells another rat. You could also be considered a rat for not being able to show the receipt. You could be working in collusion with the shop, keeping hidden the true price you paid for the gelato.

The Guardia di Finanza is the semi-militarized police force charged with the responsibility for enforcing laws related to finance. Just for your interest, Italy has four other types of police. And no, the Guardia di Finanza does not have responsibility for pursuing the mafia (there's much more about these clandestine groups in pages to come). Chasing the mafia is in the hands of the Direzione Investigativa Antimafia (Anti-Mafia Investigation Department).

So, if you step out of the shop without a receipt, it will be officers (there are always two) from the Guardia di Finanza who will 'feel your collar' and the 'collar' of those in the shop. In a country where the state is so distrusting of its citizens, avoiding being an unknowing conspirator to tax evasion can be difficult when it includes something as simple as leaving a shop without a receipt. And remember, ignorance of the laws of a country cannot be used as a defence.

But don't be too worried (non proccuparti), you don't have to buy an extra handbag or man bag to carry all your receipts. And you certainly don't have to keep them until your end of time on earth. In all the years I've been coming to Italy, I've never been stopped by the Guardia di Finanza. I've been stopped by the Carabinieri quite a few times, but never by the finance police. So no, you don't have to add to your luggage allowance.

An interesting proposition that I'm going to make is that Italians as a nation may not be the world's biggest tax avoiders. Then we'll move on to something that is most certainly and without question Italian, dubious driving.

According to those in the know, the British Virgin Islands rank as the world's top tax haven. Note the use of British in this sentence. Many of the tax havens are directly plugged into the City of London.

It's reckoned that the British Virgin Islands hold more than 5,000 times the value of its legitimate economy. This is being a cunning fox on a massive scale. Billions and billions are sifted away from the coffers of national economies by the world's super rich. Monies that should be in the hands of national governments to then provide services for their citizens. Two thirds of the biggest companies in the world have subsidiaries based in tax haven countries. If you simply want to hide money, then Switzerland is still your best bet as a result of its strict privacy laws. It's estimated, though I suspect that the figure is far bigger, that $8.7 trillion of global household financial wealth sits in tax havens. In 2016, it was estimated that the USA alone was deprived of at least $32 billion, perhaps as much as $130 billion, in tax revenue per year. The complexity of global finance and legal secrecy make it incredibly difficult to find out the true extent of what is going on.

Now, going back to Italy and the notion that Italians, as a people, have a national aversion to paying tax. If we think about things on a global scale, placing the Italian population in some sort of global rank order, are our perceptions totally justified?

Let's move on to look at the average Italian driver, another area where you would think rules are important. From my experience this is certainly one area where stereotypes unquestionably match up with fact.

I've already mentioned the use of mobile phones, so we'll leave that one alone.

The use of indicators, simple enough. It's a way to notify other road users what your intentions are. All I can think is that cars sold in Italy come with indicators that don't work. You can see what would usually be used as indicators on cars, but they appear to be purely ornamental, of no functional use for the average Italian driver. Don't expect them to be used, I'm always surprised when they are. If I were an Italian driver buying a new car, I would demand that I have one without indicators to reduce the price. Indicators would be an optional extra, like metallic paint or fluffy dice.

Seat belts, I now regard them as vital when I'm driving or simply in a car as a passenger. But then, I'm not Italian. Things have improved since I first bought my house in Umbria, most Italians do now use a seat belt if they are in the front seats. Legally seat belts must be worn in both the front and back of a car. Wherever I am in a car, I clip in the seat belt, I go through the process without even thinking. I forget the number of times I've been asked by Italians why I'm clipping in my seat belt when sat in the back of their car. One of my neighbours, with a big grin, suggesting that a real Italian man wouldn't bother.

'We'll make you into a real Italian man.'

Then going on to tell me:

'You're not in England Ghrem, why do you always do that?'

'Because I want to increase my chances of surviving the journey, and you're always on your mobile phone.'

Traffic lights and zebra crossings. You'll be incredibly pleased to know that almost all Italians do stop when the lights are red. That's reassuring, I hear you thinking. But amber is often treated as an option. You could slow down knowing the lights will change to red. You could ignore the amber light and speed up to try and get through before the red.

Stopping at zebra crossings really is treated as optional. Some have little blue flashing lights set into the tarmac to warn drivers. Almost all are slightly raised in order to slow cars down. All are the usual black and white. So, there really is no uncertainty about what they are. For you it's the uncertainty of not knowing if the driver will stop when you try to cross. If you're confident enough to step out, most drivers usually do stop, so that's alright then. There is some promising news for you. In 2021 the government made it an offence not to stop when a pedestrian wants to cross. However, don't assume the driver actually knows about the change in the law.

Parking for many Italians is a bit like an abstract painting, it appears to be randomly done. Leaving your car temporarily parked over the edge of a zebra crossing, what's wrong with that? You've made a pragmatic judgement, a balanced choice. You know that you're not supposed to do it, but you've not parked all the way across so that's fine. Anyway, you couldn't find another space and even if you could, this spot is closer to where you want to be.

Yes, in an area for parking there are designated spaces big enough for each car. We all know that they're shown by either white or blue lines, blue usually indicates a requirement to pay. Why park exactly between the lines? Just swing in and abandon the car, not recognising that you've taken up more than one space. If there is no legitimate parking space to be found, you create a space. What do you expect me to do?

And the final observation about parking, I think. Italians appear to be obsessed by the need to park as close as possible to where they want to be. I'm not suggesting that other nationalities are happy to park a great distance away, obviously not. The difference is that most other nationalities will make a compromise. If there is a space close to where they want to go, an Italian driver will fill that space. This became evident to me when I had some work done on my garden. I left those carrying out the work whilst I went out for the day doing tourist things. The purpose of the work was to stop my garden from flooding in the winter. In the words of my neighbour Aldo, to stop it becoming a lago. When I returned to the house, the garden had been completely scalped, where there had once been grass now replaced with hardcore and gravel. Aldo was pleased with the result. The builders were pleased with the result. I wasn't pleased with the result. I was consoled by those around, explaining that I would no longer have the problem of a lago. This is a lot better Ghrem, you don't have to leave your car at the edge of the garden, you can park it right next to the house. I was quite happy leaving the car at the edge of the garden, I didn't want to park my car right next to the house.

So, apart from the use of mobile phones and the non-use of indicators, how is the average Italian on rules when driving? Hold on tight.

The average Italian driver won't deliberately force you off the road, that would be ridiculous, they're not as crazy as that. In fact, they're not really crazy at all. Then again, am I so accustomed to driving in Italy that perhaps I just don't notice anymore? You need to be aware that there are two types of driver in Italy, the incredibly slow and prudent, in fact you'll see electronic signage instructing you to drive with prudenza, to drive with care. And there are those who appear to drive insanely, with a tank completely empty of prudence.

When driving on the autostrada, most Italians don't particularly drive any faster than other Europeans, but they do tend to drive in the middle or outside lane. There are two reasons for this. They hate being behind cars in the slower lane (nearside lane). And there's also a very practical reason, this being that the nearside lane tends to be the least well maintained, if kept in reasonable order at all. There's one thing for sure, you could never fall asleep whilst driving on the nearside lane of an Italian motorway. The road surface will constantly bump and roll you around.

Once away from the autostrada, this is when the empty tank of prudence shows its face. I've already hinted at the fact that Italian drivers don't like to be behind any car. You and I know that at some point you are bound to find yourself behind a car, that's the nature of being on a road. It's nothing like the car adverts where you are alone, with complete freedom, empty road ahead. But that's what the Italian driver, empty of even a drop of prudence, wants. He/she needs to see an empty road ahead. To achieve this, the less than prudent Italian driver will overtake any number of cars just to be in front. Overtaking in places where no rational person would even contemplate doing it; blind bends presenting no obstacle. They either lack any imagination of the possible consequences or they believe they are invincible. I'm no longer shocked, but I do continue to be astounded by an apparent lack of ability to picture what could happen.

Other features of Italian driving. It's less than likely that an Italian driver will give way, so don't expect it. Also, if there is a space, Italian drivers will fill it. Leave more than a car's space between you and the car in front, another car will quickly squeeze in. If there's slow moving or queuing traffic on a slip road, a road with perhaps only two lanes, the Italians will make three. Don't pull away at the very point of lights changing, you'll be left in no doubt that you were expected to have gone – loud car horns giving you a hint. However, pull up in the road to have a chat with someone, your chat blocking traffic, and people are more than happy to wait.

To sum up, just expect the unexpected when you're driving in Italy, and you'll be fine. If you drive in the south of Italy, especially in the area of Napoli, be prepared for absolutely anything.

In Italy cars must go through a safety check every two years, the equivalent of the MOT (Ministry of Transport Test) in the UK, I'm sure there must be similar rules in the US and other countries. In Italy, if you have a new car you're obliged to have it checked as it comes to the end of its fourth year. You take your car to a registered centre with the required authority to carry out checks, a revisione.

The inspection, just like in the UK, is to check the roadworthiness of a car. All makes perfect sense - thank goodness the Italians do that.

If a vehicle owner fails to have the inspection completed at the required time a fine between €150 to €570 can be imposed. But do the Italians always strictly follow the rules? No, please tell me they do. Well, they don't totally disregard the rules, but it's not uncommon for them to be bent a little.

Remember I told you that I had a brand spanking new Renault Kadjar. Well in the November of 2019 it was no longer spanking, it was four years old (I know, in the UK it's three years) and due for its first safety check. I took it along for its revisione, spending my time observing what was done.

An Italian friend had told me that 'minor' little things like headlights out of alignment would probably be ignored or the equipment to measure the alignment would be adjusted as appropriate. He also said 'appropriate adjustments' could be adopted to ensure the 'correct' exhaust emissions would be recorded and brakes would be recorded as being in acceptable limits of wear. He'd known a test centre to measure the exhaust emissions of a car that were acceptable and log them in the report of a car over acceptable limits. On another occasion, where a car had come in with brakes just below the legal limit, the owner had been told to drive the car around for a while, warm up the brakes and bring the car back. As far as I'm aware the test centre got no financial benefit from doing these things, other than owners with a few faults would be more likely to pay for the services of this centre in the future rather than another. I guess it's a kind of joining together, a collaborative approach to getting one up on the system. Collusion against what is regarded as authority does appear to be part of the Italian psyche. Rules are there as a challenge to be worked around, to be massaged. If it can bring mutual benefit, then why not? It's only a minor moral infringement – yes?

To be honest, the only thing I noticed on my car was a little tinkering around to register the headlights as being in alignment and ticking off that the tyres were within acceptable limits without first checking them.

Before I leave you with the impression that the relationship between the average Italian and rules verges at best on a pick n' mix attitude, to at worst total disregard, it's worth pointing out alongside this, there is what I can only describe as a complete contradiction in behaviour when it comes to Italians and officialdom. At times it feels as though the rule breakers have become completely docile in their conformity.

PERMIT 838

What does the term bureaucracy mean to you?

Wherever you are in the world there will be accepted procedures, appropriate forms to complete and hurdles to jump over. Officialdom eventually stamping your right to do it or at least move to the next step, permission to jump the next hurdle. That is how complex modern societies work. The slow mechanism of bureaucracy grinds away and, perhaps, at times, grinds you down. But how could a modern society operate with order if there were no bureaucratic systems in place? Don't worry, I'm not expecting you to embark on some complex doctoral thesis. I'm just posing the question, what's the alternative?

You may get to know a lot about Italy and Italians, but I doubt that you will ever really understand how things work, the system, the rules, the perhaps you can, the perhaps you can't. Go to this office, go to that office. Get a stamp for this and a stamp for that. Fill in this form. No that's the wrong one. Speak to that person who will know, only to find that you should be speaking to another person. If you want to live in Italy, you must be at one with frustration. You need to quickly learn to be able to shrug your shoulders, all will be fine, eventually – perhaps.

Never forget your marca da bollo. You almost always need a marca da bollo for any paper/document that you want to be regarded as official. This is a special stamp, so magical that without it stuck to your paper/document you will get no further in your endeavours. Now where do you think you would go to buy such an important stamp? Yes, obviously, you go to a tobacconist.

Next time you're in an Italian town keep a look out for a blue sign (sometimes black) with a big T. Below the T, you should see the words, 'SALI E TABACCHI VALORI BOLLATI'. A literal translation of this gives you, Salts, Tobacco, Revenue Stamps. Why Salt? Apparently, at some time in the past, tobacconists, along with being officially sanctioned to sell tobacco, as they still are, were also an official outlet for the sale of salt. For some Italian reason, the salt bit has never been removed from the signs.

A marca da bollo is basically a government tax that you must pay on anything that is official, say for example something like a marriage certificate or a passport. They've been around since 1863. Along with Italians breaking rules, the other thing you'll find is that many rules live forever. However, today the marca da bollo is more likely to be a sticker rather than an actual stamp. The last thing to be aware of is that there is no standard price for a marca da bollo, it all depends on what you are doing.

You may well complain about Italian bureaucracy, but if you genuinely want to enjoy life here, you have no alternative but to surrender into the arms of its frustrating foibles. Sit at a bar in a medieval piazza, warm sun on your face, glass of wine in your hand, watching Italian life go by, congratulating yourself on each occasion that you come out of the Italian machine of officialdom having had some measure of success.

And here comes the Italian paradox. Faced with bureaucratic officialdom, those treating rules as simply suggestions fall into conformity. A visit to the main post office in Gubbio finds people waiting patiently, usually without complaint, having taken, hopefully, the correct numbered ticket. People wait for their number to light up on the digital screen, at last they can approach one of the staff, that member of staff dealing with the needs of the customer. I've sat in this post office for over thirty minutes. Mornings waiting, even though the congregation was by no means large. The picture I'm painting could easily give an impression of a place full of dullness, of Italian souls having simply given in. But that's a totally false impression to take away. For the people of Gubbio it's an opportunity to meet friends, to quietly sit and gossip. An opportunity to exchange greetings with those you may not have seen for some time. The waiting is almost treated as a community event. The post office certainly offers a cool escape from the heat of an Umbrian summer. Those employed in the post office are always polite as they go about their work in a slow, unharried fashion.

Do I still use the post office in Gubbio? No, it takes too long. I now go to the little post office in Casacastalda, the village just five kilometres (three miles) from Case Colle. The post office staffed by just one person, this one person dealing with all your post office needs. Your waiting time, no longer than a few minutes. I don't go when it's pension day.

So, to simply think of Italians as rule breakers is just too easy. At times Italians display a level of conformity that can appear to the foreign eye as almost stupefying. I think I've discovered why the average Italian lives so long. A Mediterranean diet and climate may contribute, but the real reason for Italian longevity results from the need to live long enough to see something completed. You have to stay alive to a grand old age if you have any hope of seeing something through to its end. To have lived long enough to have taken the journey through the very bowels of Italian bureaucracy, coming out the other end successful and with a feeling of relief.

I've never come across any genuine feeling of despair when speaking to Italian neighbours and friends about the complexity of rules and bureaucracy in Italy. There's more a sense of resignation, that's just how things are, what can you do about it? There's no alternative but to get on with living and, if at all possible, find some way of bending round whatever may be placed in front of you. It tends to be foreigners living in Italy, especially those trying to operate a business, who find that they are driven mad by the machinations of Italian officialdom. There are a few I know who having spent so long tackling the hurdles only to find that these were never the acceptable and correct hurdles; in the end giving up. Sadly, for them and for Italy, sacrificing their Italian dream and leaving the country. I guess Italians have no alternative, they have to stick with it. Italy truly is a wonderful place to live, in many ways magnificent and beguiling. But don't assume your dream of La Dolce Vita will automatically be an easy journey.

Obviously, I have no idea of your age, it would perhaps be rude of me to ask. But do you remember the French cartoon Astérix le Gaulois (Asterix the Gaul)? The cartoon set within the Roman empire. In The Twelve Tasks of Asterix, the little Gaul has to first enter 'The Place That Sends You Mad'. Asterix, speaking cheerily to a rather gloomy administrator:

'What do we have to do in this place that sends you mad?'

'Nothing much. You have to obtain a certain permit which will then allow you to go onto the next task.'

'I see, nothing but a simple administrative formality.'

'That's right, a formality, a simple formality. You merely have to ask for Permit 838.'

I'll not give away the outcome, I think you've probably guessed it already. Anyway, who told you to ask me? You're in the wrong place. Who told you that you have the correct form?

If you're sitting there thinking this is an exaggeration, sadly it's not.

A couple I know, living in Umbria, close to Gubbio, have experience of entering the place, the system that sends you mad. He's English, but originally born in Italy, she is Swedish, both speak excellent Italian. Their hope, more than a hope, they had already started to achieve it, the ambition of living in the Italian countryside, renting out a holiday cottage. The first year had been a real success. Then bureaucracy started to kick in, the unfathomable tentacles of Italian officialdom began to wrap around their world. Now, as I've said already, every country has to have systems in place. Nothing wrong with that, at times the systems can feel frustrating, but you work through them; in the end all comes good. And that's one of the problems of Italy, trying to find the end.

Andrew first applied for residency and then an Italian passport. With the correct documentation to support your claim to Italian citizenship, the documents proving that you are Italian by blood, the process should be straightforward. For Andrew, the process appeared to be almost a formality, he was born in Italy but had never had an Italian passport. Eventually, Andrew had all the documentation required. He had a copy of his birth certificate from Napoli, what problem could there be?

On the birth certificate there was one wrong letter in the spelling of his last name. A little bit of a hassle, but that can be sorted. It should just be a formality, a simple formality – yes?

Andrew travelled to Napoli, Gubbio, London, Perugia and then back to Napoli in an attempt to sort out the one letter. Signatures here, signatures there. Other papers completed, all with any number of bolli, the official payment stamp that I explained earlier. Sent to one place, only to be told that he had to go elsewhere. Eventually success! The end had arrived in the post. Napoli had officially accepted the change of one letter. Phew, all done. Think again.

For some reason, he still had to go to the police headquarters in Perugia; he was told to do this. Having arrived there, he was told no, he needed to go back to Napoli and then to his local town, Gubbio, to finalise everything. Andrew, speaking excellent Italian, contacted Gubbio first. You're not going to believe this. He's told that the document he has may not be the correct one, he must come into Gubbio for a face-to-face appointment at 10am the following morning. Surely all should be sorted now? What have I said? Think again.

The administrator, a cog in the system that is the place that sends you mad, informs Andrew that he will have to go back to Napoli and make an appointment with a person who will put the correct document in place. Phew, at last! The putting of the correct document in place could take up to three months to be validated. Once validated there, he must go again to Gubbio where it will again be officially validated. This could take another three months.

If you plan to live in Italy, be prepared. At some point you will be tasked with entering the place that sends you mad.

Almost forgot. Back to the question I asked you about Italians and smoking. Remember the ban became law in 2005. Has the average Italian smoker simply ignored the law? To my great surprise, the answer is no. Since 2005, I have only twice noticed someone having a crafty smoke inside. You see, Italians can and do follow some rules.

RITUAL, CUSTOM & PRACTICE

If there is one thing you soon learn about Italians, they can be almost rigidly traditional. They can be just as inventive and creative as any other nationality, but there are certain areas of life where change is most certainly treated as an unwelcomed guest. Let's use the humble cappuccino as an example.

The cappuccino has now become a common part of life well beyond the borders of Italy. You perhaps know this, perhaps not, but how can you assess the credentials of a true Italian with the cappuccino test? I know the answer, my sister, Katherine and her husband, Peter, did not.

We're in Perugia. It's about 9.30 in the evening. We've just enjoyed delicious food in the same place, Bottega del Vino, where I enjoyed wonderful tiramisu with Alex and Samantha. We relax, happy and content in our fullness. I ask Katherine and Peter if they would like a little drink to settle our meal. Not really being a spirit drinker, Peter declines. Rather than alcohol, Katherine says that she would like a cappuccino. I reply that it's 9.30 in the evening, I'm not asking for a cappuccino. But that's what I'd like, a cappuccino, she replies. I'm not asking for a cappuccino. But I'd like a cappuccino. In the end I give in. The waiter approaches. I ask for an espresso, a grappa and a cappuccino.

An espresso and a grappa, yes certainly. A cappuccino, no. We are not able to make a cappuccino. Now we know they have the required equipment to make a cappuccino, but it's not going to happen. No explanation is given. Just no, we are not able to make a cappuccino. The word cappuccino is having to be almost forced from between his lips. It's the first time I've known there to be a blanket refusal to make a cappuccino, most places will serve it at any time for tourists. But not this place. Having a cappuccino after a meal is simply not the Italian thing to do. It's against the rules, to ask for one is almost heretical to an Italian.

The cappuccino is part of a morning ritual. It's almost considered a breakfast by itself. Asking for a cappuccino after a meal is like asking for a bowl of cornflakes, it's unthinkable. You've just had a full evening meal, and now you want cornflakes? A cappuccino before the clock strikes 11am is perfectly fine and respectable. A cappuccino accompanied by a small pastry, the ideal breakfast. My sister was almost eleven hours past the appropriate time for a cappuccino.

What about the humble espresso? When and how?

I think it was probably my first summer in Italy after buying the house. It must have been August because it was the Festival della Polenta e Salsiccia in Carbonesca. After exchanging morning greetings with one of my Italian neighbours, Vincenzo, he asks if I would like to meet him and his wife at the festival for a drink. That evening I take the steady walk up to Carbonesca, full of expectation.

The festival is in full flow, trestle tables and benches taken, food being consumed and just a little wine being drunk. The band is on stage, the dance floor swirling around with every age. I exchange greetings with others who know the inglese, then I spot Vincenzo who calls me over. Hands shaken, smiles exchanged, good to his word, he buys the first drink – an espresso. And that's it, just an espresso. I get the strong impression that this is not going to be an evening of alcohol consumption. The espresso is swallowed in just a few sips. That's it, that's the drink. How would you feel? Call this a drink?

I now understand the significance of an Italian buying you an espresso. It signals friendship and generosity. It's a welcome, it's a real pleasure to have you here.

Drinking espresso together, although a relatively short social experience, is the equivalent of being offered a beer in the UK. In the UK, accepting the offer of a drink involves drinking at least one beer, usually more. The one espresso, the few beers, carrying the same social meaning.

Since that evening, I've lost count of the number of times I've enjoyed an espresso with Vincenzo, stood at the bar in Colpalombo. Vincenzo also has a house in the tiny hamlet of Case Colle. Only recently has he moved with his wife to the other place they have in Gubbio. The move only coming about as a consequence of Eleonora, Vincenzo's wife, showing increasing signs of dementia.

Having an espresso with Vincenzo has become a bit of a ritual. He drives past in his old, green, Opel car, stopping at the edge of my garden to see if I'm free for a drink.

'Ghrem, prendi un caffè?'

The whole process of me getting in the car, driving down to the village, ordering the espresso, drinking the espresso whilst standing at the bar, getting back in the car, return drive to Case Colle, all taking well under fifteen minutes. There have been times when my sister and her husband have been staying with me, having just made a fresh pot of tea, hearing the call from Vincenzo to go for a drink, being transported in his car, espresso whilst stood at the bar, return drive, pot of tea still hot. I think you get the picture. Espresso drinking is important to Italians. What am I saying? It's more than important, it's a way of life. But not a part of your life that takes any great time, not something you linger over. The espresso is almost as important as the Virgin Mary. You're more than welcome to add to the whole experience by having a pastry. Espresso and pastry consumed, mingled in with an exchange of quick conversation. Not to forget that there will probably be at least one person in the bar who has made no purchase at all, but still sat reading the newspaper. As you enter and leave, the usual group sat outside; almost always male.

'Caffè normale?'

One last important point to make about the espresso. If you ask for a coffee, you will automatically be served an espresso. For an Italian, coffee equals espresso. You may possibly be asked, 'Caffè normale?' Normal coffee = espresso.

Whilst we're thinking about espresso, let's also have a think about how the average Italian eats. No, I'm not talking about how they hold a spoon or a knife and fork, I don't intend to be that forensic. It's more about what is looked on as 'normal'. We'll start with the obvious, the pizza, the Hawaiian pizza as a case study.

You will never, ever see Hawaiian pizza listed on a menu in Italy; if you do, let me know. The whole notion of putting something as sweet as ananas (pineapple) on a pizza is greeted with shock and horror. My Italian neighbours cannot comprehend that anyone would even contemplate such an idea. Why would anyone want to do it? Most places will be willing to listen to your requests to adapt some of the toppings on offer, but never pineapple. Just so you understand, and I can't emphasise this enough. Pineapple on pizza is just ridiculous. Che schifo! (How disgusting!). Now chips (French fries) on a pizza, that's fine.

And don't make the mistake that I once made in my earlier visits to Italy. It's got nothing to do with tradition, more a reflection of my poor Italian at the time. I quite like salami on a pizza, pepperoni would be perfect, giving the pizza just a little kick (un po' piccante). So, that's what I asked for, a pepperoni pizza. When it arrived at the table, there was not a slice of salami in sight. You probably know what I'd ordered. The pizza came with green and red peppers – peperoni.

Bread. You always get bread with a meal, almost always white bread. This is the same if I'm eating with my neighbours or if I'm eating in a restaurant. Probably the only exception would be if you're having pizza. Don't expect the bread to come with butter, bread never comes with butter in Italy. Yes, I know you get butter with bread in your local Italian restaurant, trust me you won't get it in Italy. Bread is either drizzled with olive oil or eaten dry. And don't tell the person serving you that you didn't order bread with your meal. You always get bread. Yes, I know you may not want it, but you're getting it. And yes, you may not have ordered it, and may not even eat it – I never do. But you will be charged for it.

Whilst we're talking about the subject of charges on your bill (il conto), let me tell you about the cover charge – coperto. Your bill will, almost without exception, come with coperto, that's just how it is. As a result, it's unusual to leave a tip, you can, but it's unusual.

So, you've chosen what you want as your main meal. Let's say you've ordered salsiccia di cinghiale (wild boar sausage), sold to you as a speciality of the restaurant. Make sure you also order contorni (side dishes). If you don't, you will probably just get the sausage and nothing more. You now know this, so you decide to order insalata e patate (salad and potatoes) with the wild boar sausage. Good, you have your full main meal. Now the next bit. Being a Brit, I'm still trying to get used to this, perhaps I never will. Your salad may not come at the same time as the sausage, don't complain if it doesn't, that's how it's done in Italy. It will probably come before the sausage or after the sausage. It could be the same if you've ordered something else to 'accompany' your sausage. The potatoes, you'll be pleased to know, will probably come at the same time as the sausage. This is how Italians eat. Don't start going on about it being ridiculous, you're in Italy, accept it like it is. It's no different when I'm eating with my neighbours. I've come to terms with it, but I guess I'll never get used to it. And in the past I have made a few mistakes, nothing important. Let me give you an example.

I'd invited my neighbours for a meal. A warm, starlit summer evening, so we're eating outside, olive trees and all that. At this time, my kitchen was on the first floor, meaning that I had to transport food down two lots of stairs and out into the garden. I forget exactly what we had, but it included a salad. I do remember that we had soup first. That was fine, accompanied with bread, no butter. I then came down with a large dish of salad, obviously leaving this on the table, then returning up two sets of stairs to the kitchen to finish preparing the main dish. You already know what's going to happen.

After leaving my neighbours to chat, I returned with the main dish. Every bit of the salad had already gone. I know and you know that's how it is. You don't serve everything at the same time in Italy. That's not how it's done.

Still thinking about salad. Don't expect your salad to have a choice of dressings. Italians usually keep salads quite simple, with just a splash of extra virgin olive oil and perhaps a little balsamic vinegar.

One last point about food. I hope I'm not starting to make it sound like real Italian food is terrible. It's most certainly not. Anyway, the last point is that you should not expect your food to be served piping hot, in my experience this is rarely the case. I have seen tourists (UK tourists in particular) sending food back because, according to them, the food was not hot enough. The food comes warm, rather than piping hot.

Italians will almost always order a bottle of still or sparking water with their meal. Again, this is the same with my neighbours, they will always have water on the table. The other interesting thing is, most Italians only drink bottled water, in or out of the home. You'll probably see people sip a handful of water from a street fountain, but most often water comes from plastic bottles. There is nothing wrong with the water straight from the tap in an Italian home, well at least I've never found it to be a problem, but it's not usually something done by most Italians.

Generally, Italians are not great beer drinkers. Tastes are starting to change with the growth of specialist microbreweries, but often one bottle of beer will be shared. All restaurants and bars serve beer, they always have, the beer most likely to be the lager type. At a meal with my neighbours there will always be red wine on the table. Depending how many are eating, two or three bottles of wine. And now, most probably, a couple of beers. The beers, remember, to be shared. As a northern European, probably more likely that it's the result of being a Brit, the sharing of beer takes a bit of acclimatisation. The beer sharing thing, I guess, pretty much reflects the relationship that most Italians have with alcohol. Alcohol is enjoyed, but it's not poured down the throat just for the sake of it. It's not that Italians have an aversion to being merry and having a laugh, far from it, they just don't need the lubrication of alcohol in the way that northern Europeans do.

I remember being in my favourite little bar in Gubbio, Martintempo, with my daughter Kara and her husband Andy. Andy quite likes his beer. But before I tell you this little story, let me tell you about the bar. Trust me, I will get back to Andy.

A review I came across on TripAdvisor neatly sums up Martintempo:

'This place is not to be missed. Dropped in for an aperitivo and stayed. The bar is unique. You can tell these guys have travelled and incorporated the best of what they've seen into this inviting bar. Marco is an excellent host, the atmosphere and service great. Along with Gabriele, he made a great effort to make our evening comfortable. The impromptu tasting platter of meats and cheese they prepared was superb. If you go anywhere in Gubbio, go here.'

You'll find this brilliant little bar on Via Baldassini, less than a ten-minute walk up Via Delle Republica from Piazza 40 Martiri. In the warm Umbrian evenings, sit outside look-ing up at the towering stone buttresses that support Piazza Grande. Outside or inside, I can guarantee that you will not be disappointed.

Anyway, back to Andy. If I remember correctly it was around 11.30pm, a Tuesday evening in early winter. The first time Kara and Andy had been over to Gubbio in December, the weather very different to the hot days of an Umbrian summer. The streets of Gubbio cold, the threat of snow blowing on an icy wind. An unusually quiet evening for Martintempo, the bar never a noisy place, but by late evening most space would be taken by small groups and couples, the clientele almost always exclusively Italian. We decided that this would be our final drink. Andy drinking beer, Kara a cocktail of some description, with me, being the driver, a cocktail with the vital ingredient of alcohol missing.

Four men enter, two Italian, two American. They drink stood at the bar, in a happy mood, speaking with great animation to Marco. Martintempo always has good music playing softly in the background, and this evening had been no exception. The flatscreen TV fixed to the wall between shelves full of books, bottles of wine and expensive champagne, moves from soft music to the unmistakable sound of karaoke. We sit being entertained by the four who had been speaking with Marco. And then, with a short break between one song choice and the next, a glass of beer is presented to Andy. A beaming smile on the face of our karaoke singer as he places the beer on the table.

Clearly, we have no alternative, we reciprocate, buying a beer for our Italian karaoke singer. Kara having another cocktail, me still having the fruit drink without a drop of alcohol. After a few more songs, another beer arrives at our table for Andy, another beer offered to the singer, but the drink politely rejected. The singing continues and we're asked if we would like to join the karaoke quartet, now supported by the voice of Marco. It's not really an ask, it's more of, you will join us at the bar. Another beer for Andy.

With three previous beers already inside him and now three more, Andy asks the Italian karaoke singer why he insists on supplying him with yet another drink?

'I simply stand in admiration of the amount of beer you are able to drink' a wide beaming smile on his now red face.

'You must be English or German, Italians don't drink that much beer.'

'English', Andy replies, also with a big beaming smile.

Kara has another cocktail. I still have my fruit, without a drop of alcohol.

What was late evening, now moved on to early morning. The only people still in the bar as the clock approaches 1am, are the four original karaoke singers, Marco, Andy, Kara and a very sober me. With arms stretched across shoulders, we join voices with the others. Another song is chosen, another beer is given, voices getting louder. With hardly a drop of alcohol in my blood, I'm carried along by those around me, my voice just as loud.

During a brief interlude, Andy is asked to take a seat. The karaoke choir stands around the smiling, confused Andy, the Englishman who, apparently, drinks lots of beer. The Italian karaoke singer, a sword in his right hand, parts the circle and steps through. The sword is sometimes used by Marco to slice the top off a champagne bottle with flamboyant style. Our Italian karaoke singer asks for silence, I guess it's an attempt to mark this event as some sort of solemn occasion. Andy, a little red faced, with a slightly nervous grin, looks towards the raised sword. Will he suffer the same fate as the champagne bottle? Andy is asked to remain still.

The sword is pointed forward towards the seated Andy, the tip of the blade directly touching the tip of his nose. Sword is then lifted above Andy's head, before it comes to rest on his right shoulder and then his left.

'I crown you Andy, the KING OF BEER!'

Undoubted relief on Andy's face and laughter all around.

The circle forms back into more of a group huddle, another song is chosen, and more karaoke, even louder than before.

What time did we eventually leave?

We left Marco and the karaoke quartet, for our drive back to Colpalombo with the King of Beer, at the 'devil's hour', just a few minutes past three in the morning.

I've since been back to Martintempo any number of times, Marco remembering that impromptu evening as one of the best – they often are.

Apart from the drinking of espresso and, perhaps cappuccino, all other drinking and eating, especially eating, is done at a leisurely pace. Eating is a social event, the social gathering as important as the food being consumed. You're in Italy, you're here on holiday, a time to relax. Don't get agitated if the service feels that little bit slow.

Whilst on the topic of eating, I should say something about the choice of food available in most shops, even supermarkets in Italy. In comparison with other countries, especially the UK, the shelves of shops in Italy are relatively uninspiring in their offerings of foreign produce. Vegetables and salads are possibly an exception, well at least in Umbria. You will find a small selection of foreign beers, mainly German, but also a small number of British and Belgian brews. Instant foods and ready meals are as rare as hen's teeth. They are starting to creep in, so perhaps the hen's teeth analogy is a slight exaggeration. Breakfast cereals, yep you'll find these, most often confined to a small section of shelf. You will always find lots and lots of pasta and endless varieties of pasta sauce. Anything a little more 'exotic', having a little tiny section, perhaps next to health foods, this also being the place where you'll find gluten-free products, etc. Things are changing, just five years back foods targeted at those with specific dietary needs were certainly as rare a find. And the final food item – cheese. Italian cheese is good, especially parmigiano and mozzarella di bufala, but the variety of other Italian cheese is relatively small. You do get the basics from Holland, perhaps a little French, on rare occasions something British.

I think you get the picture - most Italians eat Italian. I'm not suggesting that this is a problem, Italian food is often exceptionally good. And just to contradict my point about Italians mostly eating Italian, every time I've invited my neighbours for lunch or dinner, they have, without exception, age of no relevance, enjoyed British food, always asking for more. Just to let you know, asking for more has nothing to do with my cooking being in any way exceptional.

With all this eating and drinking, at some point you are going to need to seek out the toilet. So as not to confuse any American readers, the bathroom/restroom. How long do Americans 'rest' when they visit the toilet? Toilets in many restaurants, cafes and bars are hidden away, often just one to be used by males and females. Separately, obviously. Don't be surprised if you have to walk past the kitchen and then sneak past miscellaneous items stored here for use in the drinking/ eating areas. Fortunately, most are relatively clean, the toilet itself separate to the small wash basin, which, on most occasions will have a hot and cold tap, but not always. Often there will be just enough room for you to squeeze yourself in, turn and manage to secure the door. If you're lucky, there will be an obvious light switch. Unlucky, and you will need to keep one hand free to wave about in order to activate the motion sensor that time limits the light given to whatever you need to do.

Now the next bit about the actual toilet is still a mystery to me. If you happen to be at home, the home of another, perhaps a hotel, just pop into the bathroom and tell me what you find sitting on and attached to the top of the actual toilet. Just put your book down for a minute and do as I ask. Yes, you can take the book with you, if you must. What can you see? Obviously, you will find a toilet seat and, I would guess, a lid that comes down to rest on the seat and cover the toilet – exactly! In every single home I have visited in Italy and in every single hotel I have stayed in Italy, I have found the same combination – toilet seat and toilet lid. So, what's your point Graham? My point, the mystery, is why do most toilets in bars, restaurants and cafes in Italy sit there totally vulnerable and naked – no toilet seat and, therefore, no cover? I just don't have the answer. If you do find out, let me know. Depending on what you need to do, I guess if you're male most of the time there is no problem. For the other thing you may want to do, it's either the kiss of cold porcelain or mastering the skill of levitation. No, really, don't try and stand on the toilet. Now all you need to do is flush the toilet and wash your hands. Yes, you do, you should always wash your hands.

'What about flushing? Well, I've counted eighteen different flushing actions, most of them camouflaged, ranging from side levers, vertical levers, wallmounted buttons and pedals, to a cord hanging from the ceiling.' Beppe Severgnini – La Bella Figura.

Who knew that the simple act of going to the toilet could be such a challenge?

Don't forget to wash your hands. You have the little hand basin, don't expect a plug. You really do want everything. You are in luck. The tap is right there in front of you, but only cold. With even more luck, you have obvious hot and cold taps. In other places you may have to search for your supply of water. If there are no obvious taps, use your foot. Yes, your foot. There will be a little pedal on the floor.

As we happen to be looking at toilets, I may as well take the opportunity to say something about that item of bathroom plumbing that you tend not to find in the

UK and the USA or, for that matter, the majority of English speaking countries. You know what I mean, that porcelain item of bathroom furniture that you, more than likely, ignore and never use. Well perhaps you use it to wash the sand from your feet. It's very unlikely that you will find this 'alien' item when you use the toilet in bars, cafes, and restaurants. But you will find one in the bathroom of all hotels and Italian private homes. I have one in my home. You will not be totally surprised to know, that I have yet to use it. We are, of course, talking about the bidet. Designed to be sat on for the purpose of washing the private bits. No, stop being timid, you know what I mean. The genitalia, inner buttocks, your anus. Why is it that we appear to be so suspicious of having these parts jetted and massaged with water? After all, bidets are not just used by Italians. The bidet is used throughout Southern Europe, France, parts of the Far East, and the entire Islamic world. What must these people think when they visit the UK and USA? The Italians and other cultures are clearly more concerned about personal hygiene. I can hear you muttering in disagreement. Go on then, give me a counter argument.

Enough about toilets, bathrooms and rest rooms, what they have and, more than likely, don't have. You can now return to the social event of eating and drinking. Saluti!

Before we move on, this could be as good a place as any to say just a little bit about Italian punctuality when it comes to social events. You need to keep in mind that, in general, Italians have a habit of being 'fashionably late'. Trust me, there really is no hidden agenda in this. Try to let go of the slight annoyance you may feel if you happen to be left waiting. Think of time being a flexible concept. I mean, what is time? See it as a minor detail. Being a little late is not deliberate. Go with the flow. Think of it as a form of Italian social etiquette. My elder daughter, Kara, must be a natural Italian, she has the exact same characteristic – amazing.

LA FAMIGLIA

Family is important to all of us, Italian or not. Are family relationships in Italy really any different? The answer is most certainly yes. Inevitably things are slowly changing, especially if you look at the bigger cities in the north of Italy. Internal migration, especially from the south, along with migration to other countries, will continue to change family relationships. But for now, just like the Catholic Church, family is central to the life of Italy.

Mamma and Papà, Nonna and Nonno, remain central to family life long after children have grown into independent adults and, in many cases, left the family home. I'll come back to 'leaving' the family home at some point, it's not quite as straightforward as it may appear. Not quite as strong, but still central to Italian life, are the ties between siblings, mia sorella and mio fratello.

The very first time my sister came to visit the house, we were invited for dinner by my immediate neighbours, Aldo and Benedetta. It was the quintessential Italian setting. A string of tables set in the shade of olive trees. Early evening, places for at least fifteen people. The sun just starting to fade, but the heat of the day still present. Bottles of wine on the tables, plus bottles of sparkling and natural water, not to forget the obligatory bread. Cicadas, just starting to warm up for their regular orchestral event. At the head of the string of tables sat Aldo, Benedetta to one side. Four generations of family members, plus l'inglese. We have Aldo and Benedetta, mamma e papà (often babbo will be exchanged for papà) and three adult daughters. The three that I've spoken of before, Paola, Alicia and Francesca. Sitting with two of the daughters, their partners, Marcello and Pietro. By the side of Paola, her young daughter, Giulietta. And sat at the opposite end of the tables to Aldo, Gina. Two extra places for any friends who may just happen to turn up. My sister was absolutely enthralled, enchanted, mesmerised – all three wrapped up into one.

That scene has been repeated again and again over the years, most often at my neighbours', but also at the house of Marcello's mamma e babbo, nonna always present. And on most occasions, those eating include sorelle e fratelli (sisters and brothers), zii e zie (uncles and aunties). Not forgetting any children and the few friends that have also been invited. Other times dinner or lunch at the house of Marcello and Alicia. I've lost count of the number of meals in gardens or inside the homes of my Italian neighbours and friends. Every single time, they have never been small gatherings. Absolutely not one scrap of food placed in front of you that has not been freshly homemade and tasting delicious.

From my observations of Italian friends that I know, the importance of family is beyond question. If not living in the same house, they live close by. Obviously if they live in the same house, they see each other daily. If they live close by, not one week will pass without the family coming together.

The central role of family extends well beyond the family home. Italy's economy is still dominated by small family-run businesses. Italy is also a country where you still find a relatively high number of companies with an annual turnover in excess of two million euro still in the hands of one family. Not sure if I should mention it here, the mafia? You may regard family loyalty here as an aberration of family ties, but in no small way it is family bonds that have given these criminal organisations such longevity. Not to worry, none of my Italian friends and neighbours are members. Then again, it could be that I just don't keep my eyes and ears open enough; no, trust me, they're not. Although Aldo does keep a suspiciously tight control of cheese whenever you are invited for dinner. Aldo, 'Capo of the Cheese'.

Something that is increasingly noticeable about Italian families is the number of adult children who remain in the family nest. The not very flattering term used to describe them, the bamboccioni (big babies). In 2018, according to studies, almost 67% of Italians aged between 18 to 34 lived in the parental home. The UK, Germany and the USA having roughly the same level of family home living, at around 35%. And guess which gender is more likely to remain in the family home in Italy? Yes, you are indeed correct, males account for almost 73% of the total. Some argue that it is the result of a cultural phenomenon, the bamboccioni lacking the will to cut free from mamma's apron strings. Others suggest that there is a more practical reason. Remaining in the family home is a logical response to the relatively high level of unemployment among young adults in Italy. Economics is undoubtedly part of the reason, but studies have also shown that 40% of those still living with parents are in employment. I am sure you can see a possible problem here in accepting the 40% at face value. Increasingly, just like in many other countries, a growing number of jobs are either part-time, time limited contracts or seasonal. Staying with mamma and babbo makes absolute sense. However, some still place the emphasis on culture rather than economics as the most important determining factor - Italian parents preferring to have their adult children at home. With some commentators going so far as to say that many Italian parents, intentionally or not, 'bribe' adult children to stay. I'm not going to make a judgement.

The relationship between parents and children is certainly different to that in the UK, but I'll leave you to decide if adult children stay in the family home because it's comfortable or because it's an economic necessity – La Stampa, an Italian newspaper, describing the family as, 'the last frontier of welfare.'

In 2010, a minister in the Berlusconi government said that there was an urgent need to deal with the culture of mummy's boys (mammoni) and big babies. Renato Brunetta added:

'All these young people think they're living in a free hotel, and actually there's a price to pay. It allows their parents to keep control of them, emotionally, socially and financially.'

Another leading member of Forza Italia, after accepting that youth unemployment was a problem, something that his party would fix, went on to declare:

'We can't do anything for the over-coddled young men and women. That is a cultural matter. Some young Italians feel it is much better to be fed and housed and cuddled by their mothers than going out to work.'

What do you think?

Whilst you think about that, let me add a not unconnected phenomenon to the mix. Some suggest that this is a stereotype of the Italian male, whilst others swear that it is more than fact. Mammismo – the term specifically applied to males who just cannot break away from being a 'mother's boy'. Some even going as far as to argue that many of the problems in Italian society, in part, result from the Italian mothers doting on their sons. The last part is most certainly an exaggeration, as for the mother son adoration bit, I'm not so sure.

One of the many contradictions of Italy, the country being no different to any other in having them, contradictions that is. Here the contradiction almost challenges what I've said about the number of young Italian adults remaining in the family home, and yet, at the same time, gives some explanation as to why they remain. In the last quarter of 2019, the unemployment rate for the under 25s stood at 29% (Eurostat, the European Statistical Office). In 2018, the number of those in the 20 to 34 age group, not in employment or education/training, also stood at 29%. I guess this relates to around 1 in 3 of Italians under the age of 34, apparently doing 'nothing'.

Some Italian economists have suggested that, in terms of economic growth, Italy is where it was back in 1861. I'm not so sure things are as desperate as that. Since 2008 some 2 million young Italians, many of them highly skilled, have left the country to pursue careers in Northern Europe and elsewhere. That's a lot of potentially lost talent in a country with a total population of about 60 million. How many intend to return to Italy at some point in the future, I'm not sure.

I have an Italian friend, with a successful career, living in London. His parents still live in Colpalombo. The last time I spoke to him, he said he could never imagine moving back to the village. He then reflected on what he'd said. Perhaps when I've retired. Colpalombo is, he feels, still his true home. He misses the people, the geography and the community, but for now London has far more to offer than Italy.

Italian commentators lament the problems of the country. 'A country that cannot keep its youth is not forward looking', says Nicola Nobile, an economist with Oxford Economics. Italy, like many other countries in Europe, has an aging population. There are many who feel that Italian politicians focus on this large group of voters and neglect the young. It really is difficult to know which direction Italy will take to resolve a situation where the young who can, leave, and many who stay, remain in the bosom of the family home.

There is one thing I am sure about. Well, ok, an observation made by this inglese. How can I put this without offending anyone? Italian children are, in general, indulged by their parents, grandparents, absolutely everyone. Done it, said it. I guess now I should qualify what I mean. Life for the average Italian child is wonderful. Yes, I realise that there will be exceptions, children in need of external support from outside the family. But in general, the Italian child is almost smothered with attention. Children in Italy have a good supply of aunties, uncles, cousins, grandparents, around and available (before you jump in, I know not all). To an outsider all appear to be more than willing to shower children with affection, to cosset, pamper, overprotect and, I suppose the best term I can use, 'mollycoddle'. This is not to suggest that this doesn't apply to other countries, all cultures regard children as something precious, to be protected and nurtured and, quite rightly, have a place at the very centre of family and community life. I'm also desperately trying not to make a value judgement. Although it does feel like I could be digging myself a deep hole here. Let me try and dig myself out.

When Italians come to the UK, they probably find the relationship between adults and children just as 'interesting' as a Brit in Italy. The average Italian is far more expressive in their fondness for children. This applies almost equally to adult males and females, to teenagers and the elderly. Adult male Italians don't shy away from publicly expressing delight at seeing a new-born baby or a cute little child. 'O Dio, che bello, che dolcezza' ('O God, how beautiful, how sweet'). No one blinks an eye, no one suggesting that such a reaction from a man is somehow unmanly. I've seen teenage males react in just the same way, absolutely without embarrassment. Just take a minute to contrast that with how the average adult male in the UK or the US reacts.

Bedtime. Those of you who have or had young children, what time do you/did you send them to bed? What would you say is a reasonable time, especially if they have school the next day? During a school week, when at primary school, my girls would be in bed by, at the latest, 8.30pm – but that could just be me. Most Italian families, including my neighbours, very rarely eat before 8 in the evening, sometimes 8.30. Grandchildren are almost always at the meal. The very earliest they are going to be tucked up in bed, will be between 10 and 10.30. Well, ok, what about weekends? What time would you have kids in bed? Saturday evening and you have invited friends or relatives for dinner. In Italy, if the parents are up, the kids are up; there is no 'grownups only time'. The children play around and interact with the adults. Go on, what do you really think?

Now look at the above as an Italian. Why do Brits bother having children if they are so eager to get them out of the way? Why are they sent to bed, especially at weekends? Surely children are there to be enjoyed, a central part of the family gathering.

The expression, 'children should be seen but not heard', a proverb dating way back to the 15th century, still applies in some shape or form in the UK today. I guess the average Brit today interprets this as, children should be well behaved and do as they are told. Just for your interest, in its original form the proverb was applied only to young women who were expected to keep quiet, but I digress.

If you had to grade restaurants and pubs in the UK on a scale of 1 to 5 for child friendliness, 1 poor to 5 excellent, what grade would you give most of them? Just for this, places with child playrooms and ball pools are excluded. In my experience most pubs and restaurants will have a 'witching hour' for children, say 9pm, when the little demons are no longer allowed to mix with adults. Post 9pm being 'grown up time'. Not so in Italy. Generally, if the adults are there, the children are there. I can go along with that; I hear you say. However, I can also hear a 'but' coming. I can go along with that, but they should be well behaved, they should do as they are told. To a certain extent an expectation of good behaviour is also expected of Italian children. But how good is good expected to be, that is the question? Let me give you an example. It's up to you to then decide.

Carnevale comes to Italy each year somewhere between early February to early March, depending on when Easter falls. Most foreigners associate it with the Venice Carnival, the world-renowned masked occasion. But Carnevale takes place across the whole of Italy, including Gubbio, obviously. The time is celebrated with a festival of parades, masquerades, entertainment, lots of music and parties. One of the main events is the carnival for children. The medieval streets of the town are taken over by a caravan of floats, each float having a different theme. Some take shape on the back of trucks; others are pulled along by tractors. As each float slowly passes spectators lining the streets, a shower of shaving foam and canned silly string comes pouring down. Confetti also cascades, ideally into outstretched hands, but more often onto the ground where children scramble around to pick it up. No, not the confetti that you could be thinking of. These confetti come in the form of sugar-coated almonds. After the parade of floats have journeyed round the medieval streets, they eventually arrive in Piazza 40 Martiri to be judged. The winning float awarded the Mascherissima Trophy – Premio Orafo Miozzi Stefano.

Hours, days, weeks and months are spent constructing the most elaborate floats. The float constructed by my friends and neighbours has won the top prize for the past two years. Marcello, Alicia and another friend, Matteo, being the main people to have put things together. For this particular carnevale, their theme is based on the Minions from the film Despicable Me. Children in the most brilliant costumes, with giant sized adults as Stuart, Kevin and Bob (no I've not seen the film either). I may be just a little bit biased, but their float is definitely one of the best, if not the best. But no, this year, 2016, the winning float is one put together by a primary school. I think there is just a little hint of local diplomacy going on, my adopted float coming second. I guess that it's only reasonable to give others the chance to enjoy the limelight.

After all the noise, excitement and fun of the floats passing by and awards being made, every adult and child involved with the Minions makes for a restaurant in the medieval heart of Gubbio. Me included, although to be honest I feel like a bit of a gate crasher, having had absolutely no involvement in constructing the float, costumes, or even taking part in the parade. I did take lots of photographs, does that count? I forget the actual number, but there must be at least forty adults and, I would say, at least, 15 Minion children of assorted size. It's quite a big restaurant, just below ground level, with beautiful, vaulted ceilings constructed of stone. The place is full to bursting with adults and children from some of the other floats, and the occasional scattering of couples, who perhaps thought they were coming out for a romantic lunch.

All the Minion adults sit either side of long, heavy oak tables. The assorted Minion children sit with a whole gaggle of children from various floats. Is there a collective noun, other than group, for a bunch of hungry, excited children, all gathered in one place? Any suggestions? For this little tale, rather than just a group of children, let's refer to them as a gaggle of children.

The place is incredibly busy, lively, overflowing with excitement. Staff take orders, parents ordering for their children. Wine and bottled water are speedily delivered to tables, a range of soft drinks to the gaggle of children. Most people order pizza, just a few preferring a dish of pasta. Loud conversation and laughter shoots across tables as people sip on red wine and eat.

The gaggle of children aren't particularly rowdy. No food has been thrown across tables. However, in just a short time they have left half eaten food and are darting around between tables. Sometimes over to parents and then back to rest of their pizza. At other times simply chasing each other between restaurant staff serving tables; staff carrying food and drink swerving to avoid clashing with little bodies. And nobody appears to mind. The children are clearly happy and excited. The adults are equally happy and enjoying the company of others. The restaurant staff swerve with a smile on faces, making not one complaint. Even those out for that romantic lunch appear to be totally at ease, only having eyes and ears for each other.

Let me ask that question again from a little earlier. You know, the one that came out of the proverb, 'children should be seen but not heard.'

How good is good expected to be? I hope that you're not expecting me to offer an answer. I shall leave that debate in your capable hands.

I think I'm going to stand by my earlier statement, generally, Italian children are indulged.

To the outsider it may have appeared that the gaggle of children have simply been left to run feral in the restaurant, parents apparently negating any responsibility. As an insider, you realise that the cherished offspring are, in fact, being watched the whole time, with an eye of at least one parent. Any parent not keeping an eye on their child would be regarded as incredibly selfish. Little Giulio may fall over as he runs around. Someone needs to be paying attention, to be able to rush forward and comfort him.

The indulgence I speak of is not evidenced by an overwhelming supply of gifts and toys, of money being excessively spent. It's an indulgence of time, almost never-ending attention, bubbling pride and concern. I guess such dedication should be admired.

My hole is deep enough now, you can cover me with earth.

Although children are cherished with pride, the numbers born each year continue to go down. In 2019, approximately 435,000 babies were born, almost half the number born in the early 1970s. Italy now has the lowest birth rate in Europe. As the number of children born goes down, the number of single and non-married parents continues to rise.

Let's move on to marriage, divorce, Catholics and other such things.

In 1974, a referendum was held asking the Italian people if they supported proposals going through parliament giving legal recognition to divorce. Despite a fight from the Catholic Church, the Italian people gave their resounding support for the legal right to divorce. Just for your interest, the very first divorce was granted in Modena to Alfredo Cappi, 28 and Giorgia Luisa Benassi, 25, the two satisfying the requirement of being separated for five years. Over time, changes to family law were to follow. Women gaining new freedoms, significantly that they would no longer be under the control of their husband. Equal property rights were brought in, and equality related to the raising of children. Reforms have continued to be made to Italian divorce law, arriving at a situation where a divorce can be granted after six months if the desire is consensual. Contested divorce can be granted after a period of twelve months. Italian law now also grants divorce solely on the grounds of the 'irretrievable breakdown of a marriage' rather than 'fault'.

What could be regarded as the 'traditional' family in Italy has, over the years, undoubtedly changed. More marriages may be ending in divorce or with couples separating, fewer children per family, more single parents, and more couples cohabiting, but the core features of la famiglia prevail.

CATHOLICS

Italy is simply packed to overflowing with Catholicism. Obviously, it would be. It has the Roman Catholic Church, with the Vatican surrounded by the city of Rome. It has the home of the head of the Catholic faith throughout the world. In 2017 there were approximately 1.3 billion followers of Catholicism across the globe.

The Bishop of Rome, The Pontiff, The Pope, The apostolic successor to Saint Peter. Put simply, he represents what the Catholic Church regards as the only legitimate voice of Christ on earth.

It will come as no surprise then, that most Italians identify themselves as Roman Catholic. But what does that mean for the average Italian? 'Good Catholics' should be following the direction and teachings of the Church in all that they do. The fact that Italy has the lowest birth rate in Europe should give you a hint that this may not be the case. If regular church attendance is used as an indicator of faith, again there would appear to be a gap between belief and practice. Of those identifying as Roman Catholic, only about 30% attend church at least once per week. Religious icons are to be found everywhere, any town of a reasonable size having a plentiful supply of churches. Italians may be entwined in Catholicism, it runs through their veins, but in day-to-day life most Italians take a rather pragmatic approach to their faith.

For years, the Catholic Church in Italy has been trying to hold back the tide of change. As you already know, divorce was legally recognised as a means of ending a marriage in the mid-1970s, this, much to the dismay of the church, followed by the legal right of a woman to seek an abortion - the use of the term 'seek' of particular significance. Italian law may allow a pregnancy to be terminated, the law insisting that all hospitals should provide appropriate facilities. But the law also allows any doctor, nurse, anaesthetist and support staff the option to 'conscientiously object' to being involved in a termination. So, although abortion in Italy is legal, it can often be difficult to access.

In September 2003, the European Parliament approved a human rights resolution against discrimination on the grounds of sexual orientation. Following this, each member state of the EU had to confirm that it would move to abolishing any form of discrimination. You can imagine the joy of the Catholic Church and those on the centre-right and beyond in Italian politics. But change was coming, even if the church and others were kicking against it.

In February 2007, a left-of-centre coalition, led by Romano Prodi, introduced a bill giving legal recognition to domestic partnerships. It came as no surprise that there was considerable opposition from the church and right-wing opposition groups. Demonstrations took place in Rome supporting the bill, only to be followed a few days later with a counter demonstration organised by the Conference of Italian Bishops. Just to add to the mix, the 16th of June recorded Rome's biggest Gay Pride parade, with an attendance estimated to be around one million.

Between consenting adults, homosexuality has been legal in Italy since 1890. But I've found it hard to gauge where the average Italian is on LGBT issues. My impression is that it's not really on their agenda. I guess, not surprisingly, for the vast majority such issues are peripheral to daily life. Although I suspect that it's still more difficult to 'come out' in Italy than it is in some other European countries. I do remember one person, I won't say who, saying to me when watching something on the news:

'Communists are all gay Ghrem, aren't they?' Although in the mind of the person making the comment, it was a fact rather than a question.

Berlusconi (I did say he would keep cropping up), in an attempt to deflect attention away from his sexual exploits said:

'It's better to like beautiful girls than to be gay.'

However, in contrast to what I've just said. Over recent years there have been a number of openly LGBT individuals who have risen to prominence in both regional and national politics. Perhaps it is a sign that attitudes are starting to change. In 2012, Sicily elected Rosario Crocetta, an openly gay candidate, to the position of Governor. Not only did he not hide his sexual orientation, he was also a leading anti-Mafia campaigner. A police interception of mafia communications, once picking up orders for a hit man to, 'eliminate the communist faggot.' The main loser in the election was Berlusconi's People of Freedom Party (after only a short time the party name reverted back to Forza Italia).

Going back to attempts to push through equal rights legislation in parliament. In 2008, any progress being made was stalled with the election of a right-wing coalition, a Berlusconi-led government of the People of Freedom Party and Northern League (the People of Freedom Party had been Forza Italia). The Catholic Church could, for a brief time, breathe a sigh of relief, it had friends in power.

In May 2012, the Italy of Values party became the first political party to openly add same-sex marriage to its campaign. The Democratic Party followed in July of the same year. Beppe Grillo, leader of the supposed apolitical, anti-establishment party, the Five Star Movement, also supported same-sex marriage. Momentum was growing, the Catholic Church and its political supporters desperately trying to turn back the tide.

In June 2016, the law recognised Civil Unions as having exactly the same legal status as marriage. On the 24th of July, the first same-sex couple entered into a civil union.

Same-sex marriage is now recognised as legal across the majority of Western Europe, even in Spain and France, with Italy remaining an exception. A report published in 2017 by the Pew Research Centre based in Washington, found that about six-in-ten Italians supported the idea of same-sex marriage. Is this a further sign of the gradual weakening of the hold that the Catholic Church has on the Italian people?

The Catholic Church, the local priest, certainly don't have the same hold they once had. But still most Italians when asked, would state that they are believers in the Catholic faith. The Pope especially still having prominence in the minds of Italians. Italy would not be Italy without the Pope. Religious observance may well be weaker, with increasingly fewer Italians following the basic precepts of the

Catholic faith in their daily life, but Catholicism, in some form or other, pulses through their veins. For it not to do so would be unthinkable.

Avvenire is basically the daily newspaper of the Vatican and, unlike many other newspapers in Italy, its circulation is growing. The newspaper's growing circulation almost feels like a contradiction, Italians 'less' Catholic and yet digesting a view of the world still heavily influenced by journalism tied to the Church. Italians are no different to the general body of the population in most countries, conservative with a small c. Whatever may be happening in the world, the Catholic Church, Avvenire, and especially the Pope, offer some sense of continuity and stability. If I'm right, for Americans the same sense of continuity comes from an allegiance to the flag. For Brits it is, without doubt, an allegiance to the monarchy.

I guess that you could best describe the majority of Italians today as being pragmatic Catholics. Catholic symbolism and tradition still having massive significance, but not holding total sway over the practical details of everyday life. To non-Catholics, me included, it could appear that the faith is very doctrinal. To live life as a 'good' Catholic, you must follow certain rules. To an outsider it can appear strict and unbending. Perhaps the appeal is exactly the opposite. The Catholic Church is in fact very forgiving of human frailty. It certainly feels like the Church in Italy has an exceptionally lenient approach to marital infidelity, especially if it is the husband who has given in to some supposed human fallibility. The Church even more forgiving if the family remains together. Confess your sins and be prepared to repent. You're even provided with an intermediary between yourself and God in human form, the local priest and at the very highest level, the Pope.

Tobias Jones in The Dark Heart of Italy, neatly sums up Italian attitudes with regards to what other nationalities, certainly the British, would regard as social/sexual impropriety:

'Politicians, despite their Catholic avowals, proudly partner the most pendulous, beautiful celebrities, doing their credibility only good.'

Just a little interlude here, something to note. Much to the amusement of my neighbours, I have in the past, referred to Aldo as Papa, for me the meaning being father. It turns out that I had, on a few occasions, raised Aldo to the position of Pope. No conclave of Bishops or white smoke required. My mistake was eventually explained, but to my English ear, the words being used, and sound were the same, Papa – papà. On careful listening, I realised that it's all a matter of intonation. The difference indicated with a capital letter and accent. Aldo has now been demoted from Papa (Pope) to papà (a simple father).

One figure that it took me a little time to understand, and you see him everywhere, is Padre Pio. He was a Capuchin friar who died in 1968. I understood the obvious significance of Christ and the Virgin Mary. I also understood the obvious significance of the Pope and, especially in Umbria, San Francesco. But for a time, Padre Pio's bearded face that appears framed at the back of a bar, tucked behind the sun visor of a taxi, on sale in absolutely every gift shop, was a bit of a mystery to me.

It's believed by many that Padre Pio had, for want of a better description, supernatural gifts. The story is that he had an encounter with the devil, actually physically fighting with the evil presence. He is said to have experienced visions and suffered injuries to his hands and feet, in much the same way as Jesus Christ, the wounds on Christ coming from the crucifixion – the stigmata. But it wasn't until 2002 that Padre Pio became a saint. For quite some time there was disagreement and disbelief about the supposed happenings and the version of events told. Regardless of the controversy, San Giovanni Rotondo, found in the south-east of Italy, the friary where Padre Pio lived, has become one of the most visited Catholic shrines in the world. There is even a Padre Pio satellite TV channel, I think the devotional are desperately hoping for him to make a 'live' appearance.

For some reason, the appeal of this saint, who in addition to his other attributes, was said to be able to read minds, predict the future and even levitate, extends way beyond the devout. The appeal of Padre Pio extends to those who, for much of the time, only pay lip service to their Catholic faith. Perhaps it's the mysticism, the history of Catholicism enmeshed, as I suppose it has to be, in the supernatural. Any theologians reading this may be able to offer far better explanations than me.

NOI SIAMO ITALIANI

Nationality under Italian law, citizenship, is determined primarily by descent, I guess you could refer to it as a 'right of blood'. There is a limit on the number of generations that a person can trace back in order to claim the right of Italian citizenship. You can't go any further back than 1861. Before that date Italian citizens did not exist, the simple reason being that the Italian state did not exist. The ancestor being used to prove the right to citizenship may have been born before 1861, but to have a successful claim he/she would need to have been alive on the 17th of March of that year. A landmark court decision in 2009, changed the position for those trying to gain Italian citizenship through the maternal line, bringing it in line with those going down the paternal route. Before 2009, the applicant needed to show that the female was born after January 1st, 1948. So, if you can gather together all the proof required, gaining Italian citizenship through ancestry should be reasonably straightforward. But this is Italian bureaucracy. Remember Permit 838?

Potentially, there are millions of people born and living in other countries who could legitimately make a claim to have Italian citizenship. It's certainly not an exaggeration to suggest that the number could be many more millions than the 60 million already living in Italy. Another attractive point to keep in mind is that if a person successfully claims Italian citizenship, that individual also has the right to work and settle in any EU country. I often come across Americans claiming, through Italian ancestry, that they also have a claim to European Citizenship. In a sense they are right, but unfortunately European Citizenship (well I think it's unfortunate) doesn't technically exist. And don't hold your breath in expectation of a tsunami of millions landing on the Italian peninsula having been successfully, legally, recognised as Italian. The practical difficulty of gathering together the required documents, even if they still exist, is a big enough obstacle to dissuade most people from even thinking of applying. You'll find that there are always lots of 'buts' running through Italian bureaucracy, gathering all the 'right' documents together is just one.

The other 'but', is that even when you have all the documents that you think you need, I can almost guarantee that you will need more. One thing I have found out living in Italy, there almost always turns out to be yet another document that you weren't aware of, and nobody told you about. And here I'm talking about the simpler things of life. Let's assume that you do have all the required documents, how long will the process take? In some ways it's a bit like asking how long is a piece of string. It could be any length of time. If all goes smoothly, the whole process could be done and dusted in one to three years. If the road is a bit bumpy, for whatever reason, a reason that you won't probably understand, the process could take up to six years or more.

There is the option of applying for dual citizenship, this being dependent on the citizenship you already hold.

Another route into Italian citizenship, is to have been legally resident in Italy for a period of at least ten years if you're not an EU citizen, or if you are an EU citizen, four years. As long as you don't have a criminal record, you can then apply for and possibly be granted naturalisation, take note of the 'possibly'. You must also show that you have adequate financial resources.

And another route is via marrying an Italian. Unless you're desperately in love, you may regard this as a little bit drastic. No, don't leap on this one thinking it's a simple and automatic process, you will still be made to jump over hurdles. The process could still take up to five years. Those applying also have to take a language test up to intermediate level. If you're really desperate, have a child, naturally or through adoption, there is a chance that the length of time may be reduced.

And finally, every document you need to support whichever route you take, must be translated into Italian and officially certified, Italian officialdom style. They have to be 'legalized' with an apostille, an official certificate confirming authenticity.

The fact that your prime claim to Italianness comes through blood, rather than where you were born and grew up, may be very appealing to those around the world who would like to be recognised as being legally Italian, but it presents problems for some who actually already live in Italy. There are thousands of 'second-generation immigrants' who don't have the essential blood link. Simply being born in Italy is not enough, you need to be born to an Italian citizen. Someone, for example, born into an Italian American family, a family that could possibly have grown from emigration to the US some hundred years in the past could have a greater claim to Italian citizenship than someone born in Italy. This person may have never set foot on Italian soil, but still has more of a claim than someone born and actually living in the country. To be legally recognised as Italian, those from originally immigrant families, but born in

Italy, are expected to apply for citizenship after reaching the age of 18, but before their nineteenth birthday. If not done in this time slot, the right to Italian citizenship is lost for good.

In 2019, Italy had about 5.3 million foreign citizens legally resident in the country. This is about 8.3 percent of Italy's total population, currently standing at 60.5 million. Over half of Italy's foreign residents live in the north, roughly 58%, this followed by 25% in central Italy, about 12% in the south and roughly 5% on Italy's islands. Lombardy, with Milan as its capital, has the highest number of foreign residents, Lazio comes next with Italy's capital city, Rome (Figures taken from the Caritas-Migrants Immigration Report).

Just out of interest, in 2017, out of all the countries in the EU, Germany had the largest total number of immigrants, standing at just over 917,000, followed by the UK with just over 644,000, Italy just over 343,000. Spain and France both coming above Italy.

An estimated 30,000 to 40,000 Brits live in Italy. For comparison, Spain has well over 300,000. In 2017 there were an estimated 1.3 million Brits living in EU countries. Rome and Milan prove to be the most popular places to settle in Italy. Tuscany being the third choice. With Florence and Lucca coming top in that region.

It is reported that just over 4,000 migrants arrived in Italy by sea in the first four months of 2020. This followed on from 11,500 in 2019. Each year before, the news in Italy delivering desperate images of people trying to cross the Mediterranean, often in the most hazardous conditions. The peak coming in 2016, with 181,436. Since then, the numbers have rapidly declined. You will no doubt be familiar with the images showing washed up bodies, including small children, on Italian beaches. But still they come. Lampedusa, the closest Italian island to the coast of Africa, has taken possibly an unmanageable share of migrants desperately trying to cross the sea. Il Giornale (an Italian newspaper) reporting another 150 arriving at the beginning of March 2020. From January through to October 2019, over 1,000 unaccompanied children were amongst the migrants. Attempting to cross the Mediterranean continues to be an extremely hazardous and traumatic endeavour. In the early part of 2023, the issue became a dominant topic of debate not only for Italy but also for the EU. More migrants and more deaths featuring daily as one of the main topics for almost all Italian news outlets.

I'm guessing that it will come as no real surprise that roughly half of Italian citizens view migrants as 'a risk'. All European countries remain overwhelmingly white, with Italy whiter than many others. Yet the general population of all European countries constantly, in all research, vastly overestimate the number in the country who are not white. Are exaggerated estimates a problem? If simply left as opinion I guess not, but such perceptions have a tendency to drive political policy. Stereotypes and prejudice, adding to a feeling of 'uneasiness' with those perceived to be different.

One of the things you need to keep in mind when looking at Italy, is that until relatively recently the country was an exporter of people. Unlike countries with past empire, such as the UK and France, importing people is still relatively new to Italy. Beppe Severgnini, in La Bella Figura, describes the supposed attraction of modern Italy in the following way:

'Our peninsula dangles like a ripe fruit over the heads of the poor in Africa, the Balkans and the Near East. There are jobs we don't want to do anymore but immigrants will.'

Being a non-Catholic immigrant, of which I happen to be one, really doesn't appear to appear be an issue. The colour of your skin and where you originally came from, for some, can be just a little more problematic. Certainly, over the past few years, images on television screens have left Italians and others with the impression that most migrants arriving in the country come by rickety, dangerously overcrowded boats, risking life, with many lost at sea, some washed up with the plastic on Italian beaches. In the main they arrive unskilled, not able to speak the language, little if any money, probably without documentation, having few if any connections in Italy. It shouldn't be surprising if people have a skewed perception of immigrants, and migrants in particular. Images on television screens and stories told, do have the sympathy of most Italians, but what should be done? Somebody has to do something. And there are more than enough people at the very centre of the Italian political system who are willing to offer the Italian people 'obvious' and 'easy' solutions.

The reality is that most migrants don't arrive in Italy by boat. They enter Italy across open borders unseen and, for most part, ignored by the media. Legitimate immigrants tend to enter Italy, as the term suggests, by legitimate means. However, the focus of the media on illegal immigration, the over staying of those who may have once been legitimate, can result in unease about all who are seen as people of difference. Even with their far longer history of immigration, this is no different in the US, UK, France or Germany.

Let me tell you about an amusing but also a telling little incident. I'd been living in Umbria for almost two years, but back in the UK visiting my daughters. I was helping my younger daughter and her partner decorate their home. They'd been living there for just over twelve months and were on friendly, chatting terms, with their neighbours. During the two weeks, I'd also got into exchanging daily pleasantries with one of the neighbours. Perhaps a few years older than me, but not by much. A cheerful, friendly enough, white Yorkshireman. He knew I now lived in Italy, having been told by my daughter. One morning, he expressed how surprised he was seeing me back in England, spending my time working on my daughters house when I could be in Italy. He then said:

'I don't blame you living in another country, I would if I could. It's terrible now here. There are too many foreigners.'

I replied with a good morning and went back inside.

In all the time I have had a house in Italy, or during my time living here, I have not once been aware of any negativity coming from the fact that I'm a foreigner. The truth is I have been greeted with open arms, with warmth and undiluted friendship. I've been welcomed and made to feel very much part of the community where I live. It's that welcome and warmth that has made my experience of Italy even more beautiful. But, as you know, I'm British and I'm white. Be aware of it or not, be willing to accept or challenge what I have to say next. Those two factors, being British and being white undoubtedly bring privilege. Now I've set up a debate.

To describe Italy as a multicultural society would really be stretching reality. There are many in Italy who, for whatever reason, feel uneasy with what they regard as those who are 'not really Italian'(I guess that's no different from my daughter's neighbour). Other Western Europeans have the best chance of coming closest to being accepted. Eastern Europeans perhaps come next, 'but you have to remember to regard them with at least a little suspicion.' Then come those who look different in dress, facial features and colour of skin. You find people, we'll call them the 'uneasy citizens' for now (you can give them your own label), in all countries. I'm referring to those who are 'uneasy' with difference. They hold an expectation of what it means to be genuinely British, French, German, Italian, Chinese, or whatever the nationality happens to be. Certainly, Britain has struggled with this for some time. Perhaps now in more muted form, but it continues. Although, even in the UK, openly, vicious, racist abuse, can spill into headline news. In Italy, the 'debate' is still very much alive and very much mainstream. For many years, some of the main political parties in the Italian parliament have been more than willing to stoke racist flames. In 2022, Italy voted in a coalition government made up of three extreme right wing parties.

For many being Italian or being British, really means being white.

I remember once watching an international match in a local bar close to Case Colle. It just happened to be England playing, I forget the other country. Obviously, the commentary was in Italian. A Black English player had the ball, the Italian commentator simply saying that England have the ball. Someone in the bar looked at me and said:

'How can he be English, he's black?'

I explained that the player was as English as me. The person asking the question not looking convinced, a questioning shrug directed to his friends.

Mosie Kean, a star player with Juventus, suffers racist abuse at most of the matches he plays in. Throughout a game against Cagliari in April 2019, Kean is the victim of an almost constant chorus of monkey chants from the Cagliari supporters. On scoring a goal, Kean stands in front of those supporters with his arms out. After the game, the Juventus captain, Leonardo Bonnucci, rather than condemning the racism and supporting his team mate, he excuses it: 'I think the blame is shared 50-50. If Mosie hadn't celebrated his goal in front of the Cagliari fans, they wouldn't have reacted like that.'

Perhaps change is slowly coming. With a growing number of Italians from ethnic minority backgrounds, Italian society is having to challenge its perceptions. As you already know the numbers of Italians from minority backgrounds, compared to say the UK, is still relatively small. Although small in number, high profile visibility is growing, scratching at the perceptions of those I labelled the 'uneasy citizens'.

The popularity of people such as Matteo Salvini and Georgia Meloni on the far-right of politics, has ensured that being Italian and skin colour remains a simmering pot of prejudice and stereotyping, challenging Italy's moral compass and cohesion. In 2017, the Italian parliament debated changing Italy's citizenship laws, bringing in 'right of soil', to sit alongside 'right of blood'. The changes would have automatically given citizenship to anyone born in Italy, regardless of where their parents came from. Salvini jumped on the debate, linking it to undocumented immigrants, asylum seekers and those reaching Italy by boat. His slogan: 'Stop the Invasion.'

Before I leave this, I have to mention what is obvious and incredibly disappointing. Racist abuse is not confined to Italy. Look at the USA, where it's consequences are even more direct and violent. As for the UK, the European Football Championship final made it very clear that racism amongst some England supporters is still very much alive and virulent. Three English, Black players, receiving online racist abuse after missing penalties.

Let's move on to something a little more light-hearted.

GESTICULATION

I'm sat having a beer in the Post Card Inn, Holmfirth, Last of the Summer Wine Country. Here for an evening with friends in West Yorkshire, back in the UK for a couple of weeks. If there is one thing I miss living in Italy, it's a traditional British pub. You just don't find anything quite the same in other countries apart from, perhaps, Ireland. There is quite a large pub in Gubbio, The Village, that comes close to creating a British pub style. It can be found quite close to Piazza 40 Martiri. Italians certainly rate the place:

'Bel locale stile pub irlandese. Ottime birre. Menu ottimo con prezzi buoni.'

'Tutto buono, personale simpatico!'

To tell the truth, I've only been in twice. Not because it's not worth a visit, just that its clientele tends to be in the twenty to thirty age range. Really not an issue if you fall into that group; I definitely do not.

Anyway, I'm sat having a beer with friends, chatting, enjoying good company and catching up on life. I've been living in Italy for just over one year. There are six of us, friends and work colleagues who I have known for years. We sit, we joke, we laugh, debate, and we have another beer; perhaps another to follow the last two. I guess with each beer, I'm becoming more expressive.

'What's all this about?'

Two out of the group speaking at the same time and mimicking my actions.

'What do you mean, what's all this about?'

The whole group laughing as I speak, all mimicking my actions.

'All this with your hands, your face and your shoulders.'

Yet again mimicking the actions and laughing.

And there it was. My body language had changed, without me even recognising it had happened. In just one year, this Brit had adopted and started to absorb Italian mannerisms. A whole range of gesticulations never used before, now automatically used to add emphasis to what I had to say. Trust me, if you spend any length of time in the company of Italians, it will happen to you. It seeps through the skin, becoming part of you without you even knowing. Even when you do know, you can't stop it from happening. Italian gesticulation becomes an automated response.

This could have the feel of an Italian stereotype. Trust me it's certainly not. I would commit to saying that no other people use such a wide range of body language to express themselves as the Italians. And it feels as though it starts as soon as they leave the warmth of the womb. I've been in the company of little Italians, not yet really speaking the language, but already quite adept at visually expressing the message and intent of what they want to get across. They are little miniatures of the Italian adults around them.

Obviously, humans wherever they happen to be in the world add to the spoken word with body language. Some gestures are almost internationally recognised and understood. The Italians take it to a whole different level, with gestures and movements for just about everything. There are some who suggest that there are over 250 hand gestures alone. I'll let you do the counting and then, perhaps, you can let me know.

I guess in many ways the flamboyancy of Italian body language fits perfectly with what makes Italy what it is. The beauty of Italy is the visual, the taste, the enthusiasm and passion.

If you know Italy at all, you will totally understand what I'm talking about. If you're only just discovering Italy and the Italians, take your time over a glass of red wine to simply people watch. Better still, allow yourself to be absorbed into Italian life.

ITALIANS AND CLOTHING

This is not what most people may be thinking of; the notion that being Italian automatically equals dressing with style. Undoubtedly there are many Italians who fit their dress sense to Italian design, but equally there are many who, how can I put this? There are many who dress simply, just like the rest of us. Sometimes you can overplay the stereotype. No, here I'm talking about the way the Italians dress is determined by the month, the changing season. What do I mean?

Bare legs and t-shirts are for June, July and August. When autumn begins, by that I mean, at the latest, the end of September, this is the time to start covering up. Italians go by the turn of the season, regardless of the weather. Even if the days are still quite hot, the time has come to start covering up. Perhaps some type of warmer top, jeans and even a jacket. And the days can remain relatively hot right through to the end of October. The foreigners, including me, stand out. Still hot, then you obviously go out in shorts. Not if you are Italian. Regardless of the weather, the seasonal clock hands change, Italian dress changes.

I remember being with my neighbours by the sea, a place called Senigallia, in the region of Le Marche. The whole of my adopted Italian family present, enjoying a meal, the gathering to celebrate Benedetta's birthday. As the adults sat chatting and enjoying a drink, just to settle digestion you understand, the children played outside the restaurant on the beach. After only a few minutes they were called back in. How could they possibly be out, running around on the beach, without a jacket, hat and scarf. It was easily warm enough for the children to run around without outer clothing. But no, the seasonal clothing clock had moved on.

One important item of Italian apparel that I can't leave out – males' wearing 'budgie smugglers'. You must have noticed that the vast majority of Italian males' chosen beachwear tends to be extremely tiny, often tight fitting, swimming briefs/trunks. You know, just enough to cover the buttocks and groin, the little 'budgie' nestled inside. From the tanned Adonis to those with a beer belly almost hiding the budgie, you'll find Italian males stood at the water's edge, adding to their mahogany tan, with their 'budgie' hopefully asleep.

There are a number of Italianisms that I have absorbed without even knowing. However, trust me, you will not find me with my 'budgie' so snugly covered.

AFTERNOON CLOSURE

Almost all places of work close for lunch, lunch being 1pm onwards, for at least two hours, but often through to 4pm. It really is important that you don't forget. And please avoid complaining to yourself that this is so frustrating, how can you get things done? Remember, this is Italy. Relax, enjoy the weather, having a long leisurely something to eat and drink.

Things are changing. When I first bought my little bit of Umbria everything closed, even shops explicitly targeting tourists! Obviously, cafes and restaurants were open, but the bars, not always. Now supermarkets remain open, also the relatively new DIY stores and new indoor shopping centres. New as in there were no large DIY stores or indoor shopping centres, most certainly in Umbria, until the past few years. The other thing that's changed. Supermarkets and shopping centres open on Sunday. I know, and this a Catholic country. Almost forgot. Banks and the Post Office close at 1pm and do not open for the rest of the day. Both are also closed on Saturday. In the bigger cities, such as Milan, Rome and Florence, you will find that most shops stay open, but still not banks and the post office.

Did I hear you referring to the afternoon closure as 'siesta time', the chance for a long afternoon nap? You can enjoy the opportunity to have a nap, that is if you happen to be a tourist. Italians obviously have a break, but never ever accuse them of simply sleeping for two or three hours. I think they would be a little offended if you suggested they do.

THE HUMBLE ELECTRICAL SOCKET

Just a little practical thing to keep in mind when you visit Italy or decide to make your home here: the humble electrical socket. Plugs in Italy come with different sized pins depending on the level of current required by the appliance. Sounds reasonable enough, I think. The problem is that many homes only have sockets that accept one size of plug. If you want to use a plug with slightly fatter pins, you have to use an adapter. So, in my house I have adapters for Italian plugs and I have adapters for my UK plugs, these being totally different again. My advice is, if you are having renovations done, and you need new electrics, go for sockets that accept different size Italian pins. Alternatively, you can be like me, constantly complaining because the adapters, of which I have a few, disappear in a game of hide and seek.

THE MYSTERY CARD GAME

Put everything down and concentrate. I'm going to tell you about a card game - The Italian Card Game. I would assume that all of you will have played cards at some point, mostly for fun; it's a social 'sport'. It could be that you're exceptionally proficient and perhaps play for money. I'm asking you to concentrate, because here is a card game that I've still got to get my head round. I've played it a few times with my neighbours. As I've sat as a spectator, the rules of play have been explained to me. I'm told that the game is simple. I guess I must be a little slow. Don't feel obliged to comment. Just as I think I've grasped it; the rules appear to change. All my Italian friends and neighbours, without exception, know how to play this card game, all of them, including the children. The card game is of course – Briscola.

First you need to be aware that the cards used for Briscola are totally different to the 52 playing cards you would have in a standard pack. There are no jacks, no ace of hearts, no eight of spades or six of diamonds, etc. Well, that's not quite true, because there are jacks, but they're not called jacks and don't behave in the same way. So that's the first challenge, understanding what the different symbols mean and their relative value to others. Some of the cards have human figures, some cards have swords, chalices, round shields, others with a symbol I find difficult to describe. Unlike a standard pack of playing cards, these cards don't have numbers. The aim of the game is to gather more cards than your adversary and tot up the points. You with me so far? Good.

Usually, the game has four players. The dealer shuffles the deck, we're all familiar with that. Three cards are dealt to each person in a counter clockwise direction. The dealer than turns the first card in the deck face up. This card becomes the 'briscola', representing the trump suit for the game. Again, most of us will have started games in a similar way. The player to the right of the dealer puts a card face up on the table, followed by the other players doing the same thing. The cards on the table, face up, are won by the player who played the highest value card of the same suit as the briscola. However, they could also be won by player who played the highest card of the same suit as the card played by the first player. Still with me?

As in all card games, different cards have a different face value, it's the same here. For example, the Ace is worth 11 points, the Three is worth 10 points, the King is worth 4 points and so on. Remember there are no numbers on the cards.

The winner of each round collects the cards that are face up and places them face down in a pile. The game then continues, each player taking a card from the deck. The winner of the last round is the first to go. And so, the game continues, each player starting a round with three cards. You still following this?

In the last rounds, each player will go down to two cards and then to one, because all the cards in the deck have been drawn. Briscola is the last card of the deck to be drawn.

At the end of the game, each player counts the value of the cards collected. The player with the highest number of points being the winner. Simple.

Last bits of information. Cards with a face value from seven to two are worth zero points. Each suit has a value of 30 points and there's a total of 120 points in the deck. There are 40 cards in a pack, the cards divided into four suits. In each suit there is a King (Re), a Knight (Cavaliere) and a Knave (Fante). The game can be played with two, three, four or six players. It can also be played in teams. There are other versions of the game, one of the most popular being Briscola Chiamata. This has something to do with calling out Briscola Chiamata! I think I'll leave you to discover this version, along with Briscola Bastarda, Briscolone, Briscola Assassina and Briscola Pazza. The version of the game known as Briscola Assassina, having its origins from within the ranks of the mafia. Bastarda (Bastard) and Pazza (Crazy), you can find out the rules for these versions for yourself.

I guess if I'm really determined to fit in, I need to learn how to be a proper player of Briscola. Next time you're in Italy, take the opportunity to watch a game.

CANE OR CARNE? – BOH

You say 'cane', I say 'carne.' You get dog, I get meat.

For some reason it took me quite a few years to remember the difference for dog and meat in Italian. Thankfully, I was always given meat, even if I had asked for dog.

Penne is a type of pasta; we all know that - it's obvious. You can buy packs of penne in any supermarket in the UK and, I guess, in many other countries. But just like in any language, when words are thrown together in a sentence, spoken in speedy Italian or speedy English, as a foreigner we can easily be mistaken in what we think we hear. And believe me, I've repeated what I thought I'd absorbed from listening to Italians around me, only to find the word I was using had a whole different meaning. It becomes a lot easier when you understand the context of a conversation, realising that although some words when speedily spoken may sound exactly the same, for example, penne, pane, penna, pene; each has a very different meaning.

You are confident that you know what the Italian is for bread, you know the word is pene. So, with a pleasant smile on your face, that's what you ask for with your meal.

'Vorrei un po' di pene.'

You may see a look of surprise on the face of the person serving you. They will probably understand what you were meaning to say and bring you bread. What you actually said is:

'I would like a little bit of penis.'

You know your mistake. Pane is bread, pene refers to the male genitals. And you probably know that the word penna equals pen.

Whilst we're taking about food, something that confused me a for a time, is the Italian word for table. For years I understood the words tavolo/tavola to mean table, which indeed both words do. As you travel around, you'll probably see places inviting you in with the words, Tavola Calda. I was just a little confused. When booking a table, should I use tavolo or tavola? To my mind, it appeared to make little difference; I was always understood.

Perhaps I'm just a little slow (again, no need to comment), but finally it all fell into place.

I'd been working on building a low wall to the front of my garden with a friend, Peter Carpenter. The truth is, he was doing the skilled bit of the building, I was doing the hard labour, having already spent several days, under a hot Umbrian sun, digging out the foundations. I know, my middle name is Martyr. All the neighbours passing by each day, stopping to ask questions. What was I building and why? All commenting on how hot the weather is, especially when you're doing something as hard as this. The ground bone dry, full of rocks and stones. Some saying I should do it like this, others saying I should do it like that. Almost all stopping for a while to simply stand and watch the inglese at work. The usual invitation to have a speedy espresso at the bar in Colpalombo.

Although only a low wall, I suspect I should have applied for permission. But this is Italy. Build it first, see if anyone takes any notice. By notice, I mean official notice. If not, then all is good. If Italian officialdom does get wind of it, hang out for forgiveness. It really is not uncommon to be granted forgiveness in return for a small fine. If anyone passing should ask if I have permission, the answer is obviously yes.

Anyway, we're about to actually start doing the building bit, when Paola, if you remember, the middle daughter of Aldo, calls across two gardens asking if we want to borrow a table. My friend Peter, the skilled builder, calls back, no we don't need a table. Now I really can't see why she would think that we have need of a table. If we required a table, I have two in my garden. Any idea what she was actually asking? I'm glad you do. If you don't, let me give a very brief explanation.

Peter Carpenter, my very close friend, builder and fluent in Italian, can see my quizzical expression. He explains that she's not asking if we want a table. But that's what she said, I reply. No, listen. She asked if we want to borrow una tavola. Yes, I know, a table. We don't need a table. No, in this context it refers to una tavola di legno. A wooden table then, is my reply. Peter, smiling at my ignorance. No, on this occasion, she's asking if we want to borrow a wooden plank. I see, how stupid of me not to know. He just gives a smile in agreement. I then ask Peter about tavolo.

Il tavolo refers to the table as a piece of furniture, but without food.

But a table with food then becomes la tavola.

Learning all the time, all very simple when explained.

You will have realised, of course, that all of this means that in Italian, a table is both masculine and feminine. Don't ask why, it feels safer for my brain not to question these things. Just accept the fact that oxygen exists and simply accept that an Italian table can be of either gender.

Telling people that the food is out and ready to eat, you can simply say a tavola or è pronto in tavola. Why the food should be 'in the table', I have no idea.

Me booking a table – Vorrei prenotare un tavolo or È possibile prenotare una tavola?

On occasions, I'd been asking for a table already full of food.

Just think how confused I would have been if Paola had called to me from the beach whilst I was surfing, me balancing with great skill on my tavola da surf. Not that I've ever been surfing. Humour me for now, just imagine.

So now I know. Quindi ora lo so.

This is a good one to remember, should an Italian ask if you're hungry.

Mangerei anche le gambe del tavolo – I could eat the legs of the table.

You understand the word anni, it means years, as in due anni. But what does ani mean?

You know how to say you have a headache. 'Ho mal di testa.' Nice and simple.

'Ho mal di tetta.' What are you saying now?

Often, as you browse round a gift shop, you'll come across a sign on something asking you not to touch – 'Per favore non toccare'. You may even be waiting to be served, it's you next. 'Tocca a me' – I'm next or It's my turn. But you've said, 'Toccami.' I guess they may well do, if you insist.

What's the Italian for grapefruit? Yep, pompelmo, nice and simple. So, what would pompino be?

On sunny afternoons, I've often spied Aldo having a pisolino in the shade of his trees.

Ani = Anuses

Ho mal di tetta = I have a tit-ache

Toccami = Touch me please

Pompino = Blow job

Pisolino = Nap. No mix up of words here, just wanted to see what you thought Aldo does in his garden. The Italian for snooze sounds far more relaxing – sonnellino.

In fact, talking about Aldo, he's just called me and given me a number of big, lime green, juicy fresh figs from his tree. It's important you use the correct word in Italian for fig – fico/fichi. Don't make the mistake of saying something like, that's a nice juicy fica you have there. You've just told the person that they have a juicy pussy, and I don't mean a member of the cat family.

What would it mean to you in English for a woman to be described as 'nubile'? I have to admit, it's not a term you hear very often, I don't think it's a term I have ever used, but what does it mean? If and when the term is used, it's with reference to a young woman regarded as sexually attractive. How do you think the exact same word translates into Italian?

LIKING SOMETHING

Italians don't simply like, no, it's not as simple as that. If you like something in Italy it pleases you, you find it pleasing – 'Mi piace'. To like them becomes, 'Mi piacciono' – they please me. When you meet someone for the first time, introductions made, the expected response should be, 'Piacere' – that one word literally meaning that it, 'pleasures' me to meet you. Do you like him/her, that? 'Ti piace?'. Do you like them? 'Ti piacciono?' Do you like this? 'Ti è piaciuto questo?' Do you like those? 'Ti piacciono quelli?' Did you like? Ti è piaciuto?

Perhaps we'll leave it here; I think you get the point. Anyway, what with this and the pompino, it's starting to feel like a language lesson.

If you really want to look, or at least feel like you're an Italian, the little slang term 'Boh' is incredibly useful.

At times when you don't know something, you're not sure about something, perhaps you just don't know what to say back. Just respond with 'Boh', pronounced Bo.

Obviously, you also need to equip yourself with the appropriate Italian body language and gestures. Shrug of the shoulders, a slightly confused look on your face, arms held low and forwards, palms of your hands upturned. Just to say 'Boh' without all the dressings is never going to make you come even close to looking Italian.

One last important point. As you probably already know, Italians like to kiss. Not some sort of snog; no French kissing . Just a kiss to each cheek, sometimes little more than cheeks touching. But which side first?

I guess that will do for now. I'm sure there is plenty more to say about 'Being Italian', probably more you could add yourself. If you are Italian, I hope that you recognise at least some of the observations from this inglese as having a glimmer of truth. If not, I hope you will forgive me.

I should also let you know, so that you don't go round spreading 'fake news'. Briscola Assassina having its origins from within the ranks of the Mafia, I completely made up. There is absolutely no truth at all in what I said.

The kiss to each cheek, which side first? The right side.

Phew, this chapter is long. I can see now why most people take up an entire book trying to give a sense of what it means to be Italian.

Almost forgot – Nubile. In Italian, the same word simply means that the young woman is single, to use a very old English term, she is a maiden.

ITALIAN STYLE & FLAIR

I began this chapter with buying my first brand new car. I'm going to bring the chapter to a close by looking at cars again. No, it's not some boyish fascination with cars. I'm using cars to illustrate the talent within Italian society for high end design, imagination, fashion in its broadest sense, innovation, technical skill and engineering prowess. This being one Italian stereotype that is, without any doubt, absolutely true. The physical fabric of Italy, in general, is in desperate need of investment and repair. But the brand of Made in Italy is both internally and internationally very strong. This is especially true when it comes to the luxury end of the market, the prestige, massively expensive end of manufacturing.

Some other countries still have the odd company feeding the bespoke, status symbol, opulent, highly engineered and highly priced end of the car market. But Italy has several that have a reputation for having turned the manufacture of cars into a mechanical art form. The names of Ferrari, Lamborghini, Maserati, Bugatti and, one that's new to me, Pagani, are names known throughout the world. I've amused myself by saying, 'and one that's new to me', as if I frequent showrooms selling these cars or even know anyone who does. The cars produced by these iconic companies are literally tailor made. These are cars that the owners don't just drive, they wear them like a bespoke suit from Savile Row. They wear them to exhibit their wealth. Cars with price tags that are astronomical. The most expensive Lamborghini, the Veneno Roadster, for example, emptying your back pocket of almost €7 million (£6 million/$8.5 million).That's not an indication of the showroom price. Unlike the cars we may be able to get a loan to buy, these cars actually increase in value when they have left the billionaire temples of temptation. I bet the receipt alone is worth more than you or I could ever imagine earning. Yep, I agree, it's outrageous, even obscene that there are some people in the world that could easily pay this price for a car without even noticing the money had left their bank balance. To some, it's just small change. But closing this chapter by having a glimpse at the luxury end of Italian industry, is not intended to set up a debate about the morality of excessive wealth. These words are simply here to illustrate the undoubted talent that exists in Italy. A talent for innovation, style and flair. And some of that talent does feed down into items that we perhaps can afford.

ENJOY ITALY AND ENJOY THE PEOPLE

Let yourself be absorbed by Italy. Well, apart from perhaps the darker, shadowy side of the country. The side of Italy made famous by Hollywood. The chances of you coming into direct contact with the criminal hierarchies of the mafia are extremely remote. Although Hollywood is fictional, the stories told are certainly not totally fanciful. The mafia is very real, very much part of the Italian story. A part of Italy that can't simply be ignored. Within the pages to come, I'll try to cast some light on the bloated criminal underbelly of Italia.

Capo di Tutti Capi

Heavy is the crown of the Sicilian don,

Pinstriped Armani suit and iron hand,

He rules all the underworld's goings on.

He's the boss of all bosses lives high class,

Running all the games and cons

From his own bastion, he'll kill you so fast

There's no place to hide if you run.

He runs the families of la Cosa Nostra,

Crime syndicates feed off the illegal profits.

Climb up the ladder with the force of a gun,

If one day you get to be on the very top,

One slip of the tongue and you'll quickly fall.

In this organisation you can't ever slip up,

You can't break the rules, the Mafia's corrupt,

Pretty soon you'll be sleeping with the fishes,

On the bottom of the river in a coat of cement.

When joining the Mafia, kiss away all wishes,

Once you're in it, you are in for life,

A pact made with your blood as a seal,

They'll slaughter your family and your wife.

For no one is exempt from the Mafioso kill.

. . . .

Rick Fernandez

CHAPTER FIVE

Three Spanish Knights

'I heard you paint houses.'

Frank Sheeran, The Irishman - Martin Scorsese

From the moment he came into the world, bloody from his mother's womb, Antonio Zagari's future life in organised crime was virtually unstoppable, it was guaranteed. On show to gathered members of the brotherhood, a knife and a key lay either side of the baby boy.

'His destiny would be decided by which he touched first. If it were the key, symbol of confinement, he would become a sbirro – a cop, a slave of the law. But if it were the knife, he would live and die by the code of honour.'
John Dickie, Mafia Brotherhood.

The Sicilian Cosa Nostra, the Neapolitan Camorra and the Calabrian 'Ndrangheta. Although separate 'brotherhoods', collectively the term 'mafia' is commonly used in reference to all three.

For years, the mafia have been shrouded in secrecy, wrapped up in violence, all too often allowed to operate outside the law in connivance with those in positions of legitimate authority. The history of Italy as a unified political entity since 1861, exists in the shadow of the murky, often grotesquely violent, activities of the mafia.

They came from across the sea, so the story tellers would have you believe. Three 17th century Spanish knights, Osso, Mastrosso and Carcagnosso. Having taken bloody vengeance for the rape of their sister by a nobleman, they fled from Spain, eventually finding themselves on the tiny island of Favignana, close to the coast of Sicily.

Whilst living in caves they manufactured a code of life built on a brotherhood of honour. Once nurtured, they carried the rules, their code of an 'Honoured Society' into the outside world. If this were a film, we would have sombre, stylised, Spanish music, softly playing at this point. Our Spanish Knights, obviously ruggedly handsome, unshaven, bodies toned and tanned. The three, dark haired, with at least one having piercing blue eyes. Our blue-eyed knight first appearing on screen, bare chested, as he rises from a deep blue Mediterranean Sea.

Osso is said to have sworn allegiance to Saint George. He took the short journey to Sicily, establishing the Honoured Society of the Cosa Nostra.

Mastrosso decided to dedicate his life to the Madonna. He went to Naples and founded the Honoured Society of the Camorra.

The final knight in this trio, Carcagnosso, took the Archangel Michael as his protector. He, like Osso, made a relatively short journey, his journey taking him to Calabria. Here he gave birth to the Honoured Society of the 'Ndrangheta.

Clearly the story of the Three Spanish Knights is the stuff of fantasy. A fairy tale granting the mafia almost mystical status. In some ways I guess Hollywood has followed on, feeding our apparent fascination with the secretive, ritualistic, tightly knit, often violent and yet, at the same time, 'benevolent' criminal groups. Any supposed benevolence only extended to those willing to be totally subservient. The hand of friendship extended to those willing to turn a blind eye, or at least keep hidden any malevolent deeds in the hope of gaining some benefit.

The mafia in many ways are portrayed as the criminal elite. A criminal elite different to other crime gangs. These are no loose affiliations of criminal gang members, once you are in, you are in for life. Members of these 'elite' groups having sworn blood oaths, only the shedding of blood offering release. Probably the most important essential difference between the Honoured Societies and other criminal cartels, is the way in which the mafia have been able to extend reach and influence into the highest levels of economic and political power. In some ways, this also explains their incredible longevity.

Perhaps one of the best examples of the almost symbiotic relationship between the mafia and the supposedly legitimate elite, can be found in the shadowy links between the Cosa Nostra and Silvio Berlusconi, someone who held the office of Prime Minister on several occasions. Always vehemently denied and never satisfactorily proven, any number of people associated with the Cosa Nostra have highlighted a murky world loaded with suspicion.

Marcello Dell'Utri - a close associate of Berlusconi in both business and politics. In December 2004, Dell'Utri received a nine-year prison sentence for his association with the Cosa Nostra, tax fraud and false accounting. The judge described him as someone who provided a bridging point for the Cosa Nostra 'to come into contact with important economic and financial circles.' Not only did Dell'Utri have financial dealings with Berlusconi, he was also one of the founders of his political party, Forza Italia.

Salvatore Cancemi – in 1996, as a collaborator (a pentito) with those prosecuting mafia members, stated that Berlusconi and Dell'Utri were in direct contact with the Cosa Nostra boss at the time, Totò Riina. The supposed contacts were said to have resulted in legislation favourable to mafia 'business'. In return the Cosa Nostra would support Berlusconi's Forza Italia party. A two-year investigation eventually closed without any charges. Cancemi also stated that Fininvest, Berlusconi's media empire, through Marcello Dell'Utri, had paid the Cosa Nostra € 100,000 per year. Again, after investigation, the case was closed.

Antonino Giuffrè – another pentito. He stated that the Cosa Nostra moved its support from the Christian Democratic Party in the 1990s to Forza Italia, the expectation being that this new political party could better look after their interests. If there is any truth in this, it could explain how Berlusconi's coalition made a clean sweep of all the parliamentary seats in Sicily during the election of 2001. According to Giuffrè, Marcello Dell'Utri was the contact point between the Cosa Nostra and Berlusconi. All allegations were said not to be proven.

Gaspare Spatuzza – turned pentito in 2008. He testified that his boss, Giuseppe Graviono, had said to him, in 1994, that Silvio Berlusconi, the future Prime Minister, was bargaining with the Cosa Nostra for political benefit. It's argued that the Cosa Nostra began a spate of 'terrorist' bombings on the mainland in 1993 so that Forza Italia could present itself as the protector of the nation. When Berlusconi came to power in 1994, the bombings stopped.

In the years from 1991 to 2018, investigations by the Italian police resulted in 266 city councils being dissolved because of links with criminal organisations.

In December 2019, over 2,500 police took part in raids targeting members of the 'Ndrangheta. Over 300 arrests were made, including politicians and officials. Investigations that began in 2016 spread over Sicily, Lombardy, Veneto, Campania and Tuscany. The arrests that followed also took place in Switzerland, Germany and Bulgaria. Guess which name pops up again? You already knew, Silvio Berlusconi.

A former regional coordinator of Berlusconi's Forza Italia, a lawyer and a member of the justice commission, Giancarlo Pittelli, was listed among those arrested. Along with him, a mayor, a former regional official, a police commander and a political party official.

In total, the prosecution charged 475 alleged mafia members with a range of offences.

The massive police operation uncovered many of the 'Ndrangheta's secrets, including links to the fable of the Three Spanish Knights.

The president of the anti-mafia parliamentary commission commented:

'From today in Calabria, the air you breathe is better. It is air with the taste of freedom. Today is a beautiful day for freedom.'

If there is one thing that I've learnt about the Italian character, it is that it has a surface of momentary exuberant optimism, counterbalanced with a sense of fatalism. The pronouncements about 'beautiful freedom', another example of exuberant optimism.

However successful the authorities may be in pursuing the mafia, the tentacles are extremely resilient, spreading far and wide. Research uncovered almost 1,200 violent attacks against Italian politicians between 2013 and 2015. It's estimated that almost 70 percent of the attacks were committed by mafia members.

In 2016, the Cosa Nostra tried to kill the director of the Nebrodi national park in Sicily, Giuseppe Antoci. He had received death threats because of his attempts to clamp down on illegal activities within the boundaries of the park. Allegedly, millions of euros coming from the European Union had been lost to the Cosa Nostra. The attack came in the early hours of the morning as Antoci was travelling by car through a secluded area of the national park. It's said that two or three men came out of the darkness, opening fire with shotguns, penetrating the side of the car and hitting one of the police escorts. Having survived the attack, Giuseppe Antoci said:

'There had been huge collusion between the Cosa Nostra and local politicians who closed their eyes to widespread illegality. Large areas of the national park are still no-man's land. But I'm not going to stop what I'm doing.'

WHAT GAVE BIRTH TO THE MAFIA?

To find any answers we need to delve back into the mid-nineteenth century, the divide between the north and the south, and the forced unification of Italy that reached its culmination in 1861.

But before we begin to search for clues in the 19th century, it's important to note that the activities of the mafia are not restricted to the borders of Italy. As I've already said, Hollywood has perhaps done the most to firmly place the world of the mafia in the public mind, with The Godfather trilogy and GoodFellas undoubtedly the best-known films, followed by the Irishman in 2019. We're left in no doubt that the mafia have a solid base in the USA. But their reach spreads far wider than across the Atlantic. Evidence of this was highlighted by an incident on the 15th of August 2007, in the German town of Duisburg. On leaving Da Bruno Pizzeria, six Italian men were shot dead as they settled into their cars. This had been an eighteenth birthday celebration for one of the six, one of the others just sixteen. Another just nineteen and another twenty-one. All died instantly from a hail of bullets. It's even said that the killers took the time to administer one final shot to each, thus ensuring that the execution was complete. The six killed were said to be from a faction of the 'Ndrangheta, possibly hiding out in Germany to escape from a long running violent feud between different sections of the brotherhood. The Italian newspaper, La Repubblica, reported that those killed were members of the clan Pelle-Romeo, the killers from the clan Strangio-Nirta.

Killings on this scale were virtually unknown outside Italy. In Germany, the 'Duisburg Massacre' resulted in the birth of Mafianeindanke (Mafia – No Thanks!), a loose association reacting to the perceived growth in organised criminal gangs. Mafianeindanke inspired by organisations in Italy, Addiopizzo (Goodbye to Protection Money), Libera (Free) and Ammazzateci Tutti (Kill All of Us).

So, whilst we look back at the possible origins of the mafia, we must be aware that, in the words of John Dickie in his book Mafia Brotherhood:

'Mafia history is still being made.'

Of the three brotherhoods making up the mafia, the 'Ndrangheta has proved to be the most successful in establishing itself outside its region of birth. Being the youngest of the three, it's been suggested that it learnt lessons from the other two, developing and growing for many years hidden from serious scrutiny. It's also argued that the 'Ndrangheta has the strongest omertà (the oath of silence and secrecy, complete submission to the authority of the brotherhood) of the three mafia. Unlike the Cosa Nostra and the Camorra, very few from the ranks of the 'Ndrangheta have become informers (pentiti). Along with the centre and north of Italy, evidence suggests that the 'Ndrangheta has established itself in Germany, Switzerland, Canada, Australia, Belgium, Britain, Portugal, Argentina, Spain, Holland, Turkey, Brazil, Morocco, Chile, Colombia and the USA. The 'Ndrangheta has grown into a global corporation. The name is not one that easily slips off the tongue. The Cosa Nostra and the Camorra are far easier to pronounce and, probably with the help of Hollywood, will continue to persist in public fascination.

The only knowledge I had of the mafia came from films, gangster movies. In these only one mafia appeared to exist, the Cosa Nostra (Our Thing). And that's still very much the case today. Media outlets from around the world still don't entirely grasp the fact that there is more than one mafia. Even in Italy, for quite some time, there was relative ignorance about the Camorra and the 'Ndrangheta.

So, where can we find a starting point for the mafia? How long have they existed? What can history tell us about their origins? Unlike other criminal organisations, why have they been able to survive for so long?

The anarchic prison system of the 19th century provides us with some of the answers. The filth and degradation provided a fertile breeding ground, a criminal compost giving nourishment to mafia seedlings. Prisons operated through a 'system' of barbarism. Survival depended on brute strength, bribes, favours and exploitation of the weakest. With beatings, mutilation and death common place. Day-to-day 'policing' was left in the hands of those incarcerated, the most feared inmates imposing their will on others, often in open collaboration with those officially charged with maintaining order. It was easier, perhaps even profitable, to allow the inmates to self-police.

Although the individual histories of the three honoured societies, their development and growth, are undeniably shaped by regional characteristics, there are common features to be found. The embryonic stage of all three appear to be associated with prison life in the 19th century.

To tell the tale of how the world of prison fostered the growth of the mafia, I'm going to use the Camorra as an example.

In the early 1850s a member of the British Parliament was allowed access to the jails of Naples. Don't ask me why. Perhaps those in authority wanted to show this foreign dignitary how tough they were on crime. Given that the British system of incarceration at the time was horrendous in comparison to modern standards, things in Naples must have been barbarous. The British dignitary was said to be shocked by the 'beastly filth' he came across. Those charged with political crimes mixed with common criminals, some of these criminals having committed the most heinous acts. He reported finding a system where the prisoners were simply left to their own devices, with no apparent supervision from those in legitimate authority. Inevitably, those who were feared the most, either individually or through group strength, controlled the prison. This control was entwined with those supposedly legitimately in control, with payments made to guards and favours exchanged.

Keep in mind that those charged with political crimes were thrown together with 'ordinary' criminals, it has a significance that extended beyond the confines of the prisons. Also be aware that there was a growing international sympathy for those perceived to be freedom fighters (the political prisoners). Those fighting for what was to become Italy, fighting against foreign rulers, many fighting against those who controlled the differing states that divided up the Italian peninsula, either through fact, misinformation, or what we now refer to as 'fake news', were mythologised. To those calling for greater freedom, they were martyrs. To those calling for a united Italy, they were true patriots. These were thrown together with the Camorristi, the common criminals who controlled the prisons. For some, it was a partnership that survived into the outside world.

In the prisons of Naples, the Camorra controlled the lives of others, through a combination of punishment, bribes, extortion and favours. Apparently, camorra, a term for extortion, was used long before it came into common usage to identity any particular group. A similar regime existed in Sicily and in the region of Calabria. The spot where a prisoner slept, a space that had to be in some way paid for, was called a pizzo. The term pizzo eventually becoming synonymous with the payment of a bribe or protection money. Turn back a few pages to the reference made about Addiopizzo.

John Dickie, in Mafia Brotherhoods, refers to an old saying attributed to the Camorra:

'Facciamo caccia' l'oro de' piducchie.' ('We extract gold from fleas')

All three that today make up the mafia, operate in much the same way as in the prisons of the 19th century. The difference is that the mafia have moved way beyond tiny fleas, to small and large-scale business. From the confines of prison to international dealings. From prison guards to high-ranking officials and even politicians.

Murder became 'legitimised' as a basis of honour. Sanctioned by the boss, as part of a sham system of 'justice', the vendetta would be in defence of honour.

When we look back, we could ask the question: if those with legitimate power, authority and influence had acted in a different way, could history have resulted in other outcomes? Throughout the remainder of the 19th century the dysfunctional prison system was left to continue as a quagmire of criminal connivance. The focus of those with power and influence at a national level, almost always dominated by the interests of northern Italy. They were either completely ignorant of the burgeoning power of the three mafia groups, or simply not interested in the squalid goings on within the criminal underworld of the south.

Naples was a place wallowing in filth, disease and crime. The majority of its almost half a million population, living in squalid conditions, rife with vermin, sewage flowing into the streets. The very poorest areas without any sense of legitimate law and order. Life expectancy little beyond the mid-twenties. It was into this environment that ex-prisoners spilled out.

It's true that desperately squalid conditions found in Naples were not some exceptional malformation. In 1860, London had a population of three million, reaching six and a half million by 1900. As with Naples, the grip on life for the poor was tenuous. Unsanitary, overcrowded housing resulted in early death being all too common. Tuberculosis, cholera, scarlet fever, smallpox and typhoid were rife. Crime in the poorest areas often going unchecked. Perhaps the most notorious slum area being St Giles, an area of London crowded with even greater filth, prostitution, gin shops, violent criminals and general lawlessness. However, unlike Naples, from the mid-nineteenth century, admittedly grudgingly slowly, things did begin to change. Legislation started to be introduced that resulted in the improvement of housing, with large scale public work projects removing sewage from the streets, including the removal of an estimated 200,000 cesspools.

In 1856 the Police Act brought in legislation requiring all areas of the country to establish a police force, forces that would be overseen by a system of government inspection. In 1869, the National Criminal Record was set up and in 1877 the CID, Criminal Investigation Department. Levels of poverty were still extreme and crime levels, especially in the poorest areas, still high. I would also assume that corruption within the ranks of the police, collaboration from some with criminal groups and those with high-ranking positions of power and influence were also not unknown.

By contrast, in Naples, policing took a form shaped by trying to minimise what could only be described as anarchy. Policing was carried out through reciprocal agreement with those regarded as the toughest of the criminal underworld. Policing in this way was always going to be problematic.

Once back out on the streets, the Camorristi from the prisons soon established the same modus operandi. But there were far bigger fleas to be pressured and bribed. A reciprocal approach to policing inevitably resulted in the Camorristi creeping into the ranks of the official police. The Camorra was beginning to become firmly established and it was no closely kept secret, everyone in Naples knew of the Camorra.

But this was the south of Italy, only sporadically attracting any genuine interest from the north when northern interests were threatened. In 1861, the newly established, fragile Italian state ordered an official investigation into the goings on of the Camorra. The investigation found that the Camorra was far more organised than had been thought. It found that it was divided into chapters or clans, each having control over different parts of the city. The dominant person in each area, the Capo Camorrista, this person elected from amongst his peers. Those new to the Camorra having the label of Picciotto. The Picciotti had to prove that they were up for a fight. They were also expected to prove their loyalty by being prepared to serve time in prison for the crimes of those with the higher rank of Camorrista. With loyalty proven, a Picciotto could gain that honoured position. Masonic style rituals were also found to be an integral part of the organisation.

A clamp down followed, the authorities making many arrests and never again working in quite the same cosy way with the Camorra. But as is the case with the Italian state's dealings with the mafia in general, action taken was short lived. Repression swinging to at best indifference to, at worst, direct collaboration.

By the end of the 19the century, the Camorra, along with the other mafia, was no longer simply some criminal grouping, a hindrance to a legitimate system of law and order. All three criminal brotherhoods, to a greater or lesser extent, had slithered into the higher reaches of Italian society and even the Italian state.

THE COSA NOSTRA

From the mid-1860s, the mysterious Sicilian Mafia (only later known as the Cosa Nostra), began to percolate into the conscious mind of the Italian state. In order to avoid any confusion, I'll refer to the Sicilian Mafia as the Cosa Nostra. Uncertain of what the Italian state was dealing with, the authorities came down hard. The southern part of the Italian peninsula had always been viewed as different from the rest. The new Italian state had much the same attitude. The south was a strange, almost alien region. The island of Sicily regarded as even stranger than the rest. Sicily had a reputation of complete lawlessness and rebellion, some of this reputation based on fact, the rest based on nothing more than prejudiced stereotypes. Stories of some type of criminal association acting almost as a self-governing entity within the new state of Italy, provided justification for any type of action to be taken. Harsh repression from the north, simply acting to further entrench attitudes in Sicily that its people were being treated with extreme brutality, exploited by an illegitimate power. To resist against the harshness of the Italian state made perfect sense.

And yet at the same time there was confusion, a confusion deliberately fed by the Cosa Nostra, or simply a result of the state's complete lack of understanding. Some refused to accept that the Cosa Nostra even existed. It was simply in the nature of the islanders to resist, to take the law into their own hands. There was no single mafia, coordinated and controlled across Sicily. The behaviour of its population was simply a throwback to more primitive times, it was simply one aspect of a whole range of behaviours that you would expect from the uncivilised south. Such views were then reinforced and given credence through supposed sociological and scientific study.

The abnormal, criminally driven man and woman could be identified and separated from normal people through a range of physical characteristics. Perhaps the most well-known proponent of this 'scientific' analysis was the Italian, Lombroso. Those who engaged in criminal behaviour were said to have certain body types, clearly identifiable facial features, a range of abnormalities that placed them closer on the scale of evolutionary development to apes than to normal humans. Others supported such claims by looking for clear psychological differences. Sicilians were simply different from other Europeans, more Arab in temperament. As a result, psychologically, they were more prone to violent vendetta, cruelty, uncontrollable passion and irrationality.

The average Neapolitan was viewed in much the same way. The strange rituals of the Camorra regarded as nothing more than the behaviour of savages, similar in nature to the tribes of Africa. Fratricide (the killing of one's sibling) providing the most obvious example of a barbarous nature. Such thinking provided security for 'right thinking', 'normal people', not just in Italy, but across the modern civilised world of the time. Civilised society could feel safe in the knowledge that they were a different breed to those involved in criminal behaviours. Such perceptions hid the reality of the growing sophisticated nature of organised crime; it was just uncivilised barbarism. Sporadic purges would come and go when crime and violence reached politically unacceptable levels, enough to keep some sense of order.

As with all prejudice, stereotypes and pseudoscientific claptrap, there are contradictions in thinking. A central trait of the criminal mind, especially in the south of Italy was said to be one of irrationality and unthinking impulsivity. At the same time, they were equally cunning, resourceful, able to plan with care in order to outwit others, especially those in authority. As it turned out, resourcefulness, rationality and cunning were perhaps features found in greater amounts amongst the Cosa Nostra than amongst the Camorra of Naples.

The Cosa Nostra, from its very beginnings, merged with those who held both political and economic influence. It's argued that the Camorra had its origins in the gutters of Naples, whilst the Cosa Nostra, coming from much the same origins, climbed out of the gutter and quickly entwined itself with men of property. Collusion between the Cosa Nostra and those with property ebbed and flowed, but this mafia group soon realised that there were greater rewards to be made by focusing on those with relative wealth rather than on fleas. By the end of the 1860s serious money could be made from the citrus plantations of Sicily. The Cosa Nostra would work with some of the landowners, providing investment, whilst at the same time squeezing money from others through protection rackets. Those who worked with the Cosa Nostra could thrive, those who did not would suffer, with death being the ultimate penalty.

Sporadic interest from the state allowed the Cosa Nostra to operate relatively unmolested by those charged with maintaining a pretence of law and order. Crackdowns came and went, roundups were made, criminals killed or put behind bars. But the Cosa Nostra lived on. Once some semblance of relative calm had been restored, Sicily was forgotten. In much the same way as governing the streets of Naples, it was more convenient to work in some dubious collaboration with organised criminals. For a time, the Cosa Nostra would learn to keep its head down, attempting to moderate its level of violence. A level of violence that would not draw too much attention from the more zealous sections of the state.

It was not until the mid-1870s that evidence began to emerge of the ritualistic clandestine nature of the Cosa Nostra. Those coming new to the brotherhood had to go through a form of baptism. The recruit would have his finger or arm cut; blood then allowed to drip onto the picture of a saint. The blooded picture would then be burnt, the ashes scattered to signify the death of informers. After this, the new member would swear an eternal oath of loyalty to the Cosa

Nostra. However, for much of its early history, the structure and rituals of the Cosa Nostra remained a mystery to those in authority. The result was that by the end of the 19th century the same question was still being asked. Was there one single coordinated mafia operating in Sicily, or were there a jumble of criminal sects? It will probably come as a surprise for you to learn that it was not until the 1980s that official recognition was given to the fact that one single mafia existed in Sicily, that single entity having control over all other mafia sects.

CALABRIA

The Straits of Messina separate the region of Calabria from the island of Sicily. At its narrowest point, between Torre Faro and Villa San Giovanni, the distance is just over 3 kilometres (almost 2 miles). If you remember, one of the three Spanish knights made Calabria the home of what would become known as the 'Ndrangheta.

Calabria forms the toe of Italy, and along with Basilicata and Puglia, the three regions together are often referred to as the Mezzogiorno. Above fifty percent of Calabria is mountainous, a rugged terrain, wild in places, with only sparse areas for farming. Historically, Calabria has always been one of the poorest regions of Italy. In 1862, Calabria only had one passable road going from north to south. Most of its population living in isolated villages amongst its mountains and valleys. A government survey of 1871 found that 87 per cent of the population were illiterate. Advice for the northern European traveller of the time was to avoid Calabria. A Tuscan intellectual, after visiting the region in the 1870s, commented:

'Among the oppressed there is no middle stage between two extreme states of being: on the one hand, fear and obedience and the most abject docility; and, on the other, the most brutal and ferocious rebellion.'

However, at this time there was no real evidence of the type of organised criminal bands found in Sicily and around Naples. Nothing of any significance from government documents, or even anecdotal evidence from travellers who ventured into the region. And then, as if from nowhere, reports began to appear of a noticeable rise in the activities of criminal gangs. Was this the nucleus of a new Cosa Nostra or Camorra?

As with the Cosa Nostra, the authorities were unclear about this apparently 'new' breed of criminal, identifying them with terms borrowed from the Sicilian Cosa Nostra and Neapolitan Camorra, reference most often being made to the Picciotteria. The terms Picciotto and Picciotti, used to describe lower-level members of the Camorra. In Sicily, the term Picciotto was used to describe someone who was 'a bit of a lad', someone with an attitude above their lowly status. I guess those responsible for law and order did attempt to stamp out this fledgling band of upstart criminals. From the end of the 19th century and into the early years of the new, hundreds of arrests were made. But far away in Rome, little interest was really given to what was developing in the region. This was Calabria, who cared about Calabria? It would appear that no one really did. By the start of the new century the mysterious and often gruesome activities of the Cosa Nostra and the Camorra, although not understood (perhaps that was part of the fascination), were already becoming part of Italian folklore. However, in Calabria there were no serious investigations sanctioned at the highest level, no pseudoscientific analysis of racial and ethnic difference. Calabria, the very tip of the boot of Italy, could just as well be left to rot.

For the people of Calabria, the activities, of this 'new band' of criminals were all too real, beginning to control many parts of the region. First extorting money from gamblers, prostitutes and petty criminals. Then upping the stakes, along with taking from the 'fleas', they began to threaten landowners, farmers and those in business. The very essence of mafia culture and territorial command, protection and punishment, was beginning to spread. A visit from a Picciotto armed with a razor became a favoured practice. Most of the Picciotti were from the peasantry, some were small scale artisans, a few relatively successful in business, owners of land or small-scale manufacturing. From these few, came the Boss. Although the Carabinieri were often silenced through threats, arrests were made. The courts were in no doubt about a commonality that was emerging from a number of trials. Many of those appearing before a judge had already spent time in prison, some leaving with their high rank amongst the Camorristi already established, ready to take up that position on the outside. Although arrests continued to be made and trials held, policing slid into the same form as that in Sicily and Naples, an unspoken and most certainly unwritten code of 'joint management'.

But information on the nature and structure of this new criminal phenomenon was slowly beginning to emerge. Would anyone outside Calabria be interested? Reports going back to Rome gave accounts of actions taken and numbers of arrests being made. However, the reports did not fully grasp the nature of what the authorities were dealing with. The reasons for the high level of crime in the region were again put down to the nature of the people, their backwardness, their natural hatred and need for vendetta. Such reports simply fuelled the belief that the region typified the barbaric, savage nature of people living in the south of Italy.

It was found that the Picciotteria were locally based units, local groups. Each group was made up of lower-ranking Picciotti and higher ranking Camorristi. There was the Boss and there was a 'Bookkeeper' who controlled the money. Each recruit went through an initiation ceremony, thus entering the lower ranks of the 'Honoured Society'. In court some spoke of the origins of the society, it being born out of the tale of the Three Spanish Knights. But again, there appeared to be little interest taken in Rome. Few even bothered to plot out the similarities between what was happing in Calabria and what was occurring in Sicily and in Naples.

There were, however, some from the almost forgotten region of Calabria who gained what I can only describe as celebrity status. One such celebrity was Giuseppe Musolino, his celebrity gave him the title of the 'King of Aspromonte' (Aspromonte being a mountain range in southern Calabria).

The tale of Giuseppe Musolino starts when, after an argument, he tries to shoot Vicenzo Zoccali. Evidence is found identifying him as the would-be murderer, he responds by going on the run, hiding in the Aspromonte. Eventually being captured and sentenced to twenty-one years, he pledges a vendetta against Zoccali. Musolino protesting that he is the innocent victim of a plot.

Musolino somehow manages to escape from prison, soon going about his vendetta. Intending to shoot a male witness from his trial, by mistake he shoots and kills the man's wife. The sound of gunshots attracts the attention of her husband and another man. Musolino shoots the two dead. He then escapes back into the mountains, but his vendetta is clearly not over.

Zoccali is not his only target. He sets out to kill those who had testified against him and any who inform to the police. In the space of just a few months he's killed another two people and attempted to blow up Zoccali.

Musolino then travels some distance to kill Zoccali's brother, which he does. He then returns to the village of his birth, Santo Stefano, and kills another informer.

As Calabria moved into a new century, Musolino continued killing, along the way shooting a cousin, apparently by mistake. The next victim is shot in the legs with a shotgun, his life spared when he's able to convince his 'executioner' that he's not an informer. By March of 1900, it looks like the Carabinieri could be closing in. Musolino had been betrayed by one of his accomplices. But the plot to catch him in his hideout fails, the Carabinieri giving chase across the mountains. Almost apprehended, he's able to escape again, shooting and killing an officer of the Carabinieri.

Six months pass before Musolino strikes again, delivering death to another victim in the August of 1900.

By now the saga of murder had reached Rome, parliament debating what could be done. The answer was to swamp the south of Calabria with more police. Musolino evaded capture for another year, until at last in the October of 1901 he's captured close to his home village of Santo Stefano. At last, the state has him, the crazed killer bent on vendetta. Now you would suppose that the general population of Calabria would be relieved, no longer living with the distress and fear of having such a callous, cold-blooded, killer amongst them. Think again.

During his vendetta of killing, the story of Musolino had begun to spread. First through the mountains and valleys of Calabria, then gaining a wider audience across Italy. His infamous rampage and his evasion from capture had made him into a celebrity. Many believing that he was innocent of the original charges that had sent him to prison. He had become a victim of the system. It was understandable that he should seek out those who had done him wrong. You need to remember that the majority of people in the south regarded the state with suspicion, very few believing that it ever acted in their interests. In Musolino they had a lone hero, fighting the injustice done to him. Whilst fighting his own cause, the people of Calabria also had someone who had the courage to spit in the face of the state's authority.

Very few journalists ever ventured into Calabria. The few that did, found a world that was alien in every single way. The squalid conditions found in the remotest villages, dwellings that people called home, were described as not even being fit for pigs. The few journalists brave enough to ask, finding tales that told of gruesome acts of violence.

It became obvious that Musolino had escaped capture for so long because of the help provided by the Picciotteria. Only when there were mass arrests did his string of hiding places begin to dry up.

Tales were told of a man who never stole anything from the poor. A man who only attacked those deserving of punishment. Tales of someone visited by San Giuseppe. The tales almost created a saint like figure, noble, but at the same time viciously courageous. He was Calabria's Robin Hood. Even the more literate and better educated in Italian society began to have sympathy for this man who had been so wronged. Some even going so far as petitioning for a royal pardon.

Before his trial in the town of Lucca, northern Tuscany, further investigation appeared to throw up evidence of the truth behind the supposed killing spree of vengeance.

I'm sure that this will come as no surprise to you. Evidence uncovered, pointed to the fact that Musolino was deeply involved in the goings on of the mafia in his home village of Santo Stefano. His father and uncle holding high positions in the organisation. The supposed vendetta against Zoccali was in fact a contract killing ordered by the brotherhood, punishment for Zoccali not carrying out certain tasks as a Picciotto. Musolino was in fact an assassin, his targets assigned to him by the higher-ranking officials of the organisation.

At the trial, Musolino's defence did little to contest the evidence put forward in relation to his killings. His lawyers attempted to justify his killings as a response to the earlier injustice of imprisonment. Prosecution attempts to link the killings and Musolino to the mafia were repeatedly contested by the defence and to some extent ignored by the court. The mayor of Santo Stefano, someone known to have close links to the Musolino family, when asked questions in court, protested at the outrageous policing methods used against the people. He dismissed claims of an organised criminal group, such as the

Picciotteria, saying it was an invention of the police, a fiction used to sanction their unscrupulous behaviour.

In the end, Musolino was found guilty and sentenced to spend the rest of his life in prison. But the judgement and sentence did little to extinguish the mythology that had built up around the 'King of Aspromonte' – Giuseppe Musolino.

In many ways the trial, the evidence presented, and the verdict were overshadowed by the stereotypes and fixed prejudice relating to those who inhabited the south of Italy. 'Experts' called to give their opinions, fell back on notions of behavioural and psychological inferiority amongst the general population. The conclusion reached about the behaviour of Musolino being that he was nothing more than an extreme example of a racial type. The likelihood of any serious attempt being made to further investigate stories of a highly structured criminal organisation in the form of the Piccotteria were lost. Calabria could be left to slip out of national consciousness, its people left to their primitive way of life. From the Picciotteria, the 'Ndrangheta would be spawned.

It could be argued that either through ignorance or lack of will, perhaps a combination of both, all three of the groups that make up the mafia were given the opportunity to grow and flourish. A significant factor contributing to the apparent lack of a determined centralised effort to tackle the problem lay in the fact that Italy as a nation was still young and vulnerable, the authority of the state still fragile across many parts of the country. The minds of successive governments were focused on both internal and external threats to the new nation. From those who first fought for and imposed political unity on the Italian peninsula, to those who followed on, the same worry dominated the minds of those in power. The Italian nation existed, but a nation of people seeing themselves as truly Italian still needed to be moulded. The activities of the mafia, even if understood, were of secondary importance.

Attempts to purge Sicily, Naples and Calabria of the mafia did take place, but they lacked longevity and were certainly not consistent. What was consistent was the entrenched attitude that the south of Italy was innately different to the rest of the country. It was an attitude that blinded some to the reality of the ever-increasing influence and connections of the mafia within the higher reaches of society. A society that was both economically and politically already very much open to shady dealings and murky bartering of favours. All the mafia had to do was join in the game. When clashes came, as they inevitably did, between those who were more than willing to connive and those more principled in their dealings, the mafia were more than capable of dealing with the problem.

By the turn of the century, economic crisis, the threat of war, corruption and organised crime, all grappled for the attention of the Italian press. In Naples investigations into corruption resulted in the trials of many high-ranking officials, including Alberto Casale, a Member of Parliament. All were suspected of having close links to the Camorra. It really came as a surprise to no one when investigations threw up the fact that the whole of local government was corrupt. Most of those working in local government, from someone in an office, to someone collecting rubbish, were there through having the 'right' connections rather than being in possession of the appropriate skills. Favours and bribes, knowing who to approach and whisper in their ears, would ensure that arrangements could be made. There was still the Camorra feeding off fleas, but now there was also the Camorra feeding off public works, government contracts and bureaucracy.

Corruption had almost become an accepted feature of business and political life. The result was either total hostility towards those involved in politics or total antipathy. What could you expect? They're all doing it, whatever it was. That feeling continues to persist across Italian society today, it has a name – antipolitica. And it's certainly something I've come across in my conversations with Italian friends and neighbours when speaking about politics or the state of Italy in general.

At the very centre of national government there was an attitude of working with what you have rather than trying to dramatically change it. The mafia should simply be accepted as one part of Italian life, either work with it, or work around it. The very existence of such organised criminal groups often denied by those in high places.

FASCISM AND THE MAFIA

On January the 3rd 1925, Mussolini was welcomed by most of the political and business elite as the Fascist Dictator of Italy. It wasn't quite that straightforward, but that's a tale for another book. Perhaps a good place to start would be my first book, Lorenzo's Vest.

You may possibly think that the violent tactics employed by the fascists in coming to power would fit quite well with the violence associated with the mafia, both dictatorial in style and both demanding complete, unquestioning, loyalty. The mafia and Fascism could be quite good bedfellows. You need to think again.

The truth is, there could be only one body that controlled Italy. The new fascist dictatorship would be that body. Allowing parts of Italy to be run by the mafia would not be tolerated. Mussolini would, unlike leaders of the past, show that he had the will and the power to unite the whole of Italy. The loyalty of the people would be towards the state. Local loyalties would be swept aside, this included ties to the mafia. Mussolini, Il Duce (The Leader), would be the power to transform Italian society. He would be the leader to dismantle the mafia. He would, for the first time in centuries, impose order and stability on the Italian people. This was to be a great crusade, a crusade that would eventually place the power and prestige of Italy in its rightful place on the world stage.

Mussolini didn't waste any time. In the October of 1925, he gave full powers to attack the Cosa Nostra using whatever means were required. This was a test of the dictator's power. He appointed a police officer by the name of Cesare (Caesar) Mori, quite an appropriate first name given the nature of the campaign that was about to take place. It was soon dubbed as the Mori Operation. Mori carried out his assignment with an iron fist, gaining him the title of the Iron Prefect. Ruthlessness is probably the only adjective to describe the actions taken, women and children held as hostages just one example. Whole villages were cut off, livestock publicly slaughtered and hundreds of arrests made. The Cosa Nostra had never experienced a whirlwind on this scale.

Mussolini stated that the mafia was 'dishonouring Sicily', there would be 'no holding back.' He would cut out the cancer.

In May 1927, with his chest puffed out and with a stern jaw, he addressed a tamed parliament. Loud applause and cheers welcomed him. This was to be an important speech, not just for an Italian audience, it was also addressed to the outside world. He used it to highlight the rapid progress made since the fascists took control of government in Italy. Mussolini bragged that his government, in just a few years, had achieved more than others had done in a thousand. He lambasted all governments that had come and gone since the unification of Italy in 1861. They had been weak, shambolic, self-interested, corrupt and powerless to govern Italy effectively. In many ways he was right in his political analysis, past governments had been inept. He would bring about change, change that would dramatically reform the whole of society and give the people pride in being Italian. His approach was not just seductive to Italians. The perception that at last Italy had strong government also appealed to many in the international community. Sections of the media in both the US and the UK welcomed the strong leadership of Mussolini.

An important section of his speech focused on the operation against the Cosa Nostra. He boasted that the criminal organisation was no more, it had been ripped from the body of Sicily. It was he, Benito Amilcare Andrea Mussolini, who had done this.

In 1928 Mussolini declared that the job was complete.

Even following the onslaught from the fascist regime, the view still persisted that the Cosa Nostra had been nothing more than a malignant form of the Sicilian natural character. What is it they say about the fat lady? I think you will have guessed that the fight against the Cosa Nostra was not over.

In 1932, Cesare Mori published his memoir. He most definitely wanted history to remember him as the man who tamed the Cosa Nostra. The title given in English - The Last Struggle with the Mafia. In 2012, a TV miniseries was released with the title, Cesare Mori – Il Prefetto di Ferro (The Iron Prefect).

Mori told his readers that the people of Sicily were childlike in character. They could be easily impressed and easily manipulated. It was this psychology that was at the root of the mafia problem. But the slide into criminal debauchery was not some type of terminal cancer. With the right 'treatment' Sicilians could be 'cured' and brought into civilized society. They needed a strong hand to guide them, to shape their thinking and behaviour. Fascism would bring them awe and wonder! They would recognise the power of fascism to be inexhaustible. Fascism had the ingenuity to outwit any who stood in its way. In effect, the Cosa Nostra never stood a chance, something the people would come to accept. Fascism, with paternalism running through its veins, would bring rewards way beyond the wildest imagination of the Italian people.

If there is a feature that's common to all dictators, it's the irresistibility of boasting about supposed achievements. Mussolini proudly declared that the mission against the Cosa Nostra was complete. Thousands had been arrested, he made sure to give the figures. Murder and crime in general had been dramatically reduced. It will only be a short time before the Sicilian mafia will be nothing more than a distant memory. If you're prepared to ignore the methods used, you could say he was right to boast. There had been a massive reduction in the level of crime in Sicily. Perhaps dictatorship is not that bad after all.

In 1932, the regime celebrated the tenth anniversary of the Fascist march on Rome (the March on Rome, a bit of a smoke and mirrors event). As an indication of the state's belief that the Sicilian mafia had been destroyed, hundreds of those jailed were given amnesty and released. You see, a dictator can show a more compassionate side to his people. Strong, firm, some may even say brutal, but balanced with a sense of reasonableness. Some sections of Italian society today look back and view the fascist years in exactly that way. Worrying, I know. I'll have a look at the modern politics of Italy further on in the book. I know it's politics. All I ask you to do is stay with me. If you really want to try and get to know Italy, you have to have some understanding of its politics.

So that's the Sicilian mafia (Cosa Nostra), 'out of the way'. What about the Camorra?

The Camorra has never had a structure quite as robust as the Cosa Nostra. But over the years the Camorristi had certainly grown from just feeding off fleas, expanding its activities into the world of political corruption. However, links with the influential in politics and business were often more fragile than those enjoyed by the Cosa Nostra. If necessary, the powerful and influential were more than prepared to turn on their criminal partners.

Intrigue and gruesome murders, along with brushing shoulders with the aristocracy, resulted in greater scrutiny being given to the Camorra. Gossip has it that the King of Italy gave direct orders for the Carabinieri to come down hard.

High profile trials had also given the state the opportunity to show its supposed determination to act against organised crime. The Camorristi continued to be active, but infighting combined with a harder line being taken by the authorities, certainly shaped the future. Naples and the surrounding areas did not escape the campaign from the fascist state.

Along with Sicily, Mussolini focussed attention on an area between Naples and Rome that had a long history of lawlessness. The Mazzoni at the time was a marshy, poverty-ridden area, plagued with malaria.

Il Duce declared that he was going to clear the swamp with 'iron and fire'. The man charged with taking on the drainage was Major Vincenzo Anceschi. The campaign was equal to that in Sicily. Thousands were arrested, any and all methods employed to remove the 'vermin'.

As the twenties moved into the thirties, Mussolini declared that the criminal backwardness of southern Italy had been resolved. Any future discussion about organised crime was prohibited, there was nothing to discuss. You don't disagree with a narcissistic dictator. Dare you have asked about the 'Southern Question'? There was no Southern Question!

But what of Calabria?

The Picciotteria were still there, why would they have simply gone away? All the structures that had existed in the past were still fully intact, still oaths given in blood. Still only the shedding of blood releasing you. Releasing you in a very deadly way from the oath made and life itself.

Just as with Sicily and the region close to Naples, the fascist regime mounted a vigorous campaign. Hundreds of arrests were made, trials to show the public that something was being done. And yet, the Calabrian campaign didn't appear to generate the same attention across Italy as the other two. It was almost as though even fascism couldn't genuinely be bothered with Calabria. Was it that the regime, just like those of the past, had no real idea what it was dealing with? Perhaps the supposed success of the other two wars on the mafia had provided Mussolini with enough for him to stand with his legs apart, arms folded, jaw thrust out, sternly pronouncing the incredible magnificence that was Fascism. Calabria, a minor annoyance, a campaign badge that was not really required. Perhaps it's a peculiar personality trait of all dictators, that when at the height of their popularity, they can be delusional.

And, as with all dictators, there were those who simply wanted to please their leader with reports of good news. Reports went back to Rome giving some of the big names arrested and successfully tried. One Chief of Police stating that the criminal gangs had been all but crushed. Whilst at the same time, in the real world, the criminal network had entwined itself into the upper reaches of society, in some cases including the judiciary and the fascist apparatus itself.

The Picciotti and the Camorristi simply had to ride the storm and learn from the experience.

THE ALLIES AND 'LIBERATION'

Although Italy had effectively been at war since 1935, first in Ethiopia and Albania, then Greece, North Africa and Russia (with tokenistic involvement in France), the storm of death and destruction for the Italian people at home was just about to begin.

On the 10th of July 1943, the Allied Armies landed on the shores of Sicily. It was clear to any with only an ounce of sense that, for the Italians, the war was lost. Within sixteen days of the landings, the Fascist Grand Council had removed Mussolini from office and had him arrested. The people of Italy were told that he had 'stepped down'.

On the 3rd of September, the Allied Armies had landed in Calabria. On the 8th what was left of the Italian government declared its surrender. In a very real and bloody form, the Italians had now become the enemy of Germany. The war was far from over. As all sense of government in Italy collapsed, ordinary Italians were left in a desperate struggle to survive.

After the liberation of Naples in early October, the Allied Armies got bogged down (bogged down by rain, snow and mud during the winter months) in a slow and bloody advance through Italy. A deadly fight against the Germans supported by Italian Fascists still clinging to the dream. Fighting that would last a further twenty months, swallowing up civilians and soldiers alike.

On April 29th, 1945, the body of Clara Petacci, the 33-year-old mistress of Mussolini, could be found hanging upside down above the entry to a service station in Piazzale Loreto, Milan. By her side, the mutilated corpse of the 61-year-old Benito Mussolini. They had been caught by Italian partisans, shot on the shores of Lake Como and then, along with the bodies of other leading Fascists, thrown into the back of a truck, the bodies driven the short distance to Milan.

Mussolini's end was symptomatic of what had been happening across Italy since July 1943. Vengeance taken out on those viewed as responsible for dragging the Italian people into a war of destruction. Areas not yet occupied by Allied forces, in a state of civil war. Italians fighting and killing Italians. Italian Fascists, supported by the retreating Germans, fighting against Italian Partisans.

Italy was in total and absolute chaos. Hunger, disease, corruption and retaliation common place. Areas of the south were soon 'liberated', but that 'liberation' came at great cost to both Allied soldiers and the Italian people. Naples, for example, may have been liberated but the suffering of its people continued. Already, as you know, one of the poorest cities in Italy; air raids destroyed what poor infrastructure there was and left hundreds of thousands homeless. The ten-time Oscar-nominated film director, John Huston, served in the US army in the Signal Corps. During this time, he made numerous film reels for the US government and found himself in Naples. When interviewed some years later, he said:

'Naples was like a whore suffering from the beating of a brute – teeth knocked out, eyes blackened, nose broken, smelling of filth and vomit. Little boys were offering their sisters and mothers for sale. The men and women of Naples were bereft, starving, desperate people who would do absolutely anything to survive.' Taken from Mafia Brotherhoods – John Dickie

Set against this, a prime concern of the Allies was to try and seek out those apparently untainted by the fascist regime, someone had to try and restore some semblance of control. The mafia were ideally placed to step in and fill that position, many even being able to claim that they had been direct victims of fascism, having spent time in fascist prisons. Some form of local administration, some sense of law and order, needed to be achieved. Either out of ignorance or out of necessity, the Allies placed responsibility in the hands of leading figures from the mafia. I guess, in effect, the Allies were repeating the same mistakes made by successive Italian administrations.

I know, to us it may sound amazing. The mafia had been given new life, new opportunities, a firm foundation upon which to re-build. Let me ask you a question. What should have been done?

We come to this having some knowledge and understanding of the mafia. We know about the mistakes of past Italian administrations, at both a national and local level, in dealing with the three Brotherhoods. The Allies come to this lacking in such knowledge, with a multiplicity of other equal and, perhaps, more pressing problems. Not the least of the problems, fighting a war against the Germans. A war still far from certain to come to a successful conclusion. Fighting north through Italy was to be brutal, causing thousands of young men to die. The invasion of mainland Europe, D-Day, was still in the planning. Even when the invasion did take place, it would be a gamble on a massive scale.

So, collaboration with organised crime may not be ideal, but at least it 'got things done'. Others go so far as to suggest that the collaborative approach adopted by the Allies unravelled what little achievement the fascists had made against breaking down the mafia. Organised crime would develop new shoots and flourish once again. The hands of the mafia delving with even greater success into Italian society.

Remember Antonio Zagari, the baby having to make a choice between a key and a knife?

After spending his childhood running errands for the Brotherhood, at the age of 17, the son of a Capo (Boss), Antonio was at last deemed ready to be formally welcomed to the ranks of the 'Ndrangheta.

'The boss then took a knife and cut a cross on the initiate's left thumb so that blood from the wound could drip onto a playing card sized picture of the Archangel Michael. The Boss then ripped off the Archangel's head and burned the rest in a candle flame, symbolising the utter annihilation of all traitors.' John Dickie – Mafia Brotherhood

Gangsters & Cherries

Italian boys go through a mafia stage,
Idolizing gangsters and their ripping ways.
Dreaming in blood money, wearing a pair of snake
eyes, diamond studded vixens flashing pearl
glazed thighs.

One step behind the reaper, one ahead of the
cherries, beneath marble tombstones, the code
of honour buried.

But
Italian boys soon realise they haven't got the balls
to live life on a knife edge,
go toe to toe with the law.
I was no different and settled into a cage of mundane,
a nine to five carousel where every stallion is chained

. . . .

Anthony Slausin

ABRIDGED

CHAPTER SIX

The Three Knights Reborn

·······························

'The 'Ndrangheta was no mere gang: like the Sicilian Mafia, it was a parallel government, a parasitical creeper that had wound itself so thoroughly around the branches of the system that it now formed a more solid structure than the tree off which it fed.'

·······························

John Dickie - Mafia Republic

As the Italian nation recovered from the disaster of war, the mafia also recovered from having to deal with fascism. Eventually Italy would be transformed into a thriving capitalist economy, an Italian state shaped by the principles of democracy. Almost in unison with the growth in national economic wealth, the mafia became richer and, in many ways, more powerful than they had ever been.

Excuses of past state instability, a nation lacking a sense of unity, a country plagued by poverty, no longer provided plausible explanations for the existence of the mafia. Italy very quickly became a central figure in the coming together of European nations and yet, at the same time, still cohabiting with violently criminal corporations. It's a paradox that plagues Italy to this very day. January 2021, news headlines announcing the trial of 350 individuals associated with the mafia. Those on trial including politicians and assorted officials.

From the end of WW2 onwards, the Italian state appears to have continued with the mistakes of the past in its dealings with the mafia. Using the term 'mistakes' may be being a little too generous. The Italian state, or at least sections of the state, vacillated between clandestine collaboration with the mafia and periods of direct action against the three 'knights'. At times there have been those within the state apparatus who have deliberately allowed the mafia to flourish for their own individual gain, and/or as a tool used to subdue challenges from the political left.

By the end of the 1940s, the Sicilian Mafia (Cosa Nostra) had quickly regained a strangle hold on many parts of the island. Those in legitimate business became increasingly concerned by what they regarded as inappropriate concessions being made to ordinary workers by some political groups in central government. This resulted in conservative forces working hand in hand with the mafia. This close cooperation inevitably allowed the Cosa Nostra to seep into the political system. Some responsible for law enforcement did send warnings to Rome, highlighting the fact that it was difficult to effectively fight against the Cosa Nostra when it had so many friends within the Sicilian elite. For whatever reason, such warnings were simply ignored. Some suggest that conservative forces within the political establishment in Rome, regarded threats from the political left as more significant than any criminal activity in the south. The Cold War simply adding to fears about communist influences, a fear fed by the activities of the US and the UK.

The Camorra, never as well entrenched as the Cosa Nostra, also began to profit in the aftermath of WW2. Although the Camorra had many similarities with the Cosa Nostra, much of its activity remained around the slums of Naples, with friends in high places a little harder to find and offer the Camorra protection from the law.

The Calabrian mafia (the 'Ndrangheta) although the youngest of the mafia, quickly restored its dealings with political friends and those supposedly responsible for law enforcement. And Rome, what did Rome do? Rome did extraordinarily little. Conservative forces in parliament looked for support in Calabria to build political coalitions in the hope of holding back any potential advances made by socialists.

Whilst the power and influence of the mafia grew, there were still supposedly expert authoritative voices, at a national level, who argued that well organised criminal corporations only existed in fanciful minds. I guess this alleviated the need to put in place dedicated and consistent actions. Only when violence flared up, that could not be ignored, did the state step in. Sporadic purges, and then the south of Italy could be forgotten. But the knotweed continued to grow, indifference and ineptitude allowing it to spread. The growth of the knotweed matching the growth of the Italian economy in the 1950s through to the 1960s. Italian products had now become world leaders. From the 1950s onwards, all three organisations that made up the mafia moved into such businesses as tobacco smuggling, kidnapping, construction and illicit drugs. The mafia of the late 19th and early 20th centuries had undoubtedly transformed into business corporations. Closer business ties between the three groups were nurtured, with at least two of the three now successfully operating on an international scale.

Concrete. This became much more than the concrete boots shown in Hollywood films. From the 1950s through into the 1970s a rampant period of building speculation took place. The fingers of the mafia quickly spread into controlling building contracts and influencing planning permissions. Much of this supported by those in places of supposed legitimate authority, the mafia offering intimidation and violence.

From the 1950s onwards, Italy saw a mass migration of people from the south to the north in search of work. The mafia also continued to spread out across the country. The most successful of the three, you already know, the 'Ndrangheta.

It's in the construction of a winter sports resort in the region of Piedmont that we first get a sniff of the growing influence of the 'Ndrangheta. Those constructing the resort needed a low-cost labour force and a means of ignoring aspects of health and safety; the 'Ndrangheta could facilitate both. Those building contractors not willing to work with the 'Ndrangheta suffered unexplained fires, vandalism and threats at gunpoint. In Calabria road building brought yet more funds into the pocket the 'Ndrangheta.

From the late 1960s onwards, perhaps as the result of the increasing profits being made, the violence inflicted by all three of the mafia became more extreme and more commonplace. That violence at times being directed towards others in the same organisation, levels of violence that to us seem unimaginable. Internal mafia wars often resulting in hundreds being killed. On the 30th of June 1963, an explosion killed four Carabinieri, two engineers and a local policeman, torn to pieces in Sicily. The intended target was probably a rival within the Cosa Nostra. Public outrage resulted in the island being swamped with police and almost two thousand arrests were made. For a time, such actions almost removed the Cosa Nostra from the life of Sicily. An inquiry followed into the Cosa Nostra on the island that was to drag on for years, an inquiry that failed to take any note of the activities of the Camorra or the 'Ndrangheta. The question must be asked again, what was Rome messing about at?

The 1970s began to see closer links between the three organisations that make up the mafia. The Cosa Nostra extended its reach into Campania, establishing 'friendships' with some of the Camorra. Big money was available from a trade in illicit tobacco, money adding up to millions. This was good for a time, but then even bigger profits could be made. Have a guess as to the next market of the mafia. Kidnapping was one, although to some extent this was nothing genuinely new. The market that would really grow was to be illegal drugs.

Between 1969 through to the late 1980s an estimated seventy people simply vanished, most certainly kidnapped and killed. Probably the most high-profile kidnapping was that of the sixteen-year-old grandson of the American billionaire Jean Paul Getty. At first Getty refused to pay a ransom. The sliced off ear of his grandson received in the post, with a note saying other parts would follow, resulted in an estimated $3,200,000 being paid for his release. Kidnapping proved to be profitable, but it also resulted in lots of attention from the authorities. Trading in illegal drugs would result in even greater rewards.

A SIGNATURE OF VIOLENCE

Little Lord Fankie   Mad Dog   The Monster   Big Pasquale   King Concrete   Mad Mike   Joe Bananas Bonanno   The Prince of Villagrazia   Mr Champagne   The Professor   King of Poggioreale   Shorty   The Comet   Ciruzzo the Millionaire Baldy   The Pope   Little Shoe   The Animal   Ferocious Dwarf   The Man Who Cuts Christians   Big Kitten   Lady Camorra   Penelope

These are not names conjured up by script writers providing characters and dialogue for a Scorsese film, these are just a few of those who have held the position of Capo (Boss) over the years. Hollywood gives us a hint of the violence ordered by those within the higher ranks of the mafia, but I think it would be true to say the world of Hollywood fiction only scrapes the surface. It can do no more, the films are produced for entertainment, for our enjoyment. We're intrigued by the dark world of organised crime. True depictions of mafia violence, in all its grotesque and pathological forms, may delight a more macabre minority but probably repulse the rest of the viewing public.

With ever bigger financial rewards came increasing levels of violence. Levels of violence not just inflicted on those who stood in the way of the mafia, but also within the ranks of the three criminal organisations. Frustrations, jealousy, differing opinions on tactics, or simple grabs for power, have resulted in several internal wars, the resulting deaths in the thousands.

In 1974 internal wrangling within the ranks of the 'Ndrangheta grew into a situation where two opposing sides prepared for war. On the 24th of November, two assassins entered a bar, well known as place used by high ranking 'Ndrangheta, in Reggio Calabria. The first killer shot Giovanni De Stefano, from short range, in the head. The other killer shot the same person two more times, then turning the gun on Giovanni's brother Giorgio (The Comet). Giovanni died instantly, The Comet surviving the attack. The shootings unleashed a war that would last for two years, the eventual body count adding up to more than 200.

In January 1975, another Capo, Don Marci was killed. Four men confronted him as he left a game of bowls. The four killers blasted Marci with pistol and machine-gun fire. The killing in revenge for that of Stefano. In November 1977, The Comet's life finally came to an end, killed by some low ranking 'Ndrangheta 'soldier'. The story put about being that the reason for the killing resulted from some personal revenge, rather than ordered by yet another Capo. Plans to revenge this killing were halted by a gruesome peace gesture, the severed head of Giuseppe Suraci, the killer of The Comet. The truth is that Giuseppe Suraci was deliberately sacrificed to stop him telling the truth. Orders to kill The Comet had indeed come directly from a Capo.

I don't think you need me to tell you that for members of the mafia, delivering death is as routine as slaughtering and butchering animals for meat. Shooting, cutting throats, garrotting and torture, all tools used by some who were to become experts in their 'profession'. Knowledge of how to dispose of victims just as essential. Techniques for trussing up 'meat' so it could more easily be transported. Techniques mastered in the 'art' of disposal with quicklime and acid, to ensure that no 'refuse' would be left behind for forensic analysis. One

Gaspare Mutolo, after excelling in his apprenticeship with the Cosa Nostra in all the above, went on to become Mr Champagne, his power and wealth built upon the transatlantic trade in illegal drugs, the dealings having remarkably close links with international banking.

The King of Poggioreale - Raffaele Cutolo, a man of impetuous violence, was the Capo of the Nuova Camorra. It's said that by the early 1980s, the New Organised Camorra had well over 7,000 members. The astonishing thing is that Cutolo grew his empire whilst spending most of his time in prison. At the age of 21 he shot a man dead, the result of a road rage incident. In another incident, he deliberately drove his car at a group of women. Don't ask me why, I just know he did. A firefighter, who happened to be passing at the time, saved one of the women from being beaten by Cutolo when she challenged him about his stupid behaviour. Cutolo then followed the firefighter and shot him dead.

At times, the Italian judicial system has done little to support attempts to even clip the wings of organised crime. The system is archaic and long-winded, with trials often taking years before they come to court. Even then, cases may be referred to the Supreme Court, final judgements taking even longer. After serving only 7 years of a twenty-four-year sentence, Cutolo was allowed out of prison, the case having been referred to the Supreme Court on the grounds of his supposed mental instability. Cutolo took the opportunity to go on the run. He was eventually captured and returned to prison, whilst inside firmly establishing his hold over a criminal empire. After being transferred to a less secure prison (I know it's bizarre), he escapes and, again, is eventually recaptured. He spends the rest of his adult life in captivity. But, as you already know, this did not put an end to his power. Using the connectivity of the prison system he's able to oversee the growing business of the Nuova Camorra. On the outside, one of his most trusted commanders is his sister, Rosetta Cutolo. Through her, he was able to spend his prison life in relatively luxury, along with denying any knowledge about the murder of the deputy prison governor. Even the criminal psychologist who had provided expert statements in defence of Raffaele Cutolo, eventually became a victim. His body found in the boot of a car, his head on the front seat.

In 1978 the Nuova Camorra went to war with the Cosa Nostra.

John Dickie – Mafia Republic:

'The faster the wheels of the criminal economy turned, and the more frenetic the politicking became, the more pressure in Italy's underworld increased. The stakes and the risks grew greater and greater until, in the 1980s, there came an explosion of violence without precedent in the annals of mafia history.'

As you will appreciate, it's difficult to give accurate figures of how many died during the 'festival' of killing. Unofficial estimates place it at around 10,000. Official estimates, resulting from government enquiries, place the figure from 1981 through to 1990 at around 8,500.

Stefano Bontate, someone who enjoyed a life of expensive suits and Champagne, died from the blast of a sawn-off shotgun. Salvatore Inzerillo's head was so peppered with bullets that it took the police hours to identify him. The bloodletting was only just beginning. Abandoned bodies turned up with increasing regularity, some with all parts in place, many with parts missing, heads often separated from torso. People shot in hospital beds; others blown to pieces by bombs in Rome. A version of 'ethnic cleansing' was taking place, one group intending to annihilate the other. One 'ambush' leaving only three members of Mr Champagne's family alive. Family members of active mafia members more than often became victims of the slaughter.

Even as late as the 1970s, there were still some supposed experts, journalists and those in high office, clinging to the belief that the abnormal behaviour of these criminal gangs could be explained by some notion that it was a feature of the southern Italian mind and culture. Perhaps maintaining this pretence served the needs of some in the Italian establishment who had a great deal to hide.

If the internal slaughter within the mafia was not enough, the growing number of corpses outside the ranks of the mafia forced Italy to fully recognise what it had been living with for decades. Along with sporadic internal battles amongst the different mafia, one of the 'Three Knights', the Cosa Nostra, followed a path that was to take it into direct conflict with the Italian state.

In January 1979, a journalist working for the Giornale di Sicilia, Mario Francese, was shot dead as he left his home. His son, at the age of twenty, died by his side. Just a couple of months later, the leader of the Christian Democratic Party in Palermo, Michele Reina is shot dead. In July, Giorgio Ambrosoli, a lawyer who had been looking into the affairs of disgraced bankers, was shot dead in Milan as he arrived home. Just a few days later, in Palermo, Boris Giuliano, a high-ranking police officer is shot dead whilst drinking in a bar.

The targeted killing continued. To some extent the killings were nothing new. The mafia had a long record of liquidating those regarded to be a problem. But this was different. Never had so many been killed in such a short time. In September of the same year, Cesare Terranova, a judge, along with his bodyguard, were shot dead. In August 1980, Gaetano Costa, the Chief Prosecutor in Palermo became the next victim.

AN AWAKENING

The Italian state could no longer tackle the poison of organised crime in piecemeal fashion. Giovanni Falcone and the introduction of new anti-mafia legislation would prove to be powerful weapons in the state's more organised approach. From rigorously pursuing financial dealings related to heroin trafficking, Falcone was to go on to establish a centralised approach to tackling the mafia – but at what cost to his personal safety? New legislation allowed the sentences of those convicted of mafia related crime to be reduced if they were willing to provide useful information to the authorities. It resulted in a growing number of those convicted from the ranks of the mafia becoming a pentito. Trading information for a reduced prison sentence or even freedom, may not produce the most reliable information, but it did at last begin to uncover the secretive world of the 'Three Knights'. The one flaw in the weapons now employed by the state's anti-mafia laws, is that they almost completely ignored the 'Ndrangheta.

And then the state had one of its biggest pentiti, Pasquale Barra (The Animal). Alongside his role as judge and executioner in the prison system, he was also the second in command of the Nuova Camorra. But why would he decide to break his oath to the 'brotherhood', surely it would result in a death sentence?

Apparently, acting on the orders of Raffaele Cutolo - you remember him, The King of Poggioreale, also known as The Professor - Barra murdered a prison inmate, stabbing him sixty times. The problem is, a big problem for Barra, the inmate so savagely killed was related to Frank Coppola, a Sicilian-American in the Cosa Nostra. The murder looked like it could result in open confrontation between the Nuova Camorra and the Cosa Nostra. To avoid this, the Professor disowned the Animal. Hope you're managing to keep up with this. The Professor arguing that the actions of the Animal were his own decision. Barra was now effectively sentenced to death. To save his life, he had no alternative but to look to the state for protection. He told the authorities the whole story of the Nuova Camorra, names of people, everything. As the Nuova Camorra began to collapse, other defectors followed the path taken by the Animal.

In June 1983, an estimated 856 people were arrested across Italy. Along with known criminals, numbers from the Italian establishment were also caught in the net. But the killing was far from over. In the summer of the same year, Rocco Chinnici, a high-ranking official with the chief investigating magistrates' office, was killed outside his home, the victim of a car bomb. Those also killed included his two bodyguards and the caretaker of his apartment block.

The next breakthrough for the authorities came the following year when another important Capo of the mafia became a pentito – Tommaso Buscetta. For whatever reason, he appeared to be more than willing to give valuable information about the entire structure of the Cosa Nostra. As a result of what he had to say, 366 members of the mafia were arrested, the Italian press labelling the court proceedings that were to follow as the Maxi Trial. Of equal importance to the arrests, perhaps of even greater importance in focussing the mind of the state, information given by Buscetta at last identified the Cosa Nostra as one single and unified criminal structure – the recognition had taken a long time in coming. Still the killing continued.

Beppe Montana had a reputation for his speciality in seeking out mafia members who appeared to continually avoid arrest. Montana was very aware of the risks he and others took each day. In the summer of 1985, two killers struck as he returned from a boating trip with his girlfriend. At the age of 33, he was dead. Ninni Cassara, a deputy commander in the police, regarded himself and others like him to be 'walking cadaver'. The tactics used by those hunting the killers of Montana almost developed into a public relations disaster for the state.

Salvatore Marino was taken in for questioning, evidence appearing to implicate him in the murder of Montana. Torture techniques going back to the days of fascism were used, resulting in the death of Marino. A shambolic cover up was attempted, faking the death as a drowning. At the funeral of Marino, the streets were lined with people calling out the police as murderers. The word on the street, and picked up by the national press, was that specialist sections of the police had an intentional policy of deliberately killing mafia suspects.

Ninni Cassara, the 'walking cadaver', became the next victim of mafia killing. He, along with a twenty-three-year-old, Roberto Antochia, were killed in a hail of bullets, the killing close enough to the apartment of Cassara for his wife and children to witness the event.

Whilst all of this was going on, Giovanni Falcone, supported by Paolo Borsellino, was working tirelessly on putting prosecution evidence together for the Maxi Trial. Palermo's Ucciardone prison was to be the place of the trial, the courtroom taking the form of an underground bunker, with underground passages linking the court to the prison. Nothing was being left to chance. Thick concrete walls were further protected by high steel fencing. A staggering amount of money was spent on securing the building. Greater funds were also directed towards those on the ground fighting organised crime. The general public were also beginning to display open resistance to the clandestine criminal groups.

But still the killing continued. As one mafia grouping was taken down, another stepped in to fill the void. Nuova Famiglia, a breakaway from Nuova Camorra, flexed its violent muscle. However, within Nuova Famiglia there were also rival factions – civil war was almost inevitable. The Nuvoletta crime family, with close links to the Cosa Nostra, was ready and eager for a fight. The Nuvolettas were one of the oldest dynasties in the area that came under the influence of the Camorra, as such they were both powerful and feared. An attack on the Nuvoletta farmhouse in June 1984, sparked a bloody conflict, the body of one of the younger Nuvoletta brothers found shot in the head.

I know, who is killing who becomes difficult to follow.

The feared influence of the Nuvoletta family came to a bloody end in August of the same year. A bus, carrying at least fifteen killers, pulled up in the centre of Torre Annunziata, a town just 13 miles from Naples in the region of Campania. The bus, rather battered and old, drew little attention from the many people leaving mass. The killers calmly stepped from the bus and unleashed a barrage of bullets from machine guns, shotguns and pistols. The target was a group of men playing cards, some stood, others chatting with those who passed by. Eight were killed in the onslaught, with many who happened to be in the wrong place at the wrong time also hit. The place of the killing was a regular meeting place for Nuvoletta allies. What could only be described as a massacre resulted in severely weakening the influence of the Cosa Nostra in Campania. The most powerful amongst the Camorra was now Mr Angry (Carmine Alfieri).

September 23, 1985, yet another journalist is killed - Giancarlo Siani, aged just 26. He had come to the attention of the mafia with a string of articles linking organised crime to construction contractors and politicians. Two men approached his open top car from behind and shot him ten times in the head. At the time of his murder, he was gathering a dossier together on the killings in Torre Annunziata.

In Calabria, internal feuding within the 'Ndrangheta continued. Single incidents may have been less dramatic than the one in Torre Annunziata, but the bloodletting still resulted in an estimated 600 deaths.

The first week of April 1986 witnessed the start of the Maxi Trial. Revelations about the mafia spilled out, hidden secrets about internal organisation, evidence depicting the most barbarous acts of violence and the naming of perpetrators. And the names of those at the highest levels of society involved in nefarious dealings with the mafia also came tumbling out. Italy was gripped. An incident on the 7th of October 1986 sent a wave of anger across the country.

An eleven-year-old boy, Claudio Domino, was shot in the head from close range. The young boy lived in a rural area close to Palermo. It was clear to everyone that he had been deliberately chosen for assassination. Thousands attended the funeral. Newspaper headlines:

'And they call themselves Men of Honour'

One of those on trial in the Maxi bunker was granted permission to read out a statement. It was some sort of desperate attempt to distance organised crime from the killing of Claudio Domino. I guess even people who are willing to order executions, or even those who carry out the killing, have some kind of a 'moral regulator'. Given the accounts of the numbers of killings and the gruesome nature of some executions, I know that's hard to believe. The only other reason, and probably one closer to the truth, is that those involved in organised crime are bright enough to recognise that the deliberate execution of a young boy brings bad publicity. Anyway, Giovanni Bontate rejected any notion that those on trial had any connection with the killing. He asked people to recognise that they also had children of their own. He concluded by asking for a minute's silence.

Is it possible that those involved in cold blooded killing could indeed have some sort of moral compass, however distorted it may feel to us?

At last, at the end of five weeks, the Maxi Trial reached its conclusion. Nineteen of those in court were given a sentence of life imprisonment. Others were handed varying prison terms and, surprisingly, 114, following their acquittals, left the court as free men. Opinion as to the success of the court proceedings were mixed, some trumpeting the triumph of justice, others lamenting the fact that so many had 'escaped' prison. Remember what I said about the long-winded nature of the Italian judicial system – all was not over. There was also the very real danger of a backlash from the mafia, the Cosa Nostra in particular.

The Italian judicial system lumbered on, with many in the Cosa Nostra having good reason to have a smile on their face. Although having originally been convicted in the trial, by 1989 only 60 out of an original 342 were still behind bars. The supposed triumph of law over organised crime was beginning to look like a sham. Then came a bombshell from the Court of Appeal. Out of the original nineteen life sentences, seven were overturned, doubt being cast on the value of evidence given by informers. The judicial system dragged things on. What would the Supreme Court do? Were there people in high places, with even more secrets to be kept hidden? Could the Supreme Court wipe the smiles from the faces of the Cosa Nostra? Did there need to be a removal of those with the potential to severely damage the criminal brotherhoods?

It didn't take long for the bloody answer to come. Nino Scopelliti, a Calabrian magistrate with the responsibility of presenting evidence to the Supreme Court was murdered. How would the killing shape events?

At the end of January 1992, the Supreme Court gave its judgement on the Maxi Trial's original verdict.

Between the Maxi Trial and the final judgement of the Supreme Court, Giovanni Falcone had been hard at work. After accepting a position in the Ministry of

Justice, he set about reconfiguring the Italian state's whole approach to organised crime. If Falcone had not been at the very top of a mafia death list before, the changes he pushed through most definitely placed his name there.

Falcone set up a whole new police structure to chase down the mafia and any other organised criminal gangs. At last, a dedicated centralised structure would be in place, the Anti-mafia Investigative Directorate (Direzione Investigativa Antimafia). Special teams of magistrates were also set up, with the specific role of prosecuting mafia issues – District Anti-mafia Directorates (Direzioni Distrettuali Antimafia). The work of these regional bodies to be overseen by the National Anti-mafia Directorate (Direzione Nazionale Antimafia).

At long last, the Italian state had come to publicly recognise and accept the Cosa Nostra, the Camorra and the 'Ndrangheta as complex, highly organised, single criminal units. Hopefully, sporadic purges would be a thing of the past, replaced by a consistent and determined approach to cut the lifeblood of the 'Three Knights'.

Falcone also managed to push through changes to tackle money laundering more effectively. Changes that would keep mafia defendants behind bars while awaiting trial. And changes giving the state the power to dissolve whole bodies of local government that had been contaminated by organised crime.

Falcone had every reason to be fearful of mafia retribution.

The Supreme Court gave its judgment. The original Maxi Trial verdict was reinstated. Just six weeks after the Supreme Court ruling, a long-standing leader of the Cosa Nostra was shot dead near Palermo, not by the police, but by killers from his own organisation. Salvo Lima was, in effect, being punished for the tactical mistakes.

On the 23rd of May 1992, a massive explosion destroyed a stretch of motorway close to Palermo's airport. Three police following Falcone's car, after recovering from the force of the explosion, rushed forward to check on Falcone and his wife. Three bodyguards in the lead car were already dead. I would really like to tell you that Falcone survived. He and his wife, Francesca Morvillio, died in hospital the same evening.

Paolo Borsellino, the close friend and colleague of Falcone:

'They died for all of us. We have a great debt towards them, and we must pay that debt joyfully by continuing their work, by doing our duty, by respecting the law – even when the law demands sacrifices of us.' John Dickie – Mafia Republic

Paolo Borsellino's days were numbered.

On the 19th of July 1992, just as he was about to enter his mother's house, a car packed with explosives was detonated, the blast ripping Borsellino apart; five bodyguards died with him. Borsellino left a wife and three children.

THE ITALIAN STATE AND THE MAFIA

The relationship between the Italian state and the Italian people had never been strong. From the very time of political unity in 1861, distrust and dissatisfaction had been the key features of a country lacking any semblance of genuine unity. Proactively taking the fight to the mafia may have come too late.

Bubbling below the growing levels of violence, was a political system in continual turmoil. A political system with foundations built on shifting sand, coalitions muddled together from favours and promises, long term goals lost, and all too often, the needs of the Italian people forgotten. Governments pulled together through shady deals, offering ample opportunity for the mafia to creep in and infect. Coalitions came and coalitions went in rapid succession.

I guess you could say that a distrust of politicians, deserved or not, has become a feature of all countries. In Italy, the relationship between the general population and government is more than one of distrust, it is one of loathing; a loathing that still exists today. A sense of fatalism about Italian politics expressed time and time again by my Italian friends and neighbours. I have to say, over the last few years, I've developed the same feeling about politics in both the UK and the USA.

The early 1990s witnessed an almost total collapse of the Italian political system. Economic instability and evidence of corruption at the highest levels of government were placing the political establishment under incredible strain. 'Operation Clean Hands', the name given to the investigation into ongoing scandals, resulted in over 200 Members of Parliament coming under suspicion. The focus on tackling the mafia could have been completely lost. Within organised crime, the killing continued. Ignazio Salvo, a key member of the Cosa Nostra was found dead, punishment for not having done better in protecting the organisation from the state.

At a time of political and economic weakness, the killing of Falcone and Borsellino, brought ever increasing demands from the public for justice. Although the political apparatus may have been incredibly shaky, the full power of the state was now brought down on all three of the 'Spanish Knights'. By the end of 1994, over 5,000 people had been arrested under powers provided by anti-mafia laws. A witness protection programme was set up and a new prison regime put in place to restrict the power of mafia leaders behind bars. The Cosa Nostra was especially targeted, with thousands of troops being sent to Sicily to support the police. Top mafia names were being captured, whilst others looked to the state for protection. The murders of Falcone and Borsellino had not only angered an Italian public, the magnitude of bloodletting also shocked some in the ranks of organised crime.

Names at the very top of Italian crime fighting, those supposedly entrusted with breaking down the 'brotherhoods', along with the names of some in the political structure, began to spill from the mouths of top-ranking mafia informers. Bruno Contrada, once a Chief of Police in Palermo and later Deputy Head of Italy's internal intelligence service, was found guilty of dealings with the Cosa Nostra.

Even though the history of all three groups that make up the mafia has been one of extreme brutality, the almost unbridled violence of the Cosa Nostra had tipped over into levels that went beyond that reached before. The Camorra and 'Ndrangheta also fell victim to the backlash from the state. Both suffering from the increasing number of penitents willing, for whatever reason, to pass information to the authorities. But the three 'Spanish Knights' have long memories; retribution would come at some point.

Out of the three that make up the mafia, although damaged, the 'Ndrangheta weathered the storm better than the other two. This was partly the result of so few from its ranks, compared with the Camorra and Cosa Nostra, joining the growing number of informers. As a result ,the 'Ndrangheta remained somewhat a mystery, its inner working still difficult to penetrate, at times the organisation falling below anti-mafia radar.

Had there really been a true awakening? The mafia were certainly under attack, but was there full and clear determination from all sections of the state?

There are some who suggest that there were those within the state apparatus, for whatever reason, still willing to follow a hidden policy of negotiation with organised crime rather than a continuing 'all-out war'. Were some in government prepared to strike deals, to pursue a path leading to some sort of appeasement? There are even those who suspected the apparent ease with which killers had been able to strike at Falcone and Borsellino. Some going so far as to suggest that Borsellino was deliberately left under protected. In other words, sacrificed to ensure his silence. Attacks, bombing and killing continued. Even the Catholic Church came under direct attack, the Pope having publicly denounced the Cosa Nostra. Are you thinking what I'm thinking? Where had Catholicism been all this time?

Whatever happened between some in government and sections within the ranks of organised crime, the air did indeed begin to smell again, if not of collusion, then the old stink of co-habitation. And it's here that we find, you know who – Silvio Berlusconi and his more than dodgy associates. Nothing has ever been proven linking Berlusconi directly to the Cosa Nostra, but most certainly he would have done anything to protect and enhance his vast business interests when in office as Prime Minister. I'm surprised that, 'doing a Berlusconi', has not now become an accepted term of abuse for those operating out of nothing more than narcissistic self-interest.

If you want to give Berlusconi the benefit of the doubt, then I guess I'm reluctantly willing to go along with you. He may not have been in bed with the Cosa Nostra. But in the process of protecting his own, often dubious, economic interests, Berlusconi, when in office, ensured that legislation was put in place that not only protected him, but, either deliberately or not, also served the needs of organised crime. His statements on the mafia were at best ignorant to the danger and at worse deliberately crass.

John Dickie – Mafia Republic:

'To one British journalist, he said that he thought the anti-mafia magistrates were mad. To do that job you need to be mentally disturbed, he asserted.'

There were leading members of the mafia who openly admitted that they would give their political support to Berlusconi.

Although people like Berlusconi proved to be problematic in the fight against the mafia, the fight continued.

Better technology, increased surveillance, informers and those willing to risk life, resulted in numerous success stories against the mafia. Operation Perseus, in 2008, dragged in ninety-nine arrests from the very top of the Cosa Nostra.

The combination of a more vigorous and coordinated approach from the state, alongside the growth in grass-root groups campaigning against the mafia, has to some extent affected the power and influence of organised crime – but it is still very much alive and, at times, violently kicking.

Libero Grassi, a factory owner in Palermo felt the vengeance of the Cosa Nostra in August 1991. As he left his home, he was shot five times in the head. His 'guilt'? Publicly campaigning against organised crime, even appearing on national television. However, the killing, rather than dissuading others from taking a stand against the mafia, in many ways encouraged more people to do so. Those brave enough, given support when the courts made it a crime to pay protection money. In 2004, Addiopizzo (Goodbye Extortion), set up by a group of young men in Palermo, had growing success in encouraging businesses to refuse to pay protection money, although its founders must now endure a life with constant police protection. The equivalent of a national employer's federation, Confindustria, has also promoted anti-racket groups, expelling some found to be paying protection money.

Promising as the above may sound, and indeed it does offer hope, the mafia are still very present. In some ways the three 'Spanish Knights' have recognised that openly taking on the state was probably not the best tactical approach. During the 'war', two of the three had stood back, being more than willing to allow the Cosa Nostra to step up to the front line. The Camorra suffered casualties, but far fewer than its Sicilian cousin. The 'Ndrangheta suffering even fewer casualties, away from the front line and very much in the shadows. As for some within the body of the state, the collusion continued, Campania and the Camorra providing a good example.

Along with construction, the Camorra also crept into the disposal of waste and recycling. The result being not only massive levels of corruption, but also significant levels of environmental pollution, in some cases deadly toxic. A whole circuit of illicit dealings developed. Contracts being rigged, jobs given to those prepared to keep quiet, punishment for those less willing to conform, bribes in the direction of administrators and politicians. For some who broke rank, punishment was swift. One director, knowing that he had been implicated in corruption, decided to provide information to the authorities. His life was at an end. When out with his daughter, he was shot at least eighteen times.

You know the name that's going to crop up again, correct – Silvio Berlusconi. In 2009, the Junior Minister of Finance for Berlusconi's party in the region came under investigation. At the time, the Prime Minister of Italy – Berlusconi. Requests were made to parliament for permission to initiate action against the party bureaucrat and his links to the Camorra. The request was firmly rejected. A year passed, requests were then made for permission to tap the phone of Nicola Cosentino, the same Junior Minister of Finance. Again, the request was refused. Eventually Cosentino did resign from his post. Given his involvement in yet another scandal, his resignation was almost impossible to avoid. In 2012, he was again protected from arrest. You must be thinking the same as me. It was not just the ever-increasing levels of waste that stank. The toxic stench of political corruption appeared to be well embedded at the highest levels of government.

In the shadows, the 'Ndrangheta continued to prosper and grow. Over the years the activities of the Cosa Nostra and the Camorra, the killings, mass arrests and high-profile trials, had spread the names of the two across all news outlets. For the mass of the Italian population, the 'Ndrangheta was still relatively unknown. The events in Germany in 2007, and before that, the murder of Francesco Fortugno, the Deputy Speaker of the Calabrian Regional Assembly in 2005, began to place this third 'Spanish Knight' in the public eye. By 2010, the 'Ndrangheta had gained a significant profile on the radar of those fighting international crime. The work of this 'Spanish Knight' controlled by its main ruling body known as the Great Crime, the most powerful boss being the Capocrime. Outposts around the world reporting back to the Great Crime in Italy.

John Dickie – Mafia Republic:

'The 'Ndrangheta is without doubt contemporary Italy's most powerful mafia. The beneficiary of years of disregard by the state and public opinion, it has a remorseless grip on its home territory, an unparalleled capacity to colonise other regions and other countries, and vast reserves of narco-wealth that allow it to penetrate the lawful economy and financial institutions.'

EQUAL OPPORTUNITIES

There is one more feature of the mafia that I need to mention, this being the increasing role of women at the highest levels. Let's call this, for the sake of argument, 'equal opportunities'.

October 2015 - a mother, Nunzia D'Amico, pushes her baby in a pram. She's walking home along a street in Ponticelli, a suburb of Naples. It's an everyday scene, a mother, loaded down with shopping, just a short distance from her home.

Nunzia D'Amico will not live to prepare food for her child that evening. On approaching her home, she becomes another victim of mafia killings, shot dead.

The killing is all part of a familiar story, in this case antagonisms and disputes between rival groups within the Camorra.

The police were more than aware of who she was. Nunzia D'Amico had three brothers, Salvatore, Giuseppe and Antonio. At the time of her killing all three were in police custody. Whilst the three were not operational, their sister, Nunzia, had taken charge of the family drug business. In effect, she was the head of the D'Amico clan.

For those fighting organised crime, the killing added to growing evidence that more and more women were 'stepping up' and taking leading roles. Those in the know suggesting that there were ten times as many women operating at a high level compared to twenty years before. Female names sitting alongside and becoming just as notorious as those of males. Names such as, Anna Maria Licciardi, Raffaella D'Alterio (Big Kitten) and Rosetta Cutolo. The Big Kitten almost suffering the same fate as Nunzia D'Amico, the result of another shooting.

In the long history of the mafia, women traditionally remained in the background. Sometimes they were 'protected' by males, whilst at other times ruthlessly exploited; exploitation being a more common feature of the 'Ndrangheta.

But times change.

In a strange way you could regard the increasing role of women as a form of 'emancipation'. It's a bit of a warped way of looking at things, but a view that's been put forward. The reality is much easier to explain and understand. Women are moving into what were once regarded as the domain of men, because the men are either dead or in prison. Someone needs to step up and keep the family business going. Maria Campagna (Penelope) is said to have enjoyed the full trust of her husband, Salvatore Cappello, a top Camorra boss in prison. She held the top position of Capo, dealing with all the tactical decisions to be made in the transatlantic drugs trade.

Nunzia Graviano was another who took over the position of Capo whilst her brothers were in prison.

Another was Giusy Vitale, said to have ruled her domain with an iron fist. The media giving her the title of 'Capo in a Skirt'.

The truth is that 'emancipation' has only ever been temporary. Although a woman may be the Capo, it is rare for any to be involved in any formal affiliation into a mafia brotherhood. The position of Capo almost always on loan, once the husband or brother comes out of prison, leadership is handed back to the male. The 'emancipation' also having other boundaries. They can order the cold-blooded killing of others, but they can't take lovers or leave their man. Do the same rules apply to males? What do you think? Taking a lover, or leaving her man violates codes of honour, a violation that could result in a death sentence.

As you are already aware, when it comes to being killed or being involved in doing the killing, gender makes little difference. Erminia Giuliano (Lady Camorra) is said to have had a reputation for taking direct action against her enemies, once stabbing a female rival and, on another occasion, driving her car through the window of a shop owner who refused to pay pizzo. For a time, Lady Camorra appeared on the list of Italy's most wanted criminals, her arrest coming in December 2000.

Anna Mazza (Widow of the Camorra) met her death, at the age of 37, inside a butcher's shop in November 2004. Other than the killing being carried out on the orders of the Cosa Nostra, I'm uncertain as to the details of her 'crime'.

Perhaps her climb to the higher ranks of the Camorra had been too brash. Her insistence on only appointing women to positions of influence probably offended many of the brotherhood. Allowing others to share her bed after the death of her husband, crime enough to result in her own murder. Then again, it may have had nothing at all to do with her gender, the killing simply being a matter of 'business'.

Although women may appear to be 'doing it for themselves', the reality is that they remain very much under the will of the 'Men of Honour'.

MAFIA 2023

The shattering violence of the 1980s and early 1990s may have abated, but organised crime is still ever present. All three of the 'Spanish Knights' have an exceptional ability to regenerate after periods of intense activity from the state. The ability of all three, to a greater or lesser extent, to blend into the political and economic life of the country, providing further nourishment for growth. All three have moved on from the past, recognising that relative invisibility can bring greater benefits. Violence against high profile figures used more sparingly, the judgement being made to target such people only when there appears to be no other operational alternative.

Collusion with the mafia remains difficult to prove. Reforms to the Italian legal system have resulted in greater success, but it's still a system that is grindingly slow. The criminal system may be bewildering, Civil Law is even more time consuming, with cases dragging on for many years. It should come as no surprise if some are tempted to call on the services of the mafia to settle disputes.

In 2019 the Italian Interior Minister, Luciana Lamorgese, gave perhaps the most accurate picture of the mafia today. She set out a simple profile for each of the three 'Spanish Knights'. The 'Ndrangheta, without any doubt, identified as the most powerful of the three, its power now extending well beyond the region of Calabria and the borders of Italy. The Cosa Nostra may have lost some of its feared status, but is still a pervasive, dynamic and dangerous organisation. The tentacles of the Camorra are less widespread, but the organisation remains a constant threat within its territory.

I guess that this can feel incredibly depressing, not surprisingly leaving you with the feeling that Italy appears to stand little chance of finding a remedy for the chronic illness of organised crime. There is however one absolute positive, no longer is there the notion that the mafia are some aberration of the southern Italian mind and culture. Those directly involved in the fight understand what they have in front of them. Highly structured, powerful, single units of organised crime. This recognition resulting in ever more sophisticated methods of breaking down and prosecuting those within the organisations and their supporters on the outside. In the 1990s, a specialised mountain unit of the Carabinieri, the Cacciatori – Hunters, was set up with the specific task of hunting down the mafia in their mountain retreats. Added to a more determined use of law enforcement, there are a growing number of ordinary Italians who have decided to stand together and resist.

Lamorgese emphasised that the state was determined to hunt out the mafia and those who collude with organised crime. In 2018, mafia assets with a total value of €9 billion were seized, 60 members of the mafia arrested and over 2,000 people either taken into custody or reported for having mafia associations.

In January 2020, the Cosa Nostra suffered 94 arrests for involvement in fraud related to EU agricultural subsidies. The authorities claiming that more than €10 million had been fraudulently claimed. In November 2022, prison sentences were handed down to 91 people, many of them mafia members. Again, EU subsidies, amounting to more €5 million, had been fraudulently claimed. As Italy moved into the spring of 2023, Italian authorities announced the arrest of Pasquale Bonavota, a top Capo of the 'Ndrangheta. After escaping an arrest warrant for murder, he'd been on the run for over five years. In May 2023, more than 130 arrests were made in a number of European countries. The arrests part of a three-year investigation into the illegal drug trafficking of the 'Ndrangheta.

The long decades of the three 'Spanish Knights' operating with relative impunity are definitely part of Italian history. Although the Italian judicial system remains agonisingly bureaucratic and slow, more and more of those involved in organised crime are being brought before the courts, along with those from both politics and business who offer succour to the mafia for their own personal gain.

LIVING IN ITALY WITH THE SPANISH KNIGHTS

After having turned the pages of the past two chapters, it could easily feel that Italy is a society drenched in blood. For those living a life within the ranks of the mafia, the hold on life can most certainly be tenuous. However, for a small few the financial rewards can be enormous. The incredibly strong ties to family and clan, bringing its own rewards of power and influence. Omertà – break this and your life is at an end, there is no return to the 'brotherhood'. The last two chapters bear witness to the vengeful nature of the mafia, no compromise offered to those found guilty of betrayal, death often bloody and gruesome. As you are very aware, those taking a high-profile stance against the mafia did so/do so at incredible personal risk. At times the state (certainly in the past) appearing to offer little credible protection. Again, the liquidation of those standing in the way of the mafia, cold-blooded and callous. Knowing all of this leaves us with a question. How do you live in a country where organised crime appears to run through its very veins?

The truth, if my experience is anything to go by, you won't be aware that the mafia exist. There will be the occasional news items, highlighting anti-mafia raids and arrests. Possibly news items covering mafia members and associates on trial, but other than that, unless for some reason you actively seek out contact with one of the 'Knights', organised crime will be as distant from everyday life as it is for the average person in the UK, USA or any other country. There are crime dramas on TV. Gomorrah, based on a book by Roberto Saviano, premiered on Sky Atlantic in 2014, that has run for four seasons. The series revolves around the world of the mafia in the suburbs of Naples. There's also a series called Squadra Antimafia, the series depicting the work of Anti-Mafia police based in Palermo, Sicily. I strongly suspect that this is as close as you will ever get to the mafia.

Remember I live in Umbria, central Italy, a region of the country where mafia activity is less invasive than it is, for example, on the island of Sicily or around Naples. Perhaps it could be that I've just not listened and looked hard enough. But I don't think that's the case. Not once in all the time that I've been visiting Italy, and now living in Umbria, has anything related to the mafia even fleetingly come up in conversation. That's not to say that I'm being naive, clearly from everything I've said in these pages, the mafia are very much active and still a serious problem. I guess what I'm saying is, don't be too preoccupied by their existence, don't worry –

non preoccuparti. It's highly unlikely the influence of the mafia will directly impact on your life. Relax and enjoy all the delights that Italy offers.

There is one other organised criminal group that I've neglected to cover, the mafia in Puglia. Again, you find this region in the southern part of Italy, famous for its conical shaped white houses – trulli. This fourth member of the mafia being the Sacra Corona Unita – Sacred United Crown. The thinking is that this criminal group grew as a spin-off from the 'Ndrangheta. The reason for not mentioning the Sacra Corona Unita before, is that this group, in comparison with the 'Spanish Knights', appears to be less well embedded into the fabric of Italy.

Let me end this chapter on a positive note. Although the mafia, without doubt continue to be a major problem for Italy, the general crime rate for the whole country, when compared to many others is, perhaps surprisingly, relatively low. Although Naples keeps its position for having the highest murder rate in Europe. In 2018, within Italy, the city of Milan ranked first in terms of general crime, followed by Rimini and Florence. Most of these crimes related to theft, having little connection to the activities of the mafia. After having turned the pages of the past two chapters, perhaps you feel the need for just a little more reassurance about the general level of safety in Italy.

The Global Peace Index ranks 163 countries based on a range of indicators related to levels of peacefulness and safety. Italy is consistently ranked above both the UK and the USA. Just for your interest, Iceland was ranked as the safest country in the world in 2019, a position held since 2008. Where do you think Italy, the UK and USA come in the ranking? New Zealand comes second, followed by Austria, Portugal, and Denmark as the safest countries. Afghanistan, Yemen and Syria hold the lowest positions for safety. I suspect that the Ukraine will now be close to the bottom of the list. The GPI ranked Italy in 39th position, the UK finding itself in 45th position. So where does that leave the USA? Out of 163 countries, the USA comes 128th, squeezed between Saudi Arabia, one below, and South Africa, one above. I'm not sure if this will come as a surprise to many Americans. As a foreign tourist, would knowing this stop you visiting the USA?

Just one last point about relative safety. The Washington Post, June 2021:

'The shootings have come at relentless pace. Gun violence this year has cut through celebrations and funerals, places of work and houses of worship. It has taken lives at a grocery store and in a fast-food drive through lane.'

The USA sits alongside Brazil, Venezuela, Colombia and Guatemala for having the highest levels of gun related death in the world.

I'll stop here. I think you've got the picture. It would be perfectly reasonable to see the USA as an extremely dangerous place to live or visit. A justified perception? An exaggerated perception? Is it just me, as a Brit, who doesn't understand?

In the EU, there are approximately 6,700-gun related deaths each year, of these, 5,000 being suicides (Flemish Peace Institute).

Italy has never had a single school shooting.

In Italy, to own a gun, the law stipulates the following:

• You must be 18 or over

• You must hold certification showing you have attended a gun safety course

• You must pass a medical examination to determine mental stability

• You must show that you have a clean criminal record

• You must register all guns with the local police within 72 hours of purchase

• To carry a gun outside your home, you need either a sporting or hunting licence

• Any red flags in a person's behaviour, for example threatening physical violence, even with no gun involved, could result in firearms being seized and licence revoked

Added to the above. All military grade weapons are strictly forbidden.

So where does all this leave us?

It is an undoubtable fact that the mafia are very much alive in Italy, with at least two out of the 'Three Knights' having tentacles that spread across the world. But, as I said earlier, unless you want to go out of your way to seek out contact with the mafia, there really is little chance they are going to come into your life.

Italy is as safe as any other country, and safer than many.

Aton

With the rising of the sun in ancient Egypt, the land of
Pharaohs, mankind was given life:

Men had slept like the dead; now they lift their arms
in praise, birds fly, fish leap, plants bloom, and work
begins. Aton creates the son in the mother's womb,
the seed in men, and has generated all life. He has
distinguished the races, their natures, tongues, and
skins, and fulfils the needs of all. Aton made the
Nile in Egypt and rain, like a heavenly Nile in foreign
countries. He has a million forms according to the
time of day and from where he is seen; yet he is
always the same.

. . . .

The Hymn to Aton

CHAPTER SEVEN

Un Cane di Nome Aton

···

'I've seen that look in a dog's eyes, a quickly vanishing look
of amazed contempt, and I'm convinced that basically dogs
think humans are nuts.'

···

John Steinbeck

In 2016, I took a dog into my care. A male dog of doubtful age and pedigree – Aton.

The challenge of having a dog is that it follows you everywhere, yes, including
the toilet. Although I have to say, in his defence, Aton understands that my
toilet habits are my own individual concern and therefore no longer any of
his business. He still follows me up the stairs, but at last he accepts, perhaps
somewhat reluctantly, that he must remain at the toilet door. He appears to
have got the message, he cannot, must not, step over the threshold.

Aton is my shadow on four legs. He is super glue with a wagging tail. He is a
moving obstacle to negotiate with every step I take. He appears to take great
pleasure in twisting and turning between my legs and under my feet as I climb
up and down the stairs. He will often dash around the house at breakneck speed,
completely forgetting that his ability to come to a halt is almost completely
redundant on tiled floors. He frantically tries to gain at least the minimum
of traction with claws extended, but without success, his whole body sliding,
headfirst, into some immovable obstacle.

Amazingly he has total control of his bodily functions, a skill that has nothing at all
to do with my training. I can only assume that he just intuitively knows that such
necessary habits should be kept for outside. But I guess a more obvious reason
for such thoughtful behaviour is that he was well trained in toilet etiquette by his

previous owner. So far there have only been a couple of mishaps, even then he was good enough to leave his deposits close to the outside door.

He craves a belly rub, and when one is given his entire body drifts into a trance like state. Eyes closed, ears spread out on the tiled floor, four legs vertical and wide apart, a slight, knowing grin, on his face. Dog heaven.

I try to keep him occupied, giving him colouring books and his very own box of assorted pencils. His own DVDs, and even his own tablet. All are cast to one side, abandoned, substituted by his desire to glue himself to my legs and his craving to go for a walk. If he gets the slightest sniff that we may be going for a walk, he suddenly springs up two feet in the air and, whilst airborne, makes a complete 360° turn. I have his lead in my right hand. He sits. He knows that he should sit when I have the lead in my hand. He's expectant, questioning.

'We going walking? Yes, going walking, walking! We're going walking. Biscuits? Yes, give me biscuits, more and more biscuits. I'm trying hard to do good sitting. Another biscuit. I WANT TO JUMP! Are we going walking? So excited! Walking biscuits, walking. And - it's raining ....'

At this very moment, my shadow on four legs is asleep: snoring like an idling steam engine. He appears to be fast asleep, curled up in his bed, nose touching tail. I don't know about you, but I think it's extraordinary how bendable dogs are. The places they can reach, impossible for us humans, and not at all suitable for public viewing. And yet that's often when Aton will perform, showing off his complete pliability. Displaying that he is indeed flexible enough to reach parts of his anatomy that for you and me are completely out of bounds. And even if we could, such acts of self-indulgence would be private and concealed. Dogs are clearly not as inhibited, openly licking the most intimate parts. Whenever given the opportunity, not just licking their own intimate parts. No, the intimate parts of other dogs.

Where was I? Yes, Aton is fast asleep. But the reality is that 'fast asleep' is a bit of a misnomer for the condition of a dog with eyes closed. Like all of us, Aton dreams. He dreams of catching lizards, of sniffing out deer and wild boar, of food and treats, but most of all he dreams about running and running and running. He is the Forrest Gump of the dog world. As he dreams, his body twitches and trembles, legs give jerking movements and, just occasionally, a little whimper will escape or perhaps a half-hearted bark. But, as with all dogs, he's never fast asleep in the human meaning of being asleep. Hidden behind the snoring and the dreaming, Aton is always semi-alert. The slightest sound of a rustling packet being opened brings instant attention, Aton looks up and springs into a good sitting position, full of expectation.

So yes, I now have a dog, an English Pointer. June 2016 and I have a dog. I keep repeating this because I'm almost as surprised as anyone that I have this new responsibility in my life, my daughters especially surprised. I live in Italy, my adult daughters live in the UK.

This is my first dog. I'd been pondering the idea of having one whilst still living in the UK, but only really starting that pondering once I had fully retired from the daily routine of paid employment. Living in Italy, big open garden, miles of countryside, forest, fields, and mountains - why not?

The pondering continued until I came across a post on Facebook. An English woman, living in Umbria, posted a picture and brief details about a dog that desperately needed a new home:

HUNTING DOG

In need of regular exercise

Lovely family pet

Gentle nature

In need of a loving home

If a new owner is not found soon, the dog will have to go to the local community dog refuge.

The message had been posted in December, it's now the first week of April. Do I really want a dog? Anyway, the dog will by now have found that loving family home or it will be in the local dog refuge. I pondered on and looked for information about English Pointers.

The English Pointer is a medium sized dog. This is an English breed of dog.

It turns out that the English Pointer is a very sweet-natured dog, bred primarily for hunting. This breed of dog is packed with energy and therefore requires an active owner, a true athlete and full of muscle. That's the dog being full of muscle, it's not a requirement of the owner. I think my long ponder could be coming to an end. It's the type of dog that would fit in perfectly, what with me only last year, for the first time in my entire life, being officially recognised as an athlete. Look, that's what it states on my Gubbio Runners membership card, Graham Hofmann – Atleta Maschio.

The English Pointer is a congenial dog, but will not tolerate cats or domesticated birds, for example chickens. I have chickens. It's the type of dog that can be stubborn and easily distracted when something interesting or the scent of some wild creature catches his/her attention. When bored they can resort to destructive chewing.

Are you still pondering Graham or are you going to make your mind up?

I've made up my mind. I'm going to contact the person who put the information on Facebook.

It turns out that Louise, the English woman who has the Pointer, lives close to the medieval hilltop town of Todi. She's also a member of a Facebook group known as UmbriAliens. After contacting her, I also find out that she's married to an Italian and they have a young daughter. More importantly, I'm told that the dog is still looking for a home. So, I arrange to drive over to her place, meet her and the dog for the first time, but with no commitment that I will take him into my care.

Rather than just throwing it in, perhaps I should say a little about UmbriAliens. Then I'll move on to tell more tales (no pun intended) about my canine friend.

UMBRIALIENS – THE GREEN HEARTS

There are just two simple criteria for joining this 'closed group'. The first is that you must be foreign, you must be an 'Alien'. Being native-born Italian, departing to live in some other country, then returning to live in Umbria won't get you past the 'gatekeeper'. If you match up as an immigrant to Umbria you can join the group. The status of Umbrian immigrant applies to those who live in the Green Heart of Italy either full or part-time. That's it, no citizenship quiz. Where you are foreign from is of no consequence. UmbriAliens come from across the globe.

I stumbled across UmbriAliens via Facebook, it simply popped up one day, no request having been made by me. So, in April 2016, I asked if I could become a member, offering the required proof that I was a totally bona fide foreign Umbrian. Request accepted by 'the gatekeeper', and I'm allowed in.

Once in, I discover that the 'gatekeeper' is another English woman, Giselle. With just a little delving, I find that's she's married and lives close to the medieval town of Montefalco. This is the Montefalco of Sagrantino wine fame, more about that at some other point in the book.

A couple of weeks pass by and a post pops up on UmbriAliens, placed there by Giselle. She's asking if anyone is interested in going to the opening of a new wine bar in Torgiano, a small town about 10 kilometres southeast of Perugia, the capital city of Umbria. The town, like Montefalco, sits in a wine producing area. Sagrantino wine, however, is restricted to Montefalco alone. I respond by saying I'm interested, and it's agreed that I'll meet Giselle and her husband at the wine bar.

Torgiano is not that big, with just a few main streets, so the wine bar is easy to find. When I arrive, there are probably around thirty people there, enough to make the small bar feel full. I soon spot Giselle, and I'm introduced to her English husband Mark (the same Mark cornered at the big birthday party by the evangelical vegan). They're stood drinking and chatting with another couple who, by their accents, are very noticeably not English. I'm introduced to Tom and Alice, they're American, from Florida. All five of us are foreign Umbrians, therefore without any doubt qualifying as UmbriAliens. Unlike Giselle and Mark who live full-time in Umbria, Tom and Alice are part-timers, owning a house in Montignano. It's a chatting, nibbling, wine sipping sort of an evening, warm and friendly. There will be many other occasions to follow, where UmbriAliens come together.

So, they're you have it, my very first excursion into UmbriAliens; it was to be the first of many.

Back to the English Pointer. I'm going to visit Louise in order to assess the compatibility of myself and the dog.

CASTRATO!

Along with her Italian husband, Roberto, and their young daughter Olivia, Louise lives on what I guess you would call a smallholding. The place not big enough to be classed as a farm, but with far more land and outbuildings than your average family would have. They live in a large, stone built, typically Italian house. Smartly finished, but at the same time rustico, with a few English twists here and there. And animals, lots of animals. Assorted cats of differing colour and age, along with a couple of dogs, including Aton. Horses of different sizes, a donkey, a few sheep, chickens, and a few turkeys. Some animals are fully functioning and able, others have bits missing, like a leg or an eye. It appears that Louise can't say no to taking in animals found in distress. Not sure what her husband thinks about the menagerie of semi-disabled animals, just now he's working somewhere a little distant from the house.

We sit outside, sheltered from the warm, late April sun by large trees. Louise has made lunch. The food washed down with cool Umbrian vino bianco and aqua frizzante. It's a beautiful setting, full of rural Italian charm. As we sit, pecking chickens feed round our feet, dogs kept separated from what could be their lunch by a low wooden fence. A fence that I'm assured by Louise, Aton will not be able to jump over. Remember that assurance from Louise, I'll come back to it.

As we enjoy our surroundings, we sit and chat, enjoying the warm sun, food and wine. It's the sort of chat you have when you meet someone for the first time. Where are you originally from? How long have you lived here? What did you do when you were back in the UK? Where did you live? General chat about living in Umbria and the difference between here and where we come from. Then we get onto the main reason for me being here, my possible adoption of the English Pointer, Aton.

The chickens are ushered out of the protective enclosure with a soothing voice and the gentle clapping of hands. They scurry first in one direction and then the other, reptile-like legs carrying plump feathery bodies, slight panic in their glass eyes. Eventually all the girls are out, only then is Aton allowed in. He scampers round, running up and down along the length of the low wooden fence. He's in hunting mode, eyes set on the feathered reptiles. Eventually the chickens have spread out into the fields that surround the property, gone from Aton's view. For a while he stands looking in the direction of the last bird to have disappeared, not quite pointing but almost.

Louise brings him over to meet me. He's clear eyed, tongue hanging from the corner of his mouth. A handsome dog, keen, bright, and gentle in nature. Well gentle that is unless your body happens to be covered in feathers. His body is a patchwork of bright white and brown. How can I describe it? The sort of patchwork you get on a Friesian cow, but brown and white rather than black and white. Thankfully, Aton nothing like the size of a cow. Louise does have a dog the size of a polar bear, it really is that big. Well, perhaps not quite a polar bear, but it is big! Just accept my word, it's a white mountain of a dog, a Maremmano-Abruzzese. The breed is still used in Italy to protect sheep. It's a dog that could quite easily eat a chicken whole, feathers, bones, reptile legs and beak, the lot in one gulp. But, unlike Aton, the white mountain has not the slightest interest in the chickens.

We chat about what Louise knows of the history of Aton. She decided to take him in and find a new home when his owner decided to return to live in Sweden. Also, for some reason not known to Louise, the woman who had been the owner of Aton wasn't able to take him with her. So here he is, hoping for a new owner. She's not sure of his age, but he's still a young dog. Aton sits, brown eyes looking up. Not a hint of his chicken killer instinct.

I'm already convinced, I'll become the adoptive owner of Aton. Louise offers to make sure he has all the required injections that dogs are supposed to have. She will also have him castrated. No, don't wince, most male dogs are castrated. And no, I wouldn't delight in having it done to me. But Aton is a dog. From what I understand there is a logical reason for having it done. I'm told that it reduces levels of testosterone and, supposedly, levels of aggression. It should also stop his more amorous side kicking in, therefore reducing the chance that Aton will disappear, attracted by the scent of a female lover on heat. So, with that, it's agreed. I was to return in a couple of weeks and take ownership of my very first dog.

Forgot to mention, Aton is the name given to the dog by his Swedish owner.

Between first visit and my return to collect Aton, I have a little work to do in making my open garden dog secure. I have the feeling that he will simply disappear into the fields and forest, intent on hunting if I don't fence him in. The six chickens I have are already well protected from Aton and, hopefully, any snooping foxes who just happen to be sneaking by. Although keeping out a fox can never really be guaranteed, they have the ability to climb over and dig under. The foxes around this part of Umbria have a genuinely scavenging look about them, lighter in colour, smaller and just not as eye catching or robust as the urban foxes you regularly come across in the UK. The bright ginger of a UK fox appears to have heavily faded in the Italian sun. Faded to an almost scruffy light sand colour. Anyway, Aton could prove to be more of a hazard to the chickens than any skinny Italian fox.

One week before my planned return to collect Aton, I receive a worrying message from Louise. For some insane reason, Aton decided to torment the polar bear mountain of a dog. This is a dog three times the size of Aton. A sneeze from this dog would have the potential to blow him off his feet. In retaliation the Maremmano has grabbed hold of Aton, its large jaws, and I guess large teeth, causing significant damage to Aton's lower back. It sounds incredibly serious. The message reads that he's on various drips feeding him with drugs, drains to release any infection. It could well be that Aton, after all, may not turn out to be my first dog.

Another week goes by and there's better news from Louise. Aton is much improved, drips and drains removed, he will survive. However, he needs to recover fully before he has the unmentionable done to him. That little procedure to do with his 'manhood'.

The second week of May, another update from Louise. Aton has now fully recovered. He's had the necessary dog injections and his 'bits' have gone. I won't tell him if you don't. I can come over to collect him as soon as I want.

The day arrives. I sit enjoying an afternoon drink with Louise. Again, we're chatting about living in Umbria, the joys and, at times, the frustrations it brings. The chickens have been securely locked away for the time being, safely out of the reach of Aton. He looks to be in excellent health, a few tiny patches where hair had been removed for whatever veterinary procedures were required. His wounds have totally healed, he looks incredibly good. There's just one noticeable physical feature about him that looks a little peculiar. The polar bear's mouth is so big, it was able to clamp across the entire width of Aton's lower back. All is now fine, but on closer inspection it looks like the front end of one Pointer has been joined with the rear of another. And then, as I'm petting my 're-joined dog', an exceptionally large shire horse comes galloping to a sudden halt by the low wooden fence. It's a big, beautiful horse. It simply stands, head over the fence. Louise is almost as surprised as me, the horse should be securely enclosed in its field some distance from the house. Within a few minutes a man appears, clearly having given chase to the horse. It's my first meeting with Roberto, the husband of Louise. Once he's recovered from the chase, he comes to join us, the shire horse simply left as a spectator.

Apparently, Roberto was working in a field close to the shire horse. Something spooked the horse and away he went, crashing through the gate, galloping towards the house. I sense relief in Roberto's voice as we talk about Aton. I think he's pleased to be saying goodbye, but nothing specific is said.

Hands are shaken, kisses made to each cheek and Aton passed into my care.

The following day I'm out with Aton in my garden, Aldo by my side chatting about the fact that I now have a hunting dog. Will I be taking him hunting? He could be a good truffle dog. It's as we're chatting, that Aldo notices that Aton has bits missing.

'You've had him castrated! Why have you had him castrated?'

Hand gestures and the expression on his face suggesting that the castration of a male dog is almost as dreadful as if it had been done to himself.

'Why have you done this to him?'

Aldo is clearly not won over by my explanation, simply shrugging his shoulders in disagreement.

Well, that's out of the way. It's clear that we're not going to come to a common view about castration. As we're stood trying to understand the views of the other, someone parks a car at the edge of my garden. As he walks towards us, it's clear that he knows Aldo. They shake hands, Aldo introducing me to Alberto, he's a veterinario (to you and me, a vet). I've not asked for a vet to call. Apparently Aldo, after seeing Aton the night before, has taken it upon himself to call the vet to check over this new dog in the hamlet of Case Colle.

Alberto, the vet, looks like he's already had a hard start to the day, having been dragged through a hedge backwards by a pissed-off billy goat. His face, gnarled from countless days under an Italian sun, wearing at least three days of stubbly beard growth. I would guess at him being in his late fifties. What looks like a full head of greying hair hidden under a red Ferrari cap, the cap fading to pink, the rampant Ferrari stallion badge coming detached. He has a green vest, beneath a darker, heavily worn, 'farmer's' jacket. Both his jacket and black trousers have a patchwork of dubious looking stains, his wellington boots encrusted, with what I assume to be cow shit. I think you get the picture. We all carry round a big box of stereotypes; Alberto is not fitting any of the images I have in my mind of what a vet looks like. Then again, I don't think I've ever had any face-to-face contact with a vet.

He takes my hand in his, a very firm, earthy grip, big friendly smile on his face. We exchange greetings, Alberto then asking Aldo if I speak Italian. As is more often the case, before I get chance to respond, Aldo answers the enquiry:

'Sì, parla italiano, ma è terribile.'

Now my Italian is far less than perfect, but it's a bit harsh to describe it as 'terrible'. Aldo and Alberto then go on to talk about me whilst I stand beside them. Hello, I am here!

Conversation suddenly comes to a stop halfway through further questioning from Alberto, with me now responding to his curiosity about the inglese. He turns his attention back to Aldo, a surprised and, at the same time, worried look on his face. I think you know what he's noticed.

'The dog is castrated! (Il cane è castrato!). Why is the dog castrated?' Alberto holding his hands together, as though in prayer, thus giving further emphasis to his questioning.

Aldo offers a simple explanation, his explanation appearing to satisfy him and Alberto:

'Perchè è inglese (Because he's English).' Me, not the dog.

A shrug of Aldo's shoulders, his hands also held together as though in prayer.

He's English. This appears to explain everything. He's English, you know what they're like, they're a little peculiar.

Why try to argue against it. I smile and shrug my shoulders, but without holding my hands together as if to pray.

And then, Alberto, decides that the castrated dog needs an injection. I've not asked for the dog to have an injection and I'm not sure what it's for. But before I get chance to ask, Alberto has pinched the flesh on Aton's back and spiked him with a syringe – Aton almost leaping into my arms. A quick rub of Aton's flesh from Alberto and the reward of a biscuit, the biscuit for Aton not me.

That's it, all done. Alberto wishes me well, taking my hand in his earthy grip. You have a good hunting dog. I offer to pay for his veterinary wisdom, but not actually knowing what wisdom I've received. I guess I'm being English, you know what we're like. Alberto refuses to accept any payment. Italians, what are they like? He smiles, shakes hands with Aldo and makes his way back to the car at the edge of the garden.

Well, at least I have a bit of paper saying that Aton has been spiked by a vet.

HORNET!

Just had a hornet in the house. Big bloody thing. Sounded like a helicopter out of control. Aton not at all happy, jumping around all over the place, attempting to catch the beast. Me trying to stop him catching it, whilst at the same time trying to get the bugger to land so that I can squish it. Aton jumps in the air yet again, this time sending CDs crashing across the room. I take another swipe, but this only gets Aton more excited and even more determined to snap it between his jaws. Another failed jump from Aton, this time sending a wooden duck into flight. Another swipe in the air from me. The sound of the helicopter engine has stopped. Aton is also still, surprised by the sudden silence. Then he spots the stricken hornet on his bed. Of all the places in the room, it has to crash land on his bed. Both of us jump forward at the same time, him on four legs, me on just two – he gets there first. But for a split second he's not sure what to do. This gives me the opportunity to swiftly sweep the helicopter up, tossing it over the balcony. Gone, it is no more. Aton sits, a quizzical look on his face.

'Why has He done that?'

Now we have a moth, the size of a small bat, in the same room. As it flutters around, Aton springs into action, again making giant leaps into the air. But I've no need to have the same urgency. The bat sized moth soon comes to rest in the corner of the ceiling, well beyond the reach of Aton. And there it remains, still, I guess having a little snooze. Aton has now lost any interest, returns to his bed, joining the moth, soon fast asleep.

The hornet v Aton incident reminds me of two other confrontations with hornets in Case Colle.

It's a beautifully hot summer day in Umbria. I'm sitting with my daughters under the shade of the old walnut tree. The walnut tree doesn't belong to me, it grows in the corner of Lorenzo's garden, but the bulk of its flaky, fragile, branches hang over my garden. Anyway, it's in the shade of the tree that we're sitting, reading and chatting. Lucy, my younger daughter, occasionally taking the opportunity to cool off in the jacuzzi that sits just beyond the branches of the walnut tree (un albero di noce).

It's a quiet, almost serene morning. Our little Umbrian world wrapped in the protective arms of the tree. The tree is like an elderly, wise friend. It's the type of tree you find in fantasy films, a tree that has the power of speech, able to intelligently articulate its feelings. Obviously, a wise tree. I think I should give it a name - any suggestions would be gratefully received.

The tranquillity is suddenly shattered when my elder daughter, Kara, screams out. Perhaps it's more of a piercing cry of pain. Her book is thrown to the ground, drink tumbling over her bare feet. She jumps up, holding her right hand.

'I've been stung! God it hurts. What the hell has stung me?!'

You could say, looking back, that my response, and that of Lucy, could have been a little more sympathetic, offering at least a hint of concern. Our immediate reaction, I guess you could describe as one of unresponsiveness, coming from our almost stupor like state, the heat of the day already slowing down mental functioning. Well, that's my attempt at an excuse for not being more empathetic.

'I've been stung! Are you two simply not bothered?'

Kara is now stood over me, holding her right hand.

'Don't be so melodramatic. Is it a wasp or a bee?'

'Don't be so melodramatic! Are you being serious? I've been stung and you're not bothered.'

'It's just a wasp or a bee', Lucy calling from the jacuzzi, its bubbles frothing around. 'If it's a bee, you'll still have its backside stuck in you.'

'Thanks Lucy for your pearls of wisdom. It's not a bee or a wasp, it bloody hurts a lot more!"

I guess that we're just not taking this seriously enough. Our laughter at what we regard as an overreaction not really helping.

Kara sits by my side. She holds her right hand close to my face.

'See, this is not from a wasp or a bee. I've been stung by a wasp before.'

She could well be right. The knuckle of her index finger already quite swollen, you could almost say bloated and inflamed. The whole finger looking red and stiff.

Lucy is now out of the jacuzzi. Both of us showing more sympathy. The swelling and redness are certainly not the result of a bee or wasp sting. The only culprit I can think of is a hornet. And, as you already know, hornets are big bloody things in Umbria. As visitors, not as regular as bees or wasps, but making up for it in size.

Kara sits whilst we become very amateur paramedics, rubbing antihistamine cream on the swollen area. It soon brings some relief, but the swelling does last for a couple of days.

The other hornet incident involved Andy and Sam, the partners of Kara and Lucy. The house was still a holiday home, I was back in the UK working.

For a few days, what they thought to be big wasps kept being found in the small lounge on the first floor of the house. Sometimes they were simply dead, on their backs, on the tiled floor. At other times, they were very much alive, motoring around the room, thumping on the patio doors that open to the small balcony.

After a little investigation it was noticed that what we know to be hornets, were motoring up and down the chimney from the open fireplace (camino). After a little discussion, Andy and Sam come up with 'a cunning plan'.

They make sure that the doors opening to the patio are closed. Kara and Lucy have decided to keep well out of the way. Andy and Sam then spray copious amounts of fly spray up the chimney. And, just for good measure, even more fly spray. I forgot to mention, they also have the room door firmly closed. They stand back to see what will happen. What will happen doesn't take long.

There's the unmistakable sound of loud buzzing coming from deep inside the chimney. The 'giant wasps' are most certainly not happy.

And then, the 'giant wasps' come thundering out into the small lounge, in fighting mood, incredibly angry and looking for targets. Andy and Sam don't hang around to take a census of numbers. Both scramble for the door, the room now very unsafe territory. Angry hornet buzzing goes on for a little time, Andy and Sam listening from behind the protection of the closed door.

Only when all buzzing appears to have stopped, is Sam volunteered to step back into the room, door closed behind him. He calls Andy to follow, all appears to be safe. They find a 'killing field' of dead and almost dead hornets, about twenty in total.

Trust me. Don't be dissuaded from visiting Umbria by tales of hornets. Yes, there were quite a few in the chimney of my camino, but that's a rare occurrence. And yes, Kara was stung by one, but in all my years of being in Umbria she is the only one. I guess some people are just unlucky.

BOOT CAMP

We're in training, the two of us, Aton and He. Perhaps I should point out that the term 'He', refers to me. In my head it's how Aton identifies the one he lives with.

As I've already told you, it's the first time that I've lived in partnership with a dog. Over the past few months both of us have been coming to terms living with the other. It's a learning experience that brings frustrations for both trainees. One tiny problem at the start was that Aton appeared to have absolutely no understanding of English, not a word. I tried Italian, but still no clear and obvious response. Swedish, but the problem is I have not a word of Swedish. We both persevere and eventually things start to fall into place.

Days of walking, with Aton insisting that he is going to be the alpha male in this relationship, with me equally determined that I will be the one in charge. It's a battle of wills, there can only be one winner if Aton is to live with me. Weeks go past, every walk a battle, Aton determined to be in front, straining with all his strength, pulling, almost choking on the lead. Me pulling him back, insisting that he walks by my side. Who is the alpha male in this relationship?

Sitting when commanded, he soon picks this up, eager to please. It's the expectation of a reward that results from 'good sitting', rather than him doing this for my benefit. In the end he follows the command with just a hand gesture from me and a look in the eye. Sometimes he gets a reward, sometimes not. It's a must to keep them guessing.

Getting Aton to 'stay'! It's not that long before he will do exactly that when instructed, a command he learns to follow with voice and clear hand gestures. After a good deal of practice and patience, Aton is willing to hold one position as I walk away, perhaps as far as 100 meters. Only when I call him does he move. Obviously, just like in good sitting, he has the expectation of a reward. Again, a reward not automatically given.

Jumping up and begging round the table, are soon behaviours that he can control. He very quickly learns that the table, human food, and humans eating, are all barred to dogs. No exceptions.

After several months all is progressing well. I think we can live together. Well, we can at least tolerate each other. Most of the time he is reluctantly content to walk by my side. But there are just two little problems that I'm finding difficult to persuade out of Aton's behaviour.

He's a medium sized dog, very placid in the company of humans. He craves attention and rarely goes into a fit of barking. But, and it's a big but, he will insist on having a go at any dogs twice his size. He's clearly not learnt any lessons from his experience with the polar bear.

The other problem, I guess, comes from his innate instinct to hunt. Once that kicks in, there is no stopping him, no calling him back. Once he has the scent of a deer, wild boar, hare, or some other such animal in his nostrils, he will run and run and run. He eventually returns, but only when he decides. Never does his frantic chase result in a catch, but he always comes back with a look of happy fatigue.

It was his unstoppable desire to chase that eventually convinced me that he would have to remain on the lead when we were out walking. Up high in the mountains, away from other people and any roads, he could run free. But closer to Colpalombo there would have to be greater restriction.

We're out on our usual morning walk, about four kilometres in total. We walk just a short distance from the house to the main road that passes Case Colle, either climbing up to Carbonesca or twisting down to Colpalombo. Our walk takes us in the direction of Carbonesca, for a brief time along the road, Aton on the lead, and then into fields with forest at the edges and the occasional patches of low scrub type bushes, growing up to at least waist-height. Oak trees cover the valleys, the Apennines, with Monte Cucco, clear to see against a deep blue sky. A beautiful morning.

Once some distance from the road, in fact two or three fields from the road, Aton is given the freedom to run. It turns out to be a big mistake.

After having disappeared for about ten minutes, two large deer come rushing out from low scrub about three hundred meters from where I'm standing. Aton soon appears in hot pursuit. He's never going to catch them. He's racing over the ground. I call, but he is totally deaf to anything but his quarry. The deer run and leap, Aton following at top speed, but not gaining much ground. I call and call, but he is totally absorbed by the chase. In effect, I no longer exist.

Dodging a fence, the deer run upwards and across another field. I'm now giving chase, my run just about keeping Aton in view. This really is not good. The two deer and Aton, run into the next field and then towards the bend of the road to Carbonesca. On the opposite side of the road, oak forest. The deer are making a run for the forest. And just as they leap into the road, I can see a car approaching. There is not a hope at all that I can get to Aton before the car collides with the deer or, if missed, the dog.

By some miracle, the deer and Aton make it to the other side of the road and into the forest. My run has now slowed to a fast walk. As I approach the road, the driver of the car is stood waiting for me, and he's not pleased at all. We exchange a few words. My words are very apologetic, his more of a severe reprimand. He forcefully explains that I should have the dog on a lead. I apologise again. At that exact moment, as the apology leaves my lips, Aton emerges from the forest. I take hold of him. Shake hands with the driver of the car, him asking if I use the dog for hunting. I say no, which as you know is the truth, but I'm not sure that he believes me. With what could have been a distressful episode over, he drives away. I walk slowly back to the house with Aton.

VOICES IN ATON'S HEAD

The dog, Aton that is, has a very sorrowful look on his face when looking up at me. I often wonder, if he could think in a human way and had the ability to give voice to his thoughts, what he would say. It's quite difficult to pick out when Aton has a happy face, a bit like some teenagers, they tell you that they're fine, but give little outward sign of that being the case. Any possibility of food or going for a walk does, however, bring an expectant glow to his face. It would be stretching things to call it a smile, so we'll leave it at a brown-eyed sparkly glow.

It's March 2017. I've decided to run the Great Wall of China Marathon. You'll be thinking one of two things, I guess. Possibly, what a brilliant adventure. Possibly, are you simply mad? Anyway, my entry is accepted, everything is booked for May. And now I'm in training, running up more and more hills in Umbria. Obviously if I have to run up, I will also be running down. The down bits always the best. But I'm not feeling so good. I've got some type of bug. I guess it's nothing more than 'man flu', sore throat and all the other bits that go with it. I've medication, including antibiotics. I know, before you say anything. If it is flu, then antibiotics won't do that much, if anything at all. But I have them, along with other medicinal concoctions.

I can sense what Aton could be thinking. He has a certain look in his eyes:

'Just been out with He that I'm forced to live with. God he's been miserable company these past few days.'

In Aton's head, I'm simply known as He. I'm not sure if his thoughts are in Italian, Swedish or English. Probably after almost a year with me - English.

'Why do human men complain so much when they're not feeling well?'

'Aton, I'm feeling cold.'

'Aton get your own food.'

'Aton, I'm feeling cold again.'

'I feel exhausted and my throat hurts.'

'No, I'm not feeling hungry.'

'Aton, take yourself out for a walk.'

'Give me a break. I make him hot drinks. I make him hot soup. I turn on his electric blanket. I mean, an electric blanket at the end of March in Italia! And still, he sits around feeling sorry for himself. I know, it's pathetic. I've said to him that it's just a cold. It's not the end of the world. I know, but I should be with Gubbio Runners on the way to Turin, says He. Between you and me I think this is just an excuse so that he doesn't have to run the half marathon in Turin. Not saying that's a fact, just a suggestion.'

'I think he may be feeling a little better this morning.'

'He's very reluctantly taking me out for a walk, but still complaining all the time.'

'Human men, they're the most pathetic creatures.'

I know he's thinking these things. I can see it in his eyes, the look on his face, the drooped shoulders, the pitiful glance from his bed.

THE DEER WITH THREE FEET?

Out with Aton this morning, the dog that never stops running – all too often in the opposite direction to the direction I'm walking. I know I said following the incident of Aton chasing the two deer, that I would keep him on a lead, but we're walking in the mountains.

Today we have the mysterious case of the deer with only three feet. Do deer have feet? Well, whatever they're called, there could well be a deer with only three feet hobbling around Monte Cucco.

Just as we're walking along, Aton off the lead, he spots three large deer, with twelve feet between them, about 200 meters ahead. There is absolutely no chance of me stopping Usain Bolt. Off he goes at high speed, all four legs leaving the ground, ears pushed back as the wind sweeps over his face. He's an Exocet missile locked on his target, the white underside of deer tails disappearing into a patch of forest and gone from view. Aton follows, soon swallowed by oak trees.

Silence. I call but get nothing in return. I walk in the direction of the disappearance in some optimistic hope that Aton will return from the same spot that he vanished. I keep calling, but still nothing. Let's just hope there's nobody other than me and my speedy 'hunting' dog out walking. A good ten minutes have now gone by. I keep calling, but still nothing.

It's a beautiful Umbrian morning, clear blue sky holding a warm sun. My chosen walk covered in a carpet of buttercup like flowers. Still not a sign of Aton's return.

Suddenly he appears, you know already, from completely the opposite direction. He's good, running towards me, still at quite a pace, ears back. What's that he's carrying?

As he gets closer, he slows to a walk, panting heavily, tail wagging with the power of a wind turbine. In his mouth the foot, no leg attached, just the foot of a small deer. He comes closer and stops. He clearly has no intention of giving the hunting trophy to me. Resting, he holds the foot between his front paws, vigorously brushing it with his rasping tongue. His concentration on the foot only interrupted by him looking up to see if I'm going to attempt to take it away.

Although he would release the trophy without much fuss, I allow him to keep it. He put all the effort in.

Is there a deer hobbling around with something missing? I seriously doubt it. And the foot is certainly not from one of the fully-grown deer that he first chased amongst the oak trees. My guess is that today we have Aton the scavenger rather than Aton the killer. I'm sure you'll be pleased to know that. How could such a cute dog be a killer?

And so, my life in Umbria continues, but now with Aton the running dog.

And just like a child coming into your life, having a dog adds a whole new learning curve. You think you know, but you don't. Well, at least I didn't. Any journey involving Aton, just like when you have a child, has to be planned, do you have everything you need?

I'm travelling back to the UK; it's the first time Aton has been out of Italy. He has his own passport; he's also had his rabies jab. Just before we travel, he's had the required dose of worming medication. Passport, rabies jab and worming tablet, all required for him to be allowed to enter the UK. We arrive at British passport control, at the ferry terminal in France. My passport checked, Aton's passport checked, plus a scan to ensure he has a microchip; all is fine. The boarder official then decides, as he looks at Aton's passport again, that my Italian vet has not stated the time when Aton was given the worming medication. The date is there, the name of the drug, but not the time. I'm informed that we will not be able to travel. I try to argue that all the details required are correct. The official must be having an officious day, the time that the worming medication was given should be stated in the passport. Get this done and you can travel tomorrow. I explain the situation to the ferry company, we can travel tomorrow, no extra charge. Now I have to find a vet and a hotel, a hotel that will take a dog for the night. We find both, just outside the ferry terminal. I make sure that the French vet makes the time of medication given extremely clear. The following day, we board the ferry without a problem. Who thought it was a good idea to get a dog?

GALLINE

I don't know what it is, but there is a certain something in many of us that makes us want to have live chickens. I guess to be more precise, our own hens (galline), laying our own free-range, fresh eggs. Perhaps it's some kind of homage in all of us to 'living the good life'.

The land just across the road that passes the front of my house, the plot that Lorenzo had been telling me for years belongs to me, does indeed belong to me. The truth of his assertion was revealed after yet another minor disagreement with Benito, the one I've told you about before. Anyway, the land belongs to me, I'm allowed to fence it off and use for whatever purpose I choose, apart from building a group of expensive country homes. Well, in reality, apart from building anything.

The land is quite a reasonable size, I would estimate it to cover at least half a football pitch. The rest of the field beyond is owned by other neighbours who live about two hundred meters down from Case Colle, as the road twists to Colpalombo. It's quite common for people to own odd bits of land, but not to have a farm or some type of small holding. As far as I understand, Benedetta owns bits of land here and there, although they tend to be left wild, with nothing cultivated there and no animals left to graze. Each year the neighbours who own the land beyond my bit, pay someone to plough the field and prepare it for seeding. Crops from sweetcorn to grass (the grass cut for hay), have been grown there, the owners again paying someone to help with the harvest. Every year I hope they'll decide to grow sunflowers, providing me with the most beautiful vista from July into early August. But still waiting, hoping for next year. It's just me being a little greedy, I already enjoy magnificent views of the Umbrian countryside.

As I often do, I call on Aldo for advice and support. Where is the best place to buy fencing and posts? And, as always, Aldo is more than willing and happy to give his assistance. After making the roughest of estimates, we travel along, in my Italian reg car to pick out and place an order for enough fencing and posts to enclose the whole bit that belongs to me, plus enough to separate what will be a vegetable plot (orto), from the main bit of land that will be for chickens and fruit trees.

Once the fencing and posts are delivered, we set about digging holes, bashing in wooden posts and stretching the green wire mesh across to securely fit. We're now in the second week of October 2015, but the days are still quite warm, digging, bashing and fixing not easy work. I work together with Aldo, on and off, for a couple days before my niece, April, arrives from the UK to holiday for the week. How could I not offer her the opportunity to volunteer to help me dig holes and bash in more fence posts? She only needs give up one day of her week in Umbria. Not that long, and we have the entire area posted and fenced. Once she has left, for the return flight to the UK, I'll fence in the orto in order to keep the chickens out. The whole of this October week remains almost summer-like in its warmth. We have dinner with my neighbours, spend a day in the beautiful town of Orvieto, another day in Assisi, obviously not forgetting to enjoy an evening in Martintempo.

After April's departure, two more day's work and I have the orto completely enclosed. Hen house purchased and built, it's now time to go in search of the girls who will live there. There is only one person I can ask, yes, you already know. That person must be Aldo. He knows a good place near to the little town of Valfabbrica, just a twenty-minute drive from Case Colle and about 20 kilometres (12 miles) from Perugia.

As we make the short drive we chat about the day and the local goings on around Colpalombo. Along with the galletto (cockerel), Aldo asks how many galline I want. I respond by saying I don't need a galletto, Aldo most insistent that I do. To have a galletto or not to have a galletto that is the question? Perhaps it's a question I can ask you, well those of you who happen to keep chickens. How many of you have a cockerel, a rooster, a galletto? Our debate about the need for a galletto continues until we arrive at a small holding just on the edge of Valfabbrica. The acid smell of hen pee wafts through the air. As we walk towards, what look like two squat aircraft hangers, we're greeted by a man in his late thirties. The man dressed in t-shirt and jeans, a grey smock, buttoned up, coming level with his knees. I'm introduced to Filippo, yet someone else that Aldo knows. I think Aldo must know everyone within a ten-mile radius of Colpalombo and then, many other people beyond.

We explain that I would like to buy sei galline (six hens). You know what I'm going to be asked next. And you want a galletto, this being a statement not a question from Filippo. Here we go again. I respond by saying that I don't want and don't need a galletto. Aldo and Filippo both definite in their wisdom that I do. You need a galletto. No, I don't. They both look at each other with the same quizzical expressions that came with the discovery that Aton had been castrated. I have the feeling that to be a 'real' Italian man it is a required necessity to have a dog with balls and hens with a galletto. The dog with balls and a galletto to keep the hens under control, a reflection of Italian manhood. Filippo and Aldo look at each other bemused. Why does the inglese not want a galletto? I think you could give them the answer. Yes, it's simply because he is English. You know the English; quite nonsensical they are.

In the end I get my way, the customer is always right. Having said this, from my experience of living in Italy, a good many Italian businesses have clearly never come across that little motto. There are many wonderful things to enjoy about Italy, good customer after sales service tends not to be one of them. At best it tends to be variable and, at the other extreme, terrible.

As far as me not wanting or needing a galletto, I get my way. Six hens are chosen, payment handed over, hens placed in two cardboard boxes. Just before we leave, Filippo tries one more time to get me to take a cockerel. I shake my head for the final time, I don't need one. The two of them, Aldo and Filippo, shrug shoulders in unison and give in.

The Earthquake

The earthquake must be to everyone a most
impressive event: the earth considered from
our earliest childhood as the type of solidarity,
has oscillated like a thin crust beneath our feet;
and in seeing the laboured work of man in a moment
overthrown, we feel the insignificance of his
boasted power.

. . . .

Charles Darwin

CHAPTER EIGHT

Un Treno Sotto Casa

....

'It takes an earthquake to remind us that we walk on the
crust of an unfinished planet.'

....

Charles Kuralt

According to official statistics, 2016, on average, had the hottest twelve months
in the 137 years history of record keeping. NASA reported the year as being
almost 1°C above the 1951 – 1980 average. Umbria certainly had its above
average share of ridiculously hot days through July and August.

It's a hot evening in Umbria and, as is more than often the case, my deep sleep
is covered by nothing more than a thin cotton sheet. There's no real need to
have anything covering me to provide warmth, the room is far too hot. The white
cotton sheet simply rests, haphazardly, over my body in the hope of offering a
little protection from the odd mosquito that may have strayed into the room
intending to feed on English blood. Although, to be honest, apart from them
having the occasional snack, mosquitos have never been a major nuisance
around my little bit of Umbria.

I sleep and I dream. Hot summer days, blue skies, walking in mountains, sipping
wine with friends in the shade of olive trees, endless festivals, the calmness of
Lago Trasimeno, medieval hilltop towns and villages, terracotta tiles and cobbled
streets, early morning mists, my chickens, the dog - now a permanent shadow
in my life, a warm sunrise and sizzling amber sunsets, laughter and friendship –
my misunderstood Italian. My dream suddenly changing, jumping. The intense
perfume of truffle oil, the sound of bird song, wrenched away in exchange for
the sound of screeching, grinding wheels, carriages rocking, lights flickering,
people swaying as they stand holding leather straps, the underground tunnel

vibrating as the train passes below the house. My eyes are wide open. Through the half-darkness of the room, I see moonlight shadows cast across the ceiling. The dream has become real!

There's the unmistakable sound of a train thundering below, directly beneath the house. For no more than a matter of seconds the whole house rumbles, no discernible movement, but the sound is loud as the train roars beneath Case Colle. The floor of the bedroom vibrates, then silence, the train has gone. I pull the cotton sheet around me. My eyes wide open, looking at the ceiling above. Was that one jumbled up, disjointed and muddled dream, just one part of the nonsensical dreams that we all sleep through?

My ears are on full alert for any other sounds. It's no dream. But I don't leap out of bed. Instead, I pull the cotton sheet closer to my face. I listen. Silence. The moonlight shadows, cast from half open shutters, remain painted on the ceiling, no plaster has fallen, the house is still standing. I know it's an earthquake. I'm guessing it must be some distance away, but it must have been a big one. Then again, it could be closer than I think. Silence. I turn to my side, it's around three in the morning. I'm still listening. My eyes open and close, open again, close – stillness and silence. I stretch out under the cotton sheet and soon I've drifted back to sleep.

The underground train thunders below me again, the house vibrating as it passes through rock and earth. How long have I been asleep? It can't be more than a few minutes.

This time I know for certain that this is no dream. Seismic shocks speed through the ground, the house appearing to absorb any vibration. The bedroom door rattles, it's being tested by some intruder, it remains closed, the intruder still on the other side. The rumbling momentum of the train fades, it's thundering roar there and now gone. This time my interrupted sleep is sharp, my eyes immediately open. Silence. Nothing has fallen from the ceiling. The shadows remain untouched – the house is still standing. Should I have attempted to seek refuge, crawling beneath the bed, its metal frame and thick heavy mattress offering some possibility of protection? The house is still standing, nothing has fallen; I'm calm. The shadows are still there above me. I feel sure the quake has gone. I feel safe under my cotton sheet. My eyes are open, my eyes close, open again and close – I listen and then drift back to sleep.

Awake quite early, the day already sliding through the half open shutters. Dust particles float and dance through the air, caught in shafts of sunlight. The ceiling is still where it should be, securely and safely above my head. It's already warm, it's going to be another hot Umbrian day. I remain under the white cotton sheet, thinking about the underground train and listening to Case Colle life outside. Voices call to others and occasional cars pass as they climb to Carbonesca or travel down to Colpalombo. And the house is still standing.

Was that the main earthquake? Where was it, how far away? Could it have just been the aftershocks? There are always aftershocks. Wherever it was, it was big. The last time I experienced an earthquake whilst in Umbria was back in April 2009. Well, I only knew about the quake when I was woken by a telephone call from my sister. The call came through at about six in the morning, from the UK. If there were any rumblings around Case Colle, I'd slept through them. My deep sleep, the result of arriving late the night before, after what felt like a long drive from Pisa airport.

The earthquake causing my sister so much worry, was reported to have hit L'Aquila, a medium sized medieval town in the mountainous terrain of Abruzzo, a region nuzzling against the south east of Umbria. Confident that the quake can't have been that big, I'd simply turned over and gone back to sleep.

How wrong I was.

L' Apocalisse is the headline on the front page of La Nazione – Umbria, 7th April 2009. The paper going on to describe the power of the earthquake as, La notte dell'inferno Abruzzo devastato'. Apparently, the earthquake struck at 3.25 am, its epicentre registering a magnitude of 6.3. Images on TV looking like a war zone. The final number of deaths in and around L'Aquila totals 309 people, with around 1,600 injured and more than 60,000 buildings seriously damaged, including San Salvatore, the regional hospital. Over 67,000 are left homeless. A third are temporarily housed in hotels along the Adriatic coast, another third accommodated in almost 200 tents, whilst others find alternative accommodation with family, friends or elsewhere. Although L'Aquila, the capital of Abruzzo, took the main force of the earthquake, at least another 40 towns and villages were affected. In the village of Onna, a place with no more than 300 people, two thirds of the houses were destroyed, 40 villagers killed.

Unfortunately, Italy has a long and traumatic history of earthquakes. The position of the boot shaped peninsula sits where two large continental tectonic plates meet, the European and the African. Scattered around this area of the Mediterranean Sea are numerous micro-plates, shifting and squeezing. Compared with Northern Europe, the geology of Italy is relatively young. I guess you could say that the earth, the land, the hills and mountains that make Italy so enchanting are still growing.

Perhaps it shouldn't come as any real surprise if medieval structures collapse, it's extremely expensive to protect such buildings from the force of an earthquake. I guess it would be impossible to make them totally earthquake resistant. So, old buildings collapsing under the force of an earthquake is no great surprise, even though many of these were said to have had 'modifications' to make them earthquake resistant. More worrying is the number of more modern buildings, argued to be 'earthquake-proof', that fall victim to collapse.

Official enquiries, at government level, were quickly put together. Some found that corruption, mainly in the form of the misappropriation of earthquake funds, was not uncommon – money being 'directed away for some other use'. I guess the other major finding was widespread ignorance of effective anti-seismic building standards. Either those carrying out building work didn't really know what they were doing, and/or cheap materials were used to speed building and cut costs. The enquires also found that revisions made to building codes in 2006 had classified L'Aquila as being in a region of moderate seismic activity rather than one of high risk. Hence building practice did not have to be quite as stringent. Given the level of devastation from earthquakes in the past, it's hard to understand why. It could be argued that the level of destruction and the number of deaths resulting from the earthquake in Abruzzo was only in part a natural disaster, the catastrophe made worse than it may have been by human negligence.

August 2016, is this another big earthquake? Have any lessons been learnt from the quake in 2009?

Once out of bed, I'm quickly showered, dressed and outside eating breakfast. I've already had numerous messages from the UK asking if I'm safe, the same enquiry coming from friends in Italy. Messages keep coming through thick and fast, images of the quake already popping up on Facebook. Many of those in Italy are using a Facebook tool that lets others know that you're safe. The earthquake must have been big. I've already been in contact with my daughters and my sister in the UK.

Aldo greets me from over the fence and asks if I felt the earthquake last night. He confirms that the quake was big, with many people killed, many buildings destroyed. It happened quite early in the morning, near a place called Amatrice.

I go inside. Just like the earthquake in L'Aquila, only 40 kilometres away from Amatrice (25 miles), the news is full of devastation, bodies being dug from under the rubble of fallen buildings, people wandering around in total shock and disbelief. And just like L'Aquila, pictures, film, and commentary are of a war zone. The news tells us that seismologists had expected increased activity in the area at any time; but had not been able to predict exactly when. Unlike the earthquake in L'Aquila, there had been little seismic activity of any significance recorded. Although earthquake activity was expected, all were astonished by its strength. Houses and other buildings totally collapsed, others close to ruin with the contents of those who lived there on open view and scattered amongst the rubble covered streets, beds, bathtubs and furniture dangling precariously from upper floors. Interviews with survivors paint a picture of panic, sorrow, and pain. Rescue services clambering over broken buildings, dogs disappearing into nothing more than piles of rubble, searching for people. Crumbling buildings hampering those there to offer rescue.

We are told that the earthquake struck at 3.36 in the morning when most people were asleep, at a depth of approximately 6 kilometres. Another registering 4.8 in magnitude hitting the same area just a few hours later, and yet another of 5.5; these were the trains thundering below my house. For the next several hours almost 200 smaller aftershocks are registered following the initial quake, some making it hazardous for rescue workers, fortunately the majority not strong enough to be felt by those working tirelessly to save others. Towns and villages in the regions of Southern Umbria, Lazio and Marche suffered the most damage. They included Amatrice, Pescara del Tronto, Accumoli, and Amandola.

Sergio Pirozzi, the mayor of Amatrice, when interviewed:

'Amatrice is not here anymore, half the town is destroyed.'

The devastation includes the whole of the town's historic centre, much of it dating back to the Middle Ages. The clock on a 13th century bell tower stuck at 3.39, the time just a few minutes after the initial earthquake struck. Sergio Pirozzi, when asked how many people he thought were still trapped or dead under the debris, an impossible question to answer, he simply says, 'Molti, molti altri' (many, many others). Many of the buildings had supposedly been reinforced, in a very practical sense they should have been protected and therefore at least earthquake resistant.

Emergency services of every description, supported by many volunteers, work through both day and night in a desperate effort to find people still alive. A ten-year old girl is pulled from the rubble after being buried for almost 17 hours. Early estimates, as the search continued through the mangled wreckage of homes, put the number of dead at 241. By Wednesday evening, the head of the emergency unit for the Civil Defence Department, Immacolata Postiglione, states that over 1,000 people were expected to be placed in four camps being set up around the area. She goes on to say that an unknown number of tourists are still to be accounted for. Ambulances are filmed racing back and forth. For those who have died, a piazza in Amatrice is turned into a make-shift morgue.

Television crews continue to feed the news with images of complete devastation and interviews of despair. Luca Faccenda, 65 years of age, who has lost a cousin in the quake, says that he's never felt an earthquake like this.

'Walking around, seeing everything destroyed like this, it's terrible. Never in my life, at my age, did I expect to see something like this. It is impossible to comprehend.'

Heavy lifting equipment and bulldozers climb slowly along fractured roads. To add even more to the problems, landslides block roads and bridges are near to collapse. The village of Pescara del Tronto, close to Amatrice, is completely levelled to the ground by the quake. Bishop Giovanni D'Ercole, from Ascoli Piceno, perhaps best describes the scene.

'When I arrived at the break of day, I saw a destroyed village. The village screams of death.'

He looks into the camera, saying that he had blessed the bodies of two children who had been buried under the rubble. Other survivors from the area give vivid details of events. A male, aged 69, tells of his anguish.

'My sister and her husband are under the rubble. There is no sound from them. We are waiting for diggers, but they can't get up here. They managed to pull my sister's children out, they're in hospital now.'

Another local tells of her survival as the ceiling of her bedroom came crashing down.

'The whole ceiling fell but it did not hit me. I just managed to pull the pillow over my head – luckily, just my leg was injured.'

Tourists also tell of their experience.

Nick Mortimer, one of a family of nine, on holiday celebrating a 60th birthday in Amandola, describes the shock of the initial quake.

'The quake and at least one aftershock caused us to run out of the building in panic.'

Another tourist, just a few miles from Amatrice.

'I felt very strong shaking at about 3am, it went on for ages. Then it started again about half an hour or 45 minutes later. It was terrifying.'

As a result of criticism from the Italian media, the Italian Prime Minister, Matteo Renzi, is reported as saying that it was 'absurd' to think that Italy could build completely earthquake proof buildings. However, he also pledges that 50 million euro will be made available for reconstruction. Responding to anger about long delays in rebuilding after the L'Aquila earthquake, he states:

'Reconstruction is what will allow this community to live and to restart.'

The official number of deaths reported by the Protezione Civile (Civil Defence) eventually stands at 299. Amongst those killed are a small number of foreign tourists. Over 388 people are injured, with around 4,500 left homeless.

The little town of Amatrice is famous for its pecorino cheese and bacon and tomato pasta sauce, the sauce having the very slightest piccante kick. You find it on many menus throughout Italy, Spaghetti all'Amatriciana. In fact, at the time of the earthquake, many visitors had been attracted to the town for the annual Spaghetti all'Amatriciana Festival. The two-day event, that includes live music, theatre and dancing has been staged for over fifty years.

The state's response to the earthquakes in L'Aquila and Amatrice was immediate and overwhelming, almost placing the whole area on a war footing, the region flooded with resources, including material for temporary buildings to accommodate those unable to return home. But it feels like the state's response and policy, as is often the case with many governments, is driven by short term goals. Looking ahead it would appear that once people have been provided with housing, they can then be forgotten.

Following the L'Aquila earthquake, a satirical documentary film with the title Draquila: L'Italia che trema (Dracula: Italy Shakes), directed by Sabina Guzzanti, was released in May 2010. The film highlights what it regards as corruption and political ineptitude, caricaturing the then Prime Minister, Silvio Berlusconi (I told you he would keep coming up in my ramblings). The film was presented at the 2010 Cannes Film Festival, the festival being officially boycotted by the Italian government. The Italian Minister for Culture describing it as propaganda, even though she admitted having never seen it.

The L'Aquila earthquake and the Amatrice earthquake were officially graded as 'only' medium-powered seismic events and yet they still resulted in massive destruction and death. It throws up the question of how vulnerable Italy is. Understandably, the media and those directly affected regarded both as 'violent'.

English friends, who have had an agriturismo business close to Amandola for quite a number of years, would certainly describe the quake that struck the area as violent. Fortunately, they escaped without injury, but a number of buildings were so severely damaged that they were declared uninhabitable. In 2022, they were still waiting for notification that work on repairs could begin.

It feels like only a national disaster shakes up a government, only then is there something obvious done. Unfortunately, once the immediate disaster has passed, after some months and years, complacency and inaction sets in, well at least until the next disaster. It feels like the Italians are still waiting for the political elite to proactively recognise the vulnerability of many parts of the country and put in place long-term effective policies that will significantly reduce the destructive impact of earthquakes. Were any lessons acted upon from the L'Aquila quake? Amatrice suggests not.

From the end of August through to November 2016, central Italy rumbles to around 250 quakes and tremors. Fortunately, most of these don't have the strength of the quakes that hit Amatrice, the vast majority 'insignificant' in terms of people being aware they have even taken place. However, a few are powerful enough to yet again cause significant damage, with aftershocks inevitably keeping people on edge. The most notable quake coming on Sunday 30th of October, with the medieval centre of Norcia taking most of the damage; the quake having a magnitude of 6.6. Fresh damage also occurs in the towns and villages hit by the quakes in August.

On the Sunday, 30th of October, I'm in the bathroom going through the usual early morning ritual. I'm staying with friends, Evi and Luuk, a couple from the Netherlands, who rent a holiday home close to the village of Collemancio. The aroma of percolating espresso drifts through the house, mixed with the smell of freshly baked cornetti (croissants). It's a gentle, relaxed start to the day after an evening of drinks, food and laughter with UmbriAlien friends.

Evi calls from the kitchen, 'Graham, come and have a croissant whilst they're still warm', her call is mixed with the sudden, violent, rumbling and trembling of the house. I know it's another earthquake, my morning ablutions rapidly coming to an end. Leaving the bathroom, I find Evi and Luuk stood outside, some safe distance from the house.

There are nervous smiles between the three of us. That must have been big, the whole house shook. I'm the first to speak:

'I usually like my coffee stirred rather than shaken.'

'Well, the house is still standing; nothing has fallen off. I guess it's safe for us to go back inside and have a quiet breakfast.' Luuk responding with half a smile at my attempted joke.

And that's it, no more movement that we're aware of. The three of us breakfast together, trying to guess how close the quake was, how strong and questioning if it has caused any damage. This mixed in with how good the party was the evening before.

It does feel strange how, when you actually live in Italy, you become almost accepting of earthquakes. I guess it's accepting in much the same way that you know at times there will be really bad weather, at times forceful enough to cause destruction, even death. Is it the same acceptance of risk that you're prepared to accept each time you get into a car? I have to say that Italy's Civil Protection Agency, in combination with all of the emergency services is well rehearsed in responding quickly and professionally to such natural disasters. There's an obvious nervousness, even an understandable amount of fear (nervosismo/paura), but you don't constantly think about quakes. When they are big enough to make things move, they certainly make you stop, your heart beating just that little bit faster. Your body set to flight mode. So far I've been fortunate, the quakes that have either destroyed towns completely or resulted in significant damage, have simply rumbled below my part of Umbria doing little more than causing the house to momentarily dance.

As I'm driving home, there are reports about the quake on the radio. The beautiful medieval town of Norcia has suffered significant damage, news reports going on to say that this is the biggest earthquake in over 36 years. The quake hitting Amatrice, as you know, delivered well over two hundred deaths, how many will have lost their life in this one? The force of the quake radiated out to as far as Macerata to the north, Perugia to the north-west, again hitting Amatrice, just to the south. The beautiful little village of Castelluccio di Norcia, sitting on its hill, has also been severely damaged.

Earlier in the year, I stayed with my sister, Katherine and her husband, for a few days in the very centre of Norcia. We were able to leisurely explore the compact walled town, while sitting in the picturesque Piazza San Benedetto, having lunch and enjoying the warm June sun. Here we could see the Castellina, a fortress built in the 16th century, next to that the 14th century Basilica of San Benedetto. Close by, the Palazzo Communale, also from the 14th century. For two days we enjoyed exploring the almost traffic-free little lanes, sampling the sausages and meats from the area that are famous across the whole of Italy. Our last afternoon visiting the Piani di Castelluccio (Plains of Castelluccio) that stretch out below Monte Vettore. Thousands of visitors are attracted here at the end of May through to the end of early July, when Piano Grande (Large Plain) and Piano Piccolo (Small Plain) are absolutely smothered in a carpet of colour. The wild flowers (the fiorita) of all varieties, yellows, deep reds, purples and white, all of different shades, are spectacular. And then at one edge of the plain that stretches for over 8 kilometres (5 miles), set on a hill, is the tiny, picture-perfect village of Castelluccio di Norcia, not another building in view as far as the eye can see.

My sister calls me from the UK, having seen reports of the earthquake on the national news. She comments on how sad she feels, seeing places that she so recently visited in ruin.

News of the earthquake understandably dominates the news for a number of weeks. Although a tragedy for the victims and their families there are only three fatalities reported. The Basilica of San Benedetto is almost completely destroyed. As always reporters and cameras roam around the areas hit by the quake, feeding television channels and newspapers with graphic footage and eye witness interviews.

In comparison with the quake that hit Amatrice, people have been 'lucky'. Early into the process of recovery, the head of the National Civil Protection Agency said:

'About 20 people are injured. As far as people are concerned, the situation is positive, but many buildings are in a critical state in historic centres and there are problems with electricity and water supplies.'

Once some sense of stability has been achieved, questions are asked about rebuilding stone houses and medieval town centres that have stood for centuries. Will it be possible to maintain the region's style and heritage, the very features that attract so many visitors each year?

January 2017 records yet another disaster. On this occasion, a major avalanche on the Gran Sasso d'Italia massif in Abruzzo. The avalanche coming after four, relatively minor, earthquakes had struck the area, the weight of snow enough to completely bury and destroy Hotel Rigopiano. I hear of the incident the following day; news teams having arrived in the area almost at the same time as rescue teams. Although the earthquakes were less powerful than those in 2016, they were strong enough to worry guests and staff at the hotel, a number of guests apparently having decided to leave earlier than originally intended. However, heavy snow fall, more than three metres in places, had prevented anyone leaving. It was then that the avalanche struck, deep snow hampering rescue crews trying to reach the area, some having to travel over five miles with skis and snowshoes. In news reports, little of the hotel could still be seen, heavy snow continuing to fall. As rescue teams go about their work, it's reported that at least 30 people are missing, suspected to be buried. Estimates put the slide of snow at over 120,000 tones, ripping the hotel from its foundations. The final death count is 29, recorded as Italy's deadliest avalanche in over 100 years. The final few bodies not recovered until some weeks after the event. A further six people died as a result of the extreme weather, when a rescue helicopter crashed.

After investigations that lasted a number of years, in January 2022, 30 people faced a number of charges, including negligence, illegal construction and manslaughter. Those charged included representatives from the hotel, regional and government officials, a police chief, and some of those with responsibility for disaster prevention. At the time of writing, June 2022, legal proceedings were still ongoing.

Less than two years later, tragedy strikes Italy again. On this occasion, the deaths are not related to earthquakes. During a torrential rainstorm, a section of the Ponte Morandi (Morandi Bridge), in the city of Genoa, northern Italy, collapses. Almost 40 vehicles are reported to have fallen from the bridge. It's in the middle of the Italian main summer holiday, the 14th of August 2018. As you would expect, news channels not just from Italy, but from across the world, flock to the area. Dramatic images of the stricken bridge are displayed on screens and across the front page of newspapers. Eventually, 43 deaths are reported. On top of this, as many as 600 people are left homeless. And questions begin to be asked. Does Italy have a major problem?

Unfortunately, this is not the first bridge to collapse since I came to live in Italy. In October 2016, a bridge collapsed near Milan, completely crushing a car below. The collapse killing one person and injuring five. In March 2017 a bridge collapsed onto a stretch of motorway close to Ancona, a major coastal port on the Adriatic. It's a stretch of motorway I've driven along many times, passing under the bridge, on my way to the beautiful coastal town of Sirolo. Photographs in the media again show a car completely crushed. A married couple killed as a result of the collapse.

Italy is certainly a beautiful place to live, but earthquakes and the problematic state of the country's infrastructure certainly give a stark reminder of its fragility. After having said that, although Italy may be hit by earthquakes, it's certainly not alone when it comes to tragedy associated with human 'negligence'. On the 14 of June 2017, a fire destroyed much of a residential tower block in West London. The fire resulted in the death of 74 people, with more than 70 others injured. Cladding covering the outer skin of the building was quickly identified as the reason the fire had been able to spread with such intensity. Official inquiries still lumber on into 2023. I'm not going to go into any detail, other than to say that a catalogue of cost cutting, faulty materials, incompetence, deception and profit-making have been uncovered, all at the expense of any regard to safety.

As a result of the drive to maximise profit over safety, 'people were condemned to be suffocated, poisoned and burned to death.' Rowan Moore – Guardian Newspaper.

Initially the bridge collapse in Genoa was put down to structural weakness, the result of corrosion, the already weak bridge further damaged by a landslide. The bridge was actually undergoing maintenance work at the time of the collapse. Soon after the collapse Antonio Brencich, an expert in the use of reinforced concrete, described the bridge as 'a failure of engineering.' The Italian government quickly blamed Autostrada, the company operating the bridge. Talk of negligent homicide put forward as a possible outcome. Anger and blame flew around, all in the knowledge that there were bridges of a similar age (built in the 50s and 60s) all over Italy. Reports covering the Genoa bridge provided evidence that some parts had lacked any maintenance for at least 25 years.

In August 2020, Genoa's new motorway bridge is opened. And in early July 2022, it's announced that a number of people have been charged with a variety of offences related to the collapse of the bridge.

On May 23rd, 2021, a cable car crashes to the ground, resulting in 14 deaths, the cable car just five metres from the summit of Monte Mottarone, close to Lake

Maggiore in northern Italy. Investigators find that a cable had snapped, and the emergency brakes had failed. There was only one survivor, a five-year-old boy. Negligence and manslaughter charges have been brought against a number of individuals. This was Italy's worst cable car tragedy since a low-flying US military jet cut through the cable of car in the Dolomites, killing 20 people, in 1998.

If evidence were needed to show that deaths, either as a result of negligence, geology or climate, are not restricted to Italy, Germany suffers disastrous flooding in July 2021. There had been record rainfall across western Europe, causing a number of rivers to burst their banks. At least 243 people died in the floods, 196 of these deaths in Germany.

On July 4th, 2022, there are reports that at least seven people have been killed when caught in an avalanche sparked by the collapse of a glacier in the Italian Dolomites. Mario Draghi, Italy's Prime Minister, states that the incident was 'without doubt' linked to climate change. The eventual number found to have been killed by the avalanche, eleven.

To further confirm the impact of climate change, as if confirmation were required, Italy experiences the longest period of record high temperatures from May onwards. In Umbria, for example, from the end of May through to the end of July 2022, the time of writing, there had been just two days with rain. I've obviously experienced hot summers in Italy, at times temperatures of 40°C. But this is the longest, hottest, driest period I have ever known. Most plants in my garden and orto desperately struggling to survive, even the olive trees. By the end of June, it is officially recognised as the worst drought in over 70 years. The drought is so bad that concerns begin to grow about the Po River, Italy's longest waterway. Some experts fearing that sections could become completely dry. In Umbria, I don't think I have ever seen Lago Trasimeno so low. In early July the Italian government announces a state of national emergency, many regions and local authorities bringing in strict restrictions on the use of water. Fines for breaking the rules, ranging from €25 to €500, some towns and cities turning off public fountains.

As 2022 comes almost to its end, Italy suffers another disaster. Violent storms in Ischia, a small island close to Naples, trigger giant mud slides that crash into villages, destroying houses and carrying cars into the sea. This is not the first time for such an event. Between 2018 and 2021, there had been at least seventy landslides. Lack of preventative measures being taken, and illegal building over many years, are blamed for the scale of devastation. At the time of writing, at least 8 people had been found dead, with another 10 people missing.

Returning to deaths from earthquakes, what's to be done now and in the future in an attempt to reduce the numbers killed? Italy certainly can't stop earthquakes, it's inevitable that there will be more. But programmes and systems could be put in place to mitigate against their impact. The tragedy of Amatrice suggests that few lessons were learnt from the earlier quakes that hit the area in 2009. Does Italy just wait for the next and hope for the best?

Now this is just a suggestion, I'm certainly no structural engineer. I'm fine with a bit of DIY, but that's about as far as my 'technical expertise' goes. However, I do have a strong suspicion that concrete is not a great lover of earthquakes. I could perhaps be very simplistic in my thinking, but I suspect that concrete is very unwilling to be flexible and bend to the demands of a quake. And yet concrete is still the dominant material used in construction throughout Italy. There is massive financial investment in the production of cement. The country is still one of the top producers in the world. Italy must know that cement/concrete can't be good for its physical health. But, as with many parts of the world, there are those who are more than willing to place financial reward above risks to human life.

In the summer of 2021, I decided to drive down to the area struck by the earthquake of August 2016; I'd never been to Amatrice. What I found, after five years, was almost total devastation, very little of Amatrice still standing, some construction taking place to try and save particular buildings. Prefabricated structures had been erected, from which shops and other businesses were operating. Even a whole, wooden, prefabricated village had been built. All of this within sight of what was Amatrice. Travelling through the local countryside, I found village after village completely destroyed, in most, not one single building still standing. It looked like the aftermath of a military bombardment. What had been villages, now completely deserted, nature having already moved in. It really is a tragic and sad see, bringing tears to my eyes. Again, not that far away, prefabricated, wooden villages. At some point in the future some parts of

Amatrice may well be rebuilt, but I can't imagine that it will ever be the same as it had been. The villages are simply lost, left as piles of rubble.

So, the train that thundered below my house probably won't be the last. If you live in Italy it's something you have to accept. What I couldn't have expected in my most bizarre and wildest dreams, were the number of deaths that were to come to Italy and the rest of the world from 2020 onwards.

Romeo and Juliet

A lovestruck Romeo sang the streets a serenade
Laying everybody low with a love song
that he made
Finds a streetlight, steps out of the shade
Says something like,
'You and me babe, how about it?
. . . .

Mark Knopfler

CHAPTER NINE

Conkers in the Bedroom

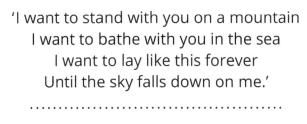

'I want to stand with you on a mountain
I want to bathe with you in the sea
I want to lay like this forever
Until the sky falls down on me.'

Savage Garden

I'm in a Chinese city, stood in the middle of a bank, with my hands on my head. From the far corner of the open floor of the bank, I have an automatic weapon pointing directly at me. The male with the gun is dressed in army green, his uniform includes a helmet and heavy black boots. He's obviously not pleased that I'm stood in only my t-shirt and shorts, perhaps it's the sandals that he finds offensive. But other than sandals, my feet are naked, no socks. He screams orders, in Chinese, his automatic weapon still pointing directly at me, his finger on the trigger. Another 'soldier', stood behind the counter of the bank, also screaming at me, he being the one who indicated that I should place my hands on my head. Trust me, at this split second in time I'm not going to complain about the bank's somewhat over assertive customer service. How will my daughters be informed of my death?

A young woman rushes out from behind the counter, first having to squeeze past the other 'soldier'. As she hurries towards me, a very worried look on her face, she speaks in very speedy, very polite Chinese, she's almost apologetic in manner. Still with my hands on my head (the 'soldier' with the automatic weapon still screaming), the words 'Bank closed' fall from my lips as a question. 'Yes, yes, bank closed', the young woman responds. Nothing more is said, apart from the screaming still coming from the gun pointing 'soldier'. With my hands still on my head, I walk backwards in the direction of the open door and my LIFE back out on the street. Parked in the road, what looks like an armoured security truck, yet another 'soldier' sat inside. Having now lowered my hands, I quickly walk away from the bank, attempting to make some sense of what just took place. The whole episode perhaps lasting less than thirty seconds. However long it was, time stood still. As I walk, in search of a more welcoming bank, I reflect on how calm I was. Possibly the shock and surprise left little opportunity for the adrenaline to kick in. Was my dress sense really so threatening? I just wanted to exchange money.

No, you haven't picked up the wrong book, it's still the one you were reading before about Italy. However, for three weeks I've left Umbria, I'll be back there, don't worry. The bank I walked into, with the screaming 'soldier', is in the city of Hangzhou, about 170 kilometres (110 miles) south of Shanghai. Why am I here? If you remember a few pages back, Aton, my dog, mentioned that I was in training. Lots of running up and down the hills of Umbria so that I would be fit enough to take part in the Great Wall of China Marathon. The marathon promoted by the Danish sports tour company as:

'The Great Wall Marathon – 5,164 STEPS INTO HISTORY.' The tour company going on to say: 'Since its inception in 1999, the Great Wall Marathon has become revered as one of the world's most challenging marathons.'

That's the reason I'm in China, having, on Saturday the 20th of May 2017, taken part in the marathon; an experience that will be forever carved into my memory. Three weeks that would see me first in the capital city of China, a city with an official population of over thirty million people, that's half the entire population of Italy. Beijing being my base for the marathon. From Beijing to Xi'an and the Terracotta Warriors, from there by sleeper train to Hangzhou. From Hangzhou, where I stood in a bank with my hands on my head, to Shanghai and my flight back to Italy.

After arriving at Beijing airport, I soon find the tour rep and the strangers I'll be spending time with for the next few days. These strangers coming from all parts of the world: Australia, the USA, Poland, Germany, Russia, the UK, Netherlands, the list goes on. Its whilst on the coach to the hotel that I get talking to an Australian couple, they're actually from the island of Tasmania. Charlie and Oliver must be in their late thirties, she's a reporter for a television station in

Hobart and he's a prosecution barrister. In the relatively short journey, we get to know quite a lot about each other, although it's only when we're stood at the hotel reception, waiting to book in, that I realise that they're actually very close friends rather than a couple. I think we already know that we're going to enjoy each other's company. It's these two that I spend most of my time with whilst in Beijing.

Before the day of the actual marathon, we're taken to a number other sites within a few hours of Beijing, including a visit to the Great Wall of China itself. It's our chance to see it as tourists rather than runners. Race officials telling us that it's a chance for us to mentally prepare for the challenge that awaits us on the day of the race. The day's temperature has already climbed to 30°C. It's forecast that on the day of the race the temperature will reach around 40°C, usually at this time of year the temperature hovers at about 27°C. Trust me to have chosen an unusually hot May.

Guidebooks will tell you that, 'hikes on sections of the wall are both spectacular and challenging'. Me being, some would say, foolhardy enough to run parts of it. One guide book describes the section of the wall that we intend to run up and down as, 'an extremely rewarding and impossibly steep section.' It's now 11am and the temperature has climbed above 35°C. The guidebook has it absolutely right, the climb is incredibly steep, up steps that vary in size and depth, perhaps a better way to describe them is that they vary in magnitude. There is absolutely no uniformity. Some of the steps are shallow, just big enough for your foot, whilst with others you take a couple of steps before literally having to stretch upwards with your leading leg to reach the next. Once up this first part, you come to wider sections of the wall that for a short time simply undulate before another challenging climb and then a drop. The downward sections are equally steep. Unknown to us on our 'tourist' visit, there are other sections of the wall, which will be part of our run, that I can only describe as idiotically steep.

The race organisers are expressing some concern about how hot it will be on race day. In all the years that the marathon has taken place, temperatures have never been this high. After some head scratching, the organisers decide that for the first time in the history of the race, those taking part in the full marathon can, at the half way point, decide to drop down to the half marathon if they are finding the heat too exhausting.

After another two days of simply being tourists, Saturday the 20th of May 2017 arrives. The challenge of running the Great Wall of China is upon us. Have I done enough training? Walking part of the wall on Thursday and knowing that the day's temperature is probably going to reach 40°C has put doubt in my mind. But I tell myself that I've always been a little nervous before the start of a long-distance race, always hoping that I've done enough training. Any doubts I may have had, always, in the end, being unfounded.

Over 2,500 runners, from more than 65 countries, crowd together for the start of the race. From elite runners, looking for fast times, to those who just hope to survive the experience. It's now 7.10am, race officials and local dignitaries on the stage welcoming people to the race, to China and the region. The officials placing importance on the need for all runners to ensure that they keep hydrated. They also explain again, because of the very unusual heat, those who have entered for the marathon distance can, at the half way point, drop down to the half marathon. I'm kitted up with energy gels, jelly babies, salt tablets and water. This is the first time, in any race, that I've bothered with anything other than water.

As race officials and dignitaries leave the stage, their place is taken by thirty or more New Zealanders. Over 2,500 runners stand, focused on the Haka, the ceremonial Māori challenge. The 'All Blacks' stand in lines, five or six in each, facing the assembled runners. There's a silence of expectation. One female New Zealander stands in front of the others, facing the crowd, explaining that this Haka is for all those who, reaching into the far distant past, gave their lives in building the Great Wall of China. History would have us believe that as many as 400,000 people died during its construction, with thousands of the dead said to be buried within the wall. I have no idea how true this is. Our New Zealander faces the mass of runners as she leads the rest of those on stage through the ceremonial challenge. I've seen the Haka on TV, but this is different. It feels as though we are absorbing the energy of those on the stage. All actions are done with force. The wide eyes of the New Zealanders looking directly into ours. Loud foot stamping and powerful arm gestures, tongue protrusions, forceful slaps on bodies, on legs and chests, with rhythmic movement accompanying loud chants. It is totally absorbing, the 2500 runners standing as one complete body. I find the experience incredibly moving, emotional, a feeling of pride running through my veins. I guess pride in being able to be part of this experience, and an awareness that I have the good fortune to still be fit enough to tackle such a challenge. The end of the Haka is greeted with rapturous applause, all are totally energised and enthusiastic to get started.

The temperature at 8am, already touching 30°C. As the heat of the sun beats down, runners spill out of the square in euphoric mood. Friends and relatives cheer people on, banners and flags waving, clapping and horns sounding. Before coming out to China, I'd watched clips of people taking part in previous Great Wall Marathons, at points, some even crawling up the steep climbs. That is not going to be me. I'm not going to have someone take a photograph of me crawling up steps. I'll be fine, we have 8 hours to complete the race.

The first few kilometres are relatively flat, running along a tarmacked road. Lots of happy, smiling runners, some exchanging greetings and encouragement as they pass. It's hot, but all feels good. Just take it steady. You have one simple aim; finish the race.

After another few kilometres, the road starts to twist and turn, climbing quite steeply. The steep climb brings us to the wall. It looks far more intimidating than it did on our tourist visit a few days earlier. Already there are very few who are actually running up the steps. I follow behind a multitude of coloured running vests, all bent forward, stretching with their leading leg to reach one step and then the next. I pass some, others pass me. One bottle of water is already empty. The climb is incredibly steep, the air dry and unbelievably hot. People, backs bent, stretching for the next step with their leading leg, placing a hand on each thigh. The trailing leg is pulled upwards, the next step is taken, hands on the thighs yet again. I manage this first climb without my legs needing a supporting hand. Eventually we come to a wide area, a gentler climb without steps, a guard tower ahead. Either side of the wall green undulating countryside and mountains. Another bottle of water consumed, a third poured over my head, body already saturated in sweat.

The guard tower offers a brief moment of shade, the chance to grab more water and have another bottle poured over me. It doesn't take long for the coolness to have evaporated. More steps to climb, just as uneven in size, just as unforgiving on thigh muscles. I'm starting to doubt myself. My legs are starting to feel like jelly. This has never happened before in a race. Another guard tower, this time I actually stop, swallowing almost a whole bottle of water in one go. You should have trained harder. You should have done far more hill running. You should have definitely built running up and down steps into your regime. There are plenty of places in Gubbio where you could have done this.

This is ridiculous Graham; you should have prepared better than this. Run with your legs! My mind wants to run. My heart wants to run. My legs are not so sure. You still have miles to cover. Another guard tower, more water swallowed, with even more poured over my head. Energy tablet being chewed. An incredibly steep descent made up of uneven steps. It feels like an almost vertical drop. This section of the race becoming a bottle neck. Groups of runners at a standstill, watching those in front slowly drop down the steps. There's little chance to be able to catch up on the slow progress and time taken when climbing up the steep sections of the wall. Without even being blocked by others in front, it would be incredibly difficult, unsafe, to attempt running down.

I now understand why this race is regarded as one of the most demanding marathons in the world. And I have done nowhere near enough training. I'm having an internal struggle with myself. An unforgiving heat of 40°C and next to no shade, multiplies the physical challenge. To tell the truth, I'm feeling incredibly disappointed. This was to be my last marathon. I have to complete it. I've never not completed a race. The massive, uneven steps of the wall feel to have drained my legs of energy. I'm actually stopping at all drink points, something I've never done before. My legs just don't want to continuing running. So, I run and walk. Run and walk. Run and walk. At the same time, psychologically beating myself up. Come on Graham, pull yourself together. You've come all the way to China for an adventure. It's an adventure that has to be enjoyed, otherwise what's the point of being here?

It becomes more than obvious that I'm not going to get back to where the race started before the cut off time that stops you continuing onto the wall again and completing the full length of the marathon. I come to terms with the fact that I'm not going to complete the entire race. I'll take the option offered by the organisers and drop down to the half marathon distance. Once I have this in my head, I decide that I'm simply going to jog along and enjoy myself. I'm going to enjoy what some running sites describe as 'the world's most picturesque endurance race.'

After feeling the 'burn' of each seemingly endless climb, the race now takes me through tiny rural villages with dirt roads and an endless supply of smiling faces. Children wanting to slap hands with you as you pass, stopping again and again to drink more water. Standing with those who live here so that they can take photographs of these mad people running through their streets. I get to the point where I have a choice. Do I continue with the entire marathon? I inform the race official that I'm dropping down to the half marathon distance.

The rest of my race is one of pure enjoyment. It's still incredibly hot and energy sapping, but I'm no longer chastising myself. This is so amazing; I'm seeing and experiencing parts of China that the vast majority of tourists never see. I stop yet again, exchanging the few jelly babies I have left for pieces of fruit held out in the hands of little children. More photographs and I jog on. Goats cross my path and solitary donkeys bake in the sun. Another group of smiling children, some running by my side; more water poured over my head.

At last, I'm on the tarmac road that will take me back into Yin &Yang square and the end of my race. Not that far to go. And the incredible thing about hitting the final few kilometres, your legs suddenly find that extra bit of energy. I'm smiling, waving to people as I pass. I turn from the road, entering through the gate that takes me into the square and the finish line. As I sprint to the line, I hear my race number and my name being called out over the speaker system. I've done it, medal round my neck. I may not have completed the whole marathon, but I can say I've run on the Great Wall of China. It's been the toughest race that I've ever taken part in.

The winner of the marathon in 2017 takes just over three hours and fourteen minutes to complete the whole race. Most marathons around the world are won with times only a little over two hours. Perhaps the difference in finishing times gives you some indication of the magnitude of the challenge. Those in the know, the really hardened marathon runners, have been quoted as saying:

'You can't win the wall, but you can lose on the wall. You can't really push yourself. If you start pushing yourself, the unrelenting incline will get to you later.'

The wall definitely punished me.

It's soon announced that presentations are about to take place. As I stand watching the medals and awards being given to the top male and female athletes, I'm getting an incredible number of texts from friends and relatives, all congratulating me on my performance, many saying that I'm far too modest. On finishing my race, I'd sent a couple messages saying that I was sorry I'd let down the many who had sponsored me (all of the money raised going to Breast Cancer Research), I'd only managed to complete half the distance. I keep getting messages saying that I'd run a fantastic, incredible race. Some of the messages coming through saying that I'd finished in 9th place for the whole marathon. Now unless I had been totally disorientated, hallucinating, feverish and delusional, I'm very confident in knowing that I only completed the half marathon distance.

My daughter, Kara, sends the results for the first 50 full marathon runners to have crossed the finishing line. And sure enough, the official results have me finishing the full marathon in 9th place! Now if this were true, I would have just become international news. Anyone with just a very basic knowledge of athletics would realise that this has to be a mistake. For someone at the age of 61 to finish in 9th place would have to be a genetic, biological and physiological miracle. But for a while I play along with this fiction, simply accepting, with humble modesty, my incredible, no, my outstanding sporting achievement. It's only when I get back to my hotel in Beijing that I explain to all the reality of the events that have taken place. Clearly, when I reached the half way point and informed the official that I was going to drop down to the half marathon distance, this information must have been lost in the system. But, for almost 24 hours I remain officially in 9th place. What a shame it is that you get nothing for coming 9th.

The following morning, as I go down for breakfast, I bump into Victor, a rep from the Danish tour company. I have to come clean, informing him that a mistake had been made. He needs to inform the race officials that I only completed the half marathon distance. By the afternoon of the same day, Graham Hofmann's name is no longer in 9th place, he's become just another runner.

On leaving Beijing, I travel by bullet train to the city of Xi'an to see the Terracotta Warriors. From Xian, I then take the sleeper train to Hangzhou, where I spend my final few days in a quiet, peaceful area close to the city. I've only experienced a very small part of this vast country. The adventure that was the Great Wall Marathon, totally unforgettable. In fact, the whole experience of being in China unforgettable, totally different to any country I had ever visited before.

After a flight of eighteen hours, including one stop over, I'm back in Italy. Told you I was coming back.

Whilst I've been away, Aton has been a guest dog, staying with Giselle and Mark who live between Montefalco and Trevi. So that's where I head for from Rome, being met by Mark at Foligno station. If you remember we first met through UmbriAliens. They have two dogs, Stella and DJ. In return, there will be times when I take care of their dogs and look after the house. Stella is about the size of a small Labrador, but apart from relative size that's about the only connection. She has a coat of thick, dark ginger hair, covering the whole of her body and hanging over her eyes. The best way I can describe her is that she has a distinct similarity to Chewbacca from Star Wars but walking on four legs rather than two. She acts as the big sister to little DJ, a short haired, white dog, perhaps just a little bigger than a Jack Russell. Both dogs are incredibly friendly, something that Aton eventually accepts after his initial agitation. You'll recall me saying that he has a bad habit of wanting to have a go at bigger dogs. But there's been no problem. All has been fine; he's willingly accepted being adopted by the other two.

This has been the longest time all three have been together. In the past I've gone over a number of times, the six of us going walking in the local area. Each dog has its very own particular characteristic. Stella's is to slide into water-filled drainage ditches and wallow in the mud. DJ is the good little boy, running ahead just a little, checking and then scampering back; at times flying over large bales of straw. In the company of the other two, Aton misbehaves, constantly pulling on his lead. When it's just the two of us he will walk at my side. I'm sure he knows that in the company of others he's less likely to be chastised. Once released from his lead he runs with the other two. The difference is, after a short distance, they stop and return, Aton just keeps on running and running and running. Eventually he disappears from view. Stella and DJ simply stand looking bewildered, looking first in the direction of Aton's disappearance, and then looking back to us, quizzical expressions on their faces:

'What the hell is he doing? Is he allowed to do that? What's wrong with him?'

Aton occasionally appears in the distance. We call, he totally ignores the calls, reappearing at some other spot. Eventually he returns, Stella and DJ asking, 'Where the hell have you been?'

The following weeks are spent cleaning up the garden, Aldo having kept an eye on my veg plot and caring for my hens. I think Paola has at last forgiven me for missing the most important event of the whole Umbrian year, the Ceri in Gubbio. It's a warm late spring, a beautiful time to be in Umbria. The days move into late June, the land green and bursting with life. A time for long walks in the mountains, visits to the coast and Italian meals with my neighbours. It feels so good to be back in Umbria.

As July moves into the first week of August, I get a long Facebook message from my friend, Martina's cousin (cugina). She asks how I am, did I enjoy China? Have I kept in contact with Martina? Hope you remember, I met Martina in Florence. Other than the occasional like of something posted on Facebook, we haven't been in contact. Why have you not kept in contact, she likes you? I thought you liked her. This is true, I did like her when we met in Florence, but not sure at all if she had a similar view of me. No, honestly she likes you. Give her a call, get together again. Is she just trying to matchmake, finding more than there really is to find?

I leave it a few weeks before I message Martina to let her know that I'll soon be travelling to the UK. My drive almost takes me past where you live, it would be good to meet again. If I book into a hotel, we could meet for a couple of days, giving us the chance to get to know more about each other. I'm really not sure how she is going to respond. Will she be interested in meeting?

I don't have to wait long. The next day I get a message back. Yes, call on your way, it will be good to see you again. I call her. We have a long conversation, Martina insisting that I don't have to book a hotel, you can stay with us, we have plenty of space. Brilliant, couldn't be better. Could I now be reading far more into this than there is? The conversation ends with me checking that she does know I have a dog; he will be travelling with me. Another week passes, several more messages are exchanged, and I start my journey north. I'll pass through Switzerland, then stopping for a few days near Koblenz in Germany, with relatives, before making the final part of the journey to the UK.

Aton is more than happy for me to do all the driving, to be his chauffeur, whilst he spends most of the road trip asleep in the back. When I say in the back, he's actually bedded down in a large cage. Technically, in Italy, if you have a dog in your car, the animal has to be safe and secured. Whisper when you use the term 'animal', I'm not sure that Aton knows he is one. He loves being in the car, being driven around. He never has to be cajoled, bribed with treats. If the car is open, he will gladly jump in. In fact, if any car door is open, he will jump in. He appears to have absolutely no regard for who may be owner of the vehicle. I'm sure there will be a day when a friend has visited, then driving away, only to arrive home and find Aton fast asleep on the back seat. On the long journey, we obviously stop a number of times for Aton to have a comfort break, a little run around. I ask if he'll take over the driving whilst I sleep. But as soon as I've opened the back of the car, he's jumped in. He sits there, looking at me. His face simply saying, what are you standing around for? You know what you have to do, get driving.

Eventually we arrive at Martina's place. She gives both of us a very warm welcome, again insisting that I stay with her and Sophia. You remember Sophia, Martina's daughter. Out of the two, it's Sophia who is smitten with Aton and his doggy eyes. That evening, the three of us enjoy an excellent meal cooked by Martina, a pasta dish. When I say we three, I'm referring to the three humans. Aton has now reluctantly accepted that he will never be allowed near the table when humans are eating. He sits at the other end of the room, looking mournful, hoping for some attention. With our meal finished, his doggy eyes win. He scampers over to Sophia; he knows who is the soft one between the three of us. After a little persuasion from Sophia, Martina agrees that Aton can sleep in her room. But not on your bed, he has to sleep on the floor.

And with the promise made by Sophia, the two of them disappear to her room. I'm just hoping he doesn't decide to pee whilst he's up there. I don't think Martina would be impressed.

With Sophia and Aton safely tucked away, we settle down to another glass of red wine. Martina sat at one end of the sofa (couch, settee, I don't mind, your choice), me sat at the other. We're incredibly relaxed in each other's company, laughter and jokes pass easily between us. We continually smile at each other. I want to move closer, but I don't. I want to kiss her, but I don't. There are any number of moments when eye contact lingers just that few seconds longer. A few seconds of incredible intimacy, making your pulse race just that little bit faster.

The time is already creeping towards two in the morning. Martina shows me my room, her room just across the small landing. We say goodnight. It's a small room, with a single bed. I guess you could call it 'a spare room'. A room that's also used as an office. I fall into bed, happy and content, my mind sifting through all the bits of conversation. I'm totally convinced that there is something between us, but will anything come of it? As I reach to turn out the light, I notice what looks like a conker, on the floor, close to the door. I get out of bed to investigate. Yes, it's definitely a conker. I place it back where it was, then noticing another conker in the far corner of the room. Strange. I climb back into bed, deciding I won't say anything about the conkers.

After having given Aton the chance to do what he needs to do, I breakfast with Martina, coffee and a pastry. Again, the atmosphere between us is warm and relaxed. It's decided that the three of us will go for a long walk, this giving Martina the chance to show me the local area. Just like Case Colle, the place where Martina lives is relatively rural. Perhaps not as rural as Colpalombo, and without the mountains, but still having plenty of countryside. So that's how we spend the bigger part of the day. Aton doing what he does when in the company of others, pulling on his lead.

That evening the two of us, Martina and myself, go for a meal in the local town. Aton will be left with Sophia. She's more than happy with this, almost begging to have time alone with him. We enjoy the warm company of the other. The food is good, the Prosecco sparkling and sweet. After returning to the house, we again sit to the early hours talking and laughing. Whilst having our meal, I've invited Martina to come and stay with me. Come and stay for a week in Case Colle. She responds by saying the two of them would love to come. They've never been to Umbria. That's fine, I don't mind if Sophia also comes along. In my head I'm thinking, no, really, I don't mind; well, not much.

The next morning, I leave to continue my journey. Aton refusing point-blank to do any of the driving. I check, just to make sure, that Martina and Sophia are coming to stay with me. We've agreed on the end of September going into October, this will allow us to celebrate Martina's birthday. They have friends in Cortona, the beautiful hilltop town sitting on the very edge of Tuscany before that region tumbles into Umbria. Also, they have friends in Viterbo, just to the south of Umbria, in the region of Lazio. It's strange how close they have come to Umbria, but never having spent any time in the region.

We give each other warm embraces, Sophia giving Aton one last cuddle. Just before I leave the house, I turn, almost standing face-to-face with Martina. We really couldn't be stood any closer. I'm looking directly into her eyes. A quick, gentle kiss passes from my lips to hers. It's a quick, impulsive kiss from me, nothing more. With Sophia standing directly to the back of Martina, I judge that one quick kiss is probably enough. Aton eagerly jumps into the back of the car. One last wave, Aton already having made himself comfortable, we drive away.

The next two weeks I spend with my daughters in the UK, visiting my sister and a few friends in and around Yorkshire. It's during this couple of weeks, that Lucy's neighbour said I'd done the right thing moving to Italy, 'too many foreigners in the UK'. Also, the time when my friends pointed out to me that much of my body language had definitely taken on an Italian slant.

By the end of August, I'm back in Italy. I've had an invite from Charlie and Oliver for me to fly out and visit them in Tasmania. We've kept in sporadic contact via Facebook since leaving China. They add that they're intending to take part in the Point to Pinnacle race on the 19th of November in Hobart, the city where they both live. Should I go? Australia will be enjoying spring weather, just as Italy is moving into winter. The whole point of me selling my house in the UK was to give me the money to travel. They're making the offer for me to stay with them. I may not get an invitation again. I've decided, I'm going to accept their kind offer. I'll spend a week in Tasmania and a couple of weeks on the mainland. I soon send a message back, yes, I'm coming! I get an enthusiastic reply from them, adding that they will enter me for the half marathon race – the Point to Pinnacle. Half marathon should be no problem, I've kept my training up since coming back from China. Nothing, I mean absolutely nothing, can be as hard as the Great Wall Marathon.

It's the final week of September. Contact between myself and Martina has been regular, but nothing more than general chat via social media. Martina and her daughter will be arriving in Perugia midmorning, Saturday, where I'll collect them and drive back to Case Colle. The journey from my house and back only sixty minutes; Prosecco and cannoli waiting at the house. Unlike my failed attempt to act as a 'tour guide' in Florence, this time I have to make a good or at least passible impression. Aton looks up from his bed, his face suggesting that he's not so sure I'll come up to scratch; then scratching parts of his anatomy that should be left until he's alone and private.

I'm excited. Will I feel the same about Martina when I visited her for just two short days? More importantly, how will she feel about me? Big smiles and hugs are given and received when we meet, followed by questions from me about their journey. Questions from Sophia about Aton. Soon at the house, I show them their respective rooms and then we sit outside in the warm Umbrian sun. Prosecco from the fridge and delicious cannoli (well I think they're delicious). Martina and Sophia have obviously had cannoli before, both agreeing that they love them. For a time, we simply sit and chat, Sophia almost smothering Aton with attention. Leaving Sophia and Aton in the garden, I go for a short walk with Martina, showing her round the little hamlet of Case Colle. Our chat, just as it was when I stayed at her place, relaxed and warm.

That evening we have a meal that I'd prepared before collecting them. Prosecco, followed by wine, has all three of us totally relaxed and uninhibited. Aton looks up from his bed. I can tell from his eyes that he's judging my performance. He's also hoping that he will be rewarded for his good behaviour by being allowed to sleep in the same bedroom as his new friend, Sophia. The evening moves to espresso. Candlelight flickers. Just one more glass of red wine. Sophia has had enough, disappearing to her room, Aton scampering up the stairs ahead of her. At last, I'm left alone with Martina. Yes, I know I should. We do, we kiss. It's a very gentle kiss. A kiss stolen between washing the dishes.

The following days are taken by visits to Gubbio and Montone. This time my tour guiding doesn't come unstuck. There's no excuse if it did, I've known the area long enough. Whilst in the town, we do all the things you do in Gubbio. Walk along its medieval stone streets, sit outside its bars in the sun, and travel in the birdcages of the Funivia to visit Sant'Ubaldo at the top of Monte Ingino. Having done that, sitting outside one of the two bars that give magnificent views over the whole of the town below.

The next day we visit Perugia, where I take them to La Pasticceria Sandri on Corso Pietro Vannucci. A tiny pastry and coffee shop that has been serving customers since 1860. Just standing outside, looking at the delicious window display, will have you drooling; rich, chocolate covered cakes and assorted candies tempting you to enter. There are places a little less expensive to have a coffee in Perugia, but the choices being offered, and the style of the place makes up for the little extra cost. The narrow space only allows a few places to sit inside, most people enjoying their drink, pastry or sandwich, at tables outside on the main medieval thoroughfare of the city. Although small, the inside has a beautifully frescoed, vaulted ceiling and walls of walnut wood. The three of us have rich, thick, hot chocolate. And we're lucky enough to be able to find space to sit inside.

After spending some time exploring the medieval heart of Perugia we drive to Castiglione del Lago and Lago Trasimeno. You already know that Trasimeno is one of my favourite places in Umbria. The four of us walk along the shore of the lake, before we take the short walk up to Castiglione. Here we do what everyone does, tempted into the many small shops selling every type of gastronomic delight.

It's the final night of their stay. We sit having a meal at the oak table in my kitchen. Aton disturbing the scene by snoring from his bed in the corner of the room. Conversation between the three of us, as always, is light-hearted and relaxed. More red wine is drunk. It's not long before we've arrived at espresso, Aton following Sophia to her room and, most probably, her bed. Just the two of us again. We sip on the last drops of red wine. The candles flicker, intense emotion dancing between the flames. We kiss. We hold the other close. Her fingers touch my lips. We retire to bed for the night. The dishes can wait.

The following morning, we breakfast relatively early. The drive to Perugia is short. We kiss, we embrace. We've already agreed that we'll spend New Year's

Eve together. One last embrace, we wave goodbye, the two of them disappearing as I turn and walk away.

DOWN UNDER

After no more than a few weeks I leave Italy, taking a number of flights to Australia. During my time there, I explore areas close to Brisbane before spending almost a week driving along Bruce Highway, stopping at a number of places along the coast of Queensland. Along the journey I step onto beaches that have clearly been plucked directly from paradise. The beaches fringed with large palm trees that lean out towards the sea. And it's whilst I'm stood with my bare feet on the hot sand, breathing in paradise, that I come to the conclusion that if God does exist, he must have a very macabre sense of humour.

DANGER! STINGING JELLYFISH. DANGER! SHARKS. DANGER! CROCODILES

He's created paradise and then stocked it with things that want to KILL ME!

On one such beach, I stand looking out to a vast ocean, a crystal-clear sea that I can't go in. That's not entirely true. There is an area protected by what I assume to be metal netting, an area where it is 'safe' to swim. Have the stinging jellyfish, crocodiles and sharks been told that they're not allowed in there? Have they been told that it's a playpen for humans only? There are just two humans in the playpen. A female lifeguard sits watching the two humans as they play. I approach the lifeguard.

'Afternoon. What a beautiful place. I was expecting sharks and possibly jellyfish. But I never expected crocodiles. Is there really a danger from crocodiles in the sea?'

She looks down from her perch, leaning to one side to speak to me.

'Afternoon. Yes, that is possible. Saltwater crocodiles come out of river estuaries and into the sea. It's very unlikely you will see one. Even more unlikely that you will be attacked by one. But we have to be careful, that's why we have the signs warning of the danger.'

From the beautiful beaches of Queensland, with things in the sea that want to kill me, I take a flight from Cairns to Sydney and from there a flight to Hobart in Tasmania.

I spend my first few days exploring Hobart, Charlie and Oliver acting as my guides. For a city, Hobart is relatively small, its main attractions found around the harbour, made up of docks and warehouses that were once used for whaling. Now the warehouses have been taken over by boutique shops, arts and craft galleries, restaurants, cafes and bars. A thriving fishing fleet still occupies one dock (no whalers), the other dock taken by yachts and craft that take you out for cruises to islands nearby or along the Derwent River. Once you walk away from the harbour, you're in the city centre, a mix of modern, Georgian and Victorian architecture. Although Hobart is a city, it has a relaxed charm, the suburbs that spread out are low rise, many areas having a village feel. Charlie has a modest place that offers great views of the bay below.

Sunday morning finds the three of us, with hundreds of other runners, waiting for the start of the race. From Hobart waterfront, we're going to climb an almost constant gradient to the very top of Mt Wellington (its Aboriginal/indigenous name being Kunanyi), its summit at a height of 1271 metres. I knew that the race was touted as one of the world's toughest half marathons. It's only now that I realise why. I'd foolishly assumed that the first half of the race would be the climb, then we would turn, the second half all being downhill. No, the whole race, just over 21 kilometres (13 miles), is one constant climb. On reaching the top, you are then bussed back down to where you started. Look for the positives, there are no steps. The race promoters go on to describe the race as, 'The Vertical Challenge'. There is no exaggeration in the description.

BANG! The front of the race is on its way. We're in the crowd of runners slowly advancing. It takes a little time before there is space for us to get into our stride. We feel invigorated, excited to be part of the event, chatting as we jog along. For the first few kilometres the run is relatively flat and easy. It's really only as we start the climb proper, that the runners start to spread out. We're still laughing and joking, exchanging comments and waves to the crowds lining the route. The sound of bagpipes spur us on as we take another steep bend in the road. Did I say it was unusually hot? Nothing like the heat in China. But at 30°C, still hot for a half marathon. Although the number of houses are now thinning out, we still enjoy the pleasure of jogging through the spray from garden hose pipes. The cold water is so unbelievably refreshing.

From the very start of the race, we had agreed that we would stay together, simply enjoy the day, no concerns about completing the challenge in a certain time. The higher we climb, the more spectacular the views become. But it's a hard climb. Charlie and Oliver are in favour of walking, they're not going to find any argument against this from me. So that's what we do. We walk and laugh, exchanging chat with spectators along the route. As we continue our climb, a rather good-looking, male, police motorcyclist pulls over to check how the three of us are doing. Brief chat and smiles are exchanged, both Charlie and Oliver claiming ownership of 'the hunk in uniform'.

The last 7 kilometres of the race feels unrelentingly steep. Although I'd said that we'd agreed to stay together, the closer we get to the finish, the more I feel the need to speed up. I'm now trying to put a little more pace into my stride, basically power walking. Head up and arms pumping. I assume Charlie and Oliver are just a short distance behind, they can't be that far. I occasionally look back. They must be hidden from view by the bends in the road. Head up, I plough on. I'm not going to be asked to pull out of the race by missing the cut off time.

It's a stunning view at the top of Mount Wellington. I chat with others who have finished, exchanging comments about the experience, about the hot weather. A few people telling me that there have been years when the end of the race has been covered in a dusting of snow. But not today, the weather is glorious. I've come from 2 metres above sea level, at the start of the race, to 1271 metres at the finish, and, surprisingly, I'm feeling quite good. A race that's advertised as physically challenging and scenically stunning, has more than lived up to its billing. Out of any races I've ever taken part in, only the Great Wall would better this. Having collected my finisher's medal and more water, I stand around for a while waiting for Charlie and Oliver. Still no sign of them, I walk a few hundred metres back down the course. They can't have been that far behind. Eventually I have to take one of the buses transporting runners back to where we started the race. Still hoping I'll spot the two of them; my transport eventually arriving at the harbourside in Hobart.

I find the shade of a small tree, the grassed area close to the quayside. It's a beautiful day. I've tried to contact the two of them, but without response. What could have possibly gone wrong? Eventually, after probably twenty minutes, I receive a call from Charlie. We agree that they'll meet me under my little tree. They walk towards me, both looking fine, smiles on each face. Apparently, with just a couple of kilometres to go, they were stopped by race officials and told that they had missed the cut off time; they must stop, board a bus, and return to the start. Although physically fine, they're incredibly disappointed. All that hard effort, and just a few kilometres to go, but no reward of a finisher's medal.

After collecting a hire car, I spend the next few days exploring Tasmania. The island has everything, mountains, dense forest, beautiful villages, history, wildlife that, in the main, is not threatening, and, to top all of this, empty, deserted beaches washed by azure seas. It feels like I'm a castaway, a Robinson Crusoe, totally alone in my very own paradise. I have warm white sand and sea all to myself. If by chance I do happen to spot another human, I want to call out: 'Get off my beach!'

My final evening in Hobart I'm at a party, celebrating Charlie's 40th birthday. It's a great evening, full of fun, laughter and drinking. The next day I leave Tasmania, my flight taking me to Sidney. Before I leave, insisting that Charlie and Oliver visit me in Umbria.

I have just seven more days in Australia. For the first three, I stay to the west of the city centre of Sydney, an inner-city suburb called Newtown. My final four days spent close to Bondi Beach.

I spend my days exploring Circular Quay and the main sites of Sydney. Including the Opera House and Sydney Harbour Bridge. And doing what I always like doing, people watching. On one of the days, I take the ferry over to Manly. Although only a short journey from Sydney, Manly has a quiet, village feel about it. I stroll around, passing surf shops, bakeries, restaurants and bars, before settling down for a coffee and pastry. With coffee and pastry inside, I set out on the most idyllic walk. And that's all I do for the entire day, passing small pristine beaches and coves. At times stopping to sit and take in the spectacular views towards Sydney. I dip into the calm waters for a swim and to snorkel, warm sun on my back and aquarium below. For rest of the day, I amble along, with lizards regularly crossing my path. Every so often dipping into the water and then stretching out on the sand to dry. A tranquil, unforgettable day. Palm trees fringing beaches, subtropical forest, birds with the most amazing colours, and chunky lizards.

The final few days in Australia are spent in an apartment close to Bronte Beach, a place not that far from Bondi. I spend the day relaxing on the beach, having a few drinks in the cafes along the beachfront. I have no intention of entering the water as an item on a shark's menu. I explore Coogee Beach and Clovelly Beach, with Coogee definitely being my favourite.

I'd travelled over 16,000 kilometres (10,000 miles) to reach Australia; with flight changes, the time taken, just over 24 hours. And on my penultimate day, I wake early in the morning feeling absolutely awful. My body aching, headache, first hot and then cold, a feeling of total fatigue. I know there will be some of you reading this and perhaps thinking, it's just a touch of man flu, get over it. Could my body not have at least waited until I was back in Umbria? After dragging myself to the nearest pharmacy, I return to my bed for the rest of the day, drugs circulating around my system in the hope of some relief. Plenty of fluids, absolutely no appetite, that's all I have to report about the day and evening. Following a restless night, the next day is much the same. My final day in Australia spent almost entirely in bed.

On the day of my return to Italy, my body has recovered a little. But I'm certainly not feeling good. And I'm definitely not looking forward to the long journey back. Taxi to the airport and eventually boarding begins for the flight that will take me to Doha, Qatar. I'm fairly certain that if I'd been making the journey during the Covid pandemic, I would not have been allowed to board the flight. Obviously at the point when you're reading this, I'm hoping that Covid is behind us or, at least, caged and under control. Anyway, my next flight takes me to Amsterdam and then a flight to Rome.

Looking back at news reports from the time, I find that Australia had been hit by the worst flu outbreak on record in 2017 (Aussie Flu). With reports stating that the outbreak had been the deadliest experienced by Australia in the last quarter of a century. We all know now that something on an absolutely unimaginable scale was to hit the entire world in 2020.

Giselle and Mark have been good enough to have Aton as a house guest again, with Mark once more collecting me from the station in Foligno. I think I'll have a good deal of house and dog sitting to do in return.

CHRISTMAS

After a week at home in Umbria, I'm fully recovered and on my way to spend Christmas with my daughters in the UK. After a few festive days with Kara and Lucy, I take the train from Leeds in West Yorkshire to Birmingham in the West Midlands. It's been agreed that I'll meet Martina at the station. So, early afternoon I'm stood above the electronic display screens showing arrivals and departures, looking down on the wide esplanade of New Street station, with its bars and places to eat. This is our agreed meeting place, on the wide balcony, just above the screens. I'm quite nervous. It's over two months since our time together in Umbria. We've kept in regular contact, messaging each day, speaking a couple of times each week. But how will Martina be feeling about the relationship? I suppose I'm also asking if I will feel the same when I see her. My nervous anticipation doesn't have to wait too long, I spot Martina below, close to one of the places to eat. I message her to say she should stay where she is, I'm stood above the electronic displays. She looks up, smiles and waves. Within less than a minute, we're stood facing each other.

Martina has booked a room in a city centre hotel, just a short walk from the station. That's where we enjoy a meal and spend the evening. The feeling and emotion between us, just as strong. There was absolutely no need for me to have been nervous. The following day we walk along the canals that cut through the city. Some suggest that Birmingham has more canals than Venice. I have no idea if this is true. We visit the Library of Birmingham, quite a spectacular place, and we have lunch in a traditional British pub.

Late afternoon, we take the short journey by train to the town where Martina and Sophia live. Sorry, did I not say? Martina is English. She lives with Sophia, close to a small town about 30 miles from the centre of Birmingham. I know, I should have said earlier. I'm here for a few days. We're spending New Year's Eve together, before I fly back to Italy.

As before, we chat and talk and chat some more. It feels like everything is included, there appear to be no hidden shadows. Welcoming in the new year is a relatively quiet affair, just the two of us in the house, Sophia having gone into town with friends. We kiss and welcome the exciting promise ahead. And then there are the conkers. No, I'd not forgotten about them. There are a few on the carpeted floor of Matina's bedroom. Each one almost hidden away in a corner of the room. I have to ask why?

I'm told that they are there to try and keep spiders away. Apparently, spiders are said to have a morbid fear of horse chestnuts. That's the reason for a couple of conkers in each room. No, I'd not heard of this before either. The thinking is that conkers contain a chemical that spiders don't like. I have absolutely no idea if this is true. But it has to be said, during my stay, I didn't see any spiders in the house. We drift into 2018, spider free. Sure, that there will be no spiders in our dreams. I'm also sure that I have fallen in love with this woman.

My stay is all too brief, just a few days. We walk around the local area, visiting the local pub in the village and a few of the bars in the town. Before I return to my daughters in Yorkshire and then the flight back to Italy, words of love slip from my lips. They escape before I've had chance to retrieve them. How will Martina respond? Should I have kept the thoughts, the emotion hidden inside? Will my words make her back away from this man who appears to be getting quite serious? I have no need for such concern and doubt. Martina responds with similar words. Plans are made for Martina to fly out to Italy mid-February, spending a week at my place in Umbria.

Glorious Umbria

It has been said that Tuscany is the land of form,
while Umbria represents the glorification of the line:
the profile of softly undulating mountains, of olive
groves and vineyards silhouetted on the slopes, of
rows of poplars, maples and elms along the course of
sparkling, meandering rivers.

. . . .

Pietro Lanzara

CHAPTER TEN

Quattro Stagioni
A Year in Umbria

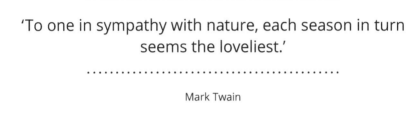

'To one in sympathy with nature, each season in turn
seems the loveliest.'

Mark Twain

INVERNO

I guess we automatically think of winter being the end of the year, short days,
long nights, icy winds, the threat of snow. But who sets the rules? So, I thought
I'd be different, just because I can. I've decided to start the year in Umbria with
winter. I mean, that's the reality; a new year starts with the weather still in
winter. I'm doing this because when most people think of Italy, they think of hot
summers, fields of sunflowers, blue skies, crystal clear seas, wine enjoyed in the
shade of olive trees, long lunches followed by an even longer siesta. Cicadas
(Cicale) providing a chorus, small lizards scurrying past, speedy Italian voices –
'Ciao Bella!'

Luigi Barzini in his book, The Italians, talks about foreign tourists being captured,
entrapped, by Italy's summer display, Italy's summer finery.

So, I'm starting with what most tourists never see. Those hooked on skiing see
Italian winters in the Alps and the Dolomites, but it's still an Italy for tourists,
fields of sunflowers exchanged for snow-covered mountains.

It's January 2017, and, as you would expect, it is cold. On this one particular
morning, it's exceptionally cold. Cold enough for the marrow to freeze in your
bones. There had been a reasonable amount of snow the previous week, enough
for the road passing Case Colle to need clearing by a snow plough, actually a

tractor with a plough on the front. But now most of the snow is on the higher mountains that can be seen from my garden, the road a little icy but clear. In fact, just last week I'd been walking on Monte Cucco with Aton, the snow up there, fresh, pristine white and deep. A cold, frosty, snow-covered land. An icy wind biting at your ears and nose, holding you just that little bit too tight.

With Aton safely snuggled down in the back of the car, I make the twists and turns as we climb Monte Cucco. Perhaps one kilometre from the top, we have to leave the car. Although it has its winter tyres, the snow is too deep. Drifts of snow completely swallow Aton as he tries to leap around but he has little real success. It's his first time in snow so deep, and he appears to relish the novelty. We walk for quite some distance, Aton's undercarriage almost the whole time brushing the snow. The sky is the deepest possible blue, not one single cloud, the sun larger than it's ever been. Trees that over the years have been forced to submit to strong winds, lean to one side, their dark, leafless branches having become icy snow sculptures: large icicles hanging like clear crystal. And not one other person on the mountain. It truly is magnificent in its isolation, the only sound a whistling wind as it blows through the green of tall fir trees, gathered snow cascading to the ground as we pass.

We continue climbing; to our left the snow-covered side of the mountain as it reaches up to touch the sky. To our right a steep drop, lower mountains and valleys below. Ahead of us deep, virgin snow merging with blueness. Aton continues to disappear from view, occasionally returning to see if I'm still alive. The unmistakable prints of a deer appear ahead in the snow. And what must surely be the prints of a wolf that has been following its prey. It has to be a wolf; they're certainly not prints created by Aton. It's incredibly unlikely that they are the prints from another dog; there are no human footprints. Will the wolf appear or, if it's been successful, will there be evidence of a kill? Aton at last returns, the usual, exhausted, excitement in his manner as a result of being allowed to run free. It's not long before we are making the walk back to the car, Aton, yet again, having recovered his energy, running ahead and out of sight. As for the wolf and its possible kill, nothing.

So, back to the morning with bone chilling coldness. Giselle and Mark had asked, some weeks before, if I would pick them up from their home close to Montefalco and drive them to Perugia airport for a flight to the UK. They'd also suggested that I stay the evening before at their place, just on the chance that we had more snow. Absolutely no snow is forecast for at least the next few weeks, so I decide to collect them the morning of their flight. I'm up and out of the house early, giving me plenty of time to get to Montefalco and transport them to the airport. And as forecast, no snow. The sky dark blue, the sun bright, not one single cloud. It is, however, minus 15°C, the coldest I have ever known it to be in Umbria.

I press the electronic ignition on the car, nothing, not a sound. I try again, nothing. And again, nothing. Now my understanding of how a car works could be written on the back of a postage stamp. My best is opening the bonnet, making it secure, then giving the engine a very stern and unforgiving look. After a few words cursing the car, I close the bonnet, trying the ignition again. Why would anything have changed? My cursing hasn't worked. Still nothing. Who would know what to do? Obviously, Aldo. He tries the ignition, nothing. After a good deal of head scratching, he calls a friend who just happens to be a mechanic. Remember it's minus 15°C. To the mechanic it's more than obvious what the problem is, the diesel has frozen in the engine. The mechanic tells us that all we can do is wait for the deiseal to defrost, if at all possible using something to warm the engine. I can't remember if it was my idea or Aldo's to use hair dryers, so I'll tell you that it was my idea. For some reason I have two, Aldo one. So, that's what's done for at least the next ninety minutes. The three dryers plugged in, all on maximum temperature and at full blast, bonnet closed, 'hot' air blowing over the frozen engine.

We always have to look for the positives in life. One absolutely positive thing about winter and freezing temperatures, is frozen dog poo. My daily routine of looking for little land mines is made so much easier when they're frozen solid. If you have a dog you'll undoubtedly know what I mean. If you don't have a dog, don't do it, I can guarantee that people will think you rather peculiar. How could I have possibly imagined that frozen dog poo would one day be a topic of conversation for me?

And the frozen engine. The hair dryers work: diesel defrosted. The next time the ignition is tried, all is fine. However, I did have to give Giselle and Mark the disappointing news that I would not be able to get them to Perugia airport on time.

Other Januarys in Umbria have been cold, with some snow, but always the promise of gloriously sunny days. Certainly, never as cold as that morning in 2018, the lowest temperatures being at the most minus 5°C, even that being unusual.

PRIMAVERA

The second week of March is a time to start working on the orto (vegetable plot) just across the narrow road that passes my house in Case Colle. It's time to fire up the motozappa purchased a few years back with the help of Aldo. A bit of a monster, as it starts to churn the soil covered in a thick blanket of weeds, believe me, it's no easy task. Better than having the back straining work of digging over every inch with a spade and garden fork, but certainly not simple. It's a heavy machine, with a mind seemingly of its own. The motozappa has to be tamed and controlled as it vibrates, jumping as it hits overly large stones. The machine reluctantly dragged round to go back in the opposite direction. Its throttle can be adjusted, low for the first traverse of the orto, its blades only cutting into the top layer of earth. An increase of the throttle, the monster cuts a little deeper, weeds being minced to mulch, rich, brown soil now turning over. Throttle increased again, the blades cut even deeper and the orto starts to look ploughed, the ground now putting up less resistance, the motozzapa is easier to manoeuvre. After a few hours a major part of the work is done, the soil now ready to be enriched with latame (manure), not something that easy to get your hands on even though we're in a rural area. But I know a man who has contacts. Yes Aldo, what would I do without my closest Italian neighbour and friend?

March moves into April. I've bought more olive trees and a variety of fruit trees, all done with the support and guidance of Aldo. He has a friend, a little distance away, who happens to be an expert in horticulture, so that's where we go, me driving. Her house has to be one of the most rustic I have ever visited in Umbria. I can imagine a wood cutter living here, large axe kept close to the door to fend off any inquisitive wolves. Part of the house is actually an old church; nothing has been removed. At some point, with the help of her husband, it will be merged with the rest of the house. Religious paintings are still where they were left, also faded frescos on the walls. For now, it appears to be a place of storage for all and everything. It's a truly wonderful place. We have coffee, a long chat and buy a number of fruit and olive trees. After the long Italian goodbye, we leave, making our way back to Case Colle. Over the next few days, I get some planting done in the vegetable plot, and with the weather now quickly warming up, the hens are providing me with at least six eggs each day. And the girls get on with this without the testosterone filled advances of a cockerel; what a surprise!

It's Easter, Good Friday, and Gubbio holds the Procession of the Dead Christ. The event, organised by the Venerable Brotherhood of Santa Croce della Force, repeated every year for centuries. It's a solemn affair, bringing in crowds of people from the surrounding area. What to an outsider look like members of the Ku Klux Klan, almost gives the whole affair a sinister feel. They are the first to be heard and seen. Dressed in white hoods and white robes, a large red cross on the front, they each carry an implement used in the crucifixion of Christ, those at the front carrying an 'instrument' that makes a rattling noise. Then come large effigies, first of the dead Christ and then the Virgin Mary, carried at shoulder height, many in the crowd wanting to touch them as they slowly pass. Following behind, male singers, the Miserere, chanting. After these, noted people of the town and then the general public. The smell of smoke fills the stone streets as bonfires are lit along the route. It's difficult for me to know what goes through the minds, the emotions felt, by those who are Catholic. But for the people of Gubbio, there is clearly a shared sense of belonging, shared emotion, almost a shared sorrow.

The first week of May finds me back in the UK to spend a week with Martina. It's so good to be together again. Aton is a house guest again with Giselle and Mark. We spend part of the week visiting friends and relatives, other days exploring the Cotswolds, the region quintessentially English; thatched cottages, half-timbered houses, little streams running through beautiful villages. Villages with names like Stinky Bottom and Itchy Scrotum. Really Graham? No, I've invented those names. Cockadilly, Honey Knob Hill, Lower Swell, not invented by me. I know, schoolboy humour. Perhaps the little boy always remains within the adult male. Umbria also has its moments in terms of place names. Bastardo, yes it does mean that. Also, not that far from the hilltop town of Trevi, you'll find Pissignano and Clitunno. No, it can't just be me, can it? Ok, if you're a little bemused by my sense of humour, you can always seek sanctuary in the village of Paradiso, close to Assisi.

Whilst I'm talking about Pissignano, I may as well tell you, for when you are in Umbria, that the first Sunday of each month, the village hosts a large 'antiques' market. How many genuine antiques you'll find I'm not so sure. More of an old furniture market, basically old anything, from toys to coins, books and jewellery. And one particular stall that sells fascist mementoes. No, it's true, this bloke is always there. He has a little stall with busts of Benito Mussolini and Adolf Hitler, these sitting by the side of old pamphlets and books with their images displayed on the front. Fascist badges and fascist caps. A range of other fascist related little trinkets. I have to point out the vendor is not a fascist. How do I know this? He has a notice telling everyone. It literally says, 'I'm not fascist, please don't spit at me. I only sell these things' (Non sono fascista, per favore non sputarmi addosso. Vendo solo queste cose). I believe him, don't you?

After another wonderful week with Martina, the passion between us growing each time we are together, I'm on an Easyjet flight from Luton to Pisa. From Pisa, the drive to Umbria.

It's early afternoon, Saturday, almost the last week of May. Out in the full heat of the sun, it's 30°C. But dark grey, almost black, impenetrable cloud is starting to swallow the higher mountains. What had been a calm, sultry, Saturday morning begins to freshen. A cooling breeze soon transforms into a wind, a wind that dramatically increases in strength. Such a change almost always brings a heavy downpour, thunder and sheets of lightning. The dry Umbrian earth will not be disappointed, the first large drops of rain beginning to fall. The olive trees bend to the will of the wind, the rain now bouncing off the ground. And then, always a surprise but not totally unusual, giant hailstones begin to thud against the terracotta tiles of the house, the car standing out in the open at risk of some really serious damage. I'm able to move it, parking it under the relative 'protection' of a tree. Hailstorms like this never last for long, thankfully, but they cover the ground with balls of ice, and leave some people with insurance claims. Fortunately, on this occasion, the tree has done its job, the car is left undamaged. Hot weather and freezing hailstone, it certainly feels like an enormous contradiction. Without getting all scientific, because my brain doesn't always understand it. What appears to be a contradiction is all to do with strong currents of warm air rising. Moisture in this air, once high enough, begins to freeze and falls back to earth at quite a speed. So, there you are, my little attempt at climatology. Please don't ask for any further detail, I wouldn't be able to give it.

Unpredictable weather or not, the end of May is always the time of Cantine Aperte (Open Cellars). It's a major event in the year when wine producers open their doors to visitors. Most vineyards offer wine tasting throughout the year, obviously, but this is the one big event. This happens in vineyards throughout Italy, an opportunity for wine producers to showcase their different wines. Many of them will also offer other locally produced products, like cheese, salami, hams and olive oil.

I'm with others from UmbriAliens, as you know, basically an international bunch of people who either live or have holiday homes in Umbria. We've gathered together, along with many others, mainly Italians, amongst the vines of Cantina Dionigi, the estate close to the beautiful little town of Bevagna. The history of Dionigi goes back to 1896. It's a gorgeously still, warm, evening. We're sat either side of long tables that have been set out amongst the grape vines, sparkling lights, draped over the vines, giving the evening a magical feel. For a set price, we have a four-course meal served at tables, the food joined by a range of wines produced on the estate. Prosecco is always offered first, this followed by white and red wines, Sagrantino being the specialty of the vineyards around Montefalco. It's a truly wonderful event. If you are ever in Italy, especially Umbria, at this time of year, it really is worth seeking out Cantine Aperte. What could be better than the sound of corks being pulled out of wine bottles, the wines flooding your taste buds, the popping corks accompanied by delicious food?

Whilst we happen to be on the subject of eating, what should you do with a half dead lizard, its tail hanging limp out the corner of Aton's mouth? No, I'm not expecting you to just read this, what would you do? This lizard is far too big for him to actually eat, which is what he normally does when they're tiny. I'm sure I noticed its tail twitch, just a little. Aton is definitely not going to give it up. After scampering round the garden, with me in hot pursuit, he eventually drops it on the ground, its half-chewed body discarded; is it dead? For Aton this is far better than any rubber toy you could possibly buy him. This toy actually moves, it's gristly and tastes of blood.

Now, a mouse in the house, a time when I need Aton's hunting, macabre, satanic, playful instinct to kick in, he simply remains oblivious. I know he knows it's there. And he knows I know he knows. The last time the mouse made an appearance, I could see Aton watching it, then turning away and going back to sleep. I'm sure he's deliberately ignoring it just to wind me up. Aton and snakes, I've yet to catch him with one. There are times when he's in the crouching dog position, barking at something, then suddenly jumping back. Then returning to the same position, barking, before again springing back. Occasionally he looks in my direction, his tongue, again, hanging out the corner of his mouth. Come and have a look. I'm already on my way, I don't need his invitation. The last thing I want is for him to get bitten by a viper. And when I get there, nothing. Whatever it was, has gone. Aton then giving me a look suggesting that, yet again, I'm too slow and too late.

The first three weeks of June have been hot and dry, today the sun appears to be having a break. Overnight the temperature has dropped from 33°C down to only 23°C, the day beginning with the rumble of thunder. A downpour looks to be threatening. What do you do if it looks like the day may well be wet? The answer is obvious, you stone the cherries that you've picked over the last couple of days. Hundreds of bright red, sweet, cherries. Last year, not one single fruit, this year a multitude. Luckily I have the mechanical means for the job. The type of metal contraption that could punch a hole in your earlobe, its use, very simple. Held in my right hand, unsuspecting cherry between the fingers of my left. Press the lever, a punch pops the stone out. Sometimes a mindless task, although laborious, can feel so rewarding. I have Radio Subasio playing to keep me company. This year I also have mulberries for the first time, from a tree planted two years before. It turns out that they are delicious.

The threatened rain doesn't come, the thunder deciding to leave. In the field across from the house, electrical engineers are erecting new power lines. One of the reasons for doing the stone popping is that I have no power in the house. No power also means no water. I know, electricity and water should never go together, but they do in Case Colle. Lorenzo is out, hacking away at thick ivy that, over the years, has grown to cover a wall and fence that's shared between the two of us. Apparently, a very large snake had disturbed his morning the previous day, sliding and winding its long body through the entangled growth.

'A snake Carlo, a big snake!' Lorenzo holding his hands and arms wide apart to give some indication of its length. Aldo had already told me of the encounter with the snake. In his telling of the tale, the snake was even bigger. It must clearly be the python that ate all the Hobbits who once lived in my little stone wood shed.

Just as I'm about to retreat into the kitchen for a drink, a scouting team of wasps having found my juicy cherries, I become aware of a rather quiet voice calling from the other side of the English gate; the road side (I'll tell you about the English gate in a bit).

'Buongiorno, mi scusi. Signore, mi scusi, buongiorno.' It would appear that the police have found me, always a little worrying. Leaning on the gate, a large envelope in his hand, is a rather elderly looking member of the Carabinieri. As I approach, 'Are you the English?' Should I say no I'm the German? I decide to go with English.

'You are Jordan, David Jordan?' 'No. Hofmann, Graham Hofmann', I reply, then pointing to my name on my letter box. The name HOFMANN in bold letters. 'Are you sure that you're not David Jordan?' Now I know that I can be forgetful and perhaps at some point in the future I will have no idea who I am, but today I'm reasonably certain that I'm not David Jordan.

'Do you know David Jordan?' 'No, do you have an address?' 'Yes, Vaccaria', he replies. I know where he means but I still don't know the name. I tell him to turn left in the direction of Colpalombo and then, after three hundred metres, turn left towards Vaccaria. Aldo now appears, he gives the officer further reassurance that I'm not the Englishman that he's after. Aldo also gives him the same directions. The officer thanks us, then back in his car, he turns right, passing the two electrical engineers who, like steeplejacks, are now at the very top of a large metal pole. The police officer is driving towards Carbonesca, in totally the wrong direction. Aldo shrugs his shoulders; I go back to my cherries. Lorenzo appears to have finished hacking away at the ivy, the monster snake not having entwined itself round his body.

ESTATE

Cicadas have spent for ever hidden away in slumber; they'll soon be warming up to orchestrate the soundtrack that welcomes the summer months. I'm sure that they have spent the colder months underground practicing their mating song. Hot summer days allowing them to release their cacophonous shrill. Apparently you can eat them, the taste similar to tofu. Gluten free, high in protein, low in fat and carbs. Perhaps I've just made that up. Let me know if it is indeed true. I'll let you try them first.

July brings the most magnificent display of tall sunflowers. Fields of green, topped with bright yellow, smiling faces. Field after field after field of the most gorgeous display of sunflowers. For a few weeks they face the sun, absorbing its light, appearing to welcome its intense heat. The sight of them can't help but make you feel happy; they look happy. The green and bright yellow, set against the deepest blue sky, is transfixing. Even though the days can sometimes feel baking hot, fields of sunflowers make you feel fresh and alive. But, eventually, even the sunflowers have had enough. By the time July has moved into August the heat is making them bow their heads. They just don't appear to have the same enthusiasm. They no longer appear to be smiling. They look tired and exhausted. 'Please, we've had enough, it's too hot. Yes, we like the sun, but enough is enough.' Over the coming weeks, the bright yellow flowers turn brown and eventually crisp.

The summer months, as you're aware, bring festivals of all kinds. Along with all the local festivals in villages, the really big events are the Festival dei Due Mondi in Spoleto (Festival of Two Worlds), Umbria Jazz in Perugia and Trasimeno Blues around the towns and villages of Lago Trasimeno. Open air music and theatre are just so perfect.

It's July and I have people staying at the house, Martina and her daughter Sophia. Sophia is here with her boyfriend Jason, and my niece, April, with her son, Ben; Martina for two weeks, the others just for one. As is the norm for Italian summers, the days are dry and hot.

We're at the Sagra di Salsiccia e Polenta (Sausage and Polenta Festival) in Carbonesca, you know the place, it's the village that forms part of my morning runs. When we arrive, the place is already busy, live music, people dancing, food and drink being served. Having exchanged greetings with those who know me, we eventually find a table with enough space for all of us. For a set price we can basically have as much sausage and polenta as our taste buds and stomachs can accommodate. Other evenings there is a choice of foods offered, all at different prices, wine and other drinks paid for separately. Tonight, the food, drinks and wine are all inclusive. We have a bottle of red and a bottle of white, along with soft drinks and water. The evening moves on and we ask for another bottle of red and another bottle of white. It's not that long before the alcohol has started to take effect, all of us at some point, joining the exclusively, apart from us, Italian revellers dancing. From the semi-formal dance that takes couples swirling round in unison, to the less formal routines of line dancing, we attempt to join in. At no point do we appear to have the 'natural' technique of all others here.

As the evening moves towards midnight, there's a pause in the music, the lead singer begins to clap, loud rhythmic clapping, at the same time calling all young people to come to the front of the dance floor, close to the stage. The music strikes up again, but now just a little faster and more furious. The young people dance, jump, clap and sing, mainly following the lead singer on stage. There is just one adult amongst this sea of youth, Martina. She's jumping, signing and clapping with just as much vigour as all those around her. She'd not understood a word that had been said when the young were invited to come to the front of the stage, so she just joined in. Why not?

By 1am people have started to leave, the music now silent. We also make our slightly tipsy walk, a couple of kilometres, back to the house, the sky bursting with stars. Left behind, on just about every table, are full and half full bottles of wine; just left. To the average Brit this is an alien concept, you almost never leave alcohol behind. The Italians far more balanced in their drinking habits.

We spend a few days by the coast and pay a visit to Lago Bolsena, in the region of Lazio, to meet Italian friends of Martina. On another day we are in Gubbio, the week almost at an end, Martina staying, the others soon leaving for the return to the UK. The penultimate night of their stay brings a dramatic change to what had been expected.

After having enjoyed a BBQ at the house, we're sat in the garden, chatting about the week, laughing about Martina joining all the young at the festival. A warm evening, starlit sky, cicadas in full chorus. Sophia and her boyfriend have gone for a walk, the rest of us continuing with our chat, just a little drink. It's as we're sat chatting that we hear a loud female scream from the back of the house, Martina immediately jumping into action!

We dash to the back of the house. It's dark, but I can already see that Martina has been able to jump over the more than a meter high fence that separates my garden from that of Benito. How she's done this, I have no idea. She's on the ground at the other side of the fence, apparently without injury. Stood on top of Benito's illegal building is Sophia's boyfriend, Jason. 'Where's Sophia?' 'She's fallen down the other side of the building', he replies. It's a drop of about three meters, the building having a concrete surround and then grass. We dash round to find Sophia on the ground and clearly in pain. It's her head and right arm that hurt. She's able to stand. We walk her back to the front of the house where we have light. She has a deep cut to the top of her head, cuts to her legs and cuts to her arms. It's her head and right arm that cause the most concern. There's no alternative but to drive her to the hospital just outside Gubbio. I drive, with Sophia and Martina in the back of the car.

On arrival at Accident & Emergency I explain what has happened, the doctor and nurse asking a number of questions and examining Sophia. Thankfully the wound to her head is superficial, as are the wounds to her arms and legs. She's taken through to X-ray, only one adult allowed to be with her, Martina not speaking Italian, the adult is obviously me. The X-rays, thankfully, show no damage to the skull, but her right arm is most definitely broken. We're then able to speak to Martina, explaining the situation, before we go into another room for the arm to be set in a cast. The doctor and nurse speaking in Italian, with me explaining to Sophia what they are going to do. With tears in her eyes, Sophia asking me to ask them questions. Her free hand holds my hand in a tight grip. I'm feeling incredibly paternal but trying not to show any anxiety in my face. Eventually we leave, Sophia now with her arm in a full cast. The whole evening clearly painful and distressing for her and understandably worrying for Martina.

After a restless night for Sophia, and after collecting a number of drugs from the pharmacy in Gubbio, it's decided that Martina will fly back to the UK with Sophia and Jason the following day. Sophia and her boyfriend would have been flying back anyway, along with, although on different flights, April and Ben.

AUTUNNO

When autumn arrives in Umbria, the temperature is still pleasantly warm, sometimes even hot. By the end of October, the Green Heart of Italy turns multi-coloured, hillsides and valleys covered in oak trees preparing for the winter months. Fields of grape vines that surround Montefalco, vines that for many months have been a vibrant green, now transform into deep crimsons, reds and oranges, the colours absolutely stunning. September is the time of the grape harvest (vendermmia), wineries across the region busy. It's a time for celebration. What you'll find, if you live in Italy for any length of time, is that there is always a time for celebration, it's something built into the DNA of Italians. On almost all occasions, celebrations and festivities having some connection to one saint or another.

Enologica Montefalco, a celebration of the grape harvest in the hilltop town of Montefalco. You already know its most celebrated red wine is Sagrantino (Montefalco Sagrantino DOCG), a grape only grown in this area. 'Enologica Montefalco, il più importante evento dedicato agli appassionati dei vini del territorio.' An event promoted as being dedicated to lovers of wine from the local area. Several days of gastronomy, music and art, days of wine tasting and workshops. Something else that you'll come to recognise, once you get to know Italians, is that they are passionate about wine. What am I saying? They're not just passionate about wine, they're also passionate about food, especially that produced and prepared locally. The event involves the whole town and well over 20 local vineyards.

I'm here with Giselle, Mark, my sister, Katherine, her husband, Pater, and others. If you remember I told you earlier in the book about the couple who run a wine tour company, a two-person operation close to Montefalco. They live in the ideal place for what they do, close to the Strada del Sagrantino, fields of vines growing to the back of their house. We're in the beautiful, historic centre of Montefalco, Piazza del Comune, the whole town teeming with people, Italians and tourists. We've already been sampling a selection of wines, now waiting for the entry into the piazza of a caravan of tractors and trailers representing the different wine producers from the area. The piazza is a buzz of excitement, a warm sun and a clear blue sky. The tractors trundle in, each trailer elaborately decorated with all manner of things related to the grape and wine. Each trailer has people dressed in full medieval costume, some trailers having the Roman god of wine, Bacchus. Most offer food or wine as they slowly pass, eventually all coming to a halt in the piazza. It's a wonderful event. Even without the festival, Montefalco is yet another hilltop Umbrian town well worth visiting. It's main piazza, encircled by restaurants and its narrow streets with even more places to eat, drink and relax, are a delight.

It's the first week of October. You know that you're starting to go 'native' when you look at the temperature outside and think, only 24°C, that's a little cool, I'd better dig out my fleece. Perhaps I could just cover my shoulders with a jumper, sleeves crossed at the front and falling over my chest. For some reason it looks good on Italian men. On a Brit, there's something not right. The dry heat of the summer months has long gone, the green of Umbria already starting to fade. It's an ideal time for getting out and walking in mountains, hills and valleys. A time for sitting by babbling rivers and streams. A time to be high above Umbria on Monte Cucco. But today it's a more local walk of just several kilometres.

Walking up towards Carbonesca, a group of cyclists pass me at speed on their downward travel towards Colpalombo. Others pass, climbing in the opposite direction, some out of their seats, legs and hearts pumping in order to stay with the rest of the pack. The green bracken that lines the road from spring into summer, at least four feet in height, is turning brown and crisp. Beyond this, the land falls steeply into the tree covered valleys below, where deer and other animals hide during the day. Tall oak trees line both sides of the road, the higher branches arching over to meet, in the spring and summer forming a wonderful canopy; a green tunnel (galleria).

I'm out with Aton. After walking no more than one kilometre, we turn left, leaving the road, walking into an open field that rises up sharply to meet the horizon. Only a short distance, but once there I have a wonderful view of the higher Apennines, Monte Cucco easily recognisable. It was here, one early morning, with a blanket of mist clinging to the ground, that I came across the most majestic looking stag. For less than a minute he stood facing me, proud and noble, wearing his great antlers as a crown, hot breath leaving his dark nostrils as clouds of steam. I'm sure he nodded a greeting before he turned and ran, soon disappearing into the forest. In all my time in Umbria, he is the only stag I have ever seen. Such moments are truly magical.

Eventually we leave the road that climbs from my place up to Carbonesca, spending the rest of the day walking along tracks that take me through forest and fields, before coming to a large pond, in the spring full of leaping frogs.

When we were there at that time, Aton inquisitive, the tip of his nose touching the water. These creatures were unknown to him, very different from the lizards he would often torment. The amphibians startled him then, diving into the water and weed. We continue, over the Chiasco river, now in full flood, Aton curious, but thankfully having absolutely no intention of going in. Eventually, quite a distance from any roads, we come to rest, to have a snack and drink aqua. It's as we sit, in almost total silence, that I become aware of movement, at the edge of the forest, across an open field, perhaps no more than eighty metres from our position. Aton, surprisingly, appears to be completely oblivious to what I see.

At the very edge of the field, coming out of the forest are three, large, wild boar. They don't look up, what slight breeze that there is blows in my direction. Why has Aton not picked up their scent? As they continue to grub around, heads down, another two appear, these two followed by five little ones. Whilst the adults feed, the little ones play, running in and out of the forest. And still Aton shows no interest, his behaviour is a mystery to me. I simply sit and watch, trying to remain as still as possible, fully expecting just one of the adults to look in my direction, snort a warning to the others, and they will be gone. In the end, it is Aton who gives away our position. Luckily, I have him on his long lead, the line pulled in. He yelps, at the same time straining to give chase. One adult looks up, snorts loudly, and with that, they've gone, vanishing back into the forest. It's the first time I have seen so many in one place, and so close. During the day it's rare to see just one wild boar.

CLIMBING OLIVE TREES
LA RACCOLTA DELLE OLIVE

I think I said, early in the book, that the olive harvest is one of my most favourite times of the year. A time when I spend whole days in the company of my Italian neighbours, the days given to picking thousands and thousands of olives. All of this done, literally, by hand, most often done with the use of little plastic rakes and a contraption that can reach up to the higher parts of a tree, flailing and shaking the branches, sending a cascade of tumbling olives to the ground. But I prefer to climb, picking olives giving me the ideal excuse to behave like a little boy. Within the branches of the olive tree, I'm in my own little world. Only a few metres from the ground, but I'm climbing. I can even sit and rest, watching others raking olives, green and black, from the lower parts of the trees. Although not really that far from the ground, between my camouflage of branches, I have the most marvellous view of the hills and mountains of Umbria. Early enough in the morning for the valleys and Colpalombo to be shrouded in white lace mist. I'm with Marcello and his family. I've never counted them (the trees, not his family), but at a rough guess, I would say that they have at least sixty mature trees. Gossip, jokes, laughter and general chat are exchanged between those hard at work.

As we move from one tree to the next, large nets, often green, with a similar look to fishing nets, but the mesh far tighter, are spread over the ground. Multiple nets are used, pegged together in an attempt to stop a single olive avoiding being caught. It's inevitable that some will escape, but there are thousands, a few hundred, throughout each day, disappearing through gaps in the nets, certainly won't be missed. There are at least six of us harvesting the olives, so we work on three or four trees at a time. You have to visualise an uneven surface, quite often the land on a slope, broken branches being used to raise parts of the netting off the ground, creating a barrier to any escaping olives. A mechanical shaker attacks the difficult to reach higher parts. I climb a different tree. Others strip olives from branches with their little rakes and by hand.

Once it's agreed that we have as many olives as it's possible to get from a tree, the nets are carefully lifted, the olives cajoled and funnelled into plastic crates. I've done this for a number of years with my neighbours. At different times, I've picked my own olives with the help of Martnia, other years with my daughters or friends who happen to be staying. Almost no one, the first time they pick olives, can resist the temptation to bite into one, the olive very quickly spat out. Raw olives, directly from the tree, are incredibly bitter, almost inedible. It's amazing that they can be transformed into olive oil that is so exquisitely flavoursome. Ignorant olive grower that I am, it's only when I went to buy a number of olive trees with Aldo, from an expert, that I discovered that there are many different varieties. We came back with three or four different types. No, don't ask me, I can't remember what they are.

At about 10.30, we have a late breakfast of scrambled egg sprinkled with black truffle, an espresso, perhaps a cappuccino, others having fruit juice. It's a real Italian family breakfast, and then back to work. More trees are climbed, most often by me. Trees are shaken and branches are stripped. Nets are gathered together, olives emptied into crates. And so, the morning continues until we stop at around 1.30 for lunch, a simple pasta. The pasta fresh, homemade, and delicious. With this we take our time, the trees and the olives won't disappear, they'll still be waiting to be shaken and picked. White wine, aqua, fruit for dolce, water melon bigger than my head, and espresso to finish. After lunch, it's back to the olive grove. Nets are moved to other trees and crates are filled with olives. At 4.30 we take another short break, a small bottle of beer, others just drinking aqua.

By early evening, at about 6.30pm, the first day of picking is done. We'll be back tomorrow, this time having lunch as a picnic, a blanket on the ground, shaded by the olive trees. Bread, cheese, prosciutto, wild boar sausage (all made by Aldo) and fresh tomatoes from the family orto. Olive oil from last year's harvest to drizzle. Wine, beer and aqua to drink. I love every minute of each day when it's the olive harvest, the precious time with my Italian neighbours and friends.

So, the harvesting has been done, the next step is to have the olives processed. I still only have a couple of mature trees, producing five or six small crates of olives, so I throw my lot in with the thousands and thousands harvested with Marcello and his family. I usually get about ten litres of oil.

For several weeks people transport their olives to small Frantoio. These are basically small processing plants. You have to call in advance to book your allotted slot. I've done this a number of times now. On this occasion I'm with Aldo and the father of Marcello, Davide. Marcello's daughter, Emma is also with us. It's a fascinating place to be, constantly busy but at the same time relaxed. We have three enormous green crates full of olives waiting to be processed. Long gone are the days when heavy stones were used to crush the olives, these days replaced by completely mechanical methods. Crates of olives are first weighed before being emptied into a large container that rumbles them, separating the olives from any leaves and unwanted bits of twig and branches. Then the olives are washed before they enter another part of the system where they are crushed, turned and mixed, eventually becoming a light brown paste. The paste is then pumped into a centrifuge where the solids are separated from the liquids. The liquids then go into other chambers before, eventually, the lime green oil starts to slowly pour out, literally through a tap. Nothing is added during the process, what you get is completely natural. What you have is fresh, authentic, extra-virgin olive oil, the air thick with its perfume. Dark, lime green and peppery to the taste.

In 'normal' times, times without Covid-19, you could walk round the plant watching each step of the process. People stood around chatting, meeting and greeting. A table set to one side where you could get an espresso or a crispy chunk of bread drizzled in a generous quantity of oil, as fresh as it's possible to get. People entering the building with crates of olives, others leaving with litres of virgin new olive oil. Covid-19 restricted access to the building, only allowing those working there to be inside.

The first week in November 2019, is a 'normal' time. A log fire burns red, bread is toasted. The toast drizzled in olive oil and offered to anyone tempted by its taste. In effect, that means everyone. Emma, Marcello's daughter, sits with a large chunk of toast soaked in olive oil, a wide grin on her face. The taste is absolutely exquisite.

MAGICAL UMBRIA

Umbria has a way of absorbing the light, storing it throughout the day, for renewal the following morning in the form of a most magnificent sunrise. It really is a magical place.

It's a beautiful start to the day, the garden littered with the colours of autumn, crisp brown, orange, red and yellow leaves. A chill is in the air, grey clouds gliding across the sky, with the occasional blue, shafts of sunlight breaking through. A deer coughs and barks from the far edge of the field, hidden from view by low scrub and trees. I'm loading the car with four winter tyres. It's time for the obligatory change from summer to winter.

In the early morning, I stood and watched him for a while, the hunter on the hillside, his dogs eagerly scampering about their business. With heads down, their incredible sense of smell searching for a scent. The loud crack of gunfire echoes over the land. What his target is I have no idea. Has he been successful? Is some unfortunate prey now motionless? I watch until the hunter disappears into low trees at the top of the steep hill just climbed. A loud call and the dogs also disappear from view. Another loud crack of gunfire. Deep in the belly of the valley, shrouded by mist, deer bark warnings to each other. Be aware, there is a human killer on the loose. Just below my feet, hidden by trees, the unmistakable sound of a wild boar snorting as it grubs around in the dark earth. And high above, in the pale blue, autumn sky, the clouds take on the appearance of a phoenix, fine feathers spread wide.

A tractor ploughs a field, ready for autumn seed. It's propelled on caterpillar tracks. When hidden from view, in the folds of the land, it has the ominous sound of a WW1 tank. It comes into view again, the driver relaxed, cigarette in the corner of his mouth as the plough, pulled behind, digs deep into the dark earth. As I continue my walk, the clanking sound of a tank fades, its place taken by the sound of small bells. Suddenly I have at least fifteen goats of varying size and colour, heading towards me, some with small bells. No human is with them, just a dog, the dog quietly running round, trying to keep the goats moving in the same direction, some preferring to stop and eat whatever happens to be available. The goats pass me. Having left some behind, the dog chases back. There's no actual contact between the dog and the goats, just a taken for granted familiarity. All appear to know and accept who is in charge. I continue my walk, the goats and the dog disappear, only the sound of bells giving some sense of where they are.

A bird of prey hovers in the sky, head looking down, its wings frantically beating to maintain its position over the possibility of breakfast. My walk takes me from a solid, dirt track, onto tarmac. A lizard scurries out, unusual for this time of year. As the tarmac reverts back to compacted gravel, a snake slithers out from the long grass at the edge of the road. Almost one metre in length, it twists and turns its body, taking on the shape of a meandering river as it gains propulsion. It's fast, crossing the gravel road in seconds, before disappearing into the grass on the other side.

Throughout the year, whatever the season, you'll find me walking in my own company, I enjoy the freedom and the solitude. At other times I'll be with friends, Marcello and Matteo. My own company, the company of others, I enjoy both equally. It was Marcello's idea for the three of us to go on a long walk in the local area of Colpalombo. It turned out to be longer than anticipated, a walk of just over 17 kilometres (10.5 miles). Now that may not sound like any great distance, but in Umbria it's the hills that make the region so beautiful. And, of course, it's those hills that we had to walk up and down. The walk took us along tarmac roads, along dirt tracks, across fields, through forests, at times passing abandoned Umbria, houses tumbling down, now occupied by nature, many totally beyond rescue. We eventually have to cross the river that flows through the area, something we had definitely not planned to do. At the points where we crossed, the river has no bridges, we had to wade through the water in our walking boots. Matteo comical in his attempts to keep his boots dry. The three of us eventually stumbled across, all three of us with boots full of fresh, cold, water. Our reward, at the end of over 17 kilometres, pasta, white wine and espresso at the home of Marcello. Another marvellous day in Umbria.

Another early morning. As I make my run up to the village of Carbonesca and beyond, acorns that litter the tarmac road crunch under my feet. The roots of oak trees that line my route, providing a home for truffles to germinate and thrive. A few more days and I'll be leaving Umbria for a few months. Don't worry, I'll be back, how could I not return? And when I leave, Umbria in November is still warm enough to sit outside cafes, in the sun, perhaps not in shorts, but still warm enough for a t-shirt. I spend the November and winter of 2018 with Martina in the UK, also spending time with my daughters and visiting friends.

INVERNO

We've almost come full circle, the winters of 2015, 2016 and 2020 spent in Umbria. It's December. At 8 in the morning a thick mist, full of impenetrable moisture, covers the house and the garden. The sun, not long since risen, still hidden from view. Mist drifts over the land, at first its impenetrability maintained. Slowly, as the morning moves on, it starts to divide into wispy ribbons, the sun starting to puncture through. The hills and mountains of Umbria are soon revealed, but the deep valleys are still hidden. The sky is deep blue, the sun bright, but we now have winter temperatures. If I had to vote for the one invention that I would rate supreme, it would have to be the electric blanket. On a cold winter night, to be able to jump into a bed already warmed, is absolute bliss. And believe me, the house is cold through the winter months. The central heating takes away the background chill but little more. It is the stufa (wood burner) in the kitchen that keeps me snug. It generates enough heat to keep the kitchen and the room directly above warm.

Early December in Italy is the time for St. Nicholas to arrive. I'm at the house of my neighbours', Aldo and Benedetta, the whole extended family is there. After dinner we're sitting and chatting, the children excited. I'd not noticed Marcello sneaking out, I guess the children were just as oblivious. A mysterious shadow is spotted through the opaque glass of the main outside door to the kitchen. The shadow disappears and then returns. Marcello is now back in the kitchen with the rest of us. Who could it have been outside? The children gingerly open the door. St. Nicholas has been, small gifts left for the children to gather together and bring into the house.

As you already know, Gubbio boasts to have the biggest 'Christmas tree' in the world (Il piu grande albero di Natale del mondo). The tree climbs up the side of Monte Ingino to the back of the town, so big it can be seen for miles. As you may have already guessed, this is not a real tree. The shape of a tree is outlined with hundreds of lights on the side of the mountain. On December 7th the tree comes to life, the lights remaining on until the first week of January. The tradition began way back in 1981. At the same time, some of the streets of the town become a biblical village, taken over by Le Vie del Presepe, life size figures making up the Nativity. It really is wonderful to walk around.

Christmas Day, just as in any country where it's celebrated, is a day for the family. For me, in Case Colle, it's another day spent with my extended Italian family. Too much food is eaten, gifts are exchanged, drink is enjoyed (always just enough), and games are played, the board game, Trivial Pursuit, especially testing of my Italian. Laughter and enjoyment fills the day and evening. Until the arrival of Covid-19, the foreigners that I know here would gather together at the house of Giselle and Mark to have a late celebration of Christmas in March.

New Year's Eve, you find me either in the company of my Italian family or with UmbriAliens who have become close friends. One year welcoming in the new year from Piazza Grande in Gubbio. I remember walking back to the car, that's how little I'd had to drink, some thirty minutes after midnight, passing people, just as sober as me, some with children, the adults stood in the street enjoying gelato. The excitement of being in the company of others, a magnificent fireworks display, enough without having to drink.

And we have arrived at a new year, what will it bring? All over Italy, on the night of January 5th, Befana arrives, an old woman, perhaps you could describe her as a witch, delivering gifts, supposedly only to children who have been good. It's a national holiday in Italy, officially recognising the end of Christmas. Again, it's a time I spend with my extended Italian family.

So, there you have it, a flavour, a snapshot, of a year in Umbria. A life in Italy that would become somewhat more problematic because of political decisions made elsewhere.

Pity The Nation

Pity the nation whose people are sheep,
and whose shepherds mislead them.
Pity the nation whose leaders are liars,
whose sages are silenced,
and whose bigots haunt the airwaves.
Pity the nation that raises not its voice,
except to praise conquerors and acclaim the bully
as hero and aims to rule the world with
force and by torture.
Pity the nation that knows no other language
but its own and no other culture but its own.
Pity the nation whose breath is money and
sleeps the sleep of the too well fed.
Pity the nation – oh, pity the people who allow their
rights to erode and their freedoms to be washed away.
My country, tears of thee, sweet land of liberty.

. . . .

Lawrence Ferlinghetti

CHAPTER ELEVEN

Beguiling Nationalism

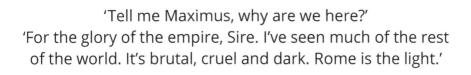

'Tell me Maximus, why are we here?'
'For the glory of the empire, Sire. I've seen much of the rest
of the world. It's brutal, cruel and dark. Rome is the light.'

Maximus speaking with the Emperor Marcus Aurelius in the film Gladiator – Ridley Scott

Early afternoon, June 16th, 2016, a young woman is lying in the street, life draining from her body. Those who happen to be passing, fight to save her. Outside a small library on Market Street, in the village of Birstall, West Yorkshire, England, tragedy unfolds. The woman has been shot and stabbed multiple times. A pathologist later describing two gunshot wounds to the head and one to the chest, along with at least 15 stab wounds, some of these in the woman's hands and arms, indicating that she was trying to defend herself. Before the attacker escapes the scene, he's confronted by an elderly male. In trying to come to the aid of the dying woman, he's also stabbed. Others at the scene try to give whatever first aid they can; it's a desperate situation.

At 1.48pm, Jo Cox, aged 41, Member of Parliament, wife, and mother to two young children, is pronounced dead. The person who carried out the attack, after disappearing into a local housing estate, is eventually confronted by two police officers, wrestled to the ground, and arrested: his name, Thomas Mair.

The murder of a British MP, killed in the street, quickly becomes international news. The Italian media, without hesitation, reporting it as a terrorist incident. It's in Italy that I first hear of the attack. Initially, the British media appear to be less willing to follow the terrorist incident line of thought, despite the fact that Mair was heard to call out, 'Put Britain First!' Instead, news outlets in the UK focus on the mental state of the killer. However, police investigations soon reveal that

Mair has links to ultra nationalist groups such as the neo-fascist National Front and the English Defence League. A search of his home uncovers Nazi regalia and far-right books. An examination of his computer showing a fascination with the Nazi Party, the Ku Klux Klan and far-right terrorists such as the Norwegian, Andres Breivik.

On the 18th of June, Mair appears at Westminster Magistrates' Court in London. When asked to give his name, he responds with the following statement:

'My name is death to all traitors, freedom for Britain.'

Mair is charged with terrorist offences under the Terrorism Act 2000.

In November 2016, Mair's trail takes place at the Old Bailey in London; he makes no attempt to offer a defence. Those who witnessed the killing in June, testify that whilst Mair was carrying out the attack, he had called out:

'This is for Britain! Keep Britain independent. Put Britain First!'

On the 23rd of November 2016, Thomas Mair is found guilty of murder and sentenced to life imprisonment. When sentencing, the judge stated that he had no doubt that Mair had been driven to commit murder through following a nationalistic ideology wrapped in violent white supremacism, a political doctrine with strong ties to modern forms of Nazism.

The murder of Jo Cox occurred just one week before the European Union membership referendum, what almost everyone now knows as 'Brexit'. In the two months following her murder, at least 25 MPs reveal that they have received death threats, the majority of those threatened being women. And even some months after the attack, the media reports that there have been more than 25,000 separate tweets in celebration of Jo's killing.

NARCISSISTIC NATIONALISM

When looking at nationalism, those in the know, identify several different types, from expansionist, the type justifying conquest and empire ('Rome is the light'), to movements striving for national independence and freedom, for example the removal of colonial control. What follows is a look at the type of nationalism that places the interests of one particular country above the interests of all others.

The type of nationalism that espouses the supposed exceptionalism of one's own nation when compared to all others. Narcissistic Nationalism, the label coined by the historian and psychologist, Jay Y. Gonen - The Roots of Nazi Psychology.

A VERY BRITISH MESS

On the 23rd of June 2016, I'm in Birstall, West Yorkshire, England, stood with about 200 people who have come together to remember Jo Cox. It's exactly one week since the killing took place. People are gathered in a circle close to a statue of Joseph Priestley, the statue itself having little real significance, other than it being a central spot on the small, cobbled, market square. We're only about fifty metres from where the attack took place, the square carpeted with thousands of flowers and messages. It's an incredibly moving experience as people join hands, making a pledge to stand against hatred and injustice. The crowd listens in silence to the words of a local vicar.

'We're meeting seven days from the tragedy that hit our community when our MP, Jo Cox, was so brutally murdered.'

I've not travelled back to the UK especially for this event, I'd returned a few days earlier to cast my vote. For me, remaining in the EU was unbelievably precious. The unity of Europe incredibly important to me. Britain's economic prosperity inextricably tied to membership of the EU. Also, I believed then and still believe now, that the stability and peace we enjoy within Europe, after centuries of war, comes from the very fact that separate and independent nations are joined together. I'm keenly aware that my generation is the first, in hundreds of years, not to have had to go to war in Europe; my father, and his generation, not being as fortunate. He experienced the horrors of war as a German soldier on the Russian front. It remains unknown what happened to his older brother, also a soldier, their mother receiving a final letter from him in February 1945.

The murder of Jo Cox, although I'd never met her, was in a sense personal to me. I'd voted for her to be my local MP. She was brutally killed just a five-minute walk from where I'd lived in Birstall before I moved to Umbria. The spot where she was shot and stabbed, I'd walked past hundreds of times. She was educated in the local area. I'd never taught her, but I had taught some of her friends. On a wider scale, her killing was unquestionably a direct consequence of the nationalistic propaganda spewed out by some campaigning for the UK to leave the EU. I don't feel that it would be an exaggeration to say that many had blood on their hands. A number of media outlets were only too willing to point the finger at those who were regarded as foreign, feeding on prejudice and stereotypes. The EU portrayed as some undemocratic monolith that had a vice like grip on the on the independence of Great Britain. Bureaucrats in Brussels determining what the British people could and could not do. Britain should be able to protect its borders, taking back control of who should be allowed in. Money wasted on the EU could be directly spent on British people. For many, such fabrications had a beguiling appeal. Jo Cox had been a keen supporter of the Remain campaign.

The day before the referendum I'm sat waiting for a haircut, the place just round the corner from where the killing took place. As I wait, the only newspaper to flick through is a copy of The SUN. The newspaper enjoys probably the widest readership in the UK. It provides its readers with what can only be described as a simplistic view of the world.

I sit flicking through page after page of spurious reasons why people should vote to leave. Absolutely no balance in what's been put down in print. But it comes as no real surprise, The SUN has never had a reputation for rigorous and independent reporting. And now it hits me in the face, people are going to vote to leave the EU.

Other newspapers join ranks with The SUN. The front page of the Daily Mail – 22nd June: 'If You Believe in Britain Vote LEAVE', its inside pages taken by rhetoric highly critical of the EU. The paper saying that the Remain side has 'failed to articulate a single positive reason for staying in the EU.' And in some ways the newspaper has this right. Taken as a whole, the Remain campaign has been shambolic, concentrating on the fears of leaving, rather than a vigorous promotion of why the UK should remain, pushing the enormous benefits membership brings for everyone. The Mail has a cartoon of a British family trapped inside a cell. The prison cell marked EU.

Those campaigning for the UK to leave, jump on what feels like the 'fear strategy' adopted by those campaigning to remain, labelling the whole thing as nothing more than: 'PROJECT FEAR.'

Other mainstream papers, just as enthusiastically, support the Leave campaign. The Express and the Telegraph, printing page after page. The only tabloid supporting Remain is the Mirror. But it feels like the paper lacks convincing enthusiasm. It's almost like someone who remains in an unhappy marriage through fear of leaving. The Mirror's editorial saying that we know that the EU is a 'difficult organisation to support with great enthusiasm.' The same editorial trying to dig itself out of a hole by saying that we shouldn't blame the EU for the problems caused by Cameron's (Prime Minister) Conservative government. The Mirror is right, but I know it's not going to convince enough to vote in favour of remaining.

Well before the date of the referendum had been announced, newspapers such as the Daily Mail had been maintaining a vicious campaign against 'foreigners'. In the autumn of 2015, the Mail adopting what many commentators described as Nazi style propaganda. A cartoon depicting ugly caricatures of what could only be regarded as the Mail's xenophobic depiction of Muslims flooding into the country. Scurrying between the feet of those supposedly swamping the country are rats. It's almost a direct lift from a Viennese newspaper of 1939. With the caption, 'Deutschland den Deutschen!' (Germany for Germans), a broom sweeping rats, caricatured as being Jewish, from the doorstep of Germany.

Others were also less than shy in adopting Nazi-style propaganda as a means of getting their message across. Nigel Farage (UKIP leader) unveils a giant poster supposedly showing a long line of Syrian refugees trying to get into Europe. The text with the image: 'BREAKING POINT. The EU has failed all of us. We must break free of the EU and take back control of our borders.' On the same day that cameras capture a smiling Nigel Farage standing proud in front of the poster, Jo Cox is murdered on the streets of Birstall. It's later shown that the lines of refugees is a fabricated image. The truth appears to be irrelevant; the damage is done.

June 23rd. The UK voted to leave the EU. The majority of voters in England and Wales backing Leave, voters in Scotland and Northern Ireland backing Remain. The vote was close, 51.9% in favour of Leave, 48.1% in favour of Remain. Although the result was not legally binding and, therefore, placed no obligation on the government to start the process of leaving the EU, Cameron, the PM and Conservative leader, addresses the British public, saying that UK will leave.

To say that I'm devastated by the result would be an understatement. For weeks I feel total grief, almost as emotionally draining as that of a death. The UK has made a massive, in all likelihood, catastrophic mistake. The consequences of this decision reverberating for many years to come. All rationality and logic screams out that leaving the EU can bring absolutely no benefits to the UK.

The reality is that the promise from the Tory (Conservative) leadership to hold a referendum on EU membership had nothing to do with popular demand. Most certainly it had nothing at all to do with what may be in the national interest. It had everything to do with internal squabbling within the Conservative party, Cameron pledging to hold the referendum in an attempt to quell the voices of those on his own extreme right. Added to internal squabbling, was a perceived threat from UKIP (United Kingdom Independence Party), and the fear that votes could drift from the Tories (Conservatives) to the party fronted by Nigel Farage.

Looking back on events it does feel incredible that Cameron was prepared to take such a gamble. The majority of Brits have never really identified themselves as European. Churchill argued for the importance of a unified body of nations in Europe at the end of WW2. His ideal was the creation of a 'European family, or as much of it as we can, and to provide it with a structure under which it can dwell in peace, in safety and in freedom. We must build a kind of United Sates of Europe.' But he still looked to the Empire as having more significance for Britain, arguing that the unity of European nations should be left in the hands of Germany and France.

The UK eventually joined the European Community (EU) on January 1st, 1973, under the Tory government of Edward Heath. But even at the moment of entry, there were divisions within the two main UK political parties. The country equally uncertain.

In 1975, with Harold Wilson as Prime Minister leading a Labour government, continued membership of the European Community was put to a referendum. For the very first time I was of a legal age to vote, voting to remain with incredible enthusiasm. Despite splits within both the main political parties, the UK returned a vote of 67% in favour of remaining. At this moment in time, the Tory (Conservative) press heavily supporting the campaign to remain.

In the same year, 1975, Margaret Thatcher became Leader of the Tory Party, and then Prime Minister in 1979, a position she held until 1990. Often regarded as a 'no-nonsense' prime minister, she was soon seen by many as someone who 'championed the cause of Britain'. Her legacy is debated by many, her detractors disdainful of her time in office, others regarding her as one of Britain's strongest leaders. Most certainly her domestic policy divided the country. In foreign policy, she was regarded by many as strong and determined, gaining her the title of 'Iron Lady'. I guess in many ways she set the tone for future UK relationships with the EU. It was to be demanding and antagonistic. She was certainly nationalistic in her determination to get the best deals out of the EU for the UK. However, on the topic of referendums, she regarded them as, 'The Devils Work'. It could well be argued that it was a Thatcherite stance that gained the UK the best membership deal of any country in the EU, the UK continually complaining and pushing for more. I don't remember the 'special perks' that the UK enjoyed featuring anywhere in the Remain campaign.

In 1988, Thatcher gave a speech directly challenging what she regarded as the growing influence of the EU in the national affairs of independent countries. In a key passage she said:

'We have not successfully rolled back the frontiers of the state in Britain, only to see them reimposed at a European level with a European superstate exercising a new dominance from Brussels.'

And yet, before what became known as the 'Bruges Speech', Thatcher had been the driving force in creating the Single Economic Market in 1986.

'Just think for a moment what prospect that is. A single market without barriers – visible or invisible – giving you direct and unhindered access to the purchasing power of over 300 million of the world's wealthiest and most prosperous people. Bigger than Japan. Bigger than the United States. On your doorstep. And with the Channel Tunnel to give you direct access to it. It's not a dream. It's not a vision. It's not some bureaucratic plan. It's for real.' Margaret Thatcher PM

In reality there is no contradiction. Thatcherism was all about shrinking the role of the state, especially in areas that related to social welfare, along with individual and employment rights. The EU, whilst eagerly embracing the Single Market, was also determined to have a commonality of rights and protections for the citizens of all member states. It's this that Thatcherism could not accept, and in many ways this position increasingly provided fuel for those within the Tory party pushing for the UK to break with the European Union. Thatcher had no desire to take Britain out of the EU. Britain would remain inside, accepting those parts regarded as in the interests of British capitalism, whilst continually kicking against social reform and protections for all EU citizens.

Spawned by Thatcher, the UK embraced a policy of deregulation, tax reduction, a shrinking of the state, and the general weakening of employee rights when set against the interests of business. The term neoliberalism is used to encompass an approach to government and economic planning that quickly took hold across the world; the UK and the USA being the vanguard. The state should step back, market forces would provide the most beneficial outcomes. In many ways the seeds were sown for the economic meltdown that was to come in 2008. Member states of the EU were also drawn into this, the increasing globalisation of business made it impossible to avoid. A major difference between the UK and other member states, is that the EU was, and remains, determined to try and find a balance between the economics of neoliberalism and the social welfare of people. It could be argued that the ultimate clash between the UK and the EU was inevitable.

The Single Market established four freedoms across all EU member states. These included the free movement of goods, services, capital and people. The free movement of people being one of the key features of the 2016 referendum. Following the Single Market came the Single European Act, this further strengthening economic ties, but also binding the UK to European Law. For increasing numbers within the Tory Party this came to be seen as a weakening of British independence/British sovereignty. This probably driven by economic interests rather than any grand notion of patriotism. John Major, who followed Thatcher to become the next Tory PM, is said to have referred to the increasing number of Euro sceptics within his own party as, 'Those Bastards!'

In 2010 the Conservative Party (Tory Party) and the Liberal Democrats formed a coalition government. The coalition policy of austerity introducing cuts in all areas of social welfare. A consistent narrative prevails. The previous Labour government had left the country in a mess, the Tory/Liberal alliance would redress the economic disaster left by Labour. The fact that increasingly unregulated market forces had resulted in economic collapse, successfully covered over; blame being directed elsewhere.

Another election in 2015 resulted in an outright Conservative win, the policy of austerity continuing with even greater severity. Continued deep cuts to government spending matched a worsening social climate across the UK. Ever increasing numbers of people feeling that they were being failed, left adrift with little hope. The continued cuts and their impact on the British people, coincided with increasing levels of immigration into the UK, with over half coming from EU countries. Voices within government, and those outside, stepping up the attention focused on the most disadvantaged, with special attention given to the 'problem' of immigration. It was against this background that the 2016 referendum took place.

In many ways the outcome of the referendum was a protest by those who felt that the main political parties had forgotten them. Cameron's government had handed the discontented, those feeling neglected, an external target – the EU. Rampant globalisation and the increasing consolidation of corporate power, the real culprits in producing the conditions where people felt forgotten, difficult concepts to easily explain. The EU far easier to identify, a visible foreign bogeyman. And there were many within government and outside, eager to feed fuel into the anti-EU flames. Ongoing problems within the UK could be resolved if the British people could be freed from foreign interference. A naïve understanding of global economics, absolutely. For global corporations there is no foreign, there are no borders, there is no loyalty to some national identity. Global capitalism towers over national borders and notions of sovereignty. 'Foreign interference' was not going to be magically swept away by voting to leave the EU. But deciding to vote Leave wasn't based on rational analysis. It was based on nothing more than a misdirected emotional response.

One week after the referendum result, I'm sat with my daughters, Kara and Lucy, their partners are also with us. We're enjoying a meal in a local pub. Somehow the conversation drifts into talking about pensions and the likelihood of them being able to benefit from a reasonable pension when they're older. A couple, probably in their mid-sixties, sit at a table close enough to be able to pick up bits of our discussion. One of them can't resist commenting on what's being said, it just happens to be the man.

'You don't know how lucky you are. In the seventies we didn't get all the benefits you get today. People today just want something for nothing. We had to work for it.'

Nobody invited him to join in our discussion. He's totally inaccurate in what he has to say, but I don't comment. I just want to enjoy my meal and the company of my daughters. Lucy challenges what's been said, pointing out that the future for young people today is far more uncertain than it was when he was young. It could be that when we're older state pensions may no longer exist. She then returns to her meal, our conversation moving on to other things.

'I suppose you all voted against Brexit.'

There's absolutely no reason why he should have brought this up. I ignore him, I really don't want to talk about Brexit. It's Lucy again who replies to his comment.

'Yes we did. We think that Brexit is a big mistake. We'd prefer not to talk about it, we'll only disagree with what you have to say.'

'Well, you were talking about pensions. Why should people in EU countries get higher pensions than people in the UK? I don't think that's right, I'm glad we're out. And the EU has for years taken our money and told us what we can and can't do.'

I can't remain silent.

'I'm sorry, but you're wrong on both points. The EU has no control over the level of pensions in each member state. Individual countries make their own decisions. State pensions are low in Britain because successive UK governments have kept them low, nothing to do with being in the EU. And secondly, the EU doesn't tell member countries what to do. Every member country influences and shapes decisions that are made, including the UK when it was inside the EU. If a country disagrees with a decision being made, it can veto that decision.'

'Well, you obviously know more about all of this than I do. I just know it's good that we've left.'

I could respond with, well stop talking bollocks then, but I don't.

'Other than the things you've already said, which aren't accurate, give me three benefits the UK will gain from leaving the EU.'

'Well, we'll have £350 million more to spend on the NHS each week.'

'But that's wrong again. All the experts agree that figure is an exaggeration of how much the UK paid in. And it doesn't tell us how much money came to Britain.'

'Oh, I see, you think you're one of those clever fuckers.'

'I'll make it easier for you. Just give me ONE positive thing that the UK will gain. That's all, just one. This time, something based on fact.'

'Borders, we get control of our borders.'

'We already had control; we've always been outside the Schengen Agreement.'

'Yep, you're one of those clever fuckers.'

I ignore his observation that I'm a 'clever fucker', suggesting that we end the conversation. It's no surprise that he's dismissive of those he sees as, 'clever fuckers'. Not that I regard myself to be a 'clever fucker', certainly no expert. During the build up to the referendum, a consistent message is driven home by those supporting the leave campaign. People are fed up with experts telling them how to think and what to do. Michael Gove, a leading Tory and Brexiteer, declared in an interview:

'I think the people of this country have had enough of experts with organisations and acronyms saying that they know what is best and getting it consistently wrong.'

It's a populist route to take. It certainly avoids having to give complex explanations about anything. It has appeal, the vast majority of people just wanting simple answers and simple ideas. It's a route taken by others, the Trump campaign and presidency a prime example.

My pub room 'debating protagonist' has to have the last word.

'Well, I'm glad that we've left.'

I don't respond.

Although certainly not inevitable, the likelihood of the Leave vote winning should have been predicted by those surrounding Cameron. The Sun, the Daily Mail, the Daily Express and the Telegraph were all vehemently in favour of Brexit. These papers combined, possibly enjoying four times the readership of those supporting Remain. Headline after headline poured scorn on the EU and anyone who supported the campaign to remain: a relentless focus on immigration. The run up to the referendum was the climax of years of nationalistic sentiment and anti-EU myths. The Eurosceptics, both in government and outside, revelled in stirring up some form of patriotic fervour. Promising the British public that Europe needed the UK far more than Britain needed the EU.

In many ways the Leave campaign simply tapped into a British sense of arrogance and belief in exceptionalism. Britain had stood alone in the past and been successful. Two world wars and past 'glories' of empire still deeply embedded within a very British mind-set; some may even argue that such a mind-set being strongest within the English.

Perhaps George Orwell had it absolutely right in The Lion and The Unicorn: Socialism and the English Genius:

'The English will never develop into a nation of philosophers. They will always prefer instinct to logic and character to intelligence. But they must get rid of their downright contempt for 'cleverness'. They cannot afford it any longer. They must grow less tolerant of ugliness and be mentally more adventurous. And they must stop despising foreigners. They are Europeans and ought to be aware of it.'

The most alluring slogan from the Leave side, repeated relentlessly: 'Take Back Control.' It was vague and never explained, but that didn't matter, it worked. The Remain campaign came up with nothing that could compete.

On the day after the referendum result being announced (June 24th) David Cameron resigned. After a good deal of infighting within the Tory party, on the 13th of July, Theresa May become the second female Prime Minister of the UK. Throughout the referendum campaign, she had been a staunch supporter of Remain, now she was charged with taking the UK out of the EU. Her time in office is characterised by one slogan after another, each one entirely meaningless and without substance.

'Brexit means Brexit – and we're going to make a success of it.' Theresa May, July 2016

May goes on to call for a 'Red, White and Blue Brexit.'

And yet this same woman in April 2015 said: 'I believe it is clearly in our national interest to remain a member of the EU.'

I still couldn't bring myself to believe that anyone holding the office of PM would want to be remembered in history for being the one to take the UK out of the EU, an act of national suicide. And yet, that's exactly where the government was taking the country, down the rabbit hole of Brexit madness. Any opposition in parliament muddled, confused and uncertain how to respond. Many in the Labour party represented areas of the country that had voted to leave. The Labour leader, Jeremy Corbyn, apparently sitting, with torn pants, stuck fast, on the fence of indecision.

On the 24th of June 2019, Theresa May resigned as Prime Minister. During her time in office, prejudicial rhetoric about 'foreigners' surged, not something that could be cast as directly her doing, but she did little to challenge it. Racism and xenophobia, that had in many ways been hidden below a thin crust of 'political correctness', were allowed to spew out. The UK was full, there's no space for yet more foreigners. And there were many within government and outside who were more than willing to ride on the back of anti-foreign sentiment. Once totally out of the EU, Britain, the public were told, could at last control its borders. And the majority of the public appeared to willingly swallow what they were told by government ministers, including Theresa May.

Those with foreign-sounding accents were increasingly targeted, including those living in the UK but from EU countries. Leading figures unashamedly, falsely stating that there were parts of the UK that were more like a foreign land than British. Even people who had lived in the UK almost all of their life, were caught up in a net of prejudice and discrimination. Despite living and working in the UK for decades, some having second and third generation families, many found themselves labelled as undocumented immigrants. Those not able to produce the appropriate official paperwork to prove British citizenship, told that they could face forced removal from the country. The Windrush Scandal hit the headlines in April 2018. Prior to becoming Prime Minister, Theresa May had been Tory Home Secretary, and as such, directly responsible for the policy of targeting individuals and forced deportation. Britishness and Whiteness had become very much mainstream. The extremism of fringe political groups such as the National Front, the British National Party and the English Defence League, had, in effect, become UK government policy.

Boris Johnson is elected to the leadership of the Conservative Party on July 23rd, 2019, automatically becoming the UK Prime Minister. In his first speech in the House of Commons, the home of British government, he tells MPs, and the country, that getting Brexit done would be the means by which the separate parts of the UK could be brought together, in Johnson's words, 're-energising our great United Kingdom and making this country the greatest place on Earth.' Not long afterwards when addressing the Tory faithful, but obviously with an eye on the general population, he went on to say that he would defend 'the most successful political partnership in history.' I guess trying to focus the populous on some supposed special qualities of a nation is nothing new, all national leaders do it. The Labour Prime Minister, Tony Blair, during his time in office, claimed that:

'The British are special. The world knows it. In our hearts we know it.'

Barack Obama's acceptance speech on becoming President, included many references to the special qualities of the USA and its people. I guess you could describe it as patriotic sugar.

In my first ramblings about Italy (Lorenzo's Vest), I described Italian politics as dysfunctional, the country not sure of its past, not confident about the present and uncertain of its future. Now, as I write in 2022, all of the above most certainly applies to the UK, perhaps even amplified. At the heart of this, what can only be described as the 'Little England Mentality'. The core of the problem is not some British feeling of exceptionalism, it is in fact a delusional belief in English exceptionalism. Those campaigning for Brexit fed off this. Taking back control would remedy the disenchantment felt by those who the establishment had left behind, those not listened to, the forgotten. Taking back control would offer a remedy for the economic insecurity felt by many people.

So, in July 2019, the UK was left in the hands of someone who had climbed the political ladder through celebrity and bluster. Somehow, despite his obvious incompetence, Boris Johnson leads the Tory party back into government in the national election of December 2019. The British electorate apparently willing to ignore Boris Johnson's buffoonery. Even more disturbing, they were willing to ignore his obvious reputation for dishonesty and his past, not only racist but also homophobic and sexist comments. Boris Johnson once referring to Black Africans as 'piccaninnies with watermelon smiles.' On another occasion, comparing some Muslim women to 'letterboxes' and 'bank robbers.'

I'm certainly not suggesting that those who voted in favour of leaving the EU were all driven by racist sentiment. Research highlights the fact that a third of British Asian voters backed Leave, along with as many as one in four Black voters. The taking back control message, placing the problems of the UK, your own economic uncertainty, the result of an external 'force', worked, to a certain extent, regardless of skin colour.

A few days after the EU referendum, I'm with friends at my favourite Indian restaurant in the village of Birstall. I still don't want to engage in any conversation related to Brexit, it feels too incredibly raw. The owner of the restaurant, an excellent host, always moving around chatting with customers. He comes to our table, asking how are things? How's your meal? The friends I'm with then ask him what he thinks of the Brexit vote. In my head I'm thinking, really, do we have to talk about this now? I just want to enjoy my meal and, for a brief time, forget about Brexit.

'Well, I voted to leave. It was the obvious thing to do.' He's just about to walk away. I'm pleased to let him go; I really don't want to respond to what he's just said. But my friends insist on continuing the conversation.

'What made you decide to vote leave?' Surprise in their voices. I really don't want to know. Let's just eat our meal. Whatever he has to say, I know I won't find any level of agreement. I'm not going to get involved in this conversation.

'Well, we have to take back control. We have to do something about immigration. The country is already full, we can't just keep allowing more and more people in. That's why I voted leave. By leaving we can have control of our borders.'

That's it, yet again, I can't remain silent.

'If I was sitting here with my eyes closed, I'd think I was listening to someone from the British National Party, the English Defence League or some other racist organisation. Don't you hear what you're saying?'

'I guess it could sound like that, I'd not really thought about it. But we do have to stop people coming in.'

Now I'm annoyed.

'So, what you're saying is, my family has done alright. My family came to the UK, and we now have a successful business. We're second or third generation British Asians, we're British. Now let's stop others coming in, the country is full.'

'I guess you could see it like that. I'd not really thought about it in that way. Anyway, enjoy your meal.' He smiles and moves to another table.

I feel like walking out of the restaurant. The taste of my meal has been totally soured.

As 2019 came to a close, the UK was left in the hands of an apparent joker, the clown, Boris Johnson. His only priority is 'to get Brexit done'. But what type of Brexit? An amicable Brexit divorce? Soft Brexit? Hard Brexit? No deal Brexit?

ITALY
'I thank God and Italians for the honour of being
able to defend my country and my children.'
Matteo Salvini

On the morning of February 3rd, 2018, Luca Traini, a 28-year-old white Italian male, drives through the town of Macerata in his Alfa Romeo. You'll find Macerata, not far from the Adriatic coast, in the region of Marche, central Italy. The town having no particular claim to fame, until now. This is to be no ordinary morning for Traini, he's got targets to shoot. His targets, anyone who looks like they come from Africa, anyone who happens to be black. Jennifer Otioto, just one year older than Traini, is shot as she waits at a bus stop. She's just one of six victims, shot by Traini that morning. Fortunately, all survive the attempt to kill them. Traini parks his car close to the Monument of the Fallen, an archway built in the time of the fascist dictator, Benito Mussolini. It's here that he's arrested.

He gives a fascist salute, the Italian flag draped around his shoulders. In 2017, Traini had stood as a candidate representing a political group known at the time as Lega Nord (Northern League) in local elections, a political party well known for its extreme stance on race and immigration. The leader of Lega Nord being Matteo Salvini.

Perhaps, before I go any further, I should try and explain a little about the Italian political system. In June 1946, after 20 years of Fascist dictatorship under Benito Mussolini, Italy became a multi-party, parliamentary, democratic republic. Following a national referendum, the monarchy was abolished. Although it's many years since Mussolini's corpse was strung upside down, on public display in Milan, his shadow still stalks Italian society. A worrying number of Italians looking back to the time of Mussolini with a sense of nostalgia. In their minds, he is someone who tried to give Italy greatness. A number of Italian political parties today, gaining popularity by associating themselves with the Mussolini brand. Although to flagrantly promote fascism as political cause is technically illegal in Italy.

Government in Italy rests in the hands of the Council of Ministers, led by the Presidente del Consiglio (President of the Council), also known as the Prime Minister. This is the executive body of government. Its role is to ensure that laws are implemented and to oversee the everyday running of the country. Then there is the Chamber of Deputies and the Senate. Members of both chambers are elected for a period of five years. In order to run the country, the Council of Ministers depends on the support of these two chambers. Hence, both bodies have a significant influence in shaping policy. Without the majority support of Parliament, the Executive Body (Council of Ministers) cannot function.

Italy also has a President of the Republic. This person is elected by Parliament in a joint session of the two chambers. For the majority of the time, the position of President of the Republic is purely ceremonial. This person is elected to serve for a period of seven years. Just to confuse you, although mainly functioning in a ceremonial capacity, this person does have significant political influence. The President of the Republic chooses who should be Prime Minister, then asking for majority support from Parliament. Members of the Council of Ministers are appointed by the Prime Minister, these appointments then 'approved' by the President. If the Prime Minister/Council of Ministers and the two chambers making up Parliament, start to fall out and argue big time, effectively meaning that government cannot function (something that has happened on a regular basis since 1946), only the President has the power to dissolve parliament, thus setting off a general election.

Are you with me so far? Good.

You have to be over the age of 25 to stand for election to the Chamber of Deputies. To stand for election to the Senate, you have to be at least 40 (I don't know why, don't ask). All Italian citizens over the age of 18 can vote for members of the Chamber of Deputies. However, to vote for members of the Senate, you have to be at least 25 (I said, don't ask). The way voting is organised is no less complicated. Italians get two votes, one for each body of parliament. Then there's a mix of first-past-the-post and proportional representation when it comes to who ends up in either the Chamber of Deputies or the Senate.

To add to the political minestrone, under the Italian constitution, the twenty regions of the country are sub-autonomous entities with defined powers.

As you can see, the Italian political system is 'easy' to understand. What appears to be a rather complex system, came into being explicitly to avoid one group or individual holding complete power.

Let me give a little more background to Italian politics, it may give you some understanding as to why the majority of Italians have almost total disdain for politicians. Yes, honestly, even more than in the UK and US, where the people have had to deal with Brexit and Trump. By the 1990s it was widely recognised that something needed to be done to try and clean up the sordid and corrupt state of Italian politics. Mani Pulite (Clean Hands Operation), exposed corruption at the very centre of government, linking much of it to big business. The dragnet pulled in a number of former prime ministers, along with hundreds of politicians and businesspeople (businessmen really). As 1993 came to a close, 251 members of Parliament were under investigation. A whirlwind was sweeping through the long-established political parties. A number of those who found themselves under investigation, committed suicide. The Italian press labelled the whole affair as 'Tangentopoli' or 'Bribe City'.

For a brief time, it looked like genuine change had come to the Italian political landscape. But the whirlwind had resulted in the complete disintegration of established politics, which in itself was no bad thing. But what would replace that which had gone? The old traditional parties fragmented, new parties appeared, some melding in with the old. And who stepped into the political void that appeared to have been left? Silvio Berlusconi. He came onto the political scene promising the Italian people something radically new. His new party, Forza Italia (Come on Italy), would save the country from collapsing into communism. The name of the party taken directly from a chant often used by football supporters to encourage the national team. Berlusconi promised to do for Italy what he had done for himself. As a multi-millionaire businessman, he would create a wealthy and prosperous Italy. He would be responsible for creating a 'new Italian miracle'. I know and you know that the Italian public should have been far more sceptical. Although he presented himself as something new and fresh, untainted by the goings on of old political groupings, much of his business success came from his very close ties to such people. He was as much a part of what many Italians regarded as the establishment as anybody, but he was able to convince enough voters of the opposite.

It's perhaps worth giving a little time to have a closer look at Berlusconi, in many ways he was the prototype for Donald Trump's election campaign and presidency.

SILVIO BERLUSCONI – Il CAVALIERE (THE KNIGHT)
'I am the Jesus Christ of politics. I sacrifice myself for everyone.'

From past pages looking at the story of the mafia, you're already familiar with Berlusconi's alleged association with organised crime. Also, when we were looking at 'Being Italian' and issues related to the payment of tax, Berlusconi appeared again.

Tobias Jones, in The Dark Heart of Italy, perhaps best describes the pervasive nature, no better still, the invasive nature of Berlusconi's influence and hold on Italian society:

'By 2010, Berlusconi appeared to be the Japanese knotweed of Italian politics. No matter what you throw at him he keeps coming back, his roots and shoots increasingly insulating themselves into the landscape.'

In 2022, Berlusconi was still one of Italy's wealthiest individuals, his fortune having grown out of building up a vast media empire, much of this done with the support of politicians who were to be swept up in Operazione Mani Pulite.

As you're already aware, unlike the UK and the US, where government and politics in general tend to be dominated by two political parties, in Italy there are numerous political groupings, all having the potential to share in government by working in coalition with others. After launching Forza Italia, Berlusconi soon climbed into bed with parties to the right and extreme right of Italian politics. An alliance between Forza Italia, Berlusconi's party, Lega Nord (having popular support in the north) and the neo-fascist Movimento Sociale Italiano (having popular support in the south) proved to be a successful partnership, giving Berlusconi electoral victory in 1994. Although his first taste at being Prime Minister of Italy was short lived, the alliance soon falling apart, Berlusconi had firmly planted his political flag with the extreme right of Italian politics.

Berlusconi came back as Prime Minister, again with the support of right-wing parties, in 2001 through to 2006. And finally, he was Prime Minister from 2008 through to 2011.Throughout his time at the very centre of Italian politics, Berlusconi presented himself as a successful man who knew how to get things done. Only remaining on the political stage to champion the cause of ordinary Italians against career politicians. His claim to be an outsider, not tainted by political intrigue, not really a politician, certainly appealed to a large number of Italians. He was a showman, crudity and womanising being very much part of his style. At all times attempting to disguise his true age, dressed in expensive designer suits, hair transplant now jet black and pasted to his head. At every opportunity associating himself with beautiful young women. In 2011, when facing allegations of underage sex with a prostitute and abusing his power as Prime Minister in a cover up, Berlusconi joked with reporters, saying that a survey had shown how incredibly popular he is with women.

'When asked if they would like to have sex with me, 30% of women said, "Yes", while the other 70% replied, "What, again?"'

His control over much of the Italian media obviously worked massively in his favour, allowing him to push the Berlusconi brand into Italian homes. A celebrity, sometimes outrageous, someone who 'told it like it is', someone who stepped outside the accepted protocols of politics. When dealing with foreign leaders, he would often come across as dismissive, arrogant, flippant in his manner; displaying few of the usual skills of tact and diplomacy expected of a national leader.

To an international audience, Berlusconi was often regarded as a clown, a showman with little genuine credibility. But his brand of what was to eventually be labelled 'Berlusconismo' by others, worked inside Italy. If we measure his success by the number of years that he held the position of Prime Minister, he was one of the most successful 'politicians' in the history of Italy. Not since Mussolini did any single individual have such dominance over the country. And in 2022, he was still around, pulling strings and doing deals. Still influencing the shape of Italian politics. The dog crap seemingly impossible to scrape off.

Although Berlusconi's climb into the ring of national politics was supposed to represent a break from corruption, it wasn't long before he was under investigation for a range of corrupt business dealings, bribes, links to the mafia, and dubious tax returns. It became clear to anyone who cared to look, that Berlusconi used his times in the office of Prime Minister to serve his own business needs and doing whatever he could to avoid being prosecuted. Any who claimed that he was guilty of being corrupt, dismissed as evidence of a left-wing conspiracy against him. Even the judiciary were portrayed by Berlusconi and his supporters as being socialist, with some having communist sympathies. Absurd yes, but it served to deflect attention away from Berlusconi, the corrupt politician. Instead, he became Berlusconi the victim. His sense of duty to the Italian people is what kept him in politics, nothing more. And what did he get in return for his sacrifice? Constant attacks from career politicians, biased reporting from some sections of the media, and unelected judges doing the bidding of the establishment. 'I'm your saviour and I'm constantly being crucified. Don't trust those who are doing this, they are not on your side.' The Berlusconi myth served him well.

During his election campaign in 2001, he looked into every living room across Italy, urging true Italians not to reject this great moment in the history of the nation. He looked the electorate in the eye, offering a personal contract, pledging to lower taxes, raise pensions, cut red tape, create greater efficiency and increase prosperity for all.

In each term as Prime Minister of Italy, Berlusconi was embattled against what he would have you believe to be 'the old guard', those who conspired to 'destroy' him. In 2010, Italy's Constitutional Court changed a law that protected a serving prime minister from prosecution. This change meant that Berlusconi could be tried for outstanding corruption and tax evasion before he left office. In February 2011, he was ordered to stand trial for allegedly soliciting sex from a 17-year-old prostitute and abusing his power whilst in office in an attempt to cover things up. In the end the trial was adjourned, the courts not sure if constitutionally the case against him could proceed. By late 2011, the Italian economy was in free fall, many having doubts that the situation could be revived under Berlusconi's leadership. Under pressure from political partners in the coalition, and what was basically a vote of no confidence in parliament, Berlusconi had no option other than to resign. But as you already know, this certainly didn't mean that he would then simply fade away. A number of criminal trials were to follow.

'I am without doubt the person who's been the most persecuted in the entire history of man.' Berlusconi

In October 2012 he was found guilty of tax fraud and sentenced to four years in prison. I remember thinking at the time, at last they have him. The reality is that endless appeals resulted in Berlusconi never actually going to prison. Throughout all of this he continued to influence and shape Italian politics inside and outside parliament. In 2013, he was found guilty of illegally acquiring and then publishing the results of a police wiretap involving a rival politician. For this he was sentenced to a year in prison, yet again the sentence never served. Before the end of 2013, Berlusconi was to be on the wrong side of the law again. This time he was found guilty of soliciting sex from an underage prostitute, sentenced to serve seven years in prison and barred from holding public office. You already know what I'm going to say. Berlusconi never went to prison, appeals against the sentence ensured that would never happen. Eventually the tax fraud case from 2012, and Berlusconi's guilt, was confirmed by Italy's highest court. Although the court upheld the guilty verdict, the sentence was reduced to one year. By this time, Berlusconi's age made it very unlikely he would ever be incarcerated. The growing number of criminal cases against him and the fact that he was barred from holding public office until 2019, didn't result in Berlusconi shying away from political and public life. He continued to shape the political scene of Italy, his face and comment still a feature of the daily news.

At the time of writing, 2022, Berlusconi appeared in the news as regular as the weather forecast. He simply refused to disappear, to slip away and eventually die. His facelifts, false tans and hair transplant appearing to ensure his longevity. His sexual antics enhancing his status of being a 'real', masculine, Italian man. Age, why should that matter? That's not a problem for someone with the sexual vigour of Silvio Berlusconi – 'Viagra is for lesser mortals.' His supporters admiring him for his apparent 'energy', his straight talking, his supposed honesty. Whatever he'd done, been accused of doing, his followers were willing to forgive him. The real, steadfast stalwarts, those who some may describe as sycophantic in their adoration, continuing to believe he was one of them. An ordinary man, fighting for them as their knight (Uomo Qualunque e Cavaliere). Someone on their side, fighting against establishment forces, giving them a voice. None of us are perfect, we all sin. At least he has the integrity to be honest about it. 'Tutti sono colpevoli di qaulcosa.'

At times, Berlusconi's apparent disregard for the Italian constitution resulted in calls from opposition leaders for his impeachment. Well, they would do that, it was all part of the grand conspiracy against him.

In May 2019, soon after his political ban had been lifted, Berlusconi, representing Forza Italia, easily won a seat in the European Parliament. In 2022, Forza Italia become part of a coalition government with other political parties on the right.

THE RISE OF MATTEO SALVINI & GIORGIA MELONI
'We will go to Europe to change the rules that have impoverished Italians.'
Matteo Salvini

In 2018, I just happened to be in Perugia when Matteo Salvini was addressing a public meeting. He stood on a platform, the sleeves of his white shirt rolled up, addressing a crowd of about 200 people, in a relaxed manner. There was little factual substance to what he was saying, but he was good at delivering his message. The crowd looked happy, applauding what he had to say. On the outer edge of those eagerly listening to Salvini speak, stood a little distance back from the crowd, were several protesters. As Salvini spoke, they repeatedly chanted, 'Fascista! Fascista!' I thought it was interesting how he responded. Rather than encouraging a violent verbal reply from the crowd listening to him, he simply said, 'Take no notice of them, they're just young fools who have no idea what they're saying. Ignore them, listen to me, they're not important.'

By 2018, there was a definite feeling in the air that the country was favouring a move to the right. After years of pouring scorn on the south of Italy and its people, Lega Nord simply became Lega, no longer speaking about breaking the country apart and casting the south out of Italy for being 'too African'. Matteo Salvini had seen his party move from being regarded as outsiders, a fringe, extremist group, only really gathering northern votes, to a position where governing the whole country could be a real possibility. Silvio Berlusconi, still very much striding the political stage with Forza Italia, pushed to one side by the more extreme rhetoric of Matteo Salvini.

Anti-immigration had always been the main focus of Lega's campaign, with Salvini scathing of centre-left governments that had, in his words, 'filled Italy with illegal immigrants.' Others, from politicians and journalists to political analysts and intellectuals, criticizing him for stirring up racism and hatred. Many directly linking his 'inflammatory' campaigning with the shootings in Macerata. Traini, the person responsible for the shootings, justified the attacks, saying that his actions were in 'revenge' for the murder and dismemberment of 18-year-old Pamela Mastropietro. The main suspect for her murder being a failed asylum seeker. Lurid details of missing body parts ensured that the killing became a central feature of the elections. Salvini pushing the argument that centre-left governments had 'blood on their hands' for allowing migrants to remain in the country. Prime Minister Gentiloni asking for calm and responsibility from all political parties, adding that 'hatred and violence' will not be allowed to divide Italy.

On March 4th Italy voted. Once all of the results had been computed, the main losers were Partito Democratico and Berlusconi's Forza Italia, the two parties gaining from their loss, MoVimento5stella and Lega. The constituency of Macerata won by a right-wing coalition led by Lega. But who would ultimately form a government? MoVimento5stella, Partito Democratico, Lega and Forza Italia may have gobbled up the majority of the votes, but no one party has won enough seats to be able to form a government alone. For months there was political deadlock, for a time it looked like the Italian president would have to ask the centre-left government of Gentiloni to remain in place until fresh elections could be organised. Italian politics is a complex and, at times, a confusing business. The Italian electorate has to sit back and wait to see what comes out of the deals that are being made. Your vote, and the political complexion of government you were hoping for could be very different when 'your' party climbs into bed with those you thought were the 'enemy'.

The eventual outcome was a marriage between a protest/anti-establishment party, MoVimento5stella, and an extreme anti-immigrant party, Lega. An outcome that I had not expected. But then, I'd not predicted or expected Brexit and I'd definitely not expected President Donald Trump. Perhaps that's one of the problems with someone who holds political leanings to the left, you expect rational and logical outcomes. I think I need to develop a more flamboyant and bizarre imagination. How could a party that promoted itself as a break from an Italy of the past, MoVimento5stella, cosy up with a party of xenophobic racists, Lega? The one thing they did have in common was a disdainful view of the EU.

So, on June 1st, 2018, Italy found itself with Matteo Salvini (Lega) and Luigi Di Maio (MoVimento5stella) as Deputy Prime Ministers. Mattarella, Italy's president, appointing Giuseppe Conte (MoVimento5stella) as Italy's Prime Minister. To put this into some sort of context. Coming out of a national election, the country had someone probably liberal leaning as Prime Minister (although, as you already are aware, this person is not elected by public vote). One Deputy Prime Minister, the leader of a party that has the capital letter V in its party name, the V symbolising, Fuck Off to Politics (Fuck Off in Italian, Vaffanculo). The other Deputy Prime Minister, the leader of a party with similar views to, for example, the English Defence League or Britain First in the UK, or the American Freedom Party in the US. Could this bizarre romance last? I guess there was one positive, Silvio Berlusconi's nose had been pushed out of place. But you already know, he was not going to go away.

Berlusconi at the age of 81: 'I'm like a good wine. I only get better with age. Now I'm perfect.'

The leader of Lega also had ambitions beyond the borders of Italy. In the months leading up to the EU elections of 2019, Salvini launched an alliance of far-right parties across Europe, many political commentators still sticking with the term 'populist' as a means of identifying those who, if not fascist in the purist sense of the term, were most certainly xenophobic and nationalistic. The consistent use of the term 'populist', intended or not, covering their true identity. These are political parties with a very strong stench of Nazism/Fascism in their DNA. Marine Le Pen, the leader of France's National Rally party (the party name recently changed from National Front), enthusiastically threw her weight behind this pan-European far-right bloc. Nationalist parties from Austria, Denmark, Belgium, Finland, Germany, the Netherlands and Estonia were already signed up, with others to follow. At its launch, Salvini calls the EU 'a nightmare, not a dream.' The slogan adopted by this far-right alliance sounded harmless enough, 'Towards a Europe of Common Sense.' Nationalist parties that had once called for their respective countries to withdraw from the EU, now intending to join together as a voting bloc in order to reform it from the inside. The early name adopted by those joining together, the European Alliance of Peoples and Nations. Again, it all sounded sensible and cosy. The reality is that this new alliance hoped to become the third, perhaps even the second, most influential and powerful group in the European Parliament, with Salvini as the self-appointed leader. Pride and patriotism would be the virtues of this new alliance, with no nation feeling the need to be apologetic for its history.

Matteo Salvini firmly refutes the claim that he is a fascist. At the same time announcing that he will not take part in celebrations commemorating Liberty Day and the defeat of fascism in Italy. Salvini arguing that it had become nothing more than a 'Fascist v Communist game.'

In April 2019, Lazio football fans raise a large Mussolini banner before a match against AC Milan. The banner reading: 'HONOUR TO BENITO MUSSOLINI'. Groups of Lazio supporters singing fascist songs and giving Nazi salutes near to Piazza Loreto, the place where Benito Mussolini's body was strung up in 1945.

Salvini's grip at almost the very top of the greasy pole of politics looked to be even more secure when the biggest Italian winner in the European elections was Lega, taking more than a third of the vote. Partito Democratico suffering almost a 50% loss from its vote in 2014. Forza Italia also suffering a 50% loss, but with

Berlusconi gaining enough support to be elected to the European Parliament. Fratelli d'Italia, the other party to see an increase in its vote. It came as no surprise that Lega would take most of northern Italy, the area of the country where it had been strong for some time. With more than a third of the vote, Lega also took areas of the country that had traditionally been left-wing, including Umbria. Even in the south, an area of the country that for years Lega had described as a 'parasite' living off the rest of Italy, the party gained a significant number of votes. With Lampedusa, Italy's closest island to North Africa and therefore at the very heart of the migrant crisis, giving Lega its biggest electoral victory. Mayoral elections bring even more rewards for right-wing parties. Salvini describing right-wing mayors being elected in the region of Emilia-Romagna, traditionally known as the 'red belt of Italy', as 'extraordinary'. In total, Lega's partnership with Forza Italia and Fratelli d'Italia added another seven provincial capitals to its portfolio.

In the August of 2019, Salvini pulls Lega out of the marriage with MoVimento5stella, his aim being to force fresh national elections, opinion polls suggesting that his party could grab hold of power. I did question how long the bizarre relationship would last. Once again, government in Italy was thrown into turmoil. As Italians went about their daily routines, political shenanigans were played out between the different groups in parliament. At times it can feel quite bewildering to actually have a clear understanding of who governs the country.

There was very little love lost between Giuseppe Conti, the Prime Minister, and Matteo Salvini. Conti accusing Salvini of being a political opportunist. Their relationship had always been one of sufferance, something forced upon them by the machinations of Italian politics. Without the support of parliament, Conti would have no alternative but to resign, his resignation probably resulting in new elections. Alternatively, Mattarella, the Italian president, could appoint an interim government, pushing any elections to the following year. Partito Democatico could stop bickering with MoVimento5stella, coming together in a coalition. This would, for now, thwart Salvini's ambitions. Salvini could throw his arms around Berlusconi, the two inviting Georgia Meloni, the leader of Fratelli d'Italia, to join them in a threesome. Are you keeping up with this? I think that you will have realised by now that the political complexion of an Italian government can change without a single Italian voter casting a vote. Although Giuseppe Conti resigns as Prime Minister, it did not result in fresh elections.

In the end Salvini was outmanoeuvred and ousted from his ministerial position when his former coalition partner, MoVimento5stella, came to some tenuous agreement with Partito Democratico and a smaller left-wing party, Liberi e Uguali (Free and Equal). Mattarella, you know who he is by now, then invited Giuseppe Conti to step back into his position as Prime Minister and form a new cabinet. Without a member of the public casting a single vote, Italy had now gone from a right leaning government to a centre-left government. Although I personally would always take up my right to vote, at times you do stop and question if there is any point. Surprisingly, Italy always has higher voter participation than the UK and the USA in national elections.

In 2020, coming to join Lega and Forza Italia, to the far-right of Italian politics, was Fratelli d'Italia (Brothers of Italy), its leader Giorgia Meloni. Her far-right credentials were clear to see when, at the age of 15, she joined the youth section of Movimento Sociale Italiano (Italian Social Movement). If you remember, I mentioned this political group before, very much the modern-day followers of the fascist leader, Benito Mussolini. Giorgia Meloni when answering a question about racism: 'Yes there is racism in Italy, against Italians.' As Covid-19 spread across the country, Fratelli d'Italia steadily climbed above MoVimento5stella in the opinion polls. By the end pf 2020, it was recognisable to anyone that a marriage with Lega and Forza Italia, could produce an unstoppable force in Italian politics. Should an election be on the cards, a coalition of the three would result in an unashamedly far-right, nationalistic, government.

As you spend more time in Italy, you'll soon notice that the birth of 'new' political parties is commonplace. Some are hybrids, whilst others are simply the same old party but rebranded. It really is a challenge to keep a check on who is who. As party names change, 'new' parties born, one party grafted onto another, it becomes difficult to sift out who is left, who is right and who is in the centre. And, according to the Italian media, there is only Centro-sinistra (Centre-left) and Centro-destra (Centre-right). The terms, extremist, far-right or far-left, appear to have disappeared from the Italian vocabulary. Lega, by any rational assessment, is on the extreme right of politics, its very soul xenophobic and ultra-nationalistic. Yet all news reporting labels Lega, Forza Italia and, the even more extreme, Fratelli d'Italia, as centre-right parties. I imagine the Ku Klux Klan launching an Italian franchise, with white supremacy and hate unashamedly, as in the US, used as its key selling point. The Italian news media reporting it as the launch of a new centre-right party.

I got into a little bit of a debate with an Italian on Facebook when I used the term Fascist in relation to Lega. Rather patronisingly, she pointed out that as a foreigner I obviously didn't really understand Italian politics. I guess it's not an unreasonable point to make. She informs me that Lega is a democratic party. Very true, I have to accept that valid point. She goes on. Lega is a democratic party; therefore, it cannot be fascist. I point out that both Mussolini and Hitler both, initially, used the democratic system. Her response is that I'm exaggerating and being ridiculous. She then goes on to 'explain' that the Italian media only uses the term 'extremist' for those who are politically extreme, like Communists and Fascists. I'm so glad that she cleared that up for me. It was our first and our last 'debate'.

Keep in mind what I've said about the political complexion of Italian government changing with bewildering regularity. In early January 2021, as Italy found itself grappling with another surge in Covid infections and resulting deaths, the country in almost complete lockdown, Italy is once again thrown into political meltdown. Matteo Renzi, leader of Italia Viva, throws a spanner in the works. People inside and outside the political system struggling to understand what Renzi hoped to gain by withdrawing his party's support from the coalition government. Renzi stating that he was withdrawing his support because of disagreements relating to the spending of money from the European Recovery Fund (Coronavirus recovery funds).

The move threw the country, in the very depths of the pandemic, into political turmoil. Italia Viva a small party, had a vital role to play in maintaining some form of stable government. The Prime Minister, Giuseppe Conti was left in a situation of having to try and cobble together enough support from a number of political groupings in order to remain in office. If that was not possible, he would have to submit his resignation to President Mattarella, who would then have to hold consultations in the hope of putting together a new government. The Italian people were yet again left simply observing the shenanigans of their political 'leaders', at the same time locked into a deadly pandemic. No public votes would be cast, the public would have no say. But the government would change.

Giorgia Meloni, Matteo Salvini and others had the scent of political power in their nostrils. Opinion polls showing that opposition parties on the right were increasingly gaining popular support.

In the end, elections were avoided. President Mattarella appoints Mario Draghi as prime minister, the appointment approved by Italy's parliament. Draghi, a technocrat rather than a politician, the ex-head of the European Central Bank, had the job of pulling a coalition cabinet together. This he did, bringing in leading figures from MoVimento5star, Lega and Partito Democratico, amongst others. It's presented to the Italian public as a unity government. A government that would fight two battles, the coronavirus pandemic and economic recovery. This was Italy's third administration in less than three years. You can easily see how it's difficult to keep up with who is in political power and who is out.

So, as Italy moved from spring into the hot summer of 2021, the covid vaccination programme having been rapidly speeded up, deaths and infection rates down, the country relatively open, Mario Draghi (sometimes known as Super Mario, the title given for his supposed role in saving the Euro) remained in the position of prime minister.

But one thing was certain, nationalistic parties to the right continued to gain popular support. Almost every single news item related to politics made reference to either Lega or Fratelli d'Italia. The media still insisting on giving them the label of centre-right. With Matteo Salvini and Giorgia Meloni competing to become the most credible leader of a right-wing coalition. By October 2021, it was Giorgia Meloni who was rapidly gaining ground. In just over two years, her party, Fratelli d'Italia, has quadrupled its support, now placed as Italy's third most popular party. A party that just a few years ago was on the fascist fringes of Italian politics, now having a significant influence over the mainstream. Giorgia Meloni had become the first woman in Italian history to lead a major political party. Opinion polls giving her an approval rating of almost 50%, way in front of Salvini. Her book release, Io Sono Giorgia – le mie radici, le mie idee (I am Giorgia – my roots, my ideas) gained massive media attention. Although increasingly popular, Meloni needed Salvini if the right were to have a chance of gaining power in government. Although her personal popularity was higher than that of Salvini, Lega still had a higher popularity rating.

Just as in the UK and the US, the Italian people were looking for change. Increasing numbers willing to ditch centrist politicians, the more traditional political parties regarded as having failed and offering nothing new. The patriotic, nationalistic, tone of Lega and Fratelli d'Italia tapping into the worries and concerns of the electorate. Hard-line positions on immigration sit at the very heart of both parties, along with very similar views on LGBTQ related issues and human rights in general. Both having a negative view of the EU. No longer threatening to withdraw Italy from membership, but both insisting that many of Italy's economic problems stem from EU austerity measures; the external bogeyman identified.

In July 2022, MoVimento5star abstains from a crucial vote on economic policy, effectively withdrawing its support for the coalition government. Once again politics was thrown into chaos. Draghi, frustrated by the political fighting that had been going on for months, offered his resignation to the Italian President, Sergio Mattarella. He rejects Draghi's resignation in the hope of holding the government together. Voices from across Europe also appealed for Draghi to remain in post, political analysts looking at Italy dumbfounded. More than a thousand mayors, from across the whole of Italy, signed an open letter asking Draghi to stay. The mayor of Milan, Beppe Sala, saying that the Italian people would not understand why the politicians had brought the county into yet another crisis. But Italy's right-wing parties were grouping together like vultures, they could smell blood. Draghi's departure from government could force an early general election, something that Berlusconi, Salvini and Meloni would very much welcome.

By the end of July, it became increasingly clear that the coalition government could not survive, Sergio Mattarella finally accepting Mario Draghi's resignation. September 25th is the date set for national elections to take place, approximately six months ahead of time. An early election having every chance of Italy finding itself with an extreme right-wing, nationalist, government. Such an outcome having serious implications way beyond the borders of Italy. Giorgia Meloni, as you know, the leader of Fratelli d'Italia , with her eyes set on becoming Italy's first female premier:

'The will of the people is expressed in one way: by voting. Let's give hope and strength back to Italy.'

In September 2022, the predicted victory of the far-right became a reality. Giorgia Meloni becoming Italy's first female PM. The national vote on Sunday September 25th had given Meloni's party, Fratelli d'Italia (Brothers of Italy), a dominant position in parliament. Governing in alliance with Salvini's Lega and Berlusconi's Forza Italia, Italy now had the most right-wing government since the time of Mussolini.

Meloni has always denied having fascist sympathies, yet willingly embraces the old fascist slogan - 'God, fatherland and family.'

Meloni's political platform:

'Yes to the natural family, no to the LGBT lobby. Yes to sexual identity, no to gender ideology. No to Islamist violence, yes to secure borders. No to mass migration. No to big international finance. No to the bureaucrats from Brussels.'

In 2018, Brothers of Italy had won little more than 4% of the national vote.

It could be argued that this is what happens when the democratic left of politics can't get its act together and offer people hope. The same could be said of the UK and the USA.

By the time you have the book in your hands we will know how extreme Italy's new government turned out to be.

DONALD JOHN TRUMP

'Donald Trump is the President of the United States. As a comedian,
it's difficult to make that sound any funnier.'
Kevin Bridges – Scottish comedian

On January 20th, 2017, a proud, 'pussy grabbing', Donald John Trump took the oath of office as the 45th President of the United States.

'From this day forward, it's going to be only America first – America First. America will start winning again, winning like never before. We will make America strong again. We will make America wealthy again. We will make America proud again. We will make America safe again. And yes, together, we will make America great again.' Donald J. Trump's Inaugural address, Washington, January 20th, 2017.

Trump's self-satisfaction at 'pussy grabbing', in a very literal sense, could be regarded as a metaphor for the whole of the USA. America was the pussy being grabbed and millions loved him for it. I'm sure that the thought of having him as president sent many into a shrieking orgasm, the rest of America feeling nauseous and incredibly embarrassed. From TV celebrity and dubiously 'successful' business tycoon to possibly the most powerful position in the world. And someone as the Vice President, Michael Richard Pence, who believed, still believes, that the world is no more than a few thousand years old. Pence who would eventually be thrown to the mob by Trump and threatened with a lynching outside the Capitol Building in Washington, the very centre of American democracy. Trump and Pence, who for more than four years had been harder to separate than shagging dogs. If only at the beginning someone had thought to grab a bucket of cold water.

To millions in America and people from around the world, the US had a buffoon, someone crude, lacking in intelligence, a misogynist, a racist, a pathological liar, a fraudster and a narcissist in the Oval Office. And yet millions of Americans truly believed that Trump was their saviour. I guess what's just as worrying for the future, is that millions of Americans still think of him in that way. The number of votes cast for Trump in the 2020 election actually increased!

I think I mentioned earlier in the book meeting my first totally devoted Trump supporters in Florence, professional and by most judgements intelligent people. They were not to be the last. It was via UmbriAliens that I came into contact with at least three others. I met them during the election campaign. Trump's campaign rallies to most rational thinking people were becoming more bizarre and outrageous. It's one of my first evening meals with quite a number of UmbriAliens, Americans, Brits, Germans, Australians, New Zealanders, Dutch and Italians. Almost a United Nations. Anyway, I'm sat at one end of a long table. At the opposite, far end of the table, above the rest of the conversation that's flowing around, I can hear a loud American voice. He's white, I would guess in his early to mid-fifties. He's justifying his support for Trump to others sat at that end of the table.

'Well, Obama has destroyed America. No, listen he has. I'm not convinced he's even American. I know he's black, obviously, but he's made racism worse than it was before. The country is a mess because of him. That's why I'm here in Italy.'

From what I can hear, it turns out that the defender of Trump is a former New York cop.

'If Clinton wins, America will be ruined. Immigrants will just flood into the country. The Democrats just can't be trusted. What are the Democrats going to do about terrorists? And the other thing is, they'll take away our guns. And look at Bernie Sanders, he's a socialist!'

I soon learn that many Americans equate the label of socialist with the worship of Lucifer, the great adversary of humanity. Socialism, the great evil, the destroyer of everything that all true patriotic American holds close to their hearts. Perhaps I'll need to hide my horns and forked tail. The ex-New York cop continues:

'Trump has my full support. He's the one who can bring change to America. He's different, he's one of us. If the Democrats win, I won't be going back.'

I'm almost hoping Trump wins, perhaps this white ex-cop will then leave Italy.

As the weeks go by, life in Umbria moving from summer to early autumn, another member of UmbriAliens, an American, increasingly posts items on Facebook in support of Trump. I guess by now you will have realised where I stand politically. If not, what's been going through your mind as you've been reading through the previous pages? I have no problem with people expressing an opinion on issues related to politics, supporting a particular political party, posting items and views on Facebook. But, if you post something then the chances are someone may question or challenge what you post; I expect that. For me it's not a problem and I don't take it personally. Most of my posts related to Trump ridiculed what he had to say, no surprise there then. Anything I said I directed at Trump and his campaign, nothing directed at anyone on Facebook. However, there are some people who do feel the need, for whatever reason, to get personal. The American posting comments and items in support of Trump being a prime example. Again, by any judgement, an intelligent and articulate individual. He'd worked in Washington where he still had contacts and friends. He very sternly pointed this out to me. I have no idea why, I'm not sure what he thought would happen.

Whatever Trump says, whatever Trump does, is supported and defended by our man who has contacts in Washington. Even Trump ridiculing and mimicking the journalist, Serge Kovaleski, is defended and justified. A mocking Trump flailing his arms around as he speaks about 'the poor man'. The rally laughing at Trump's antics. Trump threatening violence is defended and justified. It appears that Trump can do no wrong. As I've pointed out, my posts are directed at Trump. Our Washington man takes my comments personally.

'I'm a Vietnam vet. I have contacts in Washington. Stop poking the bear.'

I'm really not sure what he thought would occur if I continued to post criticism of Trump. A sudden early morning knock on the door at my home in Umbria from the CIA or some other clandestine and secretive branch of the American state.

So, after the warning to 'stop poking the bear', Washington Man then posts what I'm sure he thought was an insult:

'I bet you're one of those socialists. That's what you are, a socialist.'

I simply thanked him for his admirable insight. His response was to threaten to block me on Facebook, which is in fact what he soon did. Obviously, I thought that was the end of our very warm and amicable relationship. No, I didn't find that I was being shadowed by the CIA. The wife of Washington Man sent me a private message. The message basically said that she thought I was a nasty person. Then going on to try and explain why she and her husband supported Trump. The country had to protect its borders from illegal immigrants and terrorists. She then went on to say that she was not being racist, but when had a 'blue eyed' (honestly, her words) American committed an act of terrorism? I responded by simply asking her to look at all the mass shootings. Much to my distress, she also blocked me. And I thought we were getting along so well.

Trump's ludicrous campaign circus continued on its way, surprisingly, totally untouched by the socialist Brit living in Umbria. Surely he couldn't win the election. Regardless of his politics, he's unable to string a meaningful sentence together. I was wrong about Brexit, and I was wrong about this. How much more wrong could life get? Answer – a real, world-wide pandemic! I got that a bit wrong as well.

Not wanting to worry you and the rest of the world. I have to tell you there are some reports suggesting that Trump has been able to amass more than ten times the campaign cash he had in 2016. Apparently, as early as April 2021,

Trump's 'Save America PAC' already had $85 million in the bank. That's some bloody big crowd funding going on there. Clearly democracy is an expensive machine in America.

Trump didn't fit the expected behaviour of a president. Either by intention or by accident of character and level of intellect, he was going to break with custom. He was never going to exhibit taken for granted presidential attributes. And for the millions of Americans who follow him, this is a big part of his appeal. Trump was and remains, the Ronald McDonald of politics. Far less successful in business, but delivering quick, cheap, politics.

Throughout Trump's time in the Oval Office there were many asking questions about his mental state. Is Donald Trump mentally ill? I don't think so. Different and definitely outrageous, but is this evidence of mental instability? Perhaps asking that question is a convenient means to escape looking at what's wrong with America. It could be argued that Trump and those closest to him (Stephen Bannon having been the architect of Trump's nationalist and populist campaign and administration) simply tapped into feelings of injustice, anger and even hatred that already existed in many parts of America. Trump certainly stoked the flames and manipulated events on a massive scale, but the smoke was already there. In a sense, Trump gathered up gossip and anecdotes, then throwing them out to a receptive audience. It didn't matter if they were credible or factual. If you appear to be winning people over you amplify the fabricated stories, making them even more preposterous. Johnson in the UK, Salvini, Meloni, and Berlusconi before them, doing exactly the same. Political leaders do not exist in a vacuum, they exist within the 'order' and times that produce them. Replacing Donald J Trump will probably not be enough to 'repair' America. Many would argue that there needs to be an understanding of how the 'American Dream', in its distorted form, foments and nurtures toxic values.

I suspect that if you are American you're not going to like what I'm going to say next. Perhaps the reality is that Trumpism represents the beating heart of America. Was Trump an anomaly and a temporary hiccup, simply an ugly episode? A momentary infection that for a time distorted true American values? Or was the Trump presidency a symptom of something more pervasive and destructive? Something that highlighted the hollowness of the 'American Dream'?

The reality is that in the November election of 2020, 74 million Americans voted for Donald Trump. They were not rejecting him. He is their 'American Dream'.

For others the 'American Dream' is probably represented by the 22-year-old, Amanda Gorman, in her poem, The Hill We Climb. The poem that she read at the inauguration of Joe Biden, to an audience across the world of millions, called for all Americans to 'leave behind a country better than the one we were left.' It was certainly a powerful and beautiful message, one that perfectly fits the idealism of the liberal American Dream. The question is, can the US move on and become better than it has been? I know that I'm sounding incredibly pessimistic, but it's going to take something far more radical and charismatic than a Biden presidency to, at best, patch over the deep fissures in American society.

The abomination that was President Trump, no longer sits in the Oval Office. True American democracy was 'saved' and restored. And yet the streets of Washington, for a time, gave the appearance of a city under army occupation. Troops resting by the feet of Abraham Lincoln. The National Guard sleeping next to their weapons.

I may not be accurate in this, but I think the last time the legislators had to have the protection of fully armed troops was as far back as 1861. If armed soldiers are needed to patrol the streets of the capital city in order to protect democracy, you can be left in no doubt that something has gone seriously wrong. Armed troops patrolling the streets, evidence of a dangerously polarized country. Whatever democracy there is in America it is most certainly broken. But any God fearing, patriotic, Republican will be able to explain the storming of the Capitol. Trump supporters didn't storm America's seat of democracy, no. It was members of the violent terrorist group Antifa, masquerading as Trump supporters. And thus, the delusion continues. A delusion supported by Fox News and a bewildering number of people in the Republican party. The FBI stated that Antifa simply means anti-fascist. It has no solid membership base or national structure. Well, obviously, the FBI would say that, it's an established part of the conspiracy against the American people.

Before 2016 a Trump presidency was unthinkable. The storming of the Capitol, for the majority of Americans, unimaginable.

STOP THE STEAL RALLY & THE CAPITOL

January 6th, 2021, a date that will be etched into the American psyche alongside 9/11. The commonality between the two being one of complete shock. On that January day, a violent mob invaded the Capitol Building in Washington. A joint session of Congress, there to certify the electoral win of Joe Biden and Kamala Harris, having to run, to find hiding places. Rudy Giuliani being just one of a number who encouraged the violence: 'Let's have trial by combat!' I'm not going to recreate the storming of the building. There will be few people who didn't see what happened in media reports across the world.

Trump, as you're well aware, is no great orator, he finds difficulty engaging his brain to complete one full sentence. But he had thousands of loyal followers amassed and ready to take any necessary action to put him back in the White House. It made no difference to them if he rambled incoherently. All he had to do was press the button by stoking anger and pointing it in the direction of the Capitol. The sycophantic Pence had become one of the mob's main targets. He had betrayed Trump and he had betrayed the mob. Trump telling the crowd that Pence had to do the right thing. All he has to do is ensure that this illegal election does not place Biden in the White House. Trump convincing the mob that Pence had the legal power to do that. Constitutionally Trump knew that Pence could not, but that's not what he told his followers. In a direct conversation with Pence, Trump had told him: 'You can either go down in history as a patriot or you can go down in history as a pussy.' In Trump's mind, Pence chose to be a 'pussy'. In his ramble to his followers, he continually targeted Pence, urging them forward.

'And we fight. We fight like hell. You're not going to have a country any more ..... So, let's walk down Pennsylvania Avenue - and the Capitol.'

Trump knew the nature of the crowd. He was well aware of the potential for violence. His most loyal followers were there, the white supremacist Proud Boys. In a number of tweets prior to January 6th, Trump had all but given his direct backing to the violent behaviour of the Proud Boys. On December 18th, Trump had tweeted:

'We won the Presidential Election by a lot. FIGHT FOR IT. Don't let them take it away!'

The following day he tweeted:

'Big protest on 6 January. Be there, will be wild!'

As the mob stormed the Capitol, spearheaded by the Proud Boys, and what can only be described as a range of paramilitary groups, the violence was accompanied with the chanting of 'Hang Pence!' Some in the crowd carrying a noose for just that purpose.

On January 7th, at 3.45am, Pence officially affirmed that Joe Biden had won the election.

As a result of the riot, five people died, including a police officer.

Where was Trump when the riot was taking place? He was safe, watching events on TV. According to some who were with him, Trump looked 'excited' and 'delighted'.

How could Homeland Security, the Secret Service, the FBI, the National Guard, and a host of others, not have planned for possible paramilitary violence on January 6th? For weeks, Trump and his closest supporters had been sowing the seeds of outrageous fake news. The Trump camp would declare victory when the votes were counted, even if he lost. Trump knew that his supporters would believe anything. The success of his election campaign in 2016 and his time as president were proof of that. He once bragged that he could shoot someone on Fifth Avenue and still people would enthusiastically vote for him. When the majority of the election results had been announced, Trump had done enough to convince his followers that the whole process was fraudulent. His second term in the White House had been stolen. Trump declared victory, looking into the homes of the American people, and announced that the Democrats had concocted a giant fraud on the nation. The FBI, the CIA, the entire intelligence community had conspired against him. What more proof did he need than their lack of willingness to find evidence pointing at interference from hostile forces both within and outside the country?

The Confederate flag flew alongside the Trump M.A.G.A flag. It was more than obvious who Trump's supporters were/are, and Trump was more than happy to open his arms and embrace them. Many of those flying the Confederate flag defending it as a symbol of protest, a rebellion against the liberal elite rather than an intentional symbol of hate. I'm sure there are some who don't grasp what the flag really represents. However, anyone with even the slightest understanding of American history will recognise its true message and intention. A yearning to return to the past, when life was more predictable and ordered. A time when certain groups were expected to know their place:

Chief Gillespie - 'Well, you're pretty sure of yourself, ain't you, Virgil? Virgil – that's a funny name for a nigger boy that comes from Philadelphia! What do they call you up there?'

Detective Tibbs - 'They call me Mr. Tibbs!'

Heat of the Night 1967. Virgil Tibbs – Sidney Poitier, Chief Gillespie – Rod Steiger

'Go home, we love you, you're very special.' Trump supposedly reflecting on the events of January 6th, 2021, although I doubt that he has ever seriously reflected on any of his actions. No remorse, no apology, no condemnation for what had taken place:

'These are the things that happen when a sacred landslide election victory is so unceremoniously and viciously stripped away from the great patriots who have been badly and unfairly treated for so long. Go home with love and in peace. Remember this day forever!'

What happened on January 6th was obviously a riot, encouraged by Donald Trump and those around him. A flagrant attempt to destabilise the whole democratic system of the USA. And yet the US Senate was unable to gather together enough votes to convict Trump on a charge of incitement to insurrection for what we all witnessed. It was a triumph for Trump. He'd managed to dodge a second impeachment, denouncing it as 'the greatest witch hunt in history.' Donald Trump's lawyer, Michael van der Veen, called the proceedings a 'show trial, the Democrats being 'obsessed with impeaching Mr Trump.' He went on, 'the entire spectacle has been nothing but the unhinged pursuit of a long-standing political vendetta against Mr Trump by the opposition party.' Mr Trump saying that no president had 'ever gone through anything like it.' Following on by saying that 'the movement to Make America Great Again had only just begun.'

Fast forward to June 2022 and you have the Select Committee hearings investigating January 6th, the attack on the United States Capitol. Very much set up like a court trial, the possibility of formal criminal proceedings to follow. What is clear is that it was an attempt to build a de facto case against Trump. In his opening statement, the chairperson of the committee, Democrat, Bennie Thompson, outlined what would be, in a formal court, the prosecution's case, the 'charges' against Trump. He was at the very centre of a conspiracy aimed at overturning the lawful presidential election. Central to this conspiracy were Trump's actions in spurring a 'mob of domestic enemies of the Constitution to march down to the Capitol and subvert American democracy.' In a formal criminal case, the prosecution would then have to show evidence that the person 'charged', in this case Donald Trump, had the motive, the means, the opportunity and intent to commit illegal acts. It was made very clear at the start of the hearings that this was to be the committee's intention. In a formal criminal trial, the person charged would have the opportunity to present a defence, here that opportunity was not available. Many Americans regarded this as nothing more than a show trial, a kangaroo court. Trump being deliberately persecuted without the ability to defend himself.

Much like Berlusconi in Italy, whatever is being thrown at Trump doesn't result in him leaving the stage. On November 16th, 2022, Trump announced his bid for the White House in 2024. As I write in May 2023, Trump continued to take the centre stage of American politics. Two failed impeachments and countless accusations of public and private wrongdoing, appearing to inflict little if any damage to his approval rating. Threats of criminal charges and a whole range of civil cases against him doing little to dampen the enthusiasm of his followers.

CARRY ON BREXIT

'We are going to make a colossal success of Brexit. We are taking the machete of freedom to the brambles of EU regulation. Brexit means Brexit and we are going to make a titanic success of it.'
Boris Johnson

After a four-year transition period, on January 1st, 2021, the UK finally left the European Union. And the notion that the UK could bluff the EU into backing down by threatening to walk away without any deal, hadn't worked. Either by totally misunderstanding the political game being played, total ineptitude or deliberate sabotage on the part of the British government, the UK went over the Brexit cliff edge - a form of national tombstoning. The British people and the EU separated with the most extreme, rock-hard, Brexit.

The 'oven ready' Christmas present Brexit deal that Johnson proudly waved in front of the cameras included none of the promises made by the supporters of Brexit. Let me just remind you again of a couple of things the British public were told. The UK negotiating a free trade agreement with the EU would be remembered as 'one of the easiest in human history' - a total lie. People were told that the UK was 'going to get a great deal', a deal that would give Britain the 'exact same benefits', but without being a member of the EU and all the costs and obligations that go with it - another total lie. And yet the Brexit supporting tabloids were in jubilant spirit.

'Hallelujah! It's a Merry Brexmas' – Daily Mail

The SUN newspaper, on its front page, dressing Boris Johnson as Father Christmas.

Throughout 2020, opinion poll after opinion poll appeared to show that an increasing majority of the British people would rather have remained in the EU. Interestingly, surveys also found increasing support for EU membership across the continent. Even as early as 2019, analysts were predicting that Brexit was on course to cost the UK more than all the payments that had been made into the European Union Budget during the whole of Britain's membership. By the end of 2020, it was predicted the cost of leaving the EU would be at least £200 billion.

The dire predictions about Britain's future outside the EU didn't just come from someone like me on the left of politics. Moody, an International Credit Agency that could hardly be described as a left-wing propagandist, in 2020, downgraded Britain's international credit rating based on a number of factors, Brexit being the major contributor. Totally contradicting Boris Johnson's bluster that the UK would flourish outside the EU, Moody cited Brexit as a major factor hindering future economic growth. The New York Times, in 2020, stated that Wall Street viewed the British Pound as a second-rate currency.

And yet the British government still allowed the country to crash into the English Channel; why? From 2016 onwards, the Conservative party and Brexit became fused into one being. The party captured by its extreme right, now hostage to getting Brexit done but with absolutely no idea how to do it.

The Tory government, under Boris Johnson, promised that Brexit would liberate the UK from the 'straitjacket' of European trading regulations, releasing Britain to enjoy a bright new future on the global stage. In reality the opposite was soon shown to be true. Rather than liberating trade, Brexit resulted in a massive increase in bureaucracy for many British and European businesses. The Office for Budget Responsibility stating that the long-term effects of Brexit will be twice as damaging as those of Covid-19.

By the summer of 2021 the level of exports going from Britain to the EU had fallen by an estimated 68% compared with one year previously. The promises made that exit from the EU would bring great rewards were already being proved to be hollow, a shameful and misleading fantasy. 'Taking back control' had actually resulted in businesses having far less control. Membership of the EU, the Customs Union and the Single Market allows for easy, frictionless trade throughout the twenty-seven member states. Those inside the single market have one set of rules, British businesses, outside, have potentially twenty-seven different sets of rules to negotiate. Even UK government departments in effect admitted that leaving the EU had resulted in a nightmare for UK business, the Department for International Trade actually advising exporting businesses to register separate companies within the EU to avoid a mountain of paperwork, extra charges and taxes.

On an individual level, consumers in Europe soon found that after January 1st, 2021, they would have additional charges for VAT and customs declarations on goods purchased from UK-based companies. The tariff-free trade deal promised by Johnson was soon seen for what it was, a complete and utter sham.

Entirely as a result of Brexit, I decided to claim my German citizenship. If you remember, at the very beginning of the book I mentioned that my father originally came from Germany. It's something I had never intended to do, there was no need. Being the holder of a burgundy British/EU passport automatically made me a European citizen. As I've already said, Brexit swept that away. Those living in the EU with British passports, having to now jump through a variety of hoops to remain. The Brits I know in Italy, mourning the loss of being officially recognised as EU citizens, many thinking that it was inconceivable that the UK electorate would vote in favour of leaving. I guess there may be Americans, Australians and others reading this who may be thinking, 'well, join the club', we've always had to jump through extra hoops to live in Italy. I get that, but when you've had something torn away that for years you had thought was automatic, it gives a deep sense of loss. A loss that was totally unnecessary. Between 2016 and 2020, close to 360,000 people born in the UK applied for passports from countries within the EU.

I'm a realist, I know that the 'plight' of Brits living in the EU will be of little concern to the vast majority of those whose only home remains in the UK. Obviously, why would it bother them or even be of minor interest? But I think it has a lot to say about the supposed 'bright new dawn' of Brexit when as many as 360,000 British born citizens feel the need to claim an alternative nationality.

Sovereignty, freedom and power are nothing more than fictitious fantasy. Brexit has not made the UK stronger, and the rest of the world knows it. The rest of the world knows that the UK outside the EU is left weak and needy. Whilst the rest of the world recognises the UK's desperate position, the UK government, and some sections of media, continue to promote the fairy-tale that promised rewards will come.

Deserved, based on reality or not, prior to Brexit the UK was regarded as a rational, stable, pragmatic and open democracy. I'm not sure if the majority of people in the UK are aware of how perceptions have changed. Perhaps the average Brit is just not bothered.

Rem Korteweg from the Cligendale Institute in the Netherlands, speaking in 2020:

'For us, the UK has always been seen as like-minded: economically progressive, politically stable, having respect for the rule of law – a beacon of western liberal democracy. I'm afraid that's been seriously hit by the past four years. The Dutch have seen a country in a deep identity crisis; it's been like watching a close friend go through a really, really difficult time. Brexit is an exercise in emotion, not rationality; in choosing your own facts. And it's not clear how it will end.'

Niklolaus Blome from a leading German newspaper, Der Spiegel, is blunter about a Brexit UK:

'There is absolutely nothing good about Brexit ..... which would never have happened had Conservative politicians not, to a quite unprecedented degree, deceived and lied to their people.' He goes on to argue that much of the British media 'were complicit' in the betrayal of the British people. 'The constant trampling on fairness and facts', in effect allowing the UK to be 'captured by gambling liars, frivolous clowns and their paid cheerleaders.'

Elvire Fabry from France's Institut Jacques Delors:

'The politics promoted by Johnson and others, appears to have become detached from geopolitical reality – from the way the world is developing. It's a political vision turned towards yesterday's world.'

The vast majority of comment about Brexit has focused on its economic impact. But the European Union has always been about more than economics. At its very core is an attempt to prevent the nations of Europe, either by the design of some or as a result of unintended consequences, spiralling into war. The Europe of the second world war is part of history, with very few still alive who have personal memories. But it's certainly not something we should simply store away and forget. The history of the first half of the 20th century taught us a massively important lesson. A Europe divided can be an incredibly dangerous and deadly place. The war cemetery between Assisi and Spello provides poignant evidence of that.

The union of 27 nations will always be problematic, there will be disagreements, nations often having different priorities; no union can ever deliver perfection. But discussion, debate, bargaining, compromise and eventual agreement has to be better than the disastrous military conflicts of the past. Britain was never bullied and pushed by other members of the EU. The UK always had an equal place, with an equal voice. In fact, it enjoyed perks that other members did not have. Offering the EU as a scapegoat for Britain's internal problems remains populist propaganda.

I can't resist giving you this simple observation on some UK MPs, I have no idea where it came from:

'Listening to MPs justifying leaving the EU is like listening to men in A&E explaining why their cock is stuck in the vacuum cleaner.'

I'll leave it in the hands of Guy Vehofstadt, speaking in 2019, to conclude my dismay about Brexit and the nationalistic, verging on autocratic, Tory style of government under Boris Johnson and its extreme right.

'The world order of tomorrow is not a world order based on nation states or countries, it's a world order based on empires. China is not a nation, it's a civilisation. India is not a nation. There are two thousand nations in India, there are 20 different languages that are used there. There are four big religions. At the same time, it is the biggest democracy worldwide. The U.S is also an empire, more than a nation. And then finally the Russian Federation. The world of tomorrow is a world of empires in which we, as Europeans and you, as British, can only defend our interests, your way of life, by doing it together in a European framework and in the European Union. And those, dear friends, those who want to defend our standards of living, our social standards, our ecological standards, our labour standards, can only do that, they know it, only in the framework of Europe and inside Europe; in the centre a Britain that takes its responsibilities and not going out of this great project.'

And just to remind people that Brexit did not take place without bloodshed, this in Burgundy, France.

Rue Jo Cox

Dèputèe Britannique

Assassinèe pour ses convictions

22 juin 1974 – 16 juin 2016.

Italians

The Italians have their priorities right: They're driven,
they work, but they really enjoy the day-to-day and
don't put off the enjoyment of the everyday for some
future goal.

. . . .

Frances May

CHAPTER TWELVE

Un Paesano di Colpalombo

'Life is either a great adventure or nothing.'

Helen Keller

You've crossed over the Chiasco River, then climbing and twisting the short distance to the village. As you enter, there is little doubt where you are. Bold lettering on the side of a large stone-built house, under a terracotta tiled roof, gives you a clue.

COMUNE DI GUBBIO
Colpalombo
Sul Mare M. 424.

Although the place has a population of less than 300, Colpalombo is a thriving village, most of its inhabitants below the age of 60, with at least 100 under the age of 40. Life here is completely unhurried, every person knows every other, including the uomo inglese who lives in the hamlet of Case Colle.

The village comes under the municipality of Gubbio. The medieval town that I may have mentioned now and again. The closest airport is San Egidio – Perugia. The next closest after that is Falconara airport, Ancona, on the Adriatic coast. I'm now an 'adopted villager' of this little borgo on its hill, Colpalombo. Even before I decided to set up home in the little hamlet of Case Colle, when the house was simply a place for holidays, my feet had already been planted in Umbria. I was already being absorbed into the community, attached to the bell tower. My Italian neighbours had become close friends, my friendship with Italians reaching well beyond the village to the back of my house. On moving to live here,

I soon became a member of local associations, with invitations to participate in local events cementing my intimate connection with this part of Italy.

L'ATLETA INGLESE

You find me running through the streets of Rome, a few hundred people behind me, several hundred in front. It's November 2016. I'm taking part in a ten-kilometre race, La Corsa dei Santi. I've travelled down from Umbria with other members of Gubbio Runners, having become a fully paid-up member of the club in August. The only inglese to have ever been a member. And I think I mentioned this earlier in the book, for the first time in my life I'm given the label of being an athlete; well, at least that's what it states on my membership card. Not the easiest thing to get hold of. In Italy, to officially take part in any sporting event, you have to have undergone a brief medical check. This took place in July at a private health clinic in Gubbio, at a cost of €40. The check taking the form of questions about my general health, did I smoke, how much did I drink, how much exercise did I take each week? Any history of serious health problems in my immediate family? The health professional then listened to my lungs. Also, a check to see if my heart was beating. The final part of the health check, me having to pedal like hell on a static bike, the bike's resistance increasing as my breathing and heart rate increased. Electrodes, stuck to my chest at strategic points, feeding information to a computer and printer. 'Keep going, keep going, faster, faster, and slow down, relax, and stop.' As I sit recovering, the health professional checks if I'm likely to die in the near future. He looks slightly puzzled as he examines the results of my efforts fed into the computer. What has he found that, until now, I knew nothing about?

'Did you know that your heart is not normal?' I'm sure that's what he's asking me.

'Do you have any worries about your heart.' If he'd asked me that same question ten minutes before I would have said no. Now, yes, I have worries about my heart.

'Should I be worried? I've never had a problem.'

'Your heart does not have a regular rhythm.'

Phew, I've known that for years. I can't remember when it was first identified. In the past it's not been of any real concern. It's never caused any problems. I relate this to the person giving me the health check.

'All is fine, it's not a major problem. You are fit and healthy.'

And with that, my health check is done. I'm given an official certificate to show that I can take part in competitive running and cycling. Without this, I would have not been running through the streets of Rome. Yes, forgot to mention, I included cycling.

So, along with a couple of thousand people, I'm running through the streets of Rome, passing many of the major tourist sites; the Colosseum, the Forum, Monument of Vittorio Emanuele, crossing over the Tiber a number of times. A beautiful November day, blue sky and warm sunshine. The temperature hovering at around 18C, an ideal day for running. As we run, tourists enjoy the majesty that is Rome, some taking the time to stop, clap and give encouragement to the body of runners passing. And, finally, after covering ten kilometres, we reach the finish line. As I've said before, I've never been a fast runner, I'm in the back third of those finishing. In my younger days, I would have been in the middle. But that's not important, it's the experience of being among like-minded people, and making new Italian friends. Eventually, we find each other, our group of Gubbio Runners transforming into tourists. We sit in our running gear, enjoying gelato against the backdrop of the Pantheon. From there we walk to Fontana di Trevi, eventually making our way back to the coach and the journey back to Gubbio. Another wonderful day in the Eternal City.

Other races take place with Gubbio Runners, some in Umbria, others in different parts of Italy. There are two in particular that remain very clear in my mind. Another ten-kilometre race, this taking place near the Adriatic coast. The race covers three laps of a motor racing circuit, the name of the circuit having escaped my brain. There are runners from all parts of the central regions of Italy, Gubbio Runners being well presented. But, in total, there are only a couple of hundred runners taking part. I'm stood at the start with others from Gubbio. We nervously chat, waiting for the gun. I've always been the same, always a little nervous that I will perform at my best.

And off we go! Excuse my language, but in Yorkshire the phrase used would be, 'like shit off a shovel.' The phrase indicating something done at speed. Before we've even reached the first bend, there are only several other runners behind me, none of them from Gubbio. In all the years that I've been running, this has never happened. Will this be the very first time that I could be the last person to finish a race? It's unthinkable. What is happening? My brain is doing everything it can to encourage my legs to run faster. But the truth is that I'm running as fast as I can. With my brain putting pressure on my legs to speed up, I do start to pass a few people. The next bend and the next, the bulk of runners some distance ahead. First lap completed, the main group of runners are some 500 meters ahead of me, perhaps a dozen runners behind, certainly no more.

I'm perhaps half way round the second lap when I find the president of Gubbio Runners on my shoulder. Yes, he's lapping me. He's built for long distance running, just skin, bone and sinew. About five years younger than me, he is fast. As he leaves me in his slipstream, he calls to me with what I'm sure he thinks are words of encouragement, 'Forza Ghrem! Forza!' I acknowledge his 'encouragement' with a quick wave and a smile. Inside I'm saying, I can't go any faster, I'm running with all my strength. He's gone, already a good twenty meters ahead, flames bursting from his running shoes. Third lap, I come round the final bend, the finish line not that far ahead. A quick glance behind, about eight runners trying to catch me. Another eighty meters. I am not going to finish in last place! They shall not pass! With no more than a puff of smoke from my running shoes, I find a quick burst of energy, you could even describe it as speed. I cross the finish line, leaving the eight runners behind astonished at my athletic prowess. I'm not last. Very close, but not last.

After collecting my reward for all the effort, a t-shirt, I meet with others from Gubbio Runners, many of them already changed out of their running gear, enjoying a snack and something to drink. It's now that I discover that this was no ordinary, casual, race. No, this was a competitive race for the best club runners, finishing positions added to a league table. How did I not know this before? I guess I was just not listening when I signed up to take part. This 'new' knowledge does make me feel a little better. I'm not quite as broken down and obsolete as I thought.

Just outside the medieval walls of Gubbio are the partial ruins of the Teatro Romano, the theatre built in the 1st century B.C. It has the look of an amphitheatre, but on a much smaller scale. It was once the second largest theatre in the Roman Empire, said to have seating capable of accommodating an audience of up to 15,000 people. During the summer months, the theatre is still used for live performances, a place I've been a number of times. It stands in open park land; a car park some hundred meters to the front and Caffé del Teatro just a short distance away. I'm here with Gubbio Runners, the club being responsible for organising what I guess you could call, a festival of running. It's a Sunday, people have come from all over central Italy and beyond to participate in races of varying lengths, including a race for children. On this occasion I'm not taking part. In fact, given that the event is organised by Gubbio Runners, none of us are taking part. Our role is to mark out the different races around the streets of Gubbio, to marshal the runners, and provide all who come with food and drink. I'm on food and drink duty.

It's a busy early morning getting all the food, hot and cold drinks ready. Fortunately, marquees, tables, benches and all other essentials have already been set up. Hundreds of runners are here with family members and spectators to support them, and all would like refreshment. We have slices of different types of pizza, pasta dishes, a variety of panini, assorted slices of cake, energy bars, energy drinks and the very essential espresso. Long tables are now full of the offers available. It's behind these tables that I take up my position, the first customers soon requesting different types of food and drink. In the first hour, very few of these are runners, they're family members and spectators.

Food and other refreshments are included in the fees charged to the runners taking part in the different events. Those not taking part in any events get their food and drinks at minimal charge. With payment made at a separate till, as is almost always the case in Italy, they approach with a ticket in hand. Obviously all requests, conversation and idle chat, are in Italian. And to my surprise (I'm always surprised), I get along quite well, taking orders from people and, most of the time, giving them what they've asked for. It's not long before the first runners start to appear, the lines waiting for refreshment getting longer, the Italian being spoken, I'm sure, getting faster. But, again, the inglese does quite well. Nobody is complaining, everyone appears to be happy and smiling. Another, completely enjoyable day, with me at the very heart of the Umbrian town of Gubbio, the sun is shining, I'm with Italian friends.

A VERY ENGLISH GATE

Aton is not only the Forrest Gump of the dog world, he also turns out to be a skilled and determined escapologist. Whatever I do, he finds a way of getting through, over or under any obstacle. If you remember, when I first met Aton, I was assured that he couldn't even get over a small fence. It's not long before I realise that he is in fact the ghost of Harry Houdini. A plan is developed to build a wall, at least ten metres high, topped with an electric fence. On the garden side of the wall, a deep moat full of piranhas. I've also looked online to see if anyone manufactures straight-jackets for dogs. Yes, this is my ridiculously wild imagination, piranhas wouldn't be much use.

With the help of my friend, the very skilled builder and craftsman, Peter Carpenter, I set about building a low wall that will be topped with a low fence. No, the truth is, I help Peter. I get all the digging done, he does all of the skilled bits and I'm the labourer. As is always the case in Case Colle, my neighbours are very willing to offer tips and advice. The trench should be deeper, the mix of mortar is too wet, the mortar should have more sand, have you got permission to build a wall? All very friendly. All very inquisitive. And there has to be the speedy espresso break at the bar in Colpalombo. If you recall, I spoke about building the wall in the chapter relating to 'Being Italian'.

After slaving away in the hot sun, totally ignoring the 'helpful' advice and curiosity of my neighbours, we have the wall built, the low fence fixed in place. To give credit to my neighbours, all are extremely complimentary of our efforts. Well, yes, Peter's efforts. However, all who pass suggest that I should have an automatic gate. We reply that it's going to be a wooden gate, made by Peter, there is no need for an automatic gate. We're almost back to the debate about the cockerel. Ghrem and Peter, they're both English, what do you expect?

The gate, hand built from scratch by Peter, is the type of gate you would see on any farm in the UK. For want of a better description, a very English gate. Although surprised by the gate, my Italian neighbours are very generous and sincere in the admiration they have of Peter's skilled work. And at last, the garden is secure, Harry Houdini can no longer escape. I know that to be the case. You know that to be the case, I've just told you. Aton had other ideas, at times digging under the gate. So, a thick layer of concrete had to be poured. Now the garden is secure. Where is the straight jacket that I ordered? Aton soon realises that he can squeeze through the gaps in the English gate. That problem resolved; he then shows his skill at climbing. Yes, he climbs over the gate. Now you could come away from all this with the impression that Aton just doesn't want to live with me. The truth is that his escape attempts are only made when I'm not in the house or garden. I'll leave the dog psychiatry to you. At times someone will inform me that they have seen Aton in Carbonesca.

BABBO NATALE

It's whilst I'm on the long flight back from Australia to Italy, early December 2017, that I get a message from Marcello. He goes through the usual questions about my holiday and what I thought of Australia, joking that I'll have to adjust from the summer on one side of the world to winter in Gubbio; it's only a few weeks before Christmas. The next question comes as a complete surprise. Would I like to be Father Christmas in Gubbio? Only giving it a few seconds thought, I say yes, I'll be Babbo Natale. Great, we'll sort everything out when you're back. I then spend the rest of my journey back to Umbria drifting between feeling quite honoured to be asked to be Babbo Natale, whilst at the same time feeling a little apprehensive about what I'd volunteered to do. Me, the straniero, l'inglese, trying to fool little Italian kids that I'm Father Christmas. How convincing will I be?

As I walk through the medieval streets of Gubbio, the temperature hovers just a little above freezing. Marcello and Matteo have constructed the most elaborate Christmas grotto inside one of the giant stone arches that hold the weight of Piazza Grande above. As you enter it's a winter wonderland; it has the smell of Christmas. Hidden away, behind a heavy curtain is the world of Babbo Natale. A world of greens and reds, parcels dressed in Christmas wrapping scattered around, Christmas songs gently playing, the gentle flurry of fake snow. Set against the wall, on a low platform, facing the closed curtain, is Babbo Natale's throne. Grand and ornate, red and gold. As I enter this magical world, an Italian Father Christmas is shedding his disguise and changing into 'civilian' clothes, his brief shift now done.

I quickly change, the transformation so complete, even members of my own family wouldn't recognise me. Fully dressed in red, white trim, thick black belt to hold in my newly acquired bulk, and heavy black boots. A large red hood that almost swallows my head, a thick white beard covering the lower part of my face, gold rimmed glasses resting on the end of my nose. I have become Babbo Natale. Across from my throne, in one corner of my world, is a large wooden desk and high-backed chair. The table set out with all the things required for my Elf to answer letters arriving from expectant children. Babbo Natale's Elf is Emma, the young daughter of Marcello. She's also dressed in red and green, bright red cheeks, her thin legs ringed in Christmas colours. She acts as my helper; her main role is to slightly open the curtain and welcome each child. The stage is set, we're ready for our first child. Christmas music playing, snow gently falling.

Emma pulls back the heavy curtain. Standing there are two adults, I assume mother and father. In front of them, a small child, no more than five years of age. The adults are smiling, they look genuinely happy and excited. The young child stands frozen to the spot, apprehensive, unsure what to do, certainly no smile on her face. One of the adults gently nudges her forward. Still no smile on the child's face, more a look of worry, almost a face verging on fright. With gentle, spoken encouragement and a little more nudging from the adults, the young girl stands nervously in front of me. I smile through my thick white beard, at the same time taking hold of her tiny hand.

'What's your name?' I ask. She whispers a response.

'And how old are you?' Again, a whispered response.

'You're never fifty years old'. I reply. The young girl looking just a little confused.

'No, I'm five years old.'

'Is this your sister?' Me gesturing in the direction of her mother.

The girl looks to her mother, not sure how to respond.

'No, I'm her mother. But thank you Babbo Natale.'

'NO! I thought she was your sister.'

The young girl has now released her hand from my white glove. I'm sure she thinks that this Babbo Natale must be a bit of a fool.

'What would you like for Christmas, what would you like me to bring?'

No response. The young girl looking first at me and then her parents.

With a little encouragement, she whispers one or two things that she hopes to get.

I smile and then give a deep, Babbo Natale laugh, promising that I'll do the best I can to make sure that she gets those things. And with that the young girl and her parents turn to walk back through the curtain. Before they do, the girl, at last, gives a big smile. At last, there is a bright sparkle in her eyes. She turns to wave, I wave back, bellowing out 'Buon Natale!', this followed by another Babbo Natale deep belly laugh. They've gone, I wait with my Elf for the next unsuspecting child.

Christmas Elf pulls back the heavy curtain and welcomes the next child, each child in the company of adults. And so Babbo Natale's shift continues. Each time it's much the same, an apprehensive child and excited adults. Sometimes I pretend to be asleep, Christmas Elf having to wake me up. All feels to be going really well, my Italian holding up to the part I'm playing. My attempts at humour, if not fully understood by the children, appreciated by the adults. That is until an older child appears in front of me. After a little questioning, it turns out that he's eight. What a difference three years can make.

I go through much the same routine, my 'jokes' not working quite as well with him.

'You're not Italian. You speak funny. Where are you from?'

At least he's not questioned my role as Babbo Natale.

'Why do you think I speak funny? Where do you think I come from?'

He shrugs his shoulders, looking at the adults for an answer before looking back at me.

'I don't know, but you're not Italian. Your Italian is funny.'

'You're a very clever young man. You're right, I'm not Italian. I'm not from Italy. I'm from the cold north of the world. That's the reason why my Italian sometimes sounds strange. Everyone knows that Babbo Natale is not Italian.'

My clever young man shrugs his shoulders again. Don't you just love clever little boys? I'm not sure he's convinced. As they leave, on this occasion, I don't bother with a deep Babbo Natale belly laugh. I can hear that he's questioning the adults with him, why does that man speak funny? Other than that, my shift as Babbo Natale goes far better than I could have hoped, even with my funny Italian.

And that sets me thinking how far my Italian has come from the days when I carried a small Italian phrase book in my back pocket.

Some of you reading through the pages of this book may be at ease with Italian, in fact you may be fluent in any number of languages, if you are, I'm incredibly envious. For me, getting to grips with another language, be it Italian or German, has, at times, been both frustrating and discouraging. As my Italian developed, it often felt as though I was living in a half-understood twilight zone. My language skills rather like the zombies in apocalyptic films, slow, plodding, grasping, bewildered, grotesque and, I'm sure, often terrifying for Italians who had to decipher the broken words dripping slowly from my lips. I have to be honest and admit that I wrestle with learning another language. And at times it has felt like I'm wrestling in mud. Each time I feel my language skills are improving, the mud sucks at my self-confidence. Again and again, I become acutely aware of how faltering, for example, my Italian is compared with my native language. And I know I'm just not disciplined enough.

I once asked my father how long it took before he had the feeling that he was actually speaking English, rather than simply stumbling along. Confidently he said, 'Three years.' His learning experience was one of total immersion, deep dive, with absolutely no aids or support. I want his more regimented brain. I guess I envy his enforced diligence. I need my water wings to be taken away.

It's years ago, way back in my childhood, but I still remember with absolute clarity my father's very straightforward style of teaching me how to swim and ice skate. Not at the same time you'll be relieved to know, even he didn't throw me into frozen water. To learn how to swim, you jump into the deep end. To learn how to skate, you need to be left in the middle of the ice rink. My father clearly held to the belief that total immersion is the only way to learn. It may have worked for him; it didn't work for me. I did eventually learn to both swim and ice skate. But the learning was done at my own pace, and definitely well away from the attention of my father. Away from the observation of a teacher or competent others; escaping the potential fear of embarrassment. The other essential ingredient that enhanced my skill development, was the discovery of girls; ice skating in particular was a good way to meet them.

So, in terms of my language development, my father would be pleased. I've been in the deep end and in the middle of the ice for some time. It's worked to a certain extent, but I still have the habit of looking for the easy safety of the shallow end of the pool or the sides of the ice rink. Perhaps I need some lure, as powerful as discovering girls, to make me stay in the deep end and in the middle.

For quite some time, during my journey, the Italians around me would speak, in part, in open secrets. They were more than willing to let me into their world, but there were times when I lacked the necessary codes to successfully enter. I was in their company. I thoroughly relished being in their company, but I was still at a distance. Even now, when I speak, I do so in the half expectation that it won't be totally correct. Jhumpa Lahiri (an American with Bangladeshi origins), in her excellent book, 'In Other Words', talks about feeling 'exiled' from the Italian language even when she's in Italy. I certainly don't feel exiled. But there are times, still, when I feel like an observer rather than an active participant. My Italian has undoubtedly improved, and so it should have, I can hear you thinking. The time when my brain would automatically substitute a German word for the unknown Italian has long since gone. The Italian flicker of light is more often there than not. What at times feels like the elusive dream of fluency, does creep increasingly closer; I think.

It can't just be me who finds getting to grips with another language so frustrating? Still, there are occasions when it feels like I'm living in a half-understood twilight zone. Reluctantly I'm forced yet again to use the most familiar Italian words in my head, 'Mi dispiace, non capisco'. Again, I become acutely aware of how faltering my Italian is in comparison to my native language.

In many ways, ignorance at the beginning of my Italian experience was easier to deal with and less embarrassing. It's paradoxical. The more Italian I know, the less 'confident' I become. The more I know, the more I'm aware of my mistakes. I'm slowly coming to terms with the fact that learning another language to an acceptable degree of fluency, is not an easy relationship for my brain. There may well be lots of swearing in Italian and German; I can do that. Living in Italy I expected my brain to absorb, to soak up Italian like permeable rock - some type of osmosis. The problem with permeable rock is that it doesn't keep hold of the water. It's much the same with my brain and Italian. The Italian does indeed flow in but then soon flows out again. Perhaps I need a more watertight analogy.

The little eight-year-old boy probably had it right, I speak Italian but it's 'funny'.

If you're just starting out on your Italian language journey, take little notice of what I've related about my difficulties. In the words of Jhumpa Lahiri, I mentioned her earlier, 'A conversation involves a sort of collaboration and, often, an act of forgiveness.' Feel confident and reassured by the fact that Italians are more than willing to forgive you and help you. Throughout my journey, I've found the vast majority of Italians to be encouraging and supportive of the fledgling trying to get to grips with their language. Enjoy the mistakes you will inevitably make; at times they can be incredibly funny. And I can assure you that the Italians will laugh with you rather than at you. Let me know about your trials and tribulations, your experiences and amusing tales of moments that were lost in translation.

WILD WEST EVENING

I think I've already said, somewhere in the book, perhaps a number of times, that from June through to at least the end of September, festivals take place across the whole of Italy. Most last several days, some, occasionally, just one or two nights. You join me on a summer evening in Colpalombo. In fact, you don't just join me, you're with everyone from the village and many others from the surrounding area. It's a one evening event, promoted for the past few weeks: a Wild West Evening. Well, a local Italian version of a Wild West Evening. To tell the truth, I'm not really sure what a genuine Wild West Evening would involve, so this one will do. There's live music, Country and Western of sorts. Plenty of food and drink, there always is at any of the festivals. The food has an American theme, burgers, hot dogs and steaks, the steaks being cooked on the most enormous, wood burning BBQ. As the flames lick at the meat, the steaks sizzle, smoke infused with the smell of meat juices drifting over those gathered for the event. As always, all ages are here, with families represented by at least three generations. That's just one of the joys of being in rural Italy, there is never a hint of segregation by age, a mingling together, every age enjoying the company of all those around them. A throng of smiling faces, loud, speedy Italian, laughter and jokes, meeting friends, embracing, gossiping, chatting, eating, drinking (never to excess) and dancing. All of this for just €10. I know, it's incredible.

Along with my Italian friends and neighbours, I'm here with my cousin's son from Germany, his partner and her two teenage children. We sit with others, eating, drinking, chatting, generally enjoying the atmosphere that surrounds us. People are dressed in ways they assume equate to the wild west, to cowboys. Teenagers delivering food, dash between tables, children play, scrambling between the legs of adults. And those who know how, dance. It's always the same dance, a rhythmic waltz, that moves around in a clockwise direction. Every age glides past, at times couples turning full circle, chatting to others that they pass. All, apart from the Germans and the inglese, know this dance, all taking part with ease. A change of music and people spread out for line dancing. Again, nobody taking part puts a foot out of place. They step forward, one step to the side, a step to the other side, two steps forward, two steps back, clap, turn and repeat. And the other entertainment, something that my cousin's son, Ralph, has been begging me to have a go on throughout the evening, is a rodeo bull, a bucking bull, a mechanical bull, not really sure what it should be called. Anyway, it's providing entertainment for a good many people, adults and children. I spend most of the evening refusing Ralph's ongoing insistence that I should have a go. If I get on I'll end up breaking my neck. NO!

Ghrem! Greme! Greme! Ghrem! Italian voices calling out my name from the direction of the bucking bull. The bastard, Ralph has put my name down to have a go. Ghrem! Greme! I'm ushered over to the waiting bull, eager crowd gathered round to see the inglese make a fool of himself and break his neck. Apparently I get two rides. What fun, I think not. I'm only allowed to use one hand, holding onto a short rope, the other arm and hand held in the air. The bull soon starts to buck in different directions, quickly picking up speed, forwards, backwards, to the side and then forwards again. Me being thrown around, backside leaving the back of the bull, still with one arm in the air. Greme! Ghrem! In no more than perhaps eight seconds, I'm ejected from the bull's back, landing on mounds of inflatable padding. Ghrem! Greme! I'm back on again, this time perhaps lasting as long as ten seconds. Applause and laughter from the appreciative crowd. Well done Greme! Where the hell is Ralph?

I step to the back of the small crowd of spectators, looking over their heads. A child is now on the bucking bull, the machine tossing her around like a rag doll, and off she falls. Another victim, he maintains a grip for a surprising amount of time. But gravity will have its way, the inevitable fall soon comes.

I've found Ralph, to my surprise, he's the next one to sit astride the bucking bull. Now Ralph is a big lad, you could say that he's bulky. One arm in the air, his right hand griping the short rope, the bull goes into action. It lunges forward, then to one side, forward again, and Ralph is thrown off, disappearing from my view, seemingly swallowed by the crowd. What a moment ago had been excited cheering has suddenly changed to nervous chatter, those at the front of the crowd clambering onto the inflatable padding. I still can't see Ralph. Get up, stop being so melodramatic. Still no Ralph. I manage to squeeze through to the front. Ralph isn't moving, one person holding his head between their hands, two others questioning him in Italian. I still think he's making a very grand drama out of this.

Bending down, I ask how he is. My neck, I can't move my neck. According to those gathered around, he was thrown from the bull, landing on his head. I have to admit, I'm tempted to laugh, but I don't. Eventually we have him on his feet, Aldo, my neighbour, offering to drive him back to the house; we'd come to the event on foot. The distance is just over one kilometre, but Ralph is really in no fit state to walk. He gets into the car, holding is head rigidly still, complaining how much his neck hurts. I follow on. I walk up the hill, still thinking this will be nothing more than a sprain. When I arrive at the house, I find Ralph sat totally upright, not able to move his head in any direction. He's still complaining about how much it hurts. Me 'sympathetically' thinking, this was all your idea. We eventually, rather gingerly, taking the tiniest of steps, get him into the bedroom and onto the bed. It's agreed that we'll see how he is in the morning, if there is no change I'll drive him to the hospital. He'll be fine. His head and neck will be sore, but he'll be a little better in the morning. 'Graham, my neck really hurts.'

Very early the following day, we are in accident and emergency at Gubbio hospital. It's actually a little distance outside the town, close to the little village of Branca. Ospedale Branca di Gubbio. I've explained that Ralph has fallen over, hitting his head, with some force, on the ground. I have absolutely no idea how to explain what really happened. My Italian version of how the injury occurred will have to do. Some questioning, a brief examination of his head and neck. Was he unconscious? Has he been sick? Then he's taken trough for x-rays, I'm obviously not allowed to follow. After twenty minutes, Ralph reappears sitting in a wheelchair, his neck held firmly by a stiff plastic collar. What have they found? Ralph isn't sure? The doctor then explains to me that Ralph has fractured two vertebrae in his neck, at the very top of his spine. He has a prescription for painkillers and will need to keep the collar on for a number of weeks. The doctor then goes on to say that Ralph must go the hospital in Germany as soon as he returns home. Other x-rays will need to be taken to check how things are progressing. The hospital won't allow me to drive Ralph back to my house, insisting that he's transported by ambulance. There must be some moral to this story. I'll leave you to think of one.

My German relatives have come to stay with me, in my little bit of Italy, on a number of occasions. They've always thoroughly enjoyed everything that the region of Umbria has to offer, but it has to be said, they've not always had the best of luck. My cousin, Ralph's mother, one morning, missing the little step as you come into my kitchen, fell hard onto her back. At the time all she felt was a little bruised and a little embarrassed. On returning to Germany, on a visit to the local hospital, she found that she had fractured her coccyx.

On another occasion, Ralph and his partner were staying with me, along with their dog, a Münsterländer, about the same size as a Labrador but stockier in build. Usually a placid dog, very well behaved and trained. Their holiday was going smoothly enough. That is, until one morning when Claudia, Raph's partner, took the dog out for a short walk. Within less than five minutes she was back in tears. Giovanni's dog, the usually placid Rottweiler, giving little prior warning, had attacked the Münsterländer. The dog being attacked put up no defence, almost immediately tacking a submissive position on its back. And that was it, the attack soon over. On examining the dog, we could see a deep bite, a trickle of blood coming from the wound. Another millimetre to the left and the bite would have taken a chunk out of the Münsterländer's right testicle. I know, it makes you cringe just thinking about it. The dog was oblivious as to his injury. But there was no alternative, the trickle of blood continuing, we had to take him to my vet in Perugia. You'll be pleased to know that treatment was given, and the dog was fine.

You may not remember, earlier in the book I spoke about the need to have a Codice Fiscale for almost everything. Treatment given; Ralph needed to make payment. But the vet couldn't accept the payment without Ralph's Codice Fiscale. I explained that he was German, in Italy on holiday, and obviously doesn't have a Codice Fiscale. Then that's a problem, we can't accept the payment. Don't ask, I know it sounds ridiculous. Would they accept my Codice Fiscale? Yes, that's fine, no problem. The 'no problem' solved, payment made. That's Italy.

MONTE CUCCO

I spend a great deal of my time simply exploring the many paths, oak filled valleys, hills and mountains, crossing over babbling rivers, often passing abandoned buildings. What's the history held in these crumbling buildings; families raised? Brambles and trees being the final occupiers. The brambles multiplying in number, ripping at your skin as you attempt to explore. They act as the guardians of the skeleton that remains. Nature will survive long after we've gone. Adapted, and perhaps distorted, but it will endure. I continue on my walk at a slow pace, occasionally sitting and simply listening to nature around me. And all of this on my doorstep. The area is enchantingly beautiful. Often a deer will cross my path, on very rare occasions, a wild boar, a porcupine or a snake. I've yet to see a wolf, but they are around.

You can sometimes find me sitting at the top of Monte Cucco, very early in the morning. So early, that the sun is still sleeping. On this occasion, I'm here well before the moon has left the sky. Here to welcome the dawn rise from deep within the Apennines, to feel Umbria waking from its slumber. I've found a comfortable spot to have breakfast, to sit and wait, surrounded by solitude. The night sky, bursting with stars, hidden away, the moon soon departing. My entire vision is taken by green hills, mountains, valleys, and chiffon mists that simply float above the miniature villages far below. Close to where I'm having my early breakfast, meaty white cattle graze, chestnut horses, some still asleep, others gathering together in silence, foals feeding from their mothers. The cattle and the horses are totally indifferent to the breakfasting human. You should be able to hear the sun hissing and burning, shooting flames into the morning sky. But instead, before the sun appears, you see the tops of the mountains begin to glow bright orange, the orange glow separating the mountains from the growing blue of the sky. It's not long before the sun begins rise like a phoenix, as it climbs the cattle and horses becoming silhouettes, their dark shapes haloed by shades of red, yellow and orange. I relish the solitude, the silence. Slowly the sun separates itself from the mountains where it's been sleeping throughout the night, its warmth resting on my face. There are few trees at this height, but birdsong does begin to provide a background chorus. As the sun continues its slow ascent, the silhouetted cattle and horses come into full vision. I linger for a while, wallowing in the beauty that surrounds me, before leaving the top of Monte Cucco and making my way back to the car.

I've lost count of the number of visits to Monte Cucco, most often alone, occasionally with friends, walking and stopping to eat at one of the restaurants that you'll find up there. The main two being, Albergo Ristorante Monte Cucco da Tobia and Ristorante Il Nibbio. At other times, on calm days, sitting for hours watching hang gliders take to the sky, whilst others sweep and swoop above, the odd few coming to land on the grassy slope of the mountain.

CORSA DEI CERI
Race of the Candles

May 15th has arrived, perhaps the most important day of the year in Umbria. No, that is definitely and understatement. This is without doubt the most important date in the Umbrian calendar, and I take part dressed in the colours of Sant'Antonio! Well, I take part as a spectator, along with thousands of others. The whole of Gubbio is draped in flags and banners, every building, every window and balcony. You simply cannot escape the emotion and sense of anticipation that builds from the early hours of the morning. It's a day of massive excitement, enjoyment, passion and celebration, the ancient walls of the town fit to burst there are so many people, literally squeezed in. I'm with Paola, her partner Stefano (you remember Stefano from the visit to the warehouse on the edge of Gubbio), and Paola's daughter, Giulietta. All three are also dressed in the colours of Sant'Antonio. Before I say anymore, perhaps I need to explain a little about the Ceri.

The event is in celebration of Sant'Ubaldo, the patron saint of the town, the story being that he saved Gubbio from an invading army, way back in the 13th century. As you know, you can still pay him a visit in the Basilica di Sant'Ubaldo, his leathery remains waiting for you. There are three teams that take part in the race, these are the ceraioli. All three teams dress in the same way, white trousers, with a red sash round the waist and a red bandanna around the neck. It's the colour of the shirts that distinguish them from each other. Sant'Ubaldo a yellow/gold shirt, San Giorgio, bright blue, Sant'Antonio, black. Your allegiance to one of the saints most probably based on family tradition, although I know many families, people who are in relationships, where at least two of the saints are represented. I dress in the black shirt of Sant'Antonio, simply because Paola and her daughter do. I'm a simple man.

On the day of the race, the town is brought to life at five in the morning with the sound of drums parading through the streets. If people living in Gubbio are not already awake, at 6.15. the giant bell of the Palazzo del Consoli in Piazza Grande booms into life. The morning moves on with certain other rituals until, eventually, you find thousands of people squashed together, almost vacuum-packed, with even more people finding space that doesn't exist in Piazza Grande. It's now midday, excitement is at fever pitch. Soon the three teams will pour out of the Palazzo del Consoli into Piazza Grande. The red shirted bell ringers, high up in the bell tower, pull ropes, some swaying on the giant bell, eventually releasing its deep chime over the piazza. Although there is no space, somehow space is made, people jostled and pushed out of the way as the ceraioli run into the crowd. The piazza is an eruption of colour and joyous voices, many chanting the name of their chosen saint, thousands jumping in unison.

How the piazza is able to absorb the excited crowd and the three teams of ceraioli, if not some type of miracle, is certainly absolutely extraordinary. You have to be there to get a true sense of what I mean. The three teams are now stood side-by-side, the heavy platforms that they will eventually carry in the race are, for now, vertical. The captain of each team stands on top of their platform, the three captains in unison, each throwing a large ceramic jug high into the air, the jugs crashing into the crowd. Thousands scream, shout and jump as each captain leans forward, landing on his feet, the momentum of his 'fall' pulling the platform into a horizontal position. Each team now has a heavy platform, with candle and saint, on its shoulders. The crowd is now even crazier with excitement. People, already packed like sardines, are pushed out of the way as the three teams of ceraioli race round the centre of the piazza in a tight circle, the three candles and saints swaying from side to side. Having circled three times, the ceraioli carrying Sant'Ubaldo are the first to charge out of the piazza, quickly followed by San Giorgio and Sant'Antonio. This same order is maintained throughout the race, right up to the Basilica di Sant'Ubaldo.

I know what you're thinking, how can this be a race if they stay in the same order, Sant'Ubaldo will always win? I think I know what it's all about, let me explain. The ceraioli carrying Sant'Ubaldo try and get as far ahead as they can from the ceraioli carrying San Giorgio. The ceraioli carrying San Giorgio trying to shorten the distance between them and Sant'Ubaldo, whilst at the same time trying to leave the team carrying Sant'Antonio way behind. The ceraioli carrying Sant'Antonio, busting every blood vessel in an attempt to be almost touching the ceraioli of San Giorgio. But keep in mind that they never pass the team in front, that's not the aim.

So, it's a race, but a race without any need to try and charge past the other team. I knew you would understand. If you are a little confused, I'll confuse you a little more. The race has not started yet. Yes I know that the three saints charged out of Piazza Grande, but the actual race doesn't start until six in the evening. After leaving the piazza, yes I know in a bit of a hurry, the three saints are paraded round the town, eventually coming to rest, for a few hours, in Via Savelli. Everyone then goes off for a long lunch.

As I said, I'm with Paola, her partner and Paola's daughter. We've experienced the crush in Piazza Grande, all of us literally carried along in the excitement. We're now walking through the stone streets of Gubbio in search of a place to eat. Our walk includes visiting a friend of Stefano, Paola' partner. The outside of the medieval building is grand enough, set amongst others in the historical heart of Gubbio, inside the architecture and the décor are simply stunning. The upper floors have terracotta tiled ceilings, held in place by heavy oak beams. The walls decorated in gothic style plaster work, works of art, hundreds of years old, hanging from the walls. Much of the furniture matches the rest of the building. Although we are in a house, it feels more like a palazzo. Stefano's friend is a doctor, her husband an architect. As we chat, they show us round the rest of the house, eventually going down to the basement, other people enjoying drinks on the first floor. I guess what in days gone by would have been a cellar, is now a rather grand dining room, a long oak table set for lunch. The vaulted stone ceiling adds to the atmosphere of the place. A little to my disappointment, we've not been invited for lunch, we're just popping in to say hello. Hands are shaken, the long Italian goodbye made, and we find a modest place to eat elsewhere in the town.

Before the start of the race proper, we make the long climb up to the Basilica di Sant'Ubaldo. I'd hate to think that I would be one of those scrambling up the side of the mountain, with one of the saints on my shoulders. On the walk up free wine and water are on offer. We find a spot, close to the steps that take you into the courtyard of the Basilica. It's not that long before we know that the three teams of ceraioli are approaching. There's loud excitement from the crowd, the chanting of the saints names. I've attached myself to a lamppost, my arms wrapped around, holding on tight, the gravel track, the route of the race, almost as packed as Piazza Grande.

Above the heads of the crowd, I can see the candle carrying Sant'Ubaldo swaying from side to side. The ceraioli come charging through the crowd, their faces taught and straining with the effort. The space for them to pass, the space that didn't exist, is created, people pushed to one side, with me lifted off my feet but luckily being able to keep my arms fast around the lamppost. The giant candle is lowered, Sant'Ubaldo and the team of ceraioli gaining entry into the small courtyard of the Basilica. Although the courtyard is packed, the team charge round with the candle and saint on their shoulders. San Giorgio follows and then Sant'Antonio. We leave the ceraioli and the saints in the place of worship, making our way back down the mountain and into the town. Along our route, a festival of activity and enjoyment, food and drink on offer, people dancing and singing, the colours of the three saints mixed together arm in arm.

That night we join others, sat outside one of the little bars in Gubbio, those there a mix of the three saints. More drink, laughter and singing, some of those there having guitars. As is often the case I'm the only non-Italian. Somehow I get into a bizarre conversation about my name, Graham, the other person asking me what it means. I try to explain that it has no meaning. The person I'm speaking with responding by saying it must be the English version of Giorgio, others quite rightly explaining to him that Giorgio is simply George in English. He asks again what my name means. Nothing, I reply. It's usually a Scottish surname. I see, he responds, you're Scottish? No, I'm English. There are some conversations that you wish had never started. Luckily my inquisition is interrupted, one of those with a guitar insisting that everyone should be singing an English song for the Englishman. The whole group breaks out into a chorus of, 'We all live in a yellow submarine, yellow submarine, yellow submarine. We all live in ....' More singing, more laughter, before the evening of celebration eventually comes to a close. My day at another Ceri at an end.

FESTA DEL FUOCO

If you think that the Ceri sounds just that little bit crazy, this festival could literally set your hair on fire. A July evening in the tiny little village of Grello, up in the hills close to Gualdo Tadino. This is the local village of Peter Carpenter and his partner, Laura. I have absolutely no idea as to the origins of this festival, other than it's connected to saints, no surprise, they usually are. In this case there is also fire. Again, it's an evening of friendship, laughter, greetings and celebration.

There are three teams, each team dressed as though they had been transported from the stone age . It's around 9.50 in the evening. Speeches are given, religious blessings are made and then, one male from each team stands with an enormous straw lollipop, on a long pole, over his shoulder. The three stand side by side, the crowd of people standing well back. Someone in medieval costume steps forward and lights the straw lollipops, each one instantly ablaze. And away the 'lollipop' males go, racing round the village, flames and sparks scattered in the air and falling to the ground. In the briefest of time the fastest male appears from behind the church, the straw lollipop, over his shoulder, still fully ablaze, his fast pace adding oxygen to the flames. The next male appears and then the third, sparks and smouldering embers falling to the ground. Another circuit of the village is made, before all three appear again. Waiting for them are three pairs of males, behind each pair a large wooden sledge with an even bigger straw lollipop. The male already on fire, and arriving first, sets the straw of his two team members on fire, and away they race, burning sledge being dragged behind. The next two are set on fire and then the final two. We didn't see the end of the race, it was down the hill from the village, a big crowd following those on fire. You'll be pleased to know, as far as I'm aware, nobody actually burst into flames.

After that burning excitement there is a bit of relative quiet time, where people meet with others, most enjoying food from stalls and simple rides for children. When I say quiet, it's not actually quiet, because there is loud music playing. And to top off the blazing evening, this little village has the most magnificent display of fireworks. The display so bright, extravagant and loud, you feel the explosions thumping deep into your chest. This is the culmination of a week-long festival. I'd be surprised if there are any more than fifty people who actually live in the village of Grello.

NOCINO

Not quite sure why, but fire made me think of alcohol, homemade drinks, obviously. I'm sure there are many you could make, here we have Nocino Liqueur (Walnut Liqueur). This is a drink, introduced to me by Paola, Aldo's middle daughter. I guess if I'm living in rural Umbria, I should know how to make a few, strong drinks containing lots of alcohol; just to fit in. You pick the walnuts whilst still green, sometime in June, chop them into four parts and place them in a large jar. Then you add almost pure alcohol (I know we spoke about this earlier in the book), sugar-water syrup and flavourings - the rind of a lemon, two cinnamon sticks and a few cloves. Close the jar tightly, shake the contents, and then leave to rest for 40 days. At least once each week, shake the jar or stir the contents with a spoon. The sugar will eventually crystallise in the bottom of the jar. After the 40 days, filter through a sieve and pour into bottles. Leave the bottles for another few months. After what is really minimum effort, you end up with a dark brown liqueur of at least 40% proof and not too sweet. Those much more in the know than I, will tell you that Nocino is best served neat at room temperature. During its 40 days gestation, you can have a little try, adding a little more water or other flavourings depending on your taste buds. Saluti!

SUMMER 2019

It will come as no surprise to you if I say that some weeks are incredibly hot. Martina is here for two of them, we spend time together by the coast in the region of Marche, in Sirolo and Numana. Leisurely days by the sea, warm evenings enjoying a meal outside a restaurant. The rest of her stay taken by visits to Montefalco, Bevagna and Gubbio. Obviously we have to spend a little time in Martintempo. There are also invites from my Italian neighbours for meals. It's at one of the meals that Martina is tempted to try the sugar lumps soaked in almost pure alcohol. I can't repeat what she had to say, once she could speak again.

We're up incredibly early, 4.40 in the morning, we have a flight to catch. As we drive towards Bevagna, the sun is starting to rise from behind the Apennines, changing from deep golden to bright yellow. At this time of day, it's relatively cool, a stillness in the air. Our final destination Cantina Dionigi. Skip back a few pages, I think I mentioned the vineyard somewhere. We have a flight booked with Balloon

Adventures Italy, the advertising promising us that we will be blown away, floating high above the green heart of Italy, with breath taking views of Assisi.

At 6.30, we've arrived at Cantina Dionigi, in a field, the enormous, brightly coloured hot air balloon being inflated. Along with others, we're welcomed by our pilot, Peter, who takes us through a short safety briefing. Once that's been done, we clamber inside the massively oversized picnic basket that sits below the now fully inflated balloon. Once the balloon and basket has been released by the ground crew, we we're soon high above the rolling hills, fields, vineyards and olive groves of Umbria, the flight giving us stunning views of Assisi. Throughout the flight Peter, our pilot, chats to us, in several different languages, partly explaining what he's doing when he releases hot flames into the belly of the balloon, at other moments explaining what we see below. I can't remember how many other passengers there were, in total, perhaps twelve, including the two of us. The views as we float along are absolutely stunning, certainly one of the best experiences I have had in Umbria.

The flight lasts roughly one hour before Peter seeks out a suitable place to bring the balloon down for a safe landing. But really, I could have stayed up there for the whole day. Peter explains how he will bring the balloon down, instructing us to slightly bend our knees just before the impact of landing. It's only when we are actually on the ground again that I notice how close we have come to a detached house, literally just outside the garden. Once we've all climbed out of the picnic basket, we're driven back to Cantina Dionigi for a delicious breakfast. Just by chance we happen to be sitting next to Peter, the pilot and owner of the company, who has a fascinating background story to tell. Hungarian in origin, speaking five languages, 28 years' experience as a commercial pilot and a world record holder as an instructor. So, I guess you could say that we had been in safe hands.

MEDIEVAL PAGEANT

Remember what I said, right at the beginning of the book? At the very heart of Italian society is the bell tower, a closeness, some may even describe it as a loyalty to the local community, the village, the town and then the region. I hope I've given you a sense of that deeply held bond, that passion, when I spoke about the most important event of the year for the whole region of Umbria, the Ceri in Gubbio. Do you remember when it takes place? If not, you need to check back. It's an event that you must witness, be part of, be completely absorbed by, drenched in the passion of the people of Gubbio, at least once. Trust me, the experience will stay with you forever. Not just in Umbria, but across the whole of Italy, the deep bond with community, a connection with the past, a past totally at home with the present, is symbolised through medieval pageantry. It's September, I'm in my village of Colpalombo.

Now surrounded by a cluster of houses, Castello di Colpalombo dates back to the 12th century, the castle attacked any number of times during the years of bloody conflict between the rival cities of Gubbio, Perugia, Assisi, Spoleto, Foligno and many others. Today little remains of the castle, apart from a few sections of its broken-down walls. The village sits on a hill, surrounded by oak forests and, at a distance, the higher mountains of the Apennines. For many years it came under the protection of the Dukes of Urbino, its forests a favourite hunting place for Duke Federico da Montefeltro. And here, on this September Saturday, at least fifty people from the village are taking part in a medieval pageant, all dressed in full costume, to welcome Duke Federico da Montefeltro. The inglese, dressed as a medieval noble, has the honour of being asked take part in the festival.

We all meet in the grounds of a large stone-built house on the edge of the village. Whilst waiting for everyone to arrive we greet others, we chat, we joke and laugh, we drink wine, eventually coming together for group photographs. After photographs, are taken, we're marshalled into line for our slow procession through the streets of Colpalombo.

At the front of the procession are the leading nobles from the area, following them the lessor nobles, the inglese being one. Each male noble gently holds the hand of his lady, my left hand holding my lady's right hand in the air. We have been instructed to walk slowly; our facial expression serious. We must walk erect, no smiling at the villagers that we pass. If we feel the need, we may offer a gentle wave to the crowd. Perhaps a nod of the head. Behind the nobles come guards, in leather armour, carrying swords, lances and banners. The guards are followed by drummers beating out a slow rhythm. The drummers followed by religious dignitaries and monks. Behind them come archers, behind the archers, families of less standing. Then come jesters, jugglers and stilt walkers. At the back of the long procession are artisans, farmers, weavers, carpenters, builders, stone masons, hunters. And very last are the peasants, some carrying small animals in wooden cages, others leading goats. Along our route, other people from Colpalombo and villages close by, stand and watch. The spectators clearly know their place in the hierarchy, smiling, some clapping, many taking photographs. I give a slow wave and a slight nod of the head to the gleeful peasants lining the route.

After making a short climb, we arrive in the small piazza, by the church, at the top of the village. Here there are stalls offering food, drink and goods, crafts made from wood, others made from leather. Those selling, again in full medieval costume. Our procession assembles in the piazza to await the arrival of Duke Federico da Montefeltro. To the sound of trumpets, he arrives on horseback, the Duke flanked by two riders. Dignitaries from Colpalombo step forward to greet him and welcome him to the village. The Duke dismounts, his horse held by a guard. After dismounting he makes a short speech, thanking those present for his welcome and offering thanks to God that the hunting will be good. With a goblet of wine held in the air, the Duke announces that the festivities should begin! From early evening until late, it's a time for the whole community to come together, enjoying the company of all others. Even Benito is here, although he doesn't acknowledge my nod and wave. It's an evening of food and drink, chatting, gossip, meeting, embracing, smiling and laughter. The whole gathering entertained by jesters, fire eaters, stilt walkers and acts of magic. And the wonderful thing is, I'm part of it.

Tradition, family, friendship and community are the very heart and soul of Umbria. It's the genuine feeling of belonging that I cherish so much, the adopted inglese wrapped in the warm embrace of Colpalombo.

WILD ASPARAGUS

From pastel blues to fiery sunsets, the Umbrian sky is an artist's canvas. Is it true that sunlight ignites the sex hormone in men? And at what age does a virile young male become a lecherous old man? Just asking for a friend. I digress, as you've found, I often do. Is asparagus really an aphrodisiac? Again, I'm asking for a friend. If it is, late March through to as late as May is a good time to be hunting out wild asparagus in Umbria. Perhaps that's why Italian males have a reputation for being amorous. You sometimes find asparagus growing by the side of the road but that would make the picking far too easy. More often you'll find it as you walk through fields, open spaces in oak forests, by deserted houses on deserted land, in olive groves, sometimes between grape vines as they come into bud. Spindly and more delicate than the asparagus you tend to buy in supermarkets.

It's a Sunday morning in the middle of April, I've just returned from a short run. Showered and refreshed, I'm sat on my small balcony having breakfast, the Umbrian sun already warming the day. From my crow's nest I can watch all who pass, greetings exchanged and, as always, comments about the weather. I look out over oak forests, deep valleys and mountains that make up the Apennines, including Monte Cucco. Walking up the narrow road that passes my house is Giovanni with his cream-coloured Labrador. This is the Giovanni of spectacles and dark hair, the one who lives in a small bungalow on the bend of the main road as it passes Case Colle. His morning walk is nothing unusual. But this morning, he opens my English gate and walks up the garden, his dog quietly walking by his side.

'Buongiorno Ghrem, come va? Sarà una giornata calda.' Told you that there would be a comment about the weather.

'Ciao, Buongiorno, sto bene, grazie e tu?' I don't bother responding to his observations on the weather and he doesn't tell me how he is.

'Domenica prossima, verrai con me a colazione, alle 8, va bene?' (Next Sunday you're coming with me for breakfast, is that alright?) It's obviously an invite, a question, but it comes across more as an instruction. Next Sunday you will come for breakfast with me! He's never invited me before.

'Grazie. Si, vengo con te.'

And that's it. This Giovanni has never been one for long conversations. A quick wave from both of us and he turns to walk back down the garden. Before opening the English gate, he looks back.

'Domenica prossima. Colazione!

'Grazie, si', colazione domenica prossima!'

That's it, Giovanni then continuing his Sunday morning walk.

The week quickly goes by, plenty of work for me to do in the garden and my vegetable plot, a bit of caring for the chickens. Breakfast Sunday soon arrives, Giovanni knocking at my door. I have no idea where we are actually going. I'm assuming it will be a quick espresso, perhaps a cappuccino and a pastry in either Colpalombo or Carbonesca. The usual greetings are exchanged, plus some obligatory observations about the weather. His car is parked outside my garden, engine running. He must have decided that we'll drive to Carbonesca, perhaps Casacastalda, rather than walk. We set off in the direction of Carbonesca.

We pass through Carbonesca, climbing out of the village before levelling out and then down into Casacastalda, where we stop outside the café on the corner. It turns out to be a very brief stop, another person getting into the car, with me being introduced as the English from Case Colle. Our drive then continues in the direction of Gualdo Tadino. We soon come to a small bar along the road, park up and go inside for an espresso. Espresso quickly consumed, the three of us back in the car again. This is going to be a more elaborate breakfast than I'd been expecting.

Just before reaching Gualdo Tadino, we turn down a short dirt track, the track bringing us to what look like farm buildings. There are about thirty men, of varying age, stood around chatting, greeting others, laughing and joking, eating and drinking. Again, I'm simply introduced as the English from Case Colle, but there are one or two faces that I actually know. Tables have been set up with gas cookers, blue flames licking the bottom of a number of large pans, piles and piles of fresh wild asparagus, tray after tray of fresh eggs, large bottles of wine, a few bottles of grappa and the obligatory means for producing espresso. All male, no women. It's now about 8.45 in the morning.

A number of males chop up the asparagus, passing it to others busy making scrambled egg. The chopped asparagus mixed in with the scrambled egg, a little seasoning and just a dash of white wine, thin shavings of truffle sprinkled on top. With a disposable plastic plate in my hand, a glass of white wine in the other, I stand waiting for my asparagus and scrambled egg breakfast. I think there must have been chunks of fresh bread, there is always bread. And that's what we do for at least the next two hours. Another glass of white wine, another serving of asparagus and scrambled egg. If asparagus is an aphrodisiac, and if the sun does ignite the male sex hormone, I'm going to be rampant. I mingle with others, chatting with faces I already know, being introduced to those new. All attempt to say my name with varying degrees of success. Almost all asking the same questions. Do you like Umbria? Why did you come to live in Italy? Are you from London? The all-male breakfast moves on, with many more males arriving. By the time we eventually leave, the clock has turned well past 11am.

Why an exclusively male gathering for a breakfast of asparagus and scrambled egg, washed down with white wine, I have no real idea. If you can provide a possible answer, let me know.

GLI ARCIERI DEL COLPALOMBO

At the time of writing, 2022, there are thirty-one members, just one inglese. All others have been taking part in archery for years, for me this is definitely a first. I may have been born not that far from Nottingham Forest, but I'm certainly no Robin Hood. It's going to take me quite some time to become anywhere near expert, to be a complete toxophilite (I know, I often surprise myself with some of the terms I carry round in my head).

As I explained to you earlier, to officially take part in any sporting activity you have to pass a health check. To my surprise it's the same for archery. Once I've officially been checked, I get my little card from the president of Colpalombo archery club showing that I'm a member of the Associazione Italiana Cultura Sport. The card also identifying me as a member of Compagnia Arcieri Castrum Collis Palumb (Archers of Colpalombo). Along with completely lacking any skill in archery (Tiro con l'arco), I have no bow, no arrows, no leather quiver, no medieval dress. But, as has been the case ever since I bought my little bit of Umbria, I have Italian neighbours and friends who are more than willing to help me out. My friend Matteo, having a new bow, gives his old one to me. Marcello orders the appropriate materials and makes eight arrows, the arrows having feathers in my personal colours, blue and green. And for now, that's all I need. I have the basic necessities to begin my tutoring in the skills of archery. For the next few weeks, I practice with other members of the archery club, all being very supportive and more than encouraging. You wouldn't believe how difficult it is to get the arrows to hit the scoring parts of a target. Other members of the club make it look so easy and straightforward. We joke, we laugh together. I stand watching others, they give me tips and try to explain what I'm doing wrong.

Finally, the day has come for me to officially take part in my first archery competition. I now have a brand new bow made by a member of Colpalombo Archers, Riccardo. He is definitely the most expert and skilful member of the club. Very modest but with a special eye for the target. When he handed me the bow, made from scratch, he refused to take any money I offered. 'I made it especially for you, you're a friend and a member of the club.' I've said this a number of times throughout the book, I love Italy.

Along with my bow and arrows, I now have a leather guard to protect the lower part of my left arm, along with a leather finger guard for my right hand. I have a leather quiver for the arrows and, you'll be pleased to know, I have my full medieval garb. My medieval dress is made up of a loose-fitting, cream coloured, heavy cotton shirt, the neck open but loosely laced. A dark leather belt, round my waist, gathers the shirt together before it falls over the upper part of my heavy, dark brown leggings. The belt also loops through the leather quiver carrying the arrows. On my feet, thigh high black leather boots. I certainly look the part. The question is, will my skill with the bow come anywhere close to matching the authenticity of my dress?

I'm woken early by the heavy breathing of asthmatic love making. It's actually a couple of pigeons who appear to be going through some sort of morning courtship ritual, strutting backwards and forwards, tail fanning and bowing, directly outside my open bedroom window. The cooing sounding muffled, perhaps they were trying not to disturb me. The amorous male bird, with his chest puffed out, looks to have the female submissive to his charms. With another amber sun rising from its sleeping place behind the mountains of the Apennines, my neighbour's cockerel warming up his voice and the distinctive sound of an Ape as it climbs towards Carbonesca, my morning alarms are calling me to get out of bed. I need to be up and about anyway; I'm taking part in my very first archery tournament.

The tournament is taking place in Spello, a small, beautiful, medieval town, about a thirty-minute drive from Colpalombo. Very close by you have Assisi, the city of Perugia, and further along the valley, you have another little, beautiful, hilltop town, Trevi (nothing to do with the Trevi Fountain in Rome). There are about fifteen of us from Colpalombo Archers, travelling to Spello in a convoy of cars.

When we arrive, we find archery teams representing towns and villages from across the whole of central Italy. Although this is all serious stuff, the atmosphere is relaxed, chatty and friendly. People smile, greet friends from other teams, laugh and joke, The essential espresso quicky consumed as we all mingle together but at a little distance. This is the first competition since Covid restrictions have been relaxed. The usual close embrace when you meet others is being assiduously avoided. No kisses to each cheek, no handshakes, every single person masked. Although this is totally foreign to the nature of Italians, nobody infringes the rules of social distancing. It's the first week of July and it's hot. The sky deep blue. The tournament taking place in the most beautiful setting. All arches in full medieval costume.

I quickly realise that the custom is for us to be split into groups of eight; the eight being a mix of archers from different towns and villages. Just by chance, Marcello is in my group. A variety of targets have been set out across a wide area, each group of eight having a set route to follow. Our first target is quite straightforward. There's a life-sized deer standing about sixty meters from the archers. The 'animal' has parts of its body marked with scores of two, three and five. Each archer has three arrows. Scores being totalled after all eight archers have released their arrows. Two people have charge of the score sheets, their task to keep a tally of individual scores. Our names are already printed on the score sheets, but we take a little time for introductions. The name Graham, spoken with a foreign accent, causes quizzical looks. Sorry, what's your name? Graham, I repeat. Marcello then pointing out that I'm English and this is my first tournament. Smiling faces welcome the inglese. The names of two arches are called out, the two stepping forward and preparing to aim at the target. Others stand watching the two, all ensuring that no spectators or other archers are in the zone of fire. The arrows would certainly cause serious injury. All good, 'Vai! Vai!'

The first two have released their arrows, two other names then called out. One of the names being Carlo. We all look round, there is no Carlo in the group. Fabrizio steps forward and prepares. The person holding one of the score sheets, that person being the one who had called out Carlo, points at me and repeats Carlo, gesturing that I should step forward. All appear to accept that Graham has now become Carlo. And I don't really mind, as you already know my middle name is Carl. It's just an incredible coincidence that he chooses that name when he has difficulty grappling with the name of Graham. So, for the entire tournament I remain as Carlo. Even when Marcello, after we've moved to a number of other targets, points out that my name is Graham, I remain Carlo.

With Fabrizio by my side, the two of us fire our three arrows at the target. Fabrizio is good. The inglese, Carlo, not so good, two of his arrows missing the deer completely. We step out of the way. Two other names are called, the two releasing their three arrows when all is safe. And so, the morning continues as we move from one target to the next. After closely observing the skilful technique of others, I step forward, the bow held firmly by my left hand, arm at full stretch, my right arm pulling the arrow back. I sight the target, the arrow close to my nose. I maintain the tension. I release the arrow. My arrow hits the target. My second arrow hits the target. My third arrow hits the ground within a few centimetres of the target. Not bad, two out of three. After all archers have had their opportunity to have three shots, we all walk to the target. Scores are checked, arrows pulled out and handed back to their owners. By the time we are half way through the morning, most of those in my group have scores in triple figures. I'm trailing way behind, still to get anywhere near one hundred. This archery business is not as easy as it looks. Just to complicate things, some of the targets move. Others are a greater distance away. Some we have a set time to hit with all three arrows. And some are very small. And the day is hot, all those taking part having to seek a little comfort in the shade. My heavy cotton shirt, a patchwork of sweat, little rivulets trickling down my back, the taste of salt on my lips.

My group of archers move to the next target and then the next. Is my aim improving? Not really. More by chance than skill, I score points, others in the group offering me tips and advice. All very friendly, warm and encouraging. The next target is nothing more than a thick plaited rope. The rope hanging down, a small bell on the end. The aim, obviously, is to hit the rope, thus making the bell ring. Easy? Carlo is called first, the other archer by my side being Gaia. With rivulets of sweat running down my back, left arm at full stretch, right arm pulling the arrow back, I focus my mind on the target. Try not to over think this. Aim and release. My first arrow speeds towards the target, strikes the plaited rope and the bell rings. 'Bravo! Bravo! Carlo!' Smiles on all of the faces. I modestly accept the appreciation of my adoring fans, remaining where I am until Gaia has had three attempts to hit the target. The protocol is that you remain where you are until the archer next to you has completed his/her three shots at a target. With my first arrow, I've scored the maximum fifteen points. Others do the same, whilst for others it could be their second or third arrow before they make the bell ring. Second arrow, ten points, third arrow five points. Obviously if you miss with all three arrows, no points. My good fortune doesn't remain with me for long.

As we progress from one target to the next, my aim is haphazard. By the end of the morning, my total score has crept its way to just over one hundred. All others in the group have scores of at least two hundred plus. The very best in the group, having scores in the three hundreds. We gather round, still with an abnormal distance between us, to compare scores. All in the group are very generous, acknowledging that this is my very first tournament. 'Bravo Carlo.'

Having congratulated the other archers in our group, Marcello and myself eventually meet up with the other members of Colpalombo Archers. Excited conversation takes place, all wanting to know how others have done. It will probably come as no surprise to you that I have the lowest score. But not just the lowest score within the ranks of Colpalombo Archers, the lowest score out of all those taking part from the many different towns and villages. Well, as they say, the only way is up. And anyway, it's the taking part that counts. With practice I'm bound to improve. After all, I come from the country of Robin Hood.

Having put to one side all talk about scores, we gather together in the shade of an enormous oak tree to enjoy an Italian feast of cold meats, cheese, olives, tomatoes, salads of different types and bread drizzled with extra virgin olive oil; each person having contributed something to our afternoon picnic. The food washed down with aqua, a little white wine, a little red wine and a little Prosecco. 'Cincin!'

It's been a truly wonderful day. My immersion into the life of Colpalombo simply incredible. The people of the village, my neighbours and my friends, such a joy to be with.

'Robin Hood and Little John walkin' through the forest, laughin' back and forth at what the other has to say. Reminiscin', this-n'-thattin', having such a good time. Oo-de-lally, Oo-de-lally golly, what a day.' Disney's Robin Hood – Ooh De Lally

Since my first tournament, I've been to several more. In July 2022, you find me with Colpalombo Archers in yet another, beautiful, hilltop town, Belforte del Chienti. We've ventured outside the borders of Umbria, now in Marche. Over the year my technique has slowly improved but still some distance behind all other archers from Colpalombo. It's an incredibly hot day, as we move between targets, everyone is trying to seek shade. Surprisingly this is my best day, my aim appears to have stepped up a gear. On some of the targets I'm actually scoring top points. All other archers, be they from Colpalombo or some other town, are more than generous with their praise of the Englishman.

CALCOLI RENALI

I'm viciously woken at 2.30 in the morning by a gun shot to right side of my lower back; the pain is sudden and excruciating. It's late September 2021. I turn to my other side, but the pain simply increases. A hot knife cuts into my flesh to retrieve the bullet. God the pain is intense! I try to escape by moving round the bed. I walk to the bathroom. I search for pain killers. I hold the lower part of my back. There is no escape. What little medical understanding I have, this being very little, all I can assume is that I must be experiencing a severe problem with my right kidney, the pain feels to be in that general area. I return to bed, firmly pressing on the area of my back producing the pain, but there is absolutely no relief. It's now 3.30am, the next three hours being the most physically painful of my adult life. I'm worried, could this be something more serious than kidney stones?

By 7am I'm at the home of Peter and Laura, knocking on their door. They come to the door, clearly surprised and bemused at my early interruption of their morning routine. My face tells them that I'm in pain, that I have a serious problem. Once dressed, Alan offers, no, his insists that he will drive me to the hospital a few kilometres from Gubbio, a journey of less than thirty minutes. Once there, I explain my symptoms. Bits of paper work done, I'm being examined by a doctor and nurse. Questions are asked, prodding of each side of my lower back made, the diagnosis being that I almost certainly have kidney stones. Ultra sound and a blood sample confirm the diagnosis. The doctor explains what is going on inside my kidney. He also goes through details related to my liver, glucose levels and other bits of my insides, that came from the ultra sound and blood sample. Various drugs are prescribed, the doctor explaining that the stones should eventually pass through my system.

For the next week, the pain is, at times, just as intense. Between each spasm of moaning pain, a continual, high intensity, ache. People tell me that kidney stones are more painful than childbirth, don't believe them. I was there at the birth of my two daughters, I have never seen anything as painful. Kidney stones are most certainly painful, but nothing like childbirth.

Eventually, after several days, the pain simply stopped, almost as suddenly as it arrived. The final evening, a moment of excruciating pain, in the same part of my lower back, the following morning, nothing. I assume the stones had left my system.

One little, but significant bit of information for any American readers. Apart from payment for the drugs, the whole medical intervention was free at my point of need. No bill presented to me, no questions about medical insurance. Do you think that this could be an example of socialism?

THE CHEESE MAKER

An adopted villager of Colpalombo, of Umbria, a foreigner enjoying the most amazing life in Italy. During the hot summer months, the nights slept with my windows thrown open, the morning sunlight sweeping into my room like a flock of silent birds.

What feels like the simplicity of life can be relished and enjoyed here. Although, at times, that simplicity, perhaps some would call it honesty, can feel a little cruel. It's late afternoon, I'm sitting on my balcony enjoying a cold beer. As I most often do, I'm simply observing and listening. Coming over the low hill across from the house, and then walking diagonally down the field, is a young Italian male, dark curly hair, white shirt, sleeves rolled back revealing a dark tan. He's carrying a small baby goat, a kid, across his shoulders, two legs held fast on either side of his neck. The young goat resting on his shoulders like a milkmaid's yoke. It's the plaintive bleating of the goat that first attracted my attention. It appears to be a new addition being delivered to my neighbour Aldo. A cute little kid to join his small flock. A brief conversation takes place, the young kid given into Aldo's care. Hands are shaken, the young man then making his way back up the field and eventually disappearing from view.

The sound of bleating, once again, attracts my attention. Close to one of the out buildings, Aldo holds the young kid on the ground, what looks like a large bowl/bucket close by. Aldo is crouched on the ground with his back to me. Silence, the bleating has stopped. I collect another cold beer from the fridge, soon returning to my crow's nest, my little balcony.

On returning to my high perch, the silent kid is most certainly dead. It's been hung by its back legs from one of the out buildings, Aldo going through the process of skinning and then butchering the animal. That evening I'm invited for dinner. You already know what's on the menu.

Along with chickens and the apparently compulsory cockerel that any Italian male must have to keep his hens in check, as you already know, Aldo keeps goats. These are fed and well looked after for their milk and meat. Each year Aldo's female goats are introduced to a visiting male, a billy (sometimes known as a buck). With the wind in the right direction, I know when the billy is in temporary residence. It can just be a gentle breeze but it's enough to carry the pungent odour of the billy into my garden. And trust me, the smell has nothing at all in common with the supposedly musky scent in human male colognes. I don't want to offend any male goats, but I have to be honest. A billy goat feeling sexy, stinks! Apparently, the stink comes from scent glands located near the horns and the uncontrollable habit of the male to spray their own urine on their face, chest and front legs. It may sound disgusting to you and me, but in the animal world there is no accounting for taste. Female goats fall under its spell, sending them into heat, such a state of arousal making them more than willing to accept the billy's stinky 'foreplay'. He then mounts, whilst she stands, looking rather uninterested, in all likelihood thinking of Italy until he's had his way. The billy hangs around for a couple of weeks before moving on, I guess, to cast his spell on other female goats.

In February, the following year, Aldo has a number of extremely cute kids bouncing round the fenced field. It's not just me. Aldo also finds the young goats totally charming, always insisting that I take a number of photographs. They are full of life as they spring and play. A life that will undoubtedly be short. I know that at least one of the cute little kids will become the main food on the table over Easter.

One early morning, as I walk up the garden, my back to the English gate, I hear a very cheerful 'Ciao Ghrem, buongiorno!' Turning round I find a smiling Aldo, dressed in hunting gear, dark green: heavy boots. Strung around his waist a cartridge belt, cartridges in regimental order. Gun over his shoulder and hunting dog to his side. He has a broad smile and a twinkle in his eye.

'Have you been hunting?'

It's obvious that he has, but I have to have some way of starting the conversation.

'Yes, in the upper part of the fields, across from the house', he replies.

'Any luck?'

'I don't need luck' , then turning to one side to reveal a pheasant hidden away in the large pocket of his hunting jacket. 'Yes, a pheasant', pulling the dead bird out for display.

'Bravo', I respond.

Placing the kill back in the large pocket, Aldo walks on, still smiling.

'Alicia will be pleased when I show her what she has to cook', this said with a cheeky grin.

Aldo the hunter (cacciatore), the butcher (macellaio), the salami maker (salamiera), the crafter of the most delicious goats cheese (casaro). I now understand why, at the end of a meal, he sits at the end of the table offering cheese to others. He is, without doubt, the 'Capo of the Cheese', the blender, the cheese craftsman. The maker of the most delicious pale cream, almost yellow, large roundels of cheese. The maker of rich, creamy, ricotta. And he's justifiably proud of his endeavours. The whole process of cheese making taking almost 3 months.

Aldo the amateur fixer of almost all things. Aldo who can even turn his hand to a little hair trimming: Aldo the barber (barbiere). Barbering only conducted on the two middle aged sons of Elizabeta. You remember Elizabeta, the wife of Federico. The hair trimming done outside, under the cover of the one of the outbuildings.

Aldo my advisor, my mentor in all things practical, including the pruning of olive trees. My support when I need a fresh supply of logs, the one who has knowledge of where to buy the best trees and where I can get a delivery of manure. The Sardinian who has made his home in Colpalombo, Umbria, for the past sixty years and more. Husband to Benedetta, father to three young women, grandfather to four grandchildren. Aldo now retired from the Forestry Police. Aldo who questions why I have, in his opinion, Christmas lights outside my house all year? Aldo the joker. Aldo someone usually calm and relaxed, but on mentioning the name of Benito, be prepared to stand back. Aldo, from the very beginning, my closest neighbour and friend; not one word of English ever leaving his lips. Aldo who still insists on telling other Italians that my Italian is terrible.

Aldo is out early with his monster strimmer. Visor, heavy gloves and boots, harness over his shoulders to take some of the strain. He's now in his early 70s, apart from worrying back problems that require further surgery, he's generally fit and healthy. He grips both handles of the strimmer. The solid metal blade buzzing at high speed as he sweeps it over the ground. A blade that could easily remove your toes. The long grass and assorted weeds have no escape, minced and sprayed, clinging to the lower half of Aldo's long trousers. The smell of freshly mashed grass filling the air. It's a summer morning, early, only 7.30, but already the temperature has climbed to 26°C. Once his work is done, he'll retreat inside, the coolness of the house a refuge from the summer heat. Throughout the day he'll venture out into the garden, sit and contemplate, snooze in his hammock strung in the shade of two persimmon trees (alberi di cachi), at times engaging in conversation with all who pass his little bit of Case Colle.

LIFE & BALANCE

Millions try to find the ideal work/life balance. I know that I'm incredibly fortunate. All I have to do is focus on my life, there is no need to struggle to find 'the balance'. The restrictions of paid employment a thing of the past. Friends in the UK will sometimes ask, 'What do you do each day, don't you get bored?' My response is simple, 'As much as possible, I enjoy life.' Nothing more, that's it. And I don't feel obliged to explain. I somehow think that they expect a fuller explanation. 'You try your best to enjoy life, that's it?' And the absolute truth is, I'm never bored. I have my little bit of Umbria, the whole of Italy and beyond, to keep me occupied, simply taking up the opportunity to soak in everything on offer. And the close affinity I have with the Green Heart of Italy, my Italian friends and neighbours having totally absorbed me into the community of Colpalombo. Foreign friends that I've made and continue to make, how could I be bored?

Will I always be in my little bit of Italy? Who knows? For now, my heart is happy in the Green Heart of Italy – Umbria. Somewhere out there, there are people dreaming of Italy, I'm actually here. Our leasehold on life is relatively short. How long have humans, in the 'modern' form we now take, walked upright on this planet we call earth? It's a whisper in the history of the universe, a tiny grain of sand. We certainly have longer here than the beauty of a butterfly. All we can do is try the best we can to make the time we have worthwhile.

Phew, heavy stuff. Graham the philosopher. I don't think that philosophy very much bothers the little black scorpion that's just crept out into the middle of the kitchen floor from its hiding place. I've named him Nipper and popped a snap on Facebook. Marcello, having seen the snap, informs me that he thinks HE is a SHE and pregnant. Don't ask how he knows this; I have no idea. A pregnant scorpion, how many young do they have? I scoop SHE up, then transporting her to the end of the garden. I've decided that she'll be happier there. Although to be honest, I've not found Italian scorpions to be great talkers. Foreigners worry that they may be dangerous. They're not. They're very small, about the size of the end of my thumb. No, I don't have overly big thumbs; well, I don't think so. I'm told that a sting from one is no more painful or dangerous than, perhaps, a wasp sting. But to tell the truth, I don't know anyone who has suffered such a fate. I guess if you have the risk of suffering anaphylactic shock a scorpion sting could be a problem. The black scorpion certainly won't have been bothered by the pandemic that altered the way we've all lived during its over long stay.

Grazie

A message to the frontline medics in Bergamo
Hospital, Lombardy

Many Irish lives were saved,
Because you gave us time.

Hundreds, maybe thousands live,
Because you gave us time.

Time you didn't have yourselves,
Still sent that warning sign
And thousands live and love today,
Because you gave us time.

Your medics on the virus front,
Fighting fire with fire
Their mission just to save each life, driven by desire
Sadly many lost their lives, as
they fought to hold the line
And saving many Irish lives,
Because they gave us time.

So, as we ponder travel, not knowing when or where,
We'll journey to Bergamo and thank the people there.
Our thoughts and prayers are with you, we hope your
stars align.

Grazie

Mille Grazie

For giving us more time

. . . .

Eugene Garrihy
ABRIDGED

CHAPTER THIRTEEN

Ancora Vivo

....

'Italy looked at the example of China, not as a practical warning, but as a science fiction movie that had nothing to do with us. And when the virus exploded, Europe looked at us the same way we looked at China.'

....

Sandra Zampa, Undersecretary of Italy's Health Ministry

It's officially the warmest and driest May on record in the UK – 2020. I'm staying with my daughter, Kara, and her husband.

Early, each and every morning, a large ball of bright ginger stealthily strolls along the top of the undulating wooden fence. This feline killer stops, sits upright, still and silent, a few meters above the long grass below. The cat looks down, eyes fixed, intent. A thick ginger tail hangs, moving slightly from side to side, slowly sweeping against the ridged panelling of the fence. There must be the likelihood of a free breakfast, perhaps a small innocent mouse. The unsuspecting mouse to be crunched between sharp teeth or toyed with, perhaps even transported home as an offering. Either way, the little creature's life will soon come to an end.

The ginger ball drops, lost from view. Has torment suddenly descended from above? Will death come swift?

The ginger cat reappears, a tiny, lifeless body firmly held between its jaws. Nature can be cruel, death arriving, random and unexpected.

Saturday, June 12th, 2020 – the official number of deaths related to Covid-19 in the UK stands at 41,481. Deaths in Italy, 34,223. In the USA, 113,000. New Zealand, 22. World-wide an estimated 421,300 deaths.

When I began to put together my rambling thoughts about living in Italy, never in my most bizarre dreams did I think I would be writing about a worldwide pandemic. Possibly deaths from earthquakes, but never a contagion killing hundreds of thousands, the material of a science fiction novel.

And as I look out of my daughter's bedroom window, the ginger predator sits each morning, ready to fall on its unsuspecting prey. The sun shines and the sky is blue. As the cat drops, delivering death to a mouse, Covid-19 brings death in ever increasing numbers. The UK daily death count, the number of people taken before their time, growing exponentially.

Why am I not in Italy? The answer - Coronavirus. I'm exiled in the UK by lockdown. The World Health Organization having declared Covid-19 a worldwide pandemic on the 11th of March 2020.

The first two cases in Italy were reported between the end of January and the beginning of February 2020. An elderly man in Padua recorded as the first European to have died from the virus. The second person to die, a woman from the northern region of Lombardy. A cluster of cases quickly follow in the region, resulting in officials ordering schools, public buildings, restaurants, cafes, and bars to close in ten towns.

Friday the 24th of January, the UK government brings together a meeting of Cobra (a UK government top strategic body), such meetings only taking place at times of possible national crisis. More often than not, Cobra meetings would be chaired by the Prime Minister, in this case, Boris Johnson. However, on this occasion the meeting is left in the hands of Matt Hancock, the Health Secretary. Dire warnings are coming out of China about the serious nature of the virus, its spread already infecting and killing hundreds. A smiling Hancock speaks to the assembled media, saying that the risk to the UK is 'low'. When questioned, he states that the UK is:

'Well-prepared and well-equipped to tackle any contagion. The UK has a world-leading test for Covid-19.'

January the 14th is a big day for Johnson's Tory (Conservative) government. Boris Johnson has delivered what he had promised the British public, withdrawal of the UK from the EU. This is the focus of his government, not some virus originating in the markets of Wuhan. It's a time for Boris Johnson and his supporters to crow about the UK taking back its sovereignty, at last breaking free from the bureaucracy of the European machine. Pushing the Corona virus to the top spot would distract from what should be the main media story. The 31st of January 2020 will be known as 'Brexit Day'!

Having secured the EU withdrawal, Johnson goes on vacation for two weeks with his pregnant fiancée. It's March the 2nd before the Prime Minister attends his first Cobra meeting dealing with the issues related to the virus. He's been absent from the previous five.

By the 21st of February, the virus is estimated to have infected at least 76,000 people, killing almost 2,500 in China. The news, for most people, remains, at best, of low-level background interest. After all this is in China, thousands of miles away. There's little to worry about, even if the virus did enter the UK, we are assured that the country is well prepared. Even when the news reports that the virus has crept into Italy, with 51 cases recorded and two deaths, it's still not really absorbed by the general public as being of any genuine concern. With only two weeks before our flight to Cuba, I'm more focussed on getting the jabs suggested for our holiday. By the 26th of February, there are 13 reported cases of the virus in the UK. Unknown to the British public, the government's advisory committee is warning of a catastrophic loss of life unless drastic action is taken. The focus for me is a bit of last-minute holiday shopping for our Cuban adventure.

February 23rd. Public events, including carnival celebrations and football matches are cancelled in Italy.

March 4th. All schools and universities are closed in Italy.

There's still a temptation to play down the virus. The mayor of Milan, fronting the campaign, 'Milan Doesn't Stop', allowing bars to remain open in the evening.

March 8th. Several provinces in the north of Italy are placed under Lockdown.

March 9th. The Italian Prime Minister, Giuseppe Conte, announces a national Lockdown. This includes the restriction of movement, temporary closure of non-essential shops and businesses.

'We all must give something up for the good of Italy. We have to do it now. This is why I decided to adopt even more strong and severe measures to contain the advance of the virus and protect the health of all citizens.'

All nonessential movement is prohibited, those who do need to travel for work or for health reasons and food items, having to complete official forms.

March 11th. All bars and restaurants are closed in Italy.

March 22nd. All nonessential factories are closed.

I'd driven over from Italy in the November of 2019 to spend Christmas and New Year with Martina. Wanting to visit Cuba was something that we'd both spoken about when we very first met in Florence. The plan on arriving back in the UK from Cuba, would be another visit to see my daughters, and then the start of my long drive back to Italy. Martina would fly out to spend a week with me at the end of April.

We leave the UK from Gatwick airport, London, in the early morning of March 10th, relatively unconcerned about the virus. Our destination Havana. The UK government still taking a very relaxed approach to the outbreak. The only concrete advice being given is to ensure that you wash your hands whilst singing a few lines of 'Happy Birthday'. The main thought in my mind being, how can the virus be so deadly if the simple task of washing hands is the major form of protection. Boris Johnson at a daily news briefing on March 3rd, boasting that he was still shaking hands with everyone and didn't see this as a problem:

'I'm shaking hands with everyone. I was at a hospital the other night where I think there were a few Corona virus patients and I shook hands with everybody, you'll be pleased to know. And I continue to shake hands. People will obviously have to make up their own minds. I think the scientific evidence is, well .... Washing your hands is the crucial thing.'

On March 5th, Boris Johnson appears on breakfast TV:

'It's always worth stressing with this, the overwhelming majority of people, those who get it. This is going to be a mild to moderate illness. You know we're still at the stage where the single best thing we can do, and it will be like that for a long time, is just wash our hands.'

The presenter points out that he, Johnson, walked into the studio and immediately shook hands. Johnson brushes this to one side. People automatically shake hands.

Boris Johnson goes on to say:

'Slightly counter intuitively, things like closing schools and stopping big gatherings, perhaps don't work as well as people think.'

When further questioned, he continues with:

'One of the theories is that perhaps you can sort of take it on the chin, take it all in one go and allow the disease as it were to move through the population, without taking as many draconian measures.'

According to those close to the Italian Prime Minister, Boris Johnson had told Giuseppe Conte, on the 13th of March, that the UK was going to aim for 'herd immunity'.

As people got on with their daily routines, others flying away to holiday in foreign destinations, including myself and Martina, Covid-19 was steadily creeping into country after country.

We relax into our flight, our focus being the ten days together on Cuba. For me, the coronavirus floating somewhere in the periphery of my mind. A vague registering of the news that 71 had now died in the UK; we're told that all had underlying health problems. The impression still in the minds of many that this is no bigger problem than the yearly flu virus. In Italy, the death toll had risen to 2,503, the vast majority in the region of Lombardy. Italian experts saying that the average age of those who have died being 79.5, with only 17 people under the age of 50. All of Italy's victims under 40, we're told, had serious existing conditions.

The evening of March 10th, we arrive in Havana, our immediate concern being the loss of Martina's passport at the airport. Unknown to us, Italy is now reported as the worst affected country for Covid-19 after China. The number of coronavirus deaths in Italy having risen by 475 in one day to just under 3,000. One of the worst hit cities in northern Italy, Bergamo, has army trucks on its streets, transporting bodies to remote sites for cremation because the local morgues are struggling to cope with the rising numbers. Bergamo alone, again, unknown to us, has at least 4,500 infected with Covid-19. In this city, 93 deaths have been reported. A national Italian newspaper, Il Messaggero, showing coffins lined up in a Bergamo church.

We arrive, late evening, at our accommodation in Havana. It's a gloriously warm night. The two of us, although tired from the long flight, bubbling with excitement; the virus completely forgotten. However, Mirco Nacoti, an Italian anaesthesiologist and intensive-care specialist, estimated that perhaps 60% of Bergamo's citizens were already infected.

As we holiday in the city, we get the odd snippet of news from the UK and Italy, hearing Boris Johnson's comments to the British people with some astonishment:

'I must level with you, level with the British public. Many families, many more families, are going to lose loved ones before their time.'

To be totally honest, the gravity of what is unfolding is still not registering with either of us. Washing hands and perhaps using sanitizer is all you have to do. Havana appears to be going about its daily life unaffected by what's happening in many other countries. The only evidence of any concern was at the airport. As we went through passport control, those checking passports were wearing face masks and asking if we had recently visited China or Italy. Havana, certainly very different to any city in the UK or Italy but apparently separated from Covid-19 by thousands of miles.

Havana is a city of faded colonial splendour, crumbling buildings. As you walk around its streets, brightly coloured, classic American cars, Buicks and Chevrolets, glide past, and salsa music fills the air. Cubans seemingly finding it impossible not to sway, to sing and dance. Compared with other capital cities that I've visited, it's obvious that Havana is the capital of a poor country. This being partly the result of internal, domestic, politics and perhaps, of even greater relevance, the tight economic embargo imposed on Cuba by the USA. But it's a city that we found to be fascinating, its waterfront busy during the day and a place of tranquillity at sunset. Narrow streets and cobbled plazas, market stalls selling fresh produce, architecture, some of it gloriously splendid, much in need of a facelift. Its people, smiling, friendly and welcoming.

On our third morning in Havana, Martina, for some reason I can't remember, has already taken the rickety cage, that transports us up and down the building, to the ground floor and is waiting for me out in the street. When I arrive, she's with our one-toothed cage operator and a woman holding a clipboard and papers. Martina explains that the woman is a doctor, she's checking to see if we have any symptoms of Covid-19. Martina then says that she's told her that I live in Italy and that I speak Italian. I have to say, I'm quietly pleased in Martina's confidence in my, still faltering Italian, she gives it far more credit than I do. The knowledge that I live in Italy has put a little concern on the face of the doctor. She speaks only a few words of English, so the conversation that follows takes place in Italian and Spanish. Surprisingly, we understand most of what the other one is saying. First I make it clear that I've not been in Italy since November, this bringing a smile of relief to her face. She then asks for my passport. This she flicks through and notices the visa from my visit to China, her smile exchanged for a look of concern. I quickly reassure her that the visa is three years old, I've not been to China since 2017. Relief again, the smile returning to her face, she hands the passport back. I've already explained that we lost Martina's passport at the airport. Are both of you feeling well, no headaches or fever? I tell her that we're both feeling fine, no problems. And with that she's satisfied, leaving me a number to contact should we start to feel unwell. 'Que tenga un buen. Gracias', from her. 'Nessun problema, buona giornata' from me. And away she goes, leaving me trying to converse with our one-toothed cage attendant.

We pick up bits of information from relatives in the UK and friends in Italy. And it's becoming increasingly clear that Italy has a serious problem. The UK's main problem would appear to be a rush on toilet rolls. Although we do know that the number of people dying in the UK is increasing. The UK government, apart from Boris Johnson's prediction that members of your family will die, still appearing to take a very relaxed approach. The British public continues to be assured that the country is very well prepared. We enjoy our final day in Havana, even being able to get an emergency passport for Martina from the British Embassy. That same day we take a coach from Havana to the region of Pinar del Río. We're heading for Valle de Viñales and a small town of the same name, Viñales. A semi subtropical area, beautiful in its slow, laid-back pace. Incredibly green and lush. The place where we happen to be staying having unbroken views across the most gorgeous, wide valley, the valley peppered with hills. The only sounds we hear are the low voices of our hosts, bird song and the occasional passing cart pulled along by oxen. Horses and carts are the main form of transport, the occasional bus and the inevitable classic American car used as a taxi.

We spend our days walking and horse-riding in an area famous for its tobacco plantations. On another day, we swim in crystal clear waters and snooze on fine, white, sandy beaches. It's difficult to get your head round the fact that Florida, the USA, is only about 145 kilometres (90 miles) from the north coast of Cuba. I know, although it's close in distance, if you're American, it's virtually impossible for you to visit Cuba – sorry.

Before we leave Cuba, it's become increasingly clear that this virus is serious and causing greater and greater concern across the world. In Cuba, all still appears to be calm, but we do have news that Spain has gone into full lockdown, a term that becomes common to all of us. Why should Spain being in lockdown worry us? We have a connecting fight in Madrid. We really don't want to fly to Spain and find that we have to go into quarantine. The flight from Havana to Madrid is uneventful. The only difference from the flight we made in the opposite direction, just ten days before, is that many, but not all people on the plane are wearing masks.

After landing in Madrid, we wait for our connecting flight to Gatwick. The airport is eerily quiet, all eateries and retail outlets are closed, shutters down. No questions have been asked about our state of health. No temperature checks have been taken. Nobody has questioned why we're not wearing masks. And, thankfully, no one has said that we have to quarantine. I guess because we're transiting through, the thought is that there is little need for checks. Obviously, when we land in Gatwick, and as we go through passport control, health checks will be made, and questions will be asked about where we have just arrived from, won't they? When we arrive in Gatwick, nothing, no questions are asked, and no checks are made. It's perhaps a little less hectic than normal, but other than that, everything is as you would find in a busy international airport. Is the UK simply ignoring the coronavirus?

It's just a short train journey to Martina's friends to collect the car from their drive. Just ten days earlier, we had stayed the night before our flight the next morning, all four of us a little confused by the virus and the response from different governments. But still never imagining that it would develop into something of such magnitude. Meeting with them on our return, a surreal situation. It seemed incredible how much had changed in just under two weeks. We're welcomed back, but at a distance, Martina's friends preferring that we speak to them whilst they stand at the open door of their house. They question us about the holiday. We have even more questions about what's been going on in the UK. The usual, see you both again soon, take care. No shaking of hands and no embrace before we leave.

After spending a few days with Martina, I drive up to stay with my daughters in Yorkshire. My intention to drive back to Italy is now shrouded in uncertainty. Kara, Lucy and all other members of my family are fine. It's clear to anyone that the situation in the UK is growing in seriousness.

On March 23rd, Boris Johnson appears on TV and announces a nationwide Lockdown. There are 6,650 recorded cases of Covid-19, 335 deaths. I have yet to discover the ginger killer that every morning sits and waits for an innocent mouse. Not only am I not able to return to Italy, I also find myself separated from Martina.

Only a few weeks before, Boris Johnson had been bragging about shaking hands with Covid patients. It's now announced that he has tested positive for Covid-19 and will be self-isolating in 11 Downing Street. On April 5th, he's admitted to a London hospital, the same day being transferred to intensive care.

In Italy:

'We realised the virus was here too late. It was already spreading.' Roberto Burioni, one of Italy's leading virologists.

As for Boris Johnson, a senior government adviser gives an interesting view on his character, relating the threat from Covid-19 being equal to a country heading into war. How could the PM not have been at the Cobra meetings?

I keep in daily contact with Martina, she's now working from home, her daughter back from university. We also speak to each other at different times throughout the passing weeks. Each evening government ministers and health officials appear on TV to give Covid briefings, updates on figures and supposedly answer questions from the media. Life with my daughters, like so many people in the UK and any number of other countries, becomes almost rigidly housebound. Only leaving the house for supplies of food and brief exercise. I also start to randomly jot down my thoughts about Covid-19 and Lockdown. As my thoughts spilled onto the page, I simply couldn't imagine that the pandemic would go on for well over two years.

....

LOCKDOWN UK – DAY 13. Key politicians are still not facing up to the fact that they have been incredibly slow in reacting to the pandemic. They appear on TV each evening and speak but say very little. The level of hypocrisy is quite astonishing. After years of savage cuts to the NHS (National Health Service), we now have senior ministers singing its praise, begging the population to support it. Words come out of mouths, but deliberately avoid offering answers that would explain the different rate of deaths in the UK compared to, for example, Germany. I've lost count of the number of times they have told us that testing is vital, then avoiding answering why the numbers being tested are so low. The number of deaths in the UK yesterday, over 600. Will this level of death continue for say, the next few weeks, perhaps longer, the final total impossible to predict? Tributes appear each day to those health professionals who have died caring for others.

....

Being in lockdown in the UK, it's difficult to get a real impression of how things are going for my friends and neighbours in Italy. I do know that the Covid restrictions are far tighter than those in the UK.

Questions float around on Facebook. Will the Italian government extend Lockdown beyond the 12th of April? Will Cantine Aperte, an important time of the year for Umbrian wine producers, take place on the last weekend of May? Will Umbria Jazz go ahead in July? Even though the number of deaths and infections are daily news, I still don't think people can really comprehend what everyone is going through could continue for months, even years. Will the Ceri take place in Gubbio?

Italian friends post images and messages on Facebook, some serious, most light hearted. A dinosaur appears a number of times, running through the evening streets of Gubbio, popping out from hidden corners and then disappearing. All festivals, including the famous Ceri are eventually cancelled (they remain cancelled for almost two years). This is the first time, in its entire history, that the Ceri has not taken place. Even in the second world war, the Ceri was celebrated, women taking the place of men away fighting. People sing from balconies. Those who would have been participating in the Ceri, post music. Individuals in their own homes, dressed in the colours of the Ceri, through the wizardry of technology, coming together as one band. Joyous moments, special intermissions, set within incredibly difficult weeks and months.

....

LOCKDOWN UK – DAY 18. The life of another professional in the NHS hangs in the balance, resting in the hands of colleagues. Vicky, 38 years old, a nurse and a very close friend of Kara and Lucy, my daughters, more like a sister than a friend, is being kept alive on a ventilator in intensive care. Vicky's family is told to prepare for the strong possibility that she may not survive. She has a young daughter. The strictest barrier systems are in place, preventing any visits to Vicky's bedside. Another victim of the pandemic, brain and body existing in almost complete isolation. Vicky herself now totally oblivious to her condition, unaware of the tears and the grief felt by those close to her; Vicky's body having been placed in an induced coma. Vicky's grip on life hanging by a thread. Her body kept alive by machines and the dedicated work of hospital staff. Nights and days pass. Each time either of my daughters receive a message on their phones or a call, you can see fear etched into their faces. The next call, the next message, will be to say that Vicky has sadly died. The end of her young life feels inevitable. More days pass, Vicky existing in a twilight zone, in some place between life and death. Another message, there's slight improvement in her comatose condition. Is this really a sign of hope? The next message suggesting that there is no hope. This young mother, daughter, sister, friend will become yet another statistic. During the past 24 hours her heart has stopped a number of times, other organs showing signs of failure, her body on the edge of closing down completely.

....

April 19th, 2020, the official death toll in the UK, 15, 464, an increase of 888 from the previous day. In just one week the number of deaths has almost doubled.

Pronouncements come from leading UK ministers at the daily briefing, given at 4pm, that we are all in this together. We're reminded that this deadly virus does not differentiate on the basis of social class or wealth. And as the words spill from the lips of those in government, the stark reality is that even in the grip of a world pandemic, wealth brings privilege that is way beyond the mass of people. The UK announced its Lockdown on March 23rd. I'm deliberately using the term 'announced' rather than 'imposed', because the UK government strategy had so many holes, the restrictions placed on movement could hardly be described as an imposition on freedoms.

A report, placed in the corner of the front page of The Sunday Times, reveals not only the privilege that comes with wealth, but also the massive gaps in the Lockdown fence. From the first date of Lockdown, through to the middle of April, 545 private jets landed on UK airfields from a range of countries. A total of 767 private jets also left the UK. A private jet to, for example, the United Arab Emirates, costing up to £100,000. Many other countries had already placed restrictions on international travellers, these restrictions backed with quarantine rules. And yet, in the UK, more than 15,000 passengers arrived each day on normal flights.

When asked about the UK government's strategy, Professor Gabriel Scally, President of Epidemiology and Public Health at the Royal Society of Medicine, stated:

'It's hard to understand.' He goes on to call the strategy, 'most peculiar.'

The Sunday Times April 19th, 2020:

'Government whistle-blowers, scientists and emergency planners say there was complacency at the heart of government in late January and February, when it should have been urgently replenishing emergency stockpiles.'

'There's no way you're at war if your PM isn't there. And what you learn about Boris was that he didn't chair any meetings. He liked his country breaks. He didn't work weekends. There was a real sense that he didn't do urgent crisis planning. It was exactly like people feared it would be.'

The following comment is attributed to Dominic Cummings, the Chief Adviser to Boris Johnson:

'Herd immunity, protect the economy and if that means some pensioners die, too bad.'

Now I can't say with any certainty if he said those exact words, but I strongly suspect his advice to Boris Johnson slanted in that direction.

Those on the political right in the USA, adopted the same approach. The 70-year-old Dan Patrick, Lieutenant Governor of Texas (I have to admit, I'm not entirely sure of his role, but sounds high ranking) said:

'As a senior citizen, are you willing to take a chance on your survival in exchange for keeping the America that all America loves for your children and grandchildren? If that's the exchange, I'm all in.'

....

LOCKDOWN UK – DAY 26. We've arrived at the point where the official daily rate of death is no longer the main news item. A death rate of 800+ appears to have lost its news worthiness. Premature death has become normalised. For days headline news is taken by Boris being 'infected'. What could we expect from the UK government? Rabbits in headlights would appear to be the best. NHS staff advised to reuse PPE (Personal Protective Equipment).

....

By June 4th, 2020, there are six million confirmed cases of Covid-19 in 188 countries, with more than 380,000 people having lost their lives. The USA having the largest number of cases, almost one third of the global total. The total number of deaths in the US standing at 105,000. The UK, Italy, France and Spain are the worst-hit European countries.

Did the Corona virus escape from a lab in Wuhan? The leading theory amongst scientists is that the virus was transmitted to humans via infected animals in Wuhan's wildlife market. Really? Pangolins and bats? Close to Wuhan there is also one of China's top research laboratories into human infectious diseases. I'm really not into conspiracy theories, but it does feel like an incredible coincidence that the source of the virus and China's top laboratory just happen to be in the same city.

In the UK, government ministers repeat over and over again that they are basing policy on following the best scientific advice, that advice coming from the Scientific Advisory Group for Emergencies (SAGE). If that is in fact the case, why has the UK headed towards one of the worst per capita death rates of any developed country?

....

LOCKDOWN UK – DAY 45. The UK government appears to be determined to carry on with its 'highly successful' approach to tackling Covid-19. No sorry, apparently it's only the English government approach. Scotland doesn't agree with the approach, Wales is not sure about the approach, and N. Ireland has been forgotten. The slogans that appear at the daily briefings, reminding us of what we are supposed to do, have changed again. So, the message is very clear - BE ALERT! You should stay at home if you can, but if you can't you don't have to stay at home. You can go to work. In fact, you should go to work but don't use a bus or train. You can, however, now run there as many times as you like.

The Guardian newspaper:

'Britain is in a lonely place right now. It resembles the scene of a bad traffic accident where shocked passersby look away with pity and horror in their eyes.'

'Italians may surely be forgiven, a sense of relief that their country is no longer Europe's biggest blackspot. With this unwanted title came the unspoken inference that Italy was uniquely unprepared. Some in the UK certainly saw it that way. They thought they were immune. They were betting, as usual, on a bogus British exceptionalism. '

'Britain did not pay enough attention to what was happening here', commented Beppe Severgnini in Corriere della Sera, referring to the three-week period when Italy was ahead of the corona curve. 'The UK lost the advantage that fate and Italy gave it... when it was obvious the virus was spreading.'

....

STAY AT HOME

Government slogans change again. The STAY AT HOME slogan has disappeared. Now everyone is urged to use their common sense and be ALERT, keeping your social distance where you can. It's going to be totally your own fault now if you get Covid-19, clearly you have to use your common sense. The government has done its best, nothing to do with us now. Government ministers are following Covid-19 advice, completely washing their hands.

The response from the general public is one of confusion. A television appearance from Boris Johnson simply adding to a general feeling of bewilderment.

Even the Telegraph, usually a supporter of everything Tory, is damming of the UK government's strategy. A headline:

'Government's handling of Covid-19, is a very British disaster.'

The same newspaper goes on:

'British exceptionalism has brought an exceptional outcome. We have both an eye-watering number of avoidable deaths and a staggering amount of avoidable economic damage. The purported trade-off between lives and jobs – always a false choice – has instead spared neither. It is the worst of both.'

....

Although I'm trapped by lockdown in the UK, I obviously keep one eye on Italy, having regular contact with neighbours and friends. It really comes as no surprise when I start to pick up news stories about the mafia. It's a story as old as the Italian state itself. The story that I've attempted to tell in the pages of this book. Where the state appears to be distant, separate from the people, either unable or not willing to provide adequate support, the mafia will step in to fill the gap. The mafia as benefactors, offering a community network of support. Working in the community, rather than being distant in Rome. But, as always, working with one of the 'Spanish Knights' comes at a cost.

Reporting suggests that the mafia are plugging the gaps left by the state, offering support, and distributing free food to families in lockdown, quarantined and running out of cash. The poorest parts of Italy, the parts that you already know as having a long history of poverty, hit hard by the restrictions put in place to combat Covid-19. The regions that gave birth to the 'Knights', Sicily, Campania and Calabria. These regions of the south having a significant number of the population employed on a casual basis in the unofficial grey economy. As a result, they don't benefit from the safety net put in place by central government. Need, disquiet and growing frustration, pushing people into the hands of the mafia, criminal groups more than willing to grab control and impose their will on communities. Those in Rome are not blind to what is going on. The Italian Minister of the Interior, Luciana Lamorgese:

'The mafia could take advantage of the rising poverty, swooping in to recruit people to its organisation.'

The authorities around Naples notice an increase in the activities of the Camorra on the streets, alongside criminal activities, delivering food parcels to homes. The police stepping up their presence in the poorest parts of the city.

With almost all businesses closed for months, including shops, cafés, restaurants and bars, money for those working in the grey economy dried up altogether. It was totally understandable why some, far away from the Renaissance piazzas of tourist postcard Italy, turned to anyone offering support.

On the outer edges of Palermo, the capital of Sicily, is the neighbourhood of Zen. It's one of the poorest districts in Italy, perhaps one of the poorest in Europe. The brother of a known Cosa Nostra capo in Palermo angered when the newspaper, La Repubbica, reported that the organisation was distributing food to those in the poorest neighbourhoods. The person identified in the report arguing that this was nothing more than charitable work. As you already know, 'charitable work' on the part of the Cosa Nostra ultimately carries a cost. You're also more than aware of the risks associated with shedding light on the affairs of the mafia.

As the year moved on, mafia tentacles were noticed creeping into other parts of the country. Those struggling to survive increasingly targeted, the three mafia able to offer immediate assistance, 'saving' those not able to wait to get government support, the time required taking too long for some. La Repubblica reporting that during the pandemic crime in Italy had decreased by almost 65%, but the crime of illegally loaning money had seen a significant increase. The Prefect of Perugia and officials in other large cities issue warnings to law enforcement to look for signs mafia activity. One official when interviewed commenting, 'The mafia love a crisis.'

You know how the mafia work. In return for food and support now, be that for families or businesses, there will be something expected in the future. At some point payments having to be made. Perhaps nothing more than being deaf and blind to criminal activities. Perhaps giving your vote to a political candidate in the pocket of one of the mafia.

Although I've known Italy for quite some time now, there are occasions when I'm still surprised. I then step back, asking myself why? This is just one of those occasions. You thought Mussolini and his Fascist regime was a time in the life of Italy, now only found in the pages of history books. A number of times throughout the book I've asked you to think again.

This could be a good quiz question for the future, well at least in Italy. What links Mussolini with the Corona Virus?

So, you happen to be a company with the facility to make face masks. Without wanting to sound callous Covid-19 has provided you with money-making opportunities that you could only dream of. Everybody requires masks, throughout Italy and across the world. The profits available to you will probably never be as high again. It really is an opportunity to, for want of a more caring term, to cash in. Think hard, what could you do to add greater value to the masks you have on offer? Imagine that you're an Italian entrepreneur, a keen business mind.

That's right, it's so obvious! You don't just produce any bland face mask. You make face masks carrying the image of Benito Mussolini, Il Duce himself. I know, your business mind is a moral vacuum, you'll do anything to earn that extra euro. Along with the image of Mussolini, you may as well add fascist slogans.

'Camminare, costruire e, se necessario, combattere e vincere!' (Walk, build and, if necessary, fight and win!)

At the very height of a pandemic, with thousands having already died, what distorted mind would think that this is an acceptable idea? But this is Italia, strange things happen.

....

MINIMAL UK LOCKDOWN. Early May and Lockdown restrictions begin to be relaxed. People are allowed to leave their homes, basically, for any reason. Mask wearing, had really not found any genuine acceptance with the majority of people. Numbers of infections and deaths are coming down, but both are still quite high. June 1st, all restrictions on leaving home are removed, being replaced with the instruction to be in your home overnight. Clearly Covid-19 has vampire tendencies, more likely to strike between the hours of darkness. The advice now is to hang cloves of garlic around your house, especially bedrooms.

Outside the home, people are allowed to meet in groups of up to six. Not seven or eight, only six.

It also has to be kept in mind that the whole of the UK is unwrapped at different times. The four countries that make up the UK, yep I know it could be a little confusing for those readers not lucky enough to have been born British (I hope that you understand my sense of humour by now), England, Scotland, Wales, Northern Ireland, each have their own responsibility for health. This separation, during the pandemic, also, at times, became confusing for many Brits.

In England, on July 4th, almost all businesses that had not been open before, were again allowed to let people in. Apparently the Covid virus likes people who work out, so gyms have to remain closed. People in pubs and drunk, are fine, they can be trusted to be sensible. Take a group of English people, mix together and soak in alcohol, leave well alone for a few hours, wait for the outcome; sensible it is unlikely to be.

'LET THE BODIES PILE HIGH'
Boris Johnson accused of saying this by his former chief adviser,
Dominic Cummings.

By the end of June 2020, after most travel restrictions have been relaxed, I'm back in Case Colle, Umbria. I've been away for over six months. I've left behind a confused and bewildered England. The government now basically putting precautions to protect people from Covid-19 in the common-sense hands of the public. Remember that this is the same public that voted for Brexit, and for a Conservative (Tory) government that came with Boris Johnson as Prime Minister. Just saying, that's all. Photographs appear on the front pages of UK newspapers showing sardines, in human form, crowded onto beaches.

Umbria has reported no new Covid cases during the past two weeks. Prior to that, four cases were reported in Carbonesca, one death. About seventy cases in Gubbio, no deaths. Social distancing is still in place, masks compulsory in all public places. Shops, bars and restaurants are now open again. Schools are closed until September. And masks appear to have become new items of fashion, sometimes worn in the most peculiar way. There's the obvious and sensible, the mask covering nose and mouth. There's the just covering the mouth. There's the chin protector, the throat protector, the forehead protector, the wrist protector, the forearm protector and the elbow protector. The mask as decoration for one ear. And the mask in a car replacing fluffy dice, hanging from the rear-view mirror. Finally, there are the masks discarded as items of litter.

THE ELEPHANT AT THE BBQ

Peter Carpenter and Laura were here Saturday evening. A warm, starlit night, with just the very last, solitary firefly making a floating, twinkling encore. It's a beautifully warm evening. Food from the BBQ now consumed, we continue to sit and chat about life in general. At times, a chat that's serious and earnest; Brexit, Trump's America, Covid-19, the general move to the right in politics, relationships, especially my relationship with Martina. The three of us also laugh and joke, I'm totally relaxed in the company of the other two. Peter is the first to dip a toe into the conversation that the three of us have been avoiding, the elephant at the BBQ.

'So, what went wrong, why has it all come to an end?

I give them my account of events. My version of where, perhaps, the relationship began to unravel and eventually fall apart. They listen, mostly in silence, the odd question; still surprised and sad that it's happened. I've no intention of sharing what I had to say here. Martina had her reasons. She doesn't have the opportunity to place them in front of you.

Alcohol is clouding my brain. Unanswered questions swirling round. I'd been aware of a lack of conviction on Matina's part about our future together for some time, why did I choose not to act on what I knew to be true?

For Peter and Laura, just one final sip of wine before they leave, the three of us now confident enough to give the other a tight embrace. My fourteen days self-imposed demarcation of two meters between myself and anyone I come into contact with, now at an end. I'm more than obviously Covid free, no danger to others. Take care, see you soon; they drive away, leaving me with my thoughts.

It's 11.30, I may as well finish the almost full bottle of white wine. The darkness of the garden, still and warm. For some reason, the cicadas are silent. Stars crowd the darkest blue night sky. Citrus candles flicker. Van Morrison plays.

I'm alone with my thoughts. Where did the relationship with Martina go wrong?

'Once I had love, and it was a gas – soon found out had a heart of glass ....' Blondie

I'm deep in the beauty of a warm Italian night. I'll finish this glass, leaving the rest of the wine for another eve. Only a drop of white left in the glass. And the citrus candles flicker, the wicks having burnt down to small pools of liquid wax. The small candle flames dance and reflect on what should have been.

There's still white wine in the bottle. Just one more glass and then to bed.

It was clear that something was wrong with the relationship when we went to Cuba, the unsettled feeling, something I chose to push to the back of my mind. I guess you could label it an exercise in denial. I'd invested too much emotional energy in what I thought we had to simply let it wither away. I thought that Martina was in the same space. But, in reality, the warning signs of a disjuncture in our relationship had been building for some time. In the end, I couldn't simply dismiss and ignore the disconnection. I knew the probability of what was coming.

And then suddenly it ends. I'd already told my daughters, when I was with them in the UK, during the most stringent days of lockdown, that I thought the relationship was falling apart. I didn't expect it to come to an end so abruptly. Its life terminated by a mobile phone conversation. No relationship, no friendship, it just ends. The end is total, a joint decision. No further contact. There is little you can do when someone has decided that they no longer want to be part of the journey. It turned out that we'd not been dreaming the same dream.

It's not earth shattering. It's nothing more than another lover's tale. Yes it's one of failure, but on the map of history, it's of no significance. Something else comes to mind, entering my drunken state, one little scene from a TV series that I can't remember the name of. Two female characters are sat chatting about something related to love. One of the two shrugs her shoulders:

'If Romeo and Juliet hadn't died when they did, they'd have fallen out anyway ......'

Cynical Graham, that's not you, you're drunk! You're aimlessly rambling, tumbling random thoughts around in your mind. Bed!

Last half glass and then bed. The smell of jasmine is just astonishing. It's 1.45. This last glass to finish.

Should I be foolish enough to desire, to dream again? I thought I knew where we were going, but I was wrong. In my inebriated state, something a very close friend said to me, well over twenty years ago, comes to mind. You all know how your past will often call in for a visit, sit down and ask for a glass of wine and a chat. And not just when you're awake, it will enter, totally uninvited, into your dreams. My partner, Linden, at the age of 41, had lost her long, agonising, turmoil with cancer. I think I was in tears recounting the deep love that we had for each other. The anguish, the pain, suffered and lived through, until the end finally came. The short time we had together, the loss of what could have been. I remember my friend saying that it may possibly sound strange, but he was jealous, even happy for me. Jealous that I'd found such deep love, even though it was short and ripped away. Jealous because he didn't think he'd ever found such love with anyone. His words, his confession, made me feel sorry for him rather than myself.

I'm looking at the last drop of wine in the glass, turning over his words in my mind. He's right, we should celebrate having been in love, even if, for whatever reason, that love is lost.

Whatever circumstance you happen to be in, life continues to unfold, new days ahead, yet unknown opportunities. Everything has to move forward. Who knows where our choices will take us? There will be new friendships to be made. New adventures to be had. Perhaps even new, hopefully, long lasting love to be enjoyed.

Barking deer, must almost be in the garden. Barking deer sets off yapping dog. 'GO TO BED!'

The bottle and the glass are empty. I fall into bed and drift to sleep.

....

Sunday. And, yes, I wake up with a little hangover following my drunken reflections in the early hours of the morning. Apologies for my jumbled, rambling, feeling sorry for myself. I hope you'll forgive me.

Forgive me or not, it's Sunday and I live in Italia! It's going to be a hot day, and I've been invited for pranzo by Marcello and Alicia. How much better could life be? It's fine, I'm not expecting you to offer me an answer. One of the absolute delights of my life in Umbria, is the time I spend with my Italian extended family. As is always the case, the meal takes place below the protective branches and foliage of the giant oak tree, the long table set for twenty people: four generations. Chatter and laughter are exchanged, people still not confident enough to offer others a warm embrace. Although most restrictions have now been relaxed, Covid has not simply gone away. It's so foreign and strange, I want to greet people with a close embrace, especially in Italy: a kiss to each cheek.

Already on the table are bottles of water, jugs of red wine and the obligatory bread. Prosecco, that's been cooling in the fridge, along with a couple bottles of beer. Beer being offered as though it was wine. Four plates with prosciutto, other plates with slices of parmigiano (the parmesan better than anything you will ever taste outside Italy) and dark cinghiali smoked sausage. The wild boar sausage made by Aldo and Marcello, the taste absolutely divine. Aldo brings a big wheel of goat's cheese (formaggio di capra) to the table, the cheese made by his skilful hands. He sits at one end of the table, slicing the cheese, plates of sliced cheese then passed along. You won't be surprised to know that the flavour is exquisite, everyone asking for more. Following the ham, sausage and cheese, we have pasta with pancetta (bacon), in a thin tomato sauce. Following this, goat (capra) that's been roasted on a spit, the goat accompanied by small oven roasted potatoes (patate arrosto) and a green salad (insalata verde) tossed in nothing more than extra virgin olive oil (olio extra vergine di oliva), the oil having come from the olives picked in October the previous year. For dolce, a variety of fruit and little pastries. The whole meal ending with espresso, Sambuca to add, should that be your pleasure. Spirits of unknown strength, homemade, now on offer. It's an event that always lasts for most of the afternoon. It's the stereotype that most foreigners will have in their minds. But this is no exaggerated Italian family stereotype. This is real Italy, repeated again and again. I simply allow myself to be smothered in its warm, welcoming, joyous, embrace.

SICILIA

Italy may not mind that I've been way for so long, she knew I would return. But the house and the garden, especially the garden, have not taken kindly to my Covid-enforced absence. The hot months of July and August are spent sorting things out in the house and clearing the garden that has become a jungle. Although Covid restrictions are much reduced, there is very little chance of family or friends visiting me this year. It's a strange experience, not to have people staying. But it gives me the opportunity to explore other parts of Italy, Sicily being my intended destination. It's mid-September, Covid appears to be continuing its retreat, the only obligations now are to maintain social distancing and to wear a mask inside and when travelling by bus, train, etc. The UK, or England in particular, appears to be behaving as though the pandemic has completely gone. The only other thing that I'm obliged to do is complete a form online, stating when I will be arriving in Sicily and when I will be leaving. Once in Sicily, I'm expected to click on an app, that I've downloaded, to make my stay on the island 'live' to the authorities.

I've planned my journey down to the island with a detour to Alberobello in the region of Puglia. I guess you could describe the region as being the heel of Italy. The little town is totally enchanting and totally unique. It's famous for its conical shaped, whitewashed houses, that are built clustered together. These are the world famous trulli. A picture-postcard town and a UNESCO World Heritage Site. I give myself just two nights in this charming little place, exploring the narrow pedestrianised streets, sitting outside little bars, eating in some family run trattoria. If you are ever in the south of Italy, Alberobello is a place you have to visit. In 'normal' times I would imagine the place to be a magnet, crowded with tourists. But these are Covid times; although there are plenty of tourists they are far fewer in number, making the place feel very relaxed. But I'm moving on, Sicily being the main place for me to be.

Sicily is Italy's largest island and just a twenty-five-minute ferry crossing from the mainland. I've given myself one week, perhaps longer, I have no need to rush back. My time there takes me to Taormina, Mount Etna, Syracuse, Agrigento, Trapani, Golfo di Castellammare, and Cefalu. At times, when driving over the mountains of Sicily's interior, arguing with the total stupidity of my sat nav. It's here that you get a real sense of how locked away many of the villages and towns must have been in the past, many still having a sense of isolation, time having stood still; low cloud cover clinging to hillsides and shrouding the bottom of deep valleys. In places, ribbons of cloud being drawn into the mother cloud where the sun pierces through. It's easy to imagine how the Cosa Nostra became a focus of 'authority' on the island. Some days I'll be camping, other days I'll be using B&Bs. Although Sicily is certainly part of Italy, it feels very different; almost as though you are in another country.

During my stay, I mostly travel along the coast, each day, apart from one, bright, sunny and hot. The island has the most stunning coastline, the sea crystal clear, tiny villages and towns where you can simply sit and dream the day away, buildings draped in the brightest bougainvillea. Historically, Sicily fell victim to a succession of invaders. It was a significant part of both the Greek and Roman empires, the island scattered with magnificent architecture from those times. It really shouldn't be surprising that it has a different feel to other parts of Italy. Arabs, Normans, the French, the Spanish, all left their mark on the island. Even the Italian language is different here, at times difficult to understand.

Taormina, my first stop, is beautiful in itself, spectacular views of the rocky coastline and blue sea simply adding to that beauty. As with any Italian town, it has its piazzas, narrow streets, cafes, bars and restaurants. It's whilst I'm eating in the shade of lemon trees that I hear a French couple commit an act of sacrilege. They have just finished their meal. It's exactly 9.30 in the evening. What basic, tourist, act of treason could they have enacted?

Perhaps the main attraction of Taormina is the Greek Theatre, carved out of the hillside. Really take your time, walk slowly, close your eyes, hear voices from centuries past. The theatre also offers you almost uninterrupted views across the whole of Taormina. Below the town are beaches, grottoes, coves and what appears to be a tiny island, that's not. This is Isola Bella, attached to the coast by a thin strip of sand. I've booked two nights, my room with a balcony that offers me uninterrupted views of the would-be little island.

On the 'island' of Isola Bella, is a property, once privately owned. Apparently the place and the land were bought by a rich English woman, Florence Trevelyan, in 1890, for the grand sum of 14,000 Lire, let's say £6,000/$8,000. When Lady Trevelyan and her husband died, the island passed to her husband's cousin, he then sold the island for 30,000 Lire. And so, over the years the little island has been bought and sold many times. In 1990, the island was purchased by the Department of Cultural Heritage for an estimated sum of ten billion lire. In 2011, the site became the Museo Naturalistico Regionale di Isolabella. It really is the most delightful place to spend your days, with your evenings higher up in Taormina.

Mount Etna dominates the eastern side of Sicily and can be seen from Taormina. It's Europe's highest (more than 3327 meters), largest volcano, and still very active, something that I was to discover in the most dramatic way. Since 2013, it has been a UNESCO World Heritage Site. The Greeks, the Romans, Arabs and others, all had their own myths and gods related to the volcano. Zeus's thunderbolts came from its flames and hot lava. To the Arabs, it was the mountain of mountains. In Sicilian, it still has the Arabic name, Mongibello. Today, the rich, volcanic soil is ideal for farming, especially the growing of vines and the production of wine. It's another magnet for tourists. Walking on Mount Etna gives you the most magnificent views. But it has to be remembered that this is an active volcano. When it erupts, lava flows can reach temperatures of over 500°C. In 1928, an eruption severely damaged the railway around Etna's base and buried the village of Mascali. From the early 1970s through to the early 80s there were almost continuous eruptions.

Although Etna is still very much alive, reassuringly, there have been relatively few reported deaths resulting from its activity. Records going way back in history show only 77 deaths attributed to the volcano. Experts put this down to the fact that Etna's eruptions tend not be violently explosive and lava flow is usually slow. Almost all those who have been killed appear to have been 'in the wrong place at the wrong time'. In April 1987, two tourists were killed when a vent exploded. A similar event occurred in September 1997, killing nine tourists. On both occasions there had been warnings of activity. The most serious incident occurred in 1843 when 60 forest workers were killed.

As I join others to walk this living mountain, obviously nothing is going to happen today. Apparently there has been little 'real' activity for months. And guides wouldn't be taking groups up the mountain if there were any sign of possible eruptions.

After spending one night camping, just a few kilometres from Etna, my morning run within its view, my second night is spent in Rifugio G Sapienza, built in the very shadow of the volcano, its predecessor having been swept away by the molten lava of an eruption some years back. I'm taking part in an excursion promoted as taking you to the mouth of the volcano, its crater. We ascend part of the way by cable car (funivia), then by special off-road busses; only then does the trekking on foot begin. It's 9.30 in the morning, the sky deep blue. There are about fifteen in our group, differing in age and nationality. Our guide, I would say in his early 50s, from Gruppo Guide Alpine Etna Sud, speaks excellent English, French and Italian, interchanging between the three with exceptional ease. He assures us that although Etna continually grumbles, there are very few indications of an imminent eruption.

Even though the day temperature at sea level is still 25°C and above, at the height of the volcano, all in the group are wearing mountain gear, including good, sturdy, walking boots, boots we soon find to be essential. It's a strenuous trek, walking over a black, lunar-like landscape, but every single step well worth the effort. Our guide is expert in his knowledge of the mountain, the volcano, its geology and history. We're completely surrounded by solidified, molten, volcanic rock and ash. There are just three sounds. The voices of those in my group and our guide, the voice of the wind at this height and, the voice of Etna. A constant, low level, grumbling comes from the volcano. I expect the ground to move beneath my feet, the mountain filling its lungs, sucking in white clouds, then belching out a continuous breath of thick, grey, black and white smoke that reaches up into the blue sky. The gaping mouth of the volcano is clear to see. Etna is watching us and waiting. The size of the volcano makes other groups ahead of us look like tiny, coloured dots on a dark landscape. As we listen to our guide, another group is making an incredibly steep ascent towards the open mouth of the mountain. Dark figures, bent forward, are silhouetted against a background of blue. It's the same direction we will soon be taking. Etna is alive, continuingly grumbling about our disturbance. The dark ground beneath our boots warm, at some points too hot to touch with a naked hand. We continue on our walk.

We spend the day walking over warm, black ash, clambering over volcanic boulders and exploring deep ravines cut out by previous eruptions. One moment we have a deep blue sky and the next moment we find that we are either stood amongst or above white clouds. Etna knows that we are there.

It's as we begin to make our descent, stopping to listen again to our guide, that Etna's mood takes a dramatic change. The volcano begins to throw out black rocks, the steaming rocks climbing into the air before falling on all sides of Etna's gaping mouth. We all turn to face the volcano. Etna's grumble has become a deep roar, ever greater amounts of dark smoke reaching into the sky. More rocks are spewed out, the rocks now followed by blood red lava. We're spellbound, unable to move, totally gripped by what we are witnessing. Apart from the guide, the rest of our group is quiet, speechless. We simply stand and watch as Etna forcefully expels more rocks and increasing amounts of deep red lava. No one in our group appears to be particularly concerned, all are transfixed, some taking photographs, others filming. The guide telling us that this is a rare event, there has been no activity on this scale for over a year.

Increasing dark smoke, Etna's loud roar, more rocks and yet more lava continue for about another fifteen minutes. Then as quickly as Etna's mood changed, the volcano returns to its constant grumble, the eruption at an end. Our guide explains what has just occurred, assuring us that we were in no danger. It's reasonably obvious to me that there was little we could have actually done if we were. We continue our descent, at times having to scramble down tumbling small rocks, my boots now full of dark ash. Although conversation in the group is one of excitement, I guess the guide was right. The relative risk to us was low. At no point during the day were we any closer to the mouth of Etna than, I would guess, one kilometre. I know what you're thinking, close enough.

Obviously Etna has continued to grumble and, at times, erupt since the show she put on especially for me. Flows of lava from other vents are recorded in May and then June 7th, 2022. New fissures opening on June 13th, 2022, the vents releasing lava down parts of the mountain. The most dramatic, recent, full eruption of the volcano came in February 2022. Those witnessing the eruption described it as, 'Plumes of smoke rising from the volcano, glowing bright red and orange in the night sky. Streams of lava flowing down from the top, easily seen from the coastal town of Catania.' News reports spoke of a volcanic storm and bolts of lightning. The eruption so powerful, that it shot ash many miles into the air. It's clear to me, that when I was up there with my international group, we were in the 'right place at the right time'. Fortunate, don't you think?

Syracuse is my next destination, camping again. This was one of the first Greek colonies in Sicily. Among its many attractions are its Greek Theatre, begun in the 6th century BC, the Roman Amphitheatre, built in the 3rd century AD, the Altar of Hieron 11 and the Orecchio di Dionisio, a limestone cave shaped like a human ear. As I explore the remains of ancient Greek civilisations, the day has reached 30°C. A large lizard scurries over my sandalled foot, continuing its journey along stone paths set down hundreds of years in the past. Along with its ancient history, Syracuse is yet another beautiful coastal town. Not that far from the town is a white beach and pristine sea. I give myself two days here, enough for culture and also time for sun and sea. Close to where I'm camping, I walk through a small, wooded area, the tall trees smelling of cinnamon. Lunch is by the sea, waves crashing onto the beach. I love the sound of the sea, the constant movement.

It's 1.30 in the afternoon on the campsite. As a Brit, I'm having a cold beer. The camp bar/café is closed over lunchtime; I snuck in early. I don't know, it makes no sense at all to me, a café closing at lunchtime. A young Italian couple have just arrived on bikes, between them, carrying everything they need. Tent, clothing and, most important of all, food. They've set out their feast on the wooden table next to me. A range of salads, onions, garlic, cheese, sun dried tomatoes, crusty fresh bread, olive oil for dressing, and olives. Also, a large bottle of sparkling water. I sit with my cold beer. Why am I not more organised? Food keeps appearing as if by magic. How did they carry it all? All I can guess is that they have bags matching the one used by Mary Poppins. The smell is delicious, garlic peeled and then gently rubbed on the crusty bread. If I catch their attention with a friendly smile, perhaps they'll ask me to join them. They don't. We strike up a conversation, the result of them asking me when the café opens. A conversation continually changing between Italian and English, their English at about the same level as my Italian. It turns out that during the morning they have cycled almost as far as I've driven. But they have to admit that the day is a little too hot.

The café is now open again. This is after me informing the young Italian couple that it won't open until at least 3pm; it's now 2pm. The notice on the door stating that the place is closed until 4pm. I know, confusing. When you live in Italy, you get to know that most things are flexible, some may say unpredictable. It can be both a joy and a frustration. If you want to enjoy Italy, you have to learn to go with the flow.

Agrigento is another must-see destination for anyone seeking out ancient culture, a hilltop town, just a little distance from the sea. Here you'll find well-preserved Greek archaeology. The Valley of the Temples, Temple of Concordia, Temple of Hera Lacinia, Temple of Olympian Zeus. I spend a whole day here, then deciding to camp by the coast. The following day moving on to Trapani, where I'll spend two nights, my intention being to visit one of the Egadi Islands. On my drive to Trapani, stopping at Selinunte, where you'll find one of the largest Greek temples in the world.

Trapani gained importance as a port when under Spanish control. The modern outskirts of the town seem to sprawl a little, but the historic centre, that sits on a peninsula, is a delight to explore. I have a place overlooking the harbour, still busy with fishing boats and ferries that take people to the outlying islands. I'm on the top floor of four flights of stairs, the owner of my apartment having a unique way to transport his shopping from the entrance to the top floor of the building. A long rope hangs down, a large basket attached to its end.

It's now almost October. I'm sat outside the Happiness Café, a tidy, simple little place. But somehow the owner has got it absolutely right. This is the place where the owner of my apartment has an arrangement for his guests to have breakfast, no more than a few steps from where I'm staying. Just across the road, large ships are docked, some activity as crews prepare for the day. Behind them I can see the most magnificent sailing ship coming into port, the sun glistening as it strikes its metal masts. Inside the café, I'm struck by the signage stuck to the wooden floor, circles indicating where people should stand to maintain a safe distance between them and others, all part of Covid precautions. Countless feet have worn them away, so much so that you aren't able to read the print. It's an indication of how long we've been living with Covid, for Italy, since February. Little did I know, at this point, that the spread of Covid would return with a vengeance over the coming months. For now, I'm naively assuming that the worst is behind us. We just need to keep wearing masks and keep our distance from other people.

My plan to visit one of the islands, just off the coast, is disrupted by bad weather. That evening the weather has cleared. I'm sat outside a bar in the old part of Trapani, football is on the flatscreen TV. Inter Milan and, I forget the name of the other team. It's 9.30 in the evening, still 25°C. The usual suspects have taken prime positions to watch the game, one bottle of sparkling water and one gelato between eight of them. And nobody appears to mind that they are taking up valuable table space. It's a busy evening, lots of people around. A Saturday night, but so different to any town or city centre in the UK.

Moving on, my next two days are simply spent relaxing, camping close to Golfo di Castellammare. It's a relatively quiet area with plenty of gorgeous coves, the sea, again, crystal clear. I'm up at 6.30 and down at the small beach just below the campsite. The sea is simply mesmerising. Large waves thunder and tumble towards the shore. White horses galloping over millions of large, terracotta-coloured, pebbles, the white horses then retreating, dragging the pebbles into the sea. And the sound of the sea is never ending. It was there throughout the night; it will be there throughout the day. And the next night and the next day. The next week, next month, the next one hundred years and more. I guess it's the sound of eternity. And I simply sit and watch. The white horses galloping ashore again and again and again. I'm enraptured by the beautiful power of nature. If there is just one memory that I'll carry home from Sicily, it is that of the beautiful sea that surrounds it. A crystal clear, blue, sparkling, fish-filled sea. In some places thunderously powerful, in other parts, soft, still, warm and gentle.

My final destination, before making my way back to the mainland, is Cefalù on the northeast coast of the island. Once a small fishing village, it's now a charming holiday resort. I'm camping just a little distance from the town, along the coast, no more than a thirty-minute walk. A walk that is well worth it. Cefalù waterfront, that you see as you walk along the beach is simply picture perfect. Some rate the beautiful old town as one of the top romantic highlights of any visit to Sicily.

At 7.30 in the morning, I'm sat having breakfast by the side of my tent. I'm looking out to the Mediterranean Sea, the waves gently washing over the edge of the beach. The sun has already risen high into the deep blue sky. Two small fishing boats splutter past before coming to anchor not that far from the shore. The only other sounds are the waves and a warm breeze. Suddenly a rider appears on the beach, a beautiful chestnut brown horse beneath her. She gallops past where the sea meets the beach, water splashing as the horse meets the waves. She stops, turns the horse, and gallops away in the direction from which she first came; then gone from sight. It's a fleeting moment, one with genuine grace and power.

Sicily certainly has some of the most beautiful little coastal towns that I have ever visited in Italy. The seas that surround the island crystal clear, its rugged interior well worth taking the time to explore. BUT, and this is a Big But. Away from the resorts, which are generally clean and tidy, Sicily suffers from a terrible problem. Something that is in real danger of destroying the very beauty that attracts so many visitors. Yes it has the Cosa Nostra, but it's highly unlikely that you'll come into contact with its members or its dealings. The problem that Sicily has is the indiscriminate dumping of rubbish, garbage of every type and description. Many other parts of Italy, just like the UK, are plagued by the casual dropping of litter, but Sicily's problem is on a whole different scale, an industrial scale. Drive any distance out of a town, by the side of major roads, in lay-bys, down minor roads, along dirt tracks, you can't help but see every possible item you can think of dumped. What in all other places would be collected and then disposed of through municipal collection, in Sicily is simply piled high and left to fester and rot. Nowhere have I ever seen the dumping of refuse on this scale. Building materials, household waste, clothes, furniture, literally anything!

One evening, after I'd had the most gorgeous meal, I commended the owner on the quality of her food. In our brief chat, she asked me what I thought of Sicily. I responded by saying the same as I've said to you, the island is beautiful. However, I couldn't help but ask about the problem of rubbish dumped everywhere; why? She didn't offer an answer. Looking down, her eyes shying away from contact, she simply shrugged her shoulders and said, that's just how it is.

It's a shame that I had to leave Sicily with such images in my mind. Some have pointed the finger at the Cosa Nostra. That could be the case, but in reality, I have no idea.

POMPEI

I decided that I couldn't really be in the south of Italy and not take the opportunity to visit Pompeii (Pompei in Italian), once a thriving Roman city, devastated by the eruption of Mount Vesuvius in 79 AD. The volcano dominates this part of Italy, its large, gaping mouth, wide open. Dormant for many years, but one day it will erupt again, the explosive power deep within the mountain having the potential to completely destroy Naples. When Vesuvius erupted, after 800 years of inactivity, the hot ash, pumice and dirt raining down on Pompeii is said to have lasted for three days, covering buildings up to their roofs, toxic gas clouds further adding to the suffering of the people. So sudden and unexpected was the eruption, that few of Pompeii's citizens managed to escape. The thick layer of hot ash and dirt, burying the city, ensuring that buildings, artefacts and even people, were preserved. Two thirds of what was the Roman city of Pompeii has now been uncovered, what remains still buried, yet to be discovered. For centuries, the city remained covered and forgotten. Not until 1748 did the first excavations begin. You really do need a whole day to explore what is now available for the tourist to see, it's a vast area. It truly is one of the most amazing places I have ever visited.

Pompeii is one of the most visited archaeological sites in the world, with well over 3 million people attracted each year. In some ways the Covid pandemic, and its associated restrictions on travel, gave me an ideal opportunity to visit the site without the usual crowds that I assume would normally be there. And it really is not difficult to understand why people find the place so astonishing. You're actually allowed to walk down streets, look into homes, explore public buildings, see original decorated walls, mosaic floors and sculptures, all frozen at a moment in time. From the grand to the mundane, all Roman life can be found here. And the most poignant reminder of human fragility, the plaster casts of those who were caught in the maelstrom, bodies distorted in pain at the point of death.

I'm not going to attempt to describe Pompeii in any detail. To do so would take a whole book. For me to do the same in a few paragraphs, would be a disservice to you and not come anywhere near giving a true picture of what you find here. All I can suggest is that you get yourself there.

I've booked two nights in a family run B&B, just a ten-minute walk from the site. Accommodation, I guess you could describe as basic and clean. But what it lacked in style, made good by the friendliness of the owners and the excellent food they prepared. The two nights of my stay, I pay a little extra for home cooked evening meals. My second day is spent exploring the other Roman city destroyed by the volcano, Herculaneum. But more about that in a bit.

At the B&B, breakfast and the evening meal are taken in the garden with other guests who are staying. It's a bit of a European gathering, Italians, Dutch, Germans, Austrians, no other Brits. All very friendly, almost all paying extra for evening meals. I think it's on the second evening as we're eating and drinking, that casual chat moves to politics. I can assure you it was not a conversation started by me. Someone in the group makes a comment about the USA and Trump, honest it wasn't me. The Austrian couple with us respond by saying that they like Trump, he has the right ideas, he sticks up for his country and challenges all the nonsense about climate change and the 'pandemic'. It may surprise you, but I don't respond, I just want to enjoy the warm evening, the wine and my meal.

'So, what do you think of Brexit and Boris Johnson?', the male Austrian asks, obviously looking at me. My reply is short and swift. 'He's a buffoon, Brexit is a disastrous mistake.' Not really satisfied with my response, the Austrian male goes on to explain why in his opinion Brexit is a good idea for Britain and for Europe. He's sick of the EU telling countries what to do, including his own country, Austria. I really can't be bothered; I've been here before. Once he's exhausted his studious approach to Brexit and the EU, realising that nobody is interested in what he has to say, he turns to his expert opinion on the pandemic. Covid apparently is an elaborate hoax concocted by governments. Along with a few others, I take my glass and a bottle of wine, our little group of obviously uninformed people going over to sit at the opposite side of the garden.

The following morning, although warm, is a little grey, drizzle in the air. I'm making the relatively short drive to the site of Herculaneum, another city buried under the torrent of volcanic ash and pumice from Vesuvius. Less well known than its 'tourist rival' Pompeii, it was the first, and for a long time, the only buried city to be discovered and explored. Herculaneum is similar to Pompeii, but on a smaller scale. I've found that opinion is divided as to which is most worthy of a visit. I preferred Pompeii, perhaps the drizzle, on this particular day, made Herculaneum feel less dramatic.

My drive to the site took me through some of the satellite sprawl of Napoli. All I can say is that La Dolce Vita never lived here, visited or even gave a second wink to this part of Italy. The rubbish, simply dumped, that I described in Sicily, here you find piled high in the street, bins overflowing. There are no grand buildings; apartment blocks that look grimy and ramshackle are squeezed together, shops, cafes and bars below.

Naples itself may have its gritty and graffitied attractions, many impressive pieces of architecture, an apparent chaos that attracts tourists from around the world; my drive had none of this. That's not totally true, it did have the chaos. As a driver, a chaos that requires you to have eyes in the front, side and back of your head. If you feel a little nervous about driving in the rest of Italy, don't be tempted to drive here. My Italian neighbours and friends in Umbria had told me many times that drivers in southern Italy are crazy (pazzo). I thought they were exaggerating. How could the road sense of Italian drivers in the south be any worse than in Umbria? If anything, they had been under reporting. Driving from my accommodation to the site of Herculaneum was like driving through swirling spaghetti. The spaghetti twisting, turning and weaving in all directions. Any and all 'rules' of the road either never understood or more probably, simply ignored. Cars, vans, motorbikes, scooters and pedestrians coming from every side.

Accidents and even death, especially for those on foot, must be commonplace. Perhaps all who live and work in and around Naples, every morning, pray that all their sins will be forgiven before they leave the house, just in case death should visit them. I hear thousands of voices whispering, 'Hail Mary, full of grace, the Lord is with Thee! Blessed art Thou among women and blessed is the fruit of Thy womb, Jesus. Holy Mary, Mother of God, pray for us sinners now and at the hour of our death. Amen.' Nothing gives way, all space is used, even when there is no space. And it's the vulnerable pedestrians who surprise me the most, simply stepping into the cacophony of traffic without even one glance, never mind a second. How the metal body of my car avoided any knocks and scrapes, I will never know. I don't think I have ever been so tense when driving. Perhaps I should have accepted the Catholic faith before getting in the car. 'Oh, my Mother, preserve me this day ....' Apparently, according to Saint Alphonsus Maria Liguori, 'A devout servant of Mary shall never perish.' What I'd describe as complete stupidity (stupidità), no insanity (follia), feels relentless. Just imagine negotiating this every single day!

One final area to visit before I leave the south of Italy, the Amalfi coast. How can parts of Italy be so close to each other and so different? The Amalfi coast is just under seventy kilometres from Naples (forty-three miles). But rather than staying directly on the Amalfi coast, I've found a place within walking distance of Sorrento, staying for two nights in Hotel Del Mare. It's early morning, October

4th. With blue skies that you dream of, I know that it's going to be another warm day. And across the sea (Bay of Naples) from Sorrento, Vesuvius climbs high into the blue sky. From this distance you have a clear picture of how the mountain completely dominates the area around it, the gaping mouth of the volcano clear to see. The lower slopes taken by Pompeii and Herculaneum, the towns that lead you into Naples spreading out along the coast. The sea is calm, the sea is peaceful, the sea is blue. Yachts set sail; small boats cast nets for fish. Tourists leave the harbour of Sorrento for the Amalfi coast, Capri and Naples. And Vesuvius sits, its mouth wide open, silently waiting. One day, giving little warning, it will erupt.

Sorrento sits perched on cliffs, giving it a magnificent panoramic view over the Bay of Naples, but separating the town from its busy marina below. Piazza Tasso is its main café lined square, the rest of the town a warren of narrow, picture postcard streets. It's a town strongly related to the cultivation of lemons. Here you do find La Dolce Vita. In the narrow streets, you'll find boutiques selling locally produced goods, especially limoncello, such places sitting alongside shops selling vegetables and goods for everyday life. Mixed between these, cafes, bars and restaurants.

Marina Grande, just a fifteen-minute walk down from the town, is where I'm staying. It has the atmosphere of a tiny fishing village, one of my favourite places during my whole visit to southern Italy. Basically, a little bay, a small beach, colourful fishing boats bobbing about, and family-run restaurants. On my first day, I eat lunch as close as I can possibly be to the sea, that same evening having dinner with views over to Vesuvius. The fact that the bay is enclosed by steep cliffs has allowed it to keep its rustic charm, there is no space for further development. It's pastel-coloured buildings make it simply delightful. The film 'Pane e Amore' (Bread & Love), staring Sophia Loren was filmed here. It was also featured in a Pierce Brosnan film, 'Love Is All You Need'.

O'Parrucchiano La Favorita (O'Parrucchiano being Neapolitan dialect for Parish Priest) is perhaps the most romantic place I have ever eaten a meal, on this occasion, unfortunately, as a single man. The family-run restaurant, established in 1868, can be found in Sorrento on Corso Italia. My words will simply not do justice to the place. The most delicious food is served as you dine surrounded by lemon trees. From the street you really don't have a hint of what you can expect. After walking up a short set of marble steps that lead into a botanical glass house, you're then taken to your table, the table set in what feels like an enchanted garden, the whole place infused with the scent of lemons and oranges. This place is so good that it has been accepted into the Association of Historical Places of Italy. It is truly enchanting. Although it's not the least expensive place you will ever eat, given the setting, the quality of the food and excellent service, the prices are certainly not outrageous.

It's from my base, just a short walk from Sorrento, that I spend a couple of days exploring the Amalfi coast. It is truly, breathtakingly, stunning. The coast a UNESCO World Heritage Site, named after the town of Amalfi. The twists and turns of the narrow road, carved out of the rock, look down to a beautiful blue sea and rugged coastline. To one side you have soaring cliffs, to the other villages and towns spilling down to the Tyrrhenian Sea. It's the coastline that you've seen in countless films, the dream you have of Italy. My two favourite places, Positano and Ravello. Here rests the problem, the Amalfi coast is a desirable destination for thousands and thousands of people, including the very rich and famous (I'm definitely not either). The Covid pandemic prevented many tourists from visiting the area whilst I was there, and yet the whole coast still had a busy feel about it. I can only imagine what it's like in 'normal' times. Driving along the coast is spectacular, finding somewhere to park incredibly difficult, in or near places like Positano, almost impossible. The good news is that the narrow road, with all its sharp twists and turns, does force even the craziest Italian driver to slow down, he/she has no choice. My advice is to actually stay in one of the towns that tumble down to the sea, that is if you can find something at a reasonable cost. Obviously, what you consider 'reasonable' all depends on the size of your bank balance. Another option is to arrive by boat from other places. Your own boat if you're extremely wealthy or, probably, like most of us, by regular services that carry passengers.

With the beautiful Amalfi coast still floating through my brain, the time has come for me to make the drive back to Umbria. Where would I rather live, Sicily, Naples, Amalfi, Umbria? Where do you think? The other places are wonderful to visit, to be a tourist, but they don't match up to The Green Heart of Italy. I know, I could be accused of being just a little bit biased.

COVID RETURNS

I know that Covid never went away, it was simply loitering over the summer months, giving people, including me, a false sense that it would eventually wither. The end of June through to October 2020, felt like freedom in Italy. We were restricted but we were allowed out to play. When I was exploring the south of Italy, my brain had been predicting the start of 2021 would see the pandemic behind us. The truth, reality, soon becomes apparent. Covid cases rising exponentially, forcing governments to press the pause button on life once again. Doing almost anything that involves human contact becomes an indulgence. In fact, in Italy, it's more than an indulgence, in almost all situations it once again becomes illegal.

Although the dramatic rise in infections wasn't the most welcome news (I know - a massive understatement), the arsenal of weapons to combat the virus had dramatically changed from the first weeks of its reported outbreak in China in the early weeks of 2020. In the first few months of that year, the hope of developing a vaccine as quickly as possible felt incredibly optimistic. And yet, within the year that's exactly what had been achieved. Pharmaceutical companies racing to be first. Previous to this, the fastest any vaccine had been developed and approved was four years. Talk of spike proteins went beyond the understanding of most people, including me. I listened, but I didn't really understand. Something about something else attaching to these spike proteins, animations shown on the news in some vague expectation we would get it; I still didn't.

The very first Covid vaccine, in the world, is injected into the arm of Margaret Keenan, at the age of 90. The vaccine (Pfizer/BioNTech) administered at University Hospital in Coventry, England, on December 8th, 2020. An answer for you to impress others in a pub quiz. Now if you think having that answer will impress, this answer is even better. Who was the second person in the world to be given a Covid vaccine? Answer: William Shakespeare from Warwickshire. No, honestly, I've not made this up. And it's not the William that you're thinking of, risen from his grave. This was an 81-year-old William Shakespeare. Other vaccines soon followed, the most well-known being Oxford-AstraZeneca, Moderna, Novavax, Sputnik and Jenson (Johnson & Johnson). After possible links to blood clotting, Oxford-AstraZeneca somewhat falling from favour and, for a time, putting worry and confusion in the minds of many people. AstaZeneca being taken out of circulation in Italy and other countries, did little to ease a general anxiety about the validity and safety of Covid vaccines in general. Something that was, for a time, to severely hinder the take-up of vaccinations in Europe.

Prior to the very first vaccine being injected, Covid restrictions are reintroduced in the UK on September 14th, 'the rule of six' coming back into force. By mid-September, all hospitality is told to close between 10pm and 6am.

The UK government introduces a 'three tier system', restrictions in different parts of the country based on the levels of infection. Italy does much the same, but through a choice of colours, Red, Orange, Yellow and White. Over the winter, in Italy, very few regions are fortunate enough to be Yellow or White.

November 5th sees national restrictions reintroduced in England. As you already know, for some time, Scotland, Wales and Northern Ireland had all been doing their own thing. People only allowed to meet in their 'support bubble', non-essential high street businesses closed.

December 2nd, greater restrictions are introduced in England. Other parts of the UK increasingly going their own way. With Covid taking on a new face, the Alpha variant, on December 19th more restrictions are introduced, scientific advice calling for a full lockdown. But Christmas is on its way and Boris Johnson does not want to upset people by 'cancelling' Christmas. So, in effect, people are allowed to party on certain days in the hope that the Alpha variant isn't invited or decides to gatecrash. Surprise! Covid-19 gate-crashed all over the place.

I spend Christmas in Umbria. Visiting the UK, to be with my daughters, next to impossible because of Covid restrictions. It's a low-key Christmas and New Year's Eve, but no less enjoyable for the fact that I'm in the company of my closest Italian neighbours/friends. For most of the Christmas period, the country is Red, the tightest restrictions in place. But, bizarrely, not dissimilar to England, restrictions are reduced for one day, the 26th of December, allowing visits to families and friends. Any other movement out of your local area has to be supported by completed paperwork giving details of where you are going and why.

THE COLOUR IS ORANGE

In England, January 6th sees full lockdown restrictions back in place.

The police in Gubbio continue to issue €400 sanctions to those found not wearing masks when out in the town. On January 31st, 14 new positive covid cases are reported in the town, the total of new cases for Umbria, 294. On Monday, February 14th, the Mayor of Gubbio, Filippo Stirati, brings together the municipal council in the Palazzo Pretorio to decide on future actions, if any, that should be taken locally. After the meeting, Stirati saying that it is very likely that there will be 'further crackdowns necessary.' In the end it's decided that Gubbio as an Orange Zone will be extended until February 15th. On a wider, regional scale, there is the growing likelihood that certain parts of Perugia will go Red.

It's Sunday morning, January 17th, 2021. Looking out of the window, the garden is already white, it's snowing heavily. Strange how being in lockdown gets you excited about the most mundane things. I feel like a child. I have the urge to rush outside and play. The snow is an unexpected surprise. The forecast had only promised a chilly, grey day. I feel sorry for the short life of a snowman.

I don't see myself as an anxious person, someone who worries. But the restrictions placed upon us increasingly played on my mind. The first, the second, now the third lockdown, how many more will there be? If I had an ounce of musical talent, I would have been placing notes and words on paper: Limbo Land Lockdown Blues. I'm so tired of living with my life on pause. I desperately want things to change. And then I chastise myself again. What do I have to complain about? Stop feeling sorry for yourself, stop being so indulgent and selfish. In comparison with many people around the world you're relatively safe, living in the mountains of beautiful Umbria. I have the support of my close neighbours. I have the daily opportunity to step out of the door to my home and go on the most magnificent walks. The land is starting to come to life again. The sky is deep blue. I can keep myself occupied, gardening, working on the vegetable plot, reading, writing, going for a run. Rationally I know all this, but it's starting to feel like I'm living in a goldfish bowl. It's most certainly beautiful but it's still a goldfish bowl. I'm sure I would benefit from having the brain of a goldfish, it would be a definite positive. Each day would be a totally new and exciting experience. And the next, and the next and the next.

Human contact outside your 'bubble' is against the rules. To have close contact is illegal. Regular contact with my daughters in the UK continues, yes, but when life is in pause mode there is so little to talk about. 'What have you been doing?' feeling like a rather pointless enquiry. 'Normal' just feels so far away. Mindfulness, living for the moment, feels absolutely impossible. Although I have daily contact with my neighbours, at a distance, I feel a deep sense of isolation, my life frozen.

For a time, the EU response to the Covid crisis feels to be confused, disjointed and inadequate. Surely there should be a collective response, rather than leaving it to individual countries. In the UK there appears to be a plan, well to be exact, four slightly different plans depending on which country you live in. Boris Johnson's lips may have a vague connection with truth and reality, he may well be offering false hope, this being his most common default position, but from where I am in Italy, it at least feels like a plan. You see, lockdown restrictions must have had a severe effect on me. Have I just given Boris Johnson half- hearted 'praise'?

March 8th, England begins a phased exit from lockdown restrictions.

On March 18th, 2021, Italy remembers all those who had fallen victim to Covid-19, the media again showing the army trucks in Bergamo that carried the bodies away.

By March 2021, there had been 2.5 million Covid-19 deaths worldwide. In late February 2020, Italy had found itself the epicentre of the virus in Europe. Despite this, other countries didn't effectively respond to what was unfolding. How will history judge the way different countries tackled the pandemic? By the spring of 2021, one quarter of all Covid deaths in the UK were in care homes. And yet it would appear in the perceptions of many, that the UK had gone from being the sick person of Europe to the 'golden boy' because of the apparent success of the vaccine roll out.

For the briefest time in Italy, restrictions, although still in place, become a tiny bit more relaxed. It gives false hope. By March 2021 the whole of country is, once again, stuck in either Red or Orange, the colours for different regions changing almost on a daily basis. Only Sardinia has a choice of three colours. It really does feel that Covid will never start to weaken. And then, one morning, Aldo tells me that Claudio, part of a husband-and-wife team that runs the little café in Colpalombo, has Covid. He then goes on to say, that it's not a serious case. One week later, Claudio is in hospital in Perugia. Two days go by, and I hear news from Aldo that Claudio is in intensive care. Three days later, Aldo informs me that Claudio has sadly died.

I attended two funerals during the flux of Covid restrictions, both in 2020. Federico, my elderly neighbour, the one who remembered the Germans in Gubbio, died, not from Covid, simply the result of old age. His funeral a strange and even sadder event because of Covid restrictions. The other person was my cousin's husband in Germany, Heinz. Always a happy, cheerful person, often with a cheeky tale to tell, a cheeky grin on his face. Out walking in the forests most days, to the gym a couple of times per week. He died, not from Covid but from cancer. His funeral in Germany, restricted to an outside event in the cemetery, the male voice choir, of which he had been a member, singing by his graveside.

There had been two other deaths, well before the Covid-19 pandemic. I wasn't sure when to tell you, so I guess it may as well be here. In the summer of 2019, Aton suddenly died. The week had been incredibly hot, with everyone, animals and humans, feeling lethargic and fatigued, Aton much the same. Friday evening, he wasn't his usual, energetic self - Saturday no better. I'd decided I would take him to my vet, in Perugia, Monday morning. Sunday morning, I was out visiting friends. When I returned, Aton was in his kennel, something that was very unusual. He looked to be asleep. The sad reality is, he had died; from what, I have no idea. It was a sudden and incredibly sad loss, totally unexpected. Aton, my close companion for over three years, no longer with me. Now I'm concerned that you may think that I'm equating the death of a dog with that of humans. That's definitely not my intention, I just thought that I'd better let you know of the sad loss.

The other death that I have to report, is that of the 'evangelical vegan', Andrew. Sadly, in 2018, he died after suffering with prostate cancer.

On a much more positive note, the promising news is that by mid-May 2021, the EU's rate of vaccination has just about fallen in line with that of the UK and the US. Italy now vaccinating thousands of people each day. An army general, Francesco Paolo Figliuolo, has been put in charge of coordinating the vaccine programme. I'm not sure if he actually deserves the credit, but things definitely improve. On a less positive, personal, purely selfish note, I still don't know if I will be able, as a foreigner, to be vaccinated. Having access to a Covid vaccine becomes an exciting prize, for now, unattainable. There is one advantage to being a member of the older generation, if foreigners can get their hands on the prize, my age will push me closer to the front of those standing in line.

But there's great news from many in the US and the UK:

'Great news, I've had my Covid vaccine.'

'Great news, I'm getting my second Covid vaccine tomorrow!'

And the posts continue to be placed on Facebook. The repeated posts sending me into a mardy grumble (very much a Yorkshire term, 'mardy', I guess it equates with moody). I get that these people are excited. Honestly, I understand. I'm pleased for those who are being vaccinated; no, I'm honestly pleased. But enough already. I feel like I'm stood outside a sweet shop, looking through the window at all the smiling faces. In Italy I have no idea when I'll be invited in. So yes, I'm pleased they've had their first and even second vaccine, but do they have to keep telling everyone? And stop asking if you can now come to Italy! The country would love to see you back as a tourist, but not yet (ma non ancora). Having had the vaccine is not going to get you in. The reality is that, unlike the previous year, there is no singing from the balconies in Italy. And for a time, that's exactly how I feel. I live surrounded by the most beautiful countryside, I have the most wonderful Italian neighbours, but I really don't feel the inclination to sing; I feel depressed. Then I chastise myself again for being so selfish, in comparison to millions of people around the world I really have nothing to feel depressed about, but I still can't get rid of the feeling.

For a time, the situation continues to be confusing. Sardinia White with lingering bits of Yellow. If not in Sardinia, probably just like me, you were Red. Now this is easy to understand, you were stuffed, not able to do anything; confined to your home, bereft of almost all human contact. If not Red, then people are Orange, possibly Dark Orange, Reinforced Orange. However, Dark Orange is not officially recognised at a national level. No, I'm not making this up. To know exactly what you can and cannot do, you have to check with your local comune. But the colours can change with hardly any notice. The colours of Covid-19 are really affecting my mental wellbeing. If that's what's happening to me, what must it be like for millions of others? The colours that come from genuine human contact are the colours I want to see and feel. The colours of travel. The colours of adventure. On a happier note, I've just been listening to the first woodpecker. Spring is definitely here. Although the woodpecker didn't have much to say. I think he may have been just as sick of Covid and lockdowns as everyone else. He just kept banging his head against a tree.

I really needed to stop complaining. By the end of April most of Italy is moved to Yellow restrictions. And by the end of June, most areas have gone White, with the majority of restrictions now dropped. Safe distancing remains in place, but face masks only have to be worn indoors. The nationwide 'state of emergency' is to remain in place until December 31st. Basically this means that the government can reintroduce restrictions, if required, at short notice.

By mid-July 2021, virtually all of England's pandemic restrictions are lifted. If you remember, other parts of the UK were doing their own thing. Over 1,200 scientists back calls for the move to be delayed, the risks still too great. All concerns are ignored. At this point in time, the whole of the UK has had a total of 170,000 Covid related deaths. Although the vaccine programme has been incredibly successful, the number of serious cases significantly reduced, the vaccine does not remove all risks. A letter posted in the leading medical journal, The Lancet, supported by the 1,200 scientists states:

'We believe the government is embarking on a dangerous and unethical experiment, and we call on it to pause plans to abandon mitigations on July 19, 2021.'

I'm certainly no scientist, but I feel that removal of all restrictions is a reversion back to a position taken by Boris Johnson's government at the very start of the pandemic, the strategy of 'herd immunity'. This time, granted, with the support of mass vaccination. Over the coming months the number of serious cases certainly declines, but the numbers infected see a massive increase.

In July the Italian government introduces the country's Certificazione Verde (Green Certificate). Being in possession of what becomes known as the Green Pass is compulsory to do just about everything from August 6th. On a really, personal, positive note, I've been able to access my first and second Covid vaccinations, Pfizer/BioNTech and, as a result of this, I'm also able to get a Green Pass. At long last it really feels like life is beginning to open up again.

With restrictions on travel far less constrained, I take the opportunity to fly to the UK; it's over a year since I've seen my daughters. Now that all sounds simple enough, but as many of you will know, that turned out not to be the case, travel was still relatively complicated. Along with the Green Pass and Passenger Location Form, I'm also required to have a negative test certificate, simple enough. The thing is, the British government, in its wisdom, for some bizarre reason, will only accept evidence of a negative test in English, French or Spanish; I'm being tested in Rome. Negative in Italian = Negativo. I know, how could anyone possibly translate that? Fortunately, the Italian system has a little more common sense, my result stating Negativo and Negative.

In September the Italian government announces that all employees will be expected to be in possession of a Green Pass, a recent negative test or proof of recovery from Covid to enter the workplace. This will be implemented mid-October and last until December 31st. Non-compliance with this requirement could result in a fine ranging from €400 to €1,000. As you can well imagine, this is incredibly popular – not.

For a time, Italy goes through a few months of full-blown protests against government-imposed restrictions and sanctions, the hardships having been suffered by many, driving some people onto the streets. Although many of the protests are union-organised, they have a significant fascist presence, Forza Nuova in particular. 'No Green Pass, No Discrimination', a common slogan. Arguments about 'ultra-controlled populations' and 'freedom and liberty', used to support those who protest. I guess the main point of debate swirls around the concept of 'freedom'. A basic principle of any truly open and democratic society is the protection of individual freedoms. How far should any democratic government go in making demands on individuals and restricting certain freedoms? What do you think? Where are you in this debate?

The Italian Ministry of the Interior imposes a ban on all protests, 12th November 2021:

'From tomorrow, all marches will be prohibited, and this is true of all protests, not just the no vax ones.'

It could also be argued that such tight restrictions are a gift to the far right.

The fascists eager to ride on any discontent, representing themselves as the defenders of the people against an increasingly authoritarian state. From previous chapters you already know how cloudy and disorientating politics can be. Who decides who the 'good guys' are?

The surprising thing is, given the supposed reputation of Italians for not being that willing to follow rules, other than during the demonstrations, there had been almost total compliance with Covid restrictions, certainly more evident than in the UK. I can't think of a single situation during the whole of the pandemic, when I was indoors or on public transport where there had been a single person without a mask.

From December 6th, things become a little cloudier in relation to holding a Green Pass. There is now a requirement to have a Super Green Pass, this indicating that the holder has had a booster jab. In reality there is uncertainty about the booster being an absolute requirement. However, it is also possible to have a temporary Green Pass if you can show a negative test. As I said, a little cloudy.

On December 17th, the state of emergency, that should have ended on the 31st, is extended to the end of March 2022. I'm now back in the UK spending Christmas with my daughters. In almost all ways, England behaving as though Covid-19 had never existed. Just need to mention here, that I visited my relatives in Germany when travelling back to the UK, Passenger Location Form and negative test required in English. Negative in German = Negativ. I know, again, impossible to translate. Although I'm travelling back by car, I have to travel to Bonn airport to ensure I have a test result in English as well as German. Also, when back in England I have to have another negative test, obviously all of this done by private companies. A song by Abba comes to mind, something related to a rich man's world.

I guess you could regard this as positive news. The Economist identifies Italy as the Country of the Year. I may love lots of things about Italy, but this came as a surprise to me. According to the newspaper awarding this accolade, it's 'not given to the biggest, the richest or happiest country, but to the one that has improved the most in 2021.' It's awarded to the country for its politics. In comparison with the UK and the USA, the Economist may well have judged this right. A central figure in all of this appears to be the Italian premier Mario Draghi, described as 'a competent, internationally respected prime minister.' This is a far cry from the likes of Berlusconi and others. The eventual success of Italy's Covid vaccination rate is also singled out as 'amongst the highest in Europe.'

Whilst I'm still in the UK, the Italian government introduces another Decree, this coming in response to the Omicron variant. In February 2022, the government introduces a €100 fine for all Italians and foreigners aged over 50 living in Italy who have not been vaccinated against Covid-19. As you can imagine the mandate is highly controversial.

As Italy moves to the spring of 2022, the government is still anxious about totally relaxing Covid restrictions:

'As of March 31st, we have finished the state of emergency, but we are not out of the pandemic, we still need to act with caution.'

Plans to drop regulations about mask wearing inside public places and on transport are delayed until June.

With the vaccination programme having been in full swing since July 2021, on April 1st, 2022, Italy emerges from its two-year state of emergency, restrictions gradually being dropped. From June 1st, 2022, the Covid Green Pass is no longer required to enter Italy from EU member states or any other country.

Wearing masks when indoors is 'highly recommended' but no longer compulsory, other than in health settings, public indoor invents, public transport and schools. Other than in health settings, in England you can basically do what the hell you like.

The summer of 2022 has the definite feeling of freedom having returned.

And the most important piece of information that you'll be pleased to know, is that the very close friend of my daughters, the woman more like a sister, the nurse who found herself on life support, did, against all the odds, recover. Although in a wheelchair, after several weeks, a time that she has little memory of, she left hospital at the end of May 2020, looking weak but smiling. Did 2023 find her fully recovered? Unfortunately, that's not the case, she remains a victim of Long Covid. Like many people, Covid had ravaged her body.

CONSPIRACY

Interwoven with everything that everyone went through with the Covid-19 pandemic, from the restrictions on freedoms, the fear of debilitating illness, to the possibility of an early death, we have had to live with the conspiracy theories. Some notion that it all was, still is, a 'scamdemic' or 'plandemic'. The whole thing fabricated, foisted on an entire world population by the powerful to maintain some malign control. The vaccines yet even more proof, if more proof was needed, that global powers, in this case Big Pharma, had deliberately created a scenario in order to gather in massive profits. Not that I have any real trust in global pharmaceutical companies, clearly massive profits will have been made. And the 'craziest' of all, that the vaccines are used as a tool to track people. I don't know, some sort of bizarre notion that people are being injected with a type of liquid microchip.

Then there are those far less crazy, those who trust that their strong physical and emotional wellbeing is protection enough against any virus, including Covid. The virus accepted as real enough but you don't need a vaccine. A good healthy diet, a reasonable fitness regime and the right supplements, will ensue protection enough. All you have to do is ensure that you optimise your immune system. Obviously reasonable health, fitness and a good diet can help in all sorts of positive ways, but debilitating illness and premature death both have an annoying habit of being unpredictable, striking even the most supremely healthy person in both mind and body. Getting out the yoga mat each day and swallowing additional vitamin D won't do you any harm, but equally they won't provide anyone with an impregnable shield. But hey, look at me, I know, I'm just one amongst the millions of other 'sheeple'.

An American doctor, interviewed by the Los Angeles Times, gives us a bit of an insight:

'My patient sat at the edge of his bed gasping for air. He had tested positive for corona-virus ten days ago. He was under 50, mildly hypertensive but otherwise in good health. He finally ended up in the ER with dangerously low oxygen levels, exceedingly high inflammatory markers and patchy areas of infection all over his lungs. His wife and two young children were at home, all three infected with the virus. He and his wife had decided not to get vaccinated. My patient died nine days later of a stroke. We did everything we possibly could to save him.'

'Vaccine refuseniks': I guess some have genuine anxiety, even if the concerns are rebuffed by medical science. As I've already said, I did, in the end, get both my first and second dose of the Pfizer vaccine in Italy. After a confusing start, the whole process was eventually well organised and efficient. And I was then more than happy to have a booster dose when I visited the UK in December 2021. When I went to Cuba, I had no idea what was in the jabs. But then I don't know what's in the over-the-counter medications I take, for say, a headache, I just know they work. All the vaccines I was given as child and those I've had as an adult, put into my body without me having any understanding of what they were. Guess what? They worked. I've never had tuberculosis, polio or any other potentially life-threatening illness. I will undoubtedly, in my small way, have contributed to the enormous profits of Big Pharma, but for now what's the alternative? I still only have one head and I'm reasonably certain that Bill Gates has absolutely no interest in my daily life.

CONCLUSION

I really can't leave all of this without asking why some nations got things so dramatically wrong? Throughout the world, all governments struggled, many making misjudgements and mistakes, whilst others appear to have been simply incompetent in handling the pandemic. Covid-19 ripped through rich and powerful nations, it found them feeble and unprepared. It didn't have to be like this, there had been warnings. Barack Obama speaking in 2014, warning that countries, together, have to be ready for possible pandemics:

'We have to put in place an infrastructure, not just here at home but globally, that allows us to see it quickly, isolate it quickly, respond to it quickly. So that if and when a new strain of flu, like the Spanish flu, crops up five years from now or a decade from now, we've made the investment and we're further along to be able to catch it. Funding is needed to partner with other countries to prevent and deal with future outbreaks and threats before they become epidemics.'

Early into Obama's first term in the White House he had committed to working with scientists to put together actions for dealing with possible pandemics. Well before the election of Donald Trump in 2016, a detailed plan and supporting infrastructure had been put in place. On his very first day in the White House, Trump ordered the dismantling of the whole lot, effectively rejecting the role of science in informing the administration's policy decisions. When Covid-19 hit the USA, the Trump administration was left like a rabbit caught in the headlights. Trump had left himself with virtually no coherent scientific support. His initial response to the pandemic, 'It will go away.' The warm weather, along with sunlight, will kill the virus. Further into the pandemic suggesting that untested pharmaceuticals and strong household detergents, taken internally, could have a role to play.

And the UK?

In 2016 Exercise Cygnus took place, a government simulation of a massive flu outbreak, the scenario being that 50% of the population were infected and 400,000 had died. The whole purpose of the exercise, that brought in professionals from a whole range of agencies, was to test the preparedness for such a national emergency. The outcome:

'The UK's preparedness and response, in terms of its plans, policies and capability, is currently not sufficient to cope with the extreme demands of a severe pandemic that will have nationwide impact across all sectors.'

At the time the final Cygnus report was not published, it was said to be covered under the Official Secrets Act. In October 2020, after repeated demands from a number of bodies, its findings were made public. Previously it had been argued that such a document would be 'too terrifying' for public consumption. Apart from certain legislative proposals (such proposals allowing for the speedy implementation of the Coronavirus Act in 2020), few of its recommendations were implemented. Perhaps one of the most damning indictments, is that care homes, a significant section of the report, were never informed of its existence and therefore had no knowledge of its recommendations. The majority of those who died during the pandemic, died in care homes.

You don't become the country with one of the highest death rates in the world without terrible mistakes having been made. If the UK had been fighting a conventional war and in just ten months had 100,000 civilians killed, it would be regarded as catastrophic. The UK government must have got things outrageously wrong, with levels of negligence at the very top of the system. When Boris Johnson announced the first lockdown in March 2020, Patrick Vallance, the government's Chief Medical Adviser predicted that, 'A good result would be fewer than 20,000 deaths.' At the time I simply could not imagine the numbers would eventually move well beyond 150,000. On January 26th, 2022, Boris Johnson looked into the TV camera: 'We truly did everything we could to minimise the loss of life.' Others cast doubt on what Johnson had to say (no surprise there then). Professor Neil Fergusson, a member of the UK Scientific Advisory Group for Emergencies (SAGE) said:

'Acting earlier throughout the pandemic', would have helped cut the number of deaths. 'Had we acted earlier and with greater stringency back in September 2020, when we saw the case numbers going up .... then I think a lot of the deaths we've seen in the last four months could have been avoided.'

Johnson's statement that everything possible had been done really was nothing new. His entire professional career is a catalogue of, at best spurious claims, more often, total lies.

According to Dominic Cummings, the person mainly responsible for putting together Boris Johnson's approach to Brexit and, for some time his chief political adviser for all things related to the Covid pandemic, stated on record that Johnson had been determined not to announce another lockdown in the autumn of 2020, instead being willing to accept thousands of deaths. Cummings quoting Boris Johnson as saying, 'No more fucking lockdowns - let the bodies pile high.' When quizzed about this Cummings said, 'I heard that in the Prime Minister's study.' Did Johnson actually use these exact words? You have to keep in mind that Cummings, after some sort of squabble/power struggle with Johnson, had resigned earlier in the year and walked out of Downing Street. For quite some time he had been as close to Boris Johnson as anyone could get, he was his chief political architect. Where was his moral backbone during that time? I suspect, as with Johnson, he's never had one. Cummings then sticking in the knife, good publicity for a possible future book deal? You're well aware that I'm no fan of Boris Johnson, I'll let you decide the truth. A national group, Covid-19 Bereaved Families for Justice:

'These 'bodies' were our loved ones. Mothers and fathers, daughters and sons, brothers and sisters, grandparents, husbands and wives. Those who have lost loved ones already have to cope with the lack of dignity many of their loved ones faced as they passed.'

A report from the House of Commons Science and Technology Committee and the Health and Social Care Committee, describes the handling of the Covid-19 pandemic as 'one of the UK's worst ever public health failures.' The UK was one of the first countries to develop a test for Covid-19, if you remember, something boasted about by government ministers. Authors of the report suggest that the government 'squandered' this potential advantage, instead turning it into a 'permanent crisis.' The report concludes that some notion of British exceptionalism and what appeared to be a 'slow and gradualist' approach to the pandemic, resulted in the UK doing 'significantly worse' than many other countries.

Increasing evidence would show that the British government not only got Covid wrong, but many at the very heart of power flagrantly broke the rules, the laws they had set and all in society were expected to follow. Incompetence on the part of Johnson and his government or yet another example of outrageous arrogance towards the British public? I am, of course, talking about 'Partygate', Boris Johnson's own Ethics Adviser eventually resigning in embarrassment. An ethics adviser for Boris Johnson? I'm desperately trying not to laugh. It must either have been the cushiest job in the world, Johnson having no understanding of ethics, so therefore there is little to do, or the busiest job because you were constantly having to dig him out of holes. But the downfall of Johnson was to come, much sooner than I could have predicted.

After a high-ranking civil servant, Sue Grey, had been made responsible for looking into accusations that Downing Street had broken many of its own rules, this included Boris Johnson, the eventual report stated that:

There had been multiple breaches of Covid rules during the pandemic

Alcohol and food were consumed at a number of gatherings, where the numbers present were well above the maximum set down under Covid regulations

Responsibility for allowing these events to take place rests with those at the very top of government

Sixteen events took place between May 2020 and April 2021

Several of these events appeared to be notably drunken and rowdy

The report concluded:

'Many will be dismayed that behaviour of this kind took place on this scale at the heart of government. The public have a right to expect the very highest standards of behaviour in such places and clearly what happened fell well short of this.'

Boris Johnson had been found with chocolate all over his face yet again, something that for weeks he denied over and over again in parliament.

The Metropolitan Police in London also carried out an investigation, eventually concluding that laws had been broken. Eighty-three people, including Boris Johnson, were found to have broken the law and had fines imposed on them, this being the first time in history that a serving British PM had been sanctioned for breaking the law.

And what of Italy, the USA and any number of other countries that have suffered enormously high death rates? As of the end of November 2022, the total number of Covid related deaths for the UK stood at 196,000. Italy, 181,000. USA, 1.1 million. Other countries, for example Ireland, 8,131. Denmark, 7,500. New Zealand 3,300. Just asking - bad luck, different circumstances, poor judgement, incompetence, indifference? Looks like some important questions need to be asked.

Total Covid related deaths worldwide at the end of March 2023: OVER 6.8 MILLION.

In Memory of Palmiro Massotti – Colpalombo

Taken by Covid-19.

Italia

'It's the kind of place that can have you
fuming and then purring in the space of a hundred
metres.

People who live in Italy say they want to get out,
but those who do escape all want to come back.
As you will understand, this is not the
sort of country that is easy to explain.
Particularly when you pack a few fantasies in your
baggage and Customs waves them through.'

· · · · · · · · · · · · ·

Beppe Severgnini

CHAPTER FOURTEEN

Falling in Love
with a Prostitute

....

*'I can't live outside Italy, which is strange because
I continually get angry with Italian ineptitude, envies,
ignorance and laziness. I'm like one of those people who
falls in love with a prostitute.'*

....

Massimo d'Azeglio

It was hot last night. One crisp white sheet covering my body. With the windows wide open, shutters fastened back against the white walls of the house, a gentle morning breeze finds its way into the room. I'm awake early, my sleep disturbed by the barking of a deer; must be close to the house. The wake-up call from the deer, joined by the yapping of my neighbour's tiny dog. Apparently the little black dog, Mirtillo (Blueberry), was a gift for Benedetta in the hope that it would give her company. To tell the truth, I'm not sure she's that interested. It appears to spend most of its days scampering round the garden, incessantly yapping.

The barking deer and the yapping dog are accompanied by a chorus of birdsong, along with the faintest sound of a cuckoo in the distance. I reach across for my watch, it's 5.30am. Barking deer, yapping dog, birdsong and cuckoo, are now joined by Aldo's cockerel. Why does he need a cockerel? He has never, to my knowledge, allowed any eggs to hatch out as little yellow chicks. I'm convinced that it's a symbolic representation of his Italian manhood. If you remember, I was quizzed about my insistence that I had no need of a cockerel when I purchased my hens. A shrug of shoulders – he's English.

The sun is just about to creep from behind the Apennines, I guess I may as well crank myself out of bed. I no longer leap out. These days, it's definitely more of a slightly seized up stumble, my body needing a few minutes to adjust. I think there should be the equivalent of WD40 for human limbs, just to give the bones and muscles a little easement into the day.

I'm not complaining. Well, I guess I am, but not really. In my head I'm still no older than my mid-thirties, my body, although still relatively fit and healthy, tells a different story. The lubricant of a strong espresso should help. I'll soon be in full working order and ready to face the run to Carbonesca. After returning from my long Covid exile in the UK, I'm once again enjoying warm, dry, even hot sunny days. I know it's hot, my Italian neighbours keep telling me it is.

'Fa molto caldo oggi, non credi? Troppo caldo.'

I've benefited from the early wake up call. Most of my run is in the dappled shade of oak trees that line each side of the road, the temperature just starting to nudge 21°C. The slightly humid air forces the release of a heady perfume from yellow gorse, heavy breathing filling my nostrils with the smell. With my head down, I continue the climb. The knowledge that on reaching Carbonesca my return to the house will all be downhill, and a focused mind, keeps me going. A few hundred meters past the bar, and then you can turn for the run back. On my downward return, I pass Filippo, another of my neighbours. He's out for an early morning walk with his dog. My sister gave him the name of 'Whisky Joe' a few years back, not because he's any particular connoisseur, it's just that in comparison to most of the Italians we know, he does like a drink. Certainly no more than the average British drinker, but noticeably more than the average Italian. Filippo was Andy's drinking partner at the grande evento in 2016.

Showered, I'm sat on the small balcony having a breakfast of cereal, fresh fruit and coffee. The sun is now above the Apennines, its heat already building; the mountain tops taking on a golden glow. Some distance away, the sound of chainsaws climb out of mist covered valleys. Closer to my position, the sound of birdsong and music from Lorenzo's radio. Gentle music drifting across the garden from his basement. Giovanni walks past with his placid Rottweiler. You remember Giovanni, the 'racing driver' who transported the tower of tables for the party. The usually placid Rottweiler that decided one morning to take a bite out of Ralph's dog. Shouted conversation takes place between us, him commenting on the length of time that I've been away in England.

The jungle that the garden had become during my absence, has been tamed. The task took a few days, but no need of the Grim Reaper scythe owned by Aldo. Even in the dry heat of the day the petrol mower, purchased in 2015, made relatively easy work of it. A few more plants have been purchased, just to fill in the one or two gaps. The rest of the garden has done well in my absence. I'm told that May had been an incredibly wet month, the unusual amount of rain probably saving most of my trees and flowers. The lavender path set out and planted in late October, looks particularly good. Purple lavender have grown at least three times the size they were when planted, brushing against my legs and releasing their slight scent as I walk past.

Days gently pass. A trip into Gubbio, a visit to the bank and a cappuccino in Bar Dragoni. Another day by the beautiful Lago Trasimeno.

To be in Umbria is to be with the past and the present. In Umbria the medieval still lives. Stand in any piazza and you feel the centuries fall away. For hundreds of years Umbria slumbered, swallowed in the 14th century as a Papal State, under the total control of the Catholic Church. Political, structural and cultural development almost stagnant, held in the grip of diktats from Rome. Although the grip of Rome had long gone by the early 1960s, many parts of Umbria were still locked in a time warp.

Henry James (American/British author) called Umbria, 'The most beautiful garden in the world.' It's green, predominantly rural, wooded, a region laced with valleys and mountains. Its people identifying with their hilltop town – Gubbio, Assisi, Spello, Todi, Trevi, Orvieto, Spoleto, Montefalco, Perugia. You already know them. I introduced them to you many pages ago. For centuries Umbria's towns conspired against each other, at times forming alliances, more often falling out and going into battle.

As you know, my closest village is Colpalombo, it sits on its hill to the back of my house. On passing the hamlet of Casa Colle, you climb up the twists and turns of the oak-covered road that takes you to Carbonesca. After climbing out of Carbonesca, the road eventually levels out before dropping to the village of Casacastalda, a distance from my house of about six kilometres (just under four miles). As you drive between the two villages, you have the most magnificent views of the Apennines. Even though I've had my little house for a number of years, I still find the panorama of high mountains, in the winter covered in snow, absolutely stunning. The undulating hills, valleys shrouded in early morning mists, a brilliant sunrise and a sizzling sunset, all of it still enchants me. Each and every day I remain astonished by the beauty on my doorstep. The villages of Carbonesca and Casacastalda are just as local to me as Colpalombo. I regularly walk to both, sit outside the bars with a beer, glass of wine, a gelato or a quick espresso. Apart from the time of Covid, I've been to the summer festivals held in each village for a number of years. Both have their individual story to tell. Both just as welcoming as the village to the back of my house.

Casacastalda, the name deriving from the Castaldi family who built the castle, is just one of a number of small villages that once formed outlying defensive positions for Gubbio against the continuing military expansion of Perugia. The older parts of the village date from the 13th century, the castle then the property of the Suppolinis, a noble family in Gubbio. It's recorded that Popes stayed here en route from Rome to the port of Ancona on the Adriatic coast. In response to the murder of Afficanus Civis Perusinius, a notary from Perugia, by the local inhabitants of the village, orders were given that the whole of Casacastalda should be completely destroyed. Fortunately for us, and even more fortunate for the people who lived there at the time, the destruction was only partially completed. Apparently, in 1490, Casacastalda slammed its gates to the tax collectors from Perugia. In response to this challenge, a unit of 500 infantry and cavalry were despatched to raid the village and surrounding area, looting whatever could be found.

For several hundred years, Casacastalda had an important relationship with Perugia as a centre of civil administration, covering a number of other villages and castles. For many centuries, the castle and village remained under the control of Perugia, that is, until 1798 when French troops arrived. The overwhelming power of the French brought the temporal power of Rome to an end. However, that didn't bring an end to conflict; armies of the Pope continuing to reassert the power of the Papacy right up to the unification of Italy in 1861. Casacastalda, for a time, belonged to Gualdo Tadino. In 1860, as one part of the forced unification of the whole country, the area was attacked and came under the control of Valfabbrica, as it remains to this day.

In rural Umbria today, in the medieval towns and villages, warring alliances are long consigned to the pages of history. But history is not forgotten. There's a deep connection to community, to a shared identity, even a shared spirituality. To some extent that's one of the appeals of being here, that strong sense of tradition. Whilst this is one of its undoubted appeals, it can also build unintended barriers for those who are not the 'same'. The very thing that is a strength, that deep sense of belonging, can also nurture a sense of mistrust towards those perceived to be 'different'. The political right taps into the impulse of people who appear to be the same, who have a desire to gather together, to defend against some notional threat. More often than not, it's some notional threat to the 'white tribe'.

I question the identification I have with my country of birth, my formative years, my youth, my professional life. How important is it to have a national identity? It's a question I posed at the very start of the book; I've yet to come up with a workable answer. What's the purpose? Does it have any more value than offering you the protection of a passport? I feel quite fortunate to have both British and German nationality, to carry both passports. For me it's like having two suits. One I wear for Italy. No, more than that. One I wear for Europe and the other for the UK. One is now undoubtedly of greater value, offering me wider choice and opportunity. It's certainly not the passport of monarchy, past empire and Brexit. I'm not rejecting my British heritage. I can't wash the Britishness out of me, whatever Britishness means and whatever form that takes. And it's not something I would want to do even if I could. In truth there is much that I enjoy about the UK. I still feel strong ties to the country. I worry about its future. I have very important investments there, my daughters, both with children, trying to form a secure family life.

Becoming a grandparent for the first time in March 2022 certainly made me look again at how I live my life in Italy. Kara the mother of a baby boy, Lucy now the mother of a baby girl born in January 2023. Having two grandchildren has produced a significant magnetic pull back to the UK. But fear not, I'm not going to leave Italy. There is so much about the country and its people that I love and enjoy. I'll split my time between my life in Italia and the delights of being with my grandchildren and daughters in the UK. Unlike those who have made a home in Italy from say, the US, Canada or Australia, the UK is little more than a two hour flight away or a two day drive. And in the Spring of 2023, Georgina (Georgie) came into my life with the promise of a new and refreshing love. A budding romance taking shape.

I go back to the notion of identity. There are times when I'm not totally sure what I am. The son of an English mother and a German father, certainly not a typical Englishman, even if there is such a thing. Having grown up in a Yorkshire working class family, predominantly British, but not quite, always a little different. And now living in Italy. When I'm in Italy, at times missing things that are just so commonplace if you live in the UK. Returns to the UK, with Germany squeezed between, always enjoyed. But with a restlessness to return to Umbria, to Italy. People in the UK ask me if I feel like I'm going home when I return to Italy. I tell them I do. And it's true, Colpalombo, Umbria, Italy does feel like home, but so does Yorkshire. Is it me being greedy?

Perhaps that's the luxury of travel, it allows you to identify with more than one place. If I'm really honest about Italy, would I feel the same if I could never 'escape', if I didn't have the easy ability to be able to dip back into my life in the UK? Covid lockdowns, the inability to be able to travel back to the UK whenever I wished, gave me a jolt, a stark reality check. It's a strange thing. You only really notice something is missing when you have left it behind. Obviously, my daughters, their children, other family members, and friends, but then there are other things that are of little significance when you're there all the time. Hedgerows, farm animals actually in fields, northern towns that you never realized were so northern, the towns taking on a new milestone grit beauty. British comedy and humour. The absolute convenience of everything, from any type of food to at least reasonable after-sales service. At the same time disliking the crowded hectivity, the uniformity of almost every town centre, the Americanisation of eating out, fast food giants screaming at you. Politics having sunk completely into the gutter; little attempt being made to hide the self-interest of those in office. Then I want to return to il bel paese, even with its many frailties.

Once you get to know Italy, really know it, right down to its ancient bones, you become absorbed by its overwhelming passion and its frustrations. It becomes a love affair. You know there are faults, there are parts of the relationship that should be better, at odd times you question if it has any genuine chance of longevity. But any doubts are reduced to passing foolish mind play. This is Italy and you love all of it; even when it can be incredibly antagonistic and uncompromising, you know that this is where you want to be. I totally get what Massimo d'Azeglio is trying to say about his love for the country. Italy is well rehearsed in the art of seduction.

Dreaming of the chance to live in Italy is not enough. You have to be able to see beyond the dream. You have to also be aware of Italy's demons. I wouldn't say that Italy has more than any other country. What's happened in the UK and the USA over recent years provides palpable evidence of that. Dream and do whatever you need to do to get here but acknowledge that the Dolce Vita is only one part of Italy, some may even describe it as a mirage. Living in Italy is not the same as holidaying in Italy. This may sound like an obvious statement to make but it's a fact that you need to fully understand.

Every country has its Jekyll and Hyde, along with all the other characteristics between. You need to be prepared to peel back the Dolce Vita veil. Life in Italy is not all about 'A Place in the Sun', a popular programme on British TV promoting the dream or the idyllic tale told in 'Under The Tuscan Sun'. To truly delight in Italy, to truly know the country and its people, you have to peel back the layers. Ask questions but be prepared for answers that may not fit with what you were expecting. Come to know Italy's antagonisms, faults and frustrations. There will be times when you'll complain about her and be critical. But you'll still defend her. In the end admitting that you are totally addicted and seduced by her beautiful peculiarities. There may even be times when you leave her. But you will come back. Italy knows you will return.

Holiday weather in Italy and living weather in Italy are two different things. Most foreign holiday makers dream of an Italy with endless hot summer days, crystal clear sea, warm evenings sat under a sky bursting with stars, an orchestra of cicadas. And they're right, that's exactly what you will find. But to live here throughout the year, you'll find that winter can be as cold as the summer is hot. You tend not to get the same drizzle grey days of February that you often have in the UK, days that feel at times to be endless. You do get rain, sometimes cold icy rain, and, if you decide to set up home in the hills and mountains, snow. Something we definitely get here more than I have ever come across in the UK is hail, sometimes almost half the size of a gob stopper. Now balls of ice that big can do some damage. When you take out car insurance, there is even a section asking if you want to include damage from hailstones.

The winter days are just as short, the cold winds just as cold. People shut themselves away in their homes, houses warmed by burning logs. I guess one of the big differences is that grey, damp days don't feel to be endless. The temperature remains cold, but you can almost always count on the certainty that a couple of wet, cold, windy, grey days, will be followed with crisp, dark blue skies and bright sunshine. Such days perhaps lasting a whole week or more, before you have a few that are damp, windy and grey again. And where I live, in the hills of Umbria, where snow topped mountains can be viewed from my garden, there are the mystical mists and clouds that rest deep in the valleys, swallowing whole villages, including Colpalombo. With the clouds so low, that some days you're not able to see the English gate at the edge of the garden. But you also know, that on almost all of these days, the low clouds and the heavy mist will, before the day has come to an end, be burnt way by the sun.

In Head Over Heel – Seduced by Southern Italy, Chris Harrison describes Italy's summers in this way:

'Summer is an annual honeymoon in an otherwise unhappy marriage. Until you've lived with the Italians beyond summer you've only seen their silhouettes.'

He goes on to rest the blame with travel writers, many failing to see that life in Italy can be just as frustrating as life in any other country, at times even more frustrating. But I guess the aim of most who write about Italy is to feed the Dolce Vita dream. Most people have a holiday romance with Italy. The time spent in the country giving a tantalising glimpse of bare flesh as it leaves stockings held by suspenders. Italy is sexy, beautiful, romantic and alluring. Italy and the Italians are carefree, they appear to be less tied to the rules and norms of ordered society. For the casual visitor, Italy holds the lure of promiscuous excitement and joy.

Barzani is even more dramatic than Harrison in giving your cheek a quick pinch in the hope of bringing you out of your dream:

'The Italian way of life cannot be considered a success except by temporary visitors.'

Almost all of my Italian neighbours and friends, if you had the opportunity to ask them, would totally agree with Barzini. It's a continuing conundrum, because, at the same time, they are loyal to their country, and, as you know, even more loyal to the region, their local town and village.

Luigi Barzini, when reflecting on his words written about Italy, thinks of his country in much the same way as he thinks of his mother. 'I have known her and admired her for a long time. I love her dearly.' And yet, at the same time, he feels he has to be honest about her failings. In the foreword to his book, The Italians, Barzini reflects on how he came to feel about his country of birth:

'I became disenchanted with some of her habits, shocked by some of her secret vices, repelled by her corruption, depravity and shamelessness, hurt when I discovered that she was not, after all, the shining paragon I believed her to be when I was young. Still, I could have no other mother. I could not stop loving her.'

Unless you are totally blind to the faults of your country of birth, I guess Barzini is no different to many of us. I reject the politics of the UK; I don't reject the country and its people. The same would be true of Italy. Donnachadh McCarthy in The Prostitute State – How Britain's Democracy Has Been Bought, sets out how the corporate elite, in league with some former and current British politicians, have sold the UK's political identity.

Do I love Italy? It's a strange question to identify with a country. Are you asking the question about a particular country in its entirety, the love of a country without question, without criticism? If that's the case, then no. Ti Amo Italia! England, the best country on earth! God bless America! I certainly don't feel an automatic loyalty to any country. I'm English/British, purely by accident of birth. I have no other claim. It's not something I achieved. To proclaim complete loyalty to any one country suggests a position of absolute blind submission: to be uncritical and unquestioning. Is patriotism/nationalism blind love of country?

There are times, even for me, when my 'tribal patriotism' rises to the surface. I think I've hinted at it before in relation to international football and international athletics. In the European Championships of 2016, Italy were playing against Germany in a quarter final match. Who should I support? Marcello and myself had arranged to have a BBQ in the garden of my house. Along with Aldo, we supply the food, others bring the drink. Marcello sets up a big screen, I hang a German and an Italian flag either side. We have three Americans, a German, an Englishman, an English/German (me), and the rest are Italian. I know, it sounds like the beginning of a joke. The national anthems are played, and I, just for a laugh, stand next to the German flag, Marcello next to the Italian. It's an excited, light hearted evening, lots of jokes being thrown around. The end result is a win for Germany, 6-5. I don't make a big fuss, well perhaps just a little.

In July 2021, Italy played England in the European Championship Final (the championship having been postponed from 2020 because of Covid-19). I'm sure if you are an England fan, you will have this game engrained in your memory. Marcello and Alicia have invited people to their house to watch the game and to enjoy snacks and a few drinks. A screen has been set up in the garden by Marcello. One inglese (me), a Dutch family who have just recently bought a house within walking distance of Marcello and Alicia's place, all others are Italian. It's a pleasantly warm evening, once again chat is light-hearted, laughs and jokes. Surely England can't let me down? A good start, England score within the first two minutes. As the ball hits the back of the Italian net, everyone looks at me. I remain silent, just a 'smug' shrug of the shoulders. The game then potters along until the 67th minute when Italy equalise. After 90 minutes, the game goes to extra time and then the dreaded penalty shootout, England's nemesis. Italy were, as most of you will know, victorious. All look at me in quiet celebration. Yes, I was disappointed, but I certainly don't find the loss of a football match devastating.

My perceptions, as I've said from the start of my ramblings, come through the eyes of a straniero. Not only that, apart from the occasional excursions to other parts of Italy, they come from my intimate relationship with a predominantly rural part of the country. My biggest city is Perugia, a relatively small city in comparison to Milan, the commercial heart of Italy. Exceedingly small when matched with Manchester and Birmingham in the UK or say New York in the USA.

Although Perugia has a university that attracts students from around the world (languages being a specialism), it would be an exaggeration to describe it as cosmopolitan. As you already know, Umbria is characterised by small hilltop towns and villages, medieval in origin and seemingly unchanged by time. It's the apparently unchanging nature of the land, the towns and villages, the customs and traditions, the people, that are so appealing. All combine, making the region of Umbria such an attractive place to visit and to make a home. As you are aware, geographically, Umbria finds itself roughly at the centre of Italy. In terms of prosperity, the region is probably in the same position. Umbria doesn't enjoy the wealth of the north, but equally, it's more prosperous than some regions of the south. Some may argue that my reflections on Italy are in fact based on one particular region, rather than capturing and accurately shining a light on the whole. In some ways that is possibly true, but at the same time, what I've found in Umbria I'm sure will be reflected in almost every region of the Italian peninsula. As you explore this beautiful country, discovering more for yourself, let me know. Italy has a way of absorbing you, drawing you in, not willing to let you go.

Sorry, my flow has just been interrupted. As I'm sat typing on the wooden table outside, a large, meter long, snake has suddenly appeared on the white stone of the patio. Its green body, speckled with black spots, momentarily comes to a stop. With its head slightly lifted, it checks the warm air with its tongue. There's no sound, it's definitely not that type of snake. I'm not sure why I've even pointed that out, Italy, as far as I'm aware not having any snakes that make a sound. Its tongue flicks out a few more times and then, with surprising speed, it passes, close to my feet, before squeezing through the green fencing separating my garden from the garden that once belonged to Gina.

With the snake having passed by and gone, I go back to trying to string words together. I can hear singing coming from Lorenzo's garden. Maria, his wife, is here for the day. It's Sunday afternoon, the sound of song a change from heated exchanges in speedy Italian that had been shooting around when she first arrived. 'Ascolta, ascolta! Ascoltami!' 'Non stai ascoltando.' 'Mamma Mia!' Their daughter and partner have arrived for Sunday lunch. Calm returns to the little hamlet of Case Colle.

Italy as a country sometimes feels like it has the same qualities as a bumblebee in relation to the physics of aerodynamics. The bumblebee shouldn't be able to fly, but it does. Italy shouldn't function as a nation, but it does. At times it feels like it's held together with sticky tape. Somehow it works, Italy functions and remains gloriously intact.

I know that I'm incredibly fortunate. One of the joys of actually living in Italy, and there are many, is that, at least for me, there is no day-to-day agenda, I no longer have a limited timescale. The tourist may have a few hours here or perhaps the luxury of a few days before they have to move on. I have no rush. I live Italian slow.

Tourists survey menus: no not this place, let's keep looking for that little something special, we'll know when we find it. Unlike Rome or Florence, in Umbria there is no one trying to entice you in. You will be generously welcomed, more often than not by members of the family who own it. In the many medieval hilltop towns of Umbria, you can also allow yourself to slow down, to truly savour what you find all around you.

The extended Italian family that has adopted me overflows with generosity and love; I've introduced you to them. How could I have known, when I bought my little bit of Umbria with nothing more than a phrase book in my back pocket, I would be so fortunate. Sometimes you have to simply take a leap into the unknown.

For many people from around the world, their dream is to visit Italy, Rome, Venice, Florence, Assisi, the Amalfi coast, Sicily. I sometimes have to actually pinch myself; I live in the county others dream of. I have Assisi almost on my doorstep, I can visit any morning, any day. The capital of Italy just a short train journey away.

By the time the train from Gubbio (Fossato di Vico) to Rome has reached Spoleto, the grey, heavy sky has been replaced by a pale blue. Fortunately, it looks like the sun is going to warm up the day. It's early November, I'm meeting three British friends, it's the first time they have been to Rome. They're staying in the city for two nights, their final destination being Jordan, yes the country of Jordan. For some bizarre reason, which makes no sense to me, it's cheaper for them to get a flight to Rome, pay to spend two nights in a hotel, then get another flight to Jordan, rather than paying for a direct flight from the UK. Perhaps you understand the economics of the aviation industry, I don't.

I'm not sure how many times I've been to Rome, above ground and below. On every visit I'm still struck by its living history. My three friends are seeing it for the first time, they slowly walk along its streets enraptured by what they see. And once again I realise how fortunate I am. I can visit this place at any time. Most people will only visit once, perhaps a couple of times in their entire life. Many will have travelled from across the other side of the world to be in Rome. The vast majority only able to spare the city a few days before they have to move on to see some other part of Italy.

In a little over two hours, for the price of €12.50, I can be in the city that millions dream of visiting. Within two hours I can be in Florence. A few more hours and I can be in Venice. A few more the Amalfi coast. Close to Switzerland, the Italian lakes. Towards the French border, Liguria and the Cinque Terre. Just under three hours by train to Bologna, a little more to Pisa, Lucca, Verona, the list is endless. To the very north the Dolomites, to the west Sardinia and Elba, to the very south Puglia, Calabria and Sicily. There are so many places that I don't have enough pages in this book to tell you about them. I've been lucky enough to visit many, there are still many I have to see. Being in Umbria, the very centre of Italy, its Green Heart, is the ideal place to be.

Umbrian towns and villages were most often built on hilltops for protection, and in the hope of being able to escape the malaria wetlands in the valleys below. The misfortunes of Umbria's history have become our medieval treasure. Although in the very centre of Italy, the region was for centuries forgotten, hurriedly passed through by nervous travellers. As you know, at times fought over by competing armies, eventually left in the uncompromising grip of the Papacy before becoming part of an Italian nation in 1861. Its history has left Umbria's medieval towns and villages almost unadulterated by change, and yet able to accommodate the modern.

It's in one of these medieval towns that you find me. It's July 2022 and I'm in the beautiful, honey-coloured, hilltop town of Montone (Uno dei Borghi più belli d'Italia), I think that I've mentioned the place before. Every year, this little town, with a population of less than 2,000, becomes host to the Umbria Film Festival. Five days of movies, discussions and workshops. The roots of the festival go back to 1995, a collaboration between the Italian Film Association and Terry Gilliam of Monty Python fame; apparently he has a house in the area. The festival has international appeal, each year attracting international stars. This year Stanley Tucci, the American actor, director and film producer, is in town, he's to be awarded with the keys to Montone and his film, Supernova, will be shown on the big, open-air screen in Piazza San Francesco. I've had lunch in probably my favourite restaurant in Montone, Ristorante Taverna del Verziere (Cucina Tradizionale – Sapori Autentici). The food here is delicious, eaten outside on a terrace overlooking terracotta rooftops and green hills. Can I tempt your taste buds with what I had?

Deep fried zucchini flowers with chickpea hummus and mortadella

Beef and pork dumplings with parmigiano cream, hazelnuts
and black truffle

Montefalco Rosso

Aqua frizzante

Espresso

After having walked round the town in an attempt to digest my lunch, I'm now enjoying a cold beer outside Aries Café in the main piazza. It's a hot day, the square filling with both locals and tourists. Mixed in with Italian, there are a number of American voices. And then, by pure coincidence, Stanley Tucci sits at the next table. People approach him, asking for a photograph, his autograph, a brief chat. He's polite, charming, very accommodating. Should I be yet another to interrupt his glass of wine? He smiles, obviously recognising that I'm a Brit, asking me where I'm from, questioning why I came to live in Umbria. We shake hands and he introduces me to his agent, she's just as easy going and polite. He talks about his connection to Italy and the film Supernova. I hand him a copy of my book, Lorenzo's Vest. He appears to be genuinely interested and delighted. Is this Stanley Tucci the actor or Stanley Tucci the person? I also give a copy to his agent, her response being that she will make sure that he reads it. With that, we shake hands and I leave him to be disturbed by other people.

You see, even in rural Umbria, even if it's for the briefest moment, you could also have the opportunity to 'mix' with the stars. The only other celebrity I've ever spoken with is Mick Jagger, he just happened to be walking towards me in a little village in Tuscany, I forget the name. We shook hands and that was about it.

Another hilltop town, just as beautiful as the last. As you drive towards the town of Trevi, it looks like its pastel colours have burst out of a volcano, a lava flow of homes and buildings spilling down the mountain. I'm here on a busy Friday morning in June, sat outside Caffè Roma, in one corner of Piazza Mazzini, with an obligatory cappuccino and pastry for breakfast. Don't worry, it's well before 11.30, the cappuccino cut off point. To the right of the piazza, from the position of the café, is the Town Hall, across the other side is Ristorante La Vecchia Posta. Around the edges of the piazza, a number of little shops and another couple of small restaurants.

I find that I'm being entertained by the loud, verbal, confrontation taking place between a female police officer from the town and the very irate, male recipient of a parking ticket. Despite the increasing verbal aggression from him, she remains very calm and polite, long dark hair falling from beneath her brimmed hat, her slight profile standing firm. She's explaining yet again why he has a ticket. He fakes walking away. He does this a number of times, but after only a few steps he returns, his outrage even louder than before. The small audience that has now gathered is clearly on the side of the police officer. All appear to know her, some chastising the irate male for his behaviour. He has little option, he has to walk away, she was always going to win. The people of Trevi go about their morning business, an unrushed calm has returned.

Give yourself at least a couple of hours to visit this little town. It won't take you long to explore its ancient, narrow streets, then stopping for a drink and something to eat. The whole area surrounded by olive groves.

Could Umbria be your Mediterranean idyll, your La Dolce Vita dream? Sun, wine, food, terraced vineyards and olive groves, lakes and mountains, medieval hilltop towns. From May into June, fields and roadsides peppered with gloriously red poppies, meadows thick with wild flowers. A land not just populated by people. A land populated by wild boars and deer, porcupines, wolves, and the occasional bear. Umbria offering endless diversions from the anxieties of modern life. A region that allows you to be pampered. In Umbria, the modern and the medieval share the same space. There is no contradiction in the juxtaposition of centuries. In Umbria the past sits side by side with the present. You can touch, taste and breathe Umbria. To be in Umbria is to be embraced in green, oak-covered comfort. But, as you know from the pages of a previous chapter, Umbria, just like many parts of Italy, can at times tremble, evidence of the peninsula's geological fragility.

The final week of June 2022, I'm walking through fields carpeted with millions and millions of brightly coloured wild flowers, bright reds, purples, shades of violet, pinks, yellows, whites and crimsons. You know of it already; I've spoken about it earlier in the book. It's known as Castelluccio Fioritura. From a distance, the floor of this wide flat valley, created from tectonic collapse, looks like it has been woven or hand stitched, a patchwork quilt, stretched out between the high mountains that enclose it. At points, the reds so bright that they look like fresh blood smeared over the land. This is the Piani di Castelluccio, part of the Monti Sibillini National Park, one of the most stunning areas of the Apennines in Umbria. Between the blanket of flowers, there is pasture and the cultivation of lentils. You may even hear the area spoken of as 'Castelluccio, the land of the lentils.' Wooded areas are sparse at this height, 1,300 metres. The area has deer, wild boars, wolves, wildcats, birds of prey and chamois. There are also brown bear and lynx, the two species wondering in from the even more mountainous region of Abruzzo.

The wide basin, with its surrounding high mountains, attracts visitors throughout the year, but it is the particular months of June into early July, when they come in their greatest numbers. Its highest mountain, at a height of 2,475 metres, is Monte Vettore. At one edge of the basin is the little village of Castelluccio di Norcia, that I've mentioned before, more often simply known as Castelluccio. At a height above sea level of 1,452 metres, it's one of the highest settlements in the Apennines, for many centuries, this tiny village must have been almost totally isolated. The village sits on its hilltop island, surrounded by the pasture and agricultural land below.

As I approached along the single road that stretches along the valley bottom, it was early morning, Castelluccio still hidden in low, white cloud. And then, as if by magic, the village arose, a string of white linen remaining around its base, a tranquil sea soon gone, evaporated by the sun. The village is tiny, just a few, steep narrow lanes, with names such as Via delle Fate (The Way of The Fairies). For centuries people lived here trying to make a living from cultivating the land and from grazing sheep and cattle.

You'll not be surprised to know that, just like many other parts of Umbria and the rest of Italy, the Sibillini Mountains are rich in folklore, stories of witches, medieval knights, wizards and necromancers, many of the tales now built into religious festivals; Catholic and pagan entwined. Tales of knights disappearing into underground caves never to be seen again.

Lago di Pilato, close to the summit of Monte Vettore, is said to have witnessed magical and demonic happenings. Legend has it that the lake led into the underworld, religious rulings forbidding access to the area, gallows placed close to the entrance of the valley. Other tales tell of fairies and beautiful maidens dancing on the shores of the lake, only to then quickly disappear, running over the edges of Monte Vettore. Religious 'scholars' from the middle ages stated that, 'Devils abide there and answer those who ask questions of them.' If you feel that you have the energy, walk up to the lake at 1,940 metres, perhaps you'll have the chance to sit and have a chat. Of course, there is always the possibility that you may never be seen again.

Unfortunately, as a result of the powerful earthquakes that shook the area in 2016, especially one on October 30th, there is now very little left of the original village. Few buildings survive apparently undamaged. The little village, on its little hill, is semi abandoned. Out of the 100 people who lived there full time, only a few now remain, others returning each day to open their business to tourists. Almost all business outlets are now found in prefabricated buildings. At the time of my visit in June 2022, there was just one building where any work was taking place in an attempt to rebuild. To say that there is no hive of activity to rebuild what has been destroyed would be an understatement.

What's left of the village is very different to the beautiful little town of Norcia, just some 28 kilometres (17 miles) away, the town hit by the same earthquake. At the end of June 2022, it felt like the whole of Norcia was held in a tight girdle of heavy scaffolding. As you know, I'd visited Castelluccio with my sister and her husband in June 2016, staying in Norcia for two evenings. At that point Castelluccio was as charming and solid as it had been for many years. It was only two months after this, in August, that the train thundered below my house in Colpalombo, a quake with a magnitude measuring 6,5. The quake that wiped out much of Castelluccio, shaking it to its very core, in October, slightly more powerful at 6.6. If you remember I was with friends near Assisi at the time.

The village of Castelluccio 'remains' where it has always been, although now much of it is broken and in rubble. Almost six years since the quake, it was sad to see the village still shattered. But there is a vibrancy about the place, visitors returning now that Covid restrictions have been lifted. The beauty of the natural area where it stands, is simply irresistible. Certainly, in the months of June into July, the wide valley, smothered in flowers, feels like perfection, breathtakingly beautiful.

Norcia, most of it built between the 14th and 17th centuries, famous for its architecture and its celebrity status for producing the best cured meats in the whole of central Italy and beyond. In fact, any butchers in Italy who specialise in pork meat, sausages, salamis and hams are called Norcini. Until October 2016 the town had been 'relatively' untouched by earthquakes, even the quake that devastated Amatrice produced little significant damage. But as you're already aware, October 30th changed all of that. Previous tremors, over a number of weeks, had sent people running into the streets. But this one was big. It struck the town on a Sunday morning, at around 7.40am, destroying or severely damaging buildings that had stood for centuries. The Basilica of San Benedetto, almost completely gone. Reports, at the time, showing nuns scrambling for safety as rubble and dust fell around them. Roads split apart, the walls of the town in partial collapse.

This may sound like a rather callous question to ask. Do you think Italian building companies 'relish', rub their hands together, just a little bit, at the thought of an earthquake?

In June 2022, tourists were starting to return to Norcia. Businesses and restaurants were open, but significant damage still remained. A good deal of the town still completely covered in scaffolding. As I walked around, I had the impression that much of this was in place simply to keep the most significant buildings standing, stopping them from falling into complete collapse, rather than any reconstruction taking place. The cost of rebuilding the Basilica alone, stands at an estimated ten-million-euro, half of this coming from the EU's European Regional Development Fund. There were still areas of the town with no access allowed, Zone Rosse (Red Zones), because buildings are unsafe. A number of the businesses that were once in the town are now accommodated in a street of wooden buildings outside its walls, for how long, it's really difficult to tell. They're said to be temporary, but in Italy temporary can last a long time.

Fortunately, my experience of earthquakes, so far, has been from some little distance, but still enough to make the ground tremble and the house shake. The country is without doubt beautiful, but a beauty that is fragile, at times literally breaking apart. Thankfully those moments are not that often. There has been very little, 'noticeable', seismic activity since 2016.

I don't really need to tell you that Italy has many foreigners enraptured, you're probably one of them. Often frustrating, sometimes confusing and at times even exhausting. Italy's cavalier ways, the boisterous, warm, nature of its people intoxicating. Italy has a way of stirring emotions; you feel life blooming inside you.

It's potential fragility, the possibility of the ground shaking beneath your feet, something that you have to accept as part of its unpredictable character.

I'm still delighted by all of Italy's magnificence, the occasional bad weather and even its many bugs. The supersized insects that you find sitting by your side. Beetles with horns, protected by black armour and wearing heavy boots. Grasshoppers that are enormous, with the habit of entering the kitchen through the open door, for a time still, then suddenly springing from one surface to another. Small black scorpions that creep out from hidden corners. The motionless praying mantis, with unmoving alien like eyes, who, when at last it does move, moves in robotic slow motion in the hope that you won't notice. I've never been witness to one striking at its prey, I assume it's done with speed, the same when the female bites the head off her lover. And, of course, there are the snakes of varying length.

In Umbria clouds appear as dreams floating across a deep blue sky. Unless those clouds are the opening act for a coming storm. August, as it usually is, has been hot, a number of weeks with no rain at all. But on this afternoon, thunder creeps menacingly closer from the direction of Gubbio. Thick, boiling, dark grey clouds swallowing the hills and more distant mountains to the back of the house. Another deep, vibrating, heavy drum beat of thunder coming from the very belly of the clouds. The first big drops of rain begin to fall. You could almost dance between them, they're so large in size and separate from each other. What had been a gently building breeze, gathers into a stronger wind, pushing the clouds directly over Case Colle. The sky darkens to black. The temperature pleasantly warm but with a fresher feel after the weeks of intense heat.

Rumbling thunder echoes around, bouncing off the hills. The downpour that's threatening, still to be released. Giant boulders being tumbled around in the thick darkness that hovers above. The rumble of thunder vibrating like the aftershock of some mini explosion. For a brief moment there's an interlude, each dark rumble appearing to weaken. The large drops of rain have stopped, the black sky teasing. When will the downpour empty over the house and garden?

The bombardment of thunder intensifies again, now appearing to come from all directions. The wind strengthens, gusting over the garden. It feels like anything not rooted to the ground will be swept away. Younger olive trees bend, desperately trying to resist its force. The almost storm-force gusts at last deliver the promised rain, a torrential downpour of biblical proportions sweeping almost horizontally over the garden. Giant sheets of metal rattle and vibrate above the house. Each shake bringing even stronger gusts of wind and even heavier rain. It's a torrent that the ground struggles to gulp down. A clap of thunder shakes the house with explosive force. The rumble of thunder then appearing to retreat, the wind lessening, the rain almost stopped. And, as is almost always the case, what felt like doomsday begins to slowly fade. Wisps of moisture-filled air now lifting from the ground. The smell of warm dampness soon dries, what had been impenetrable cloud cover begins to part, shafts of sunlight piercing through. The summer heat of August will be back tomorrow to accompany my morning run to Carbonesca.

So, I continue to be entrapped by the seductive power of this Mediterranean country, its people, its natural and structural beauty, at times its trembling fragility. Living with the pleasures and accepting the frustrations. Many beautiful memories have now been made here. All my thousands of words, put down in print, could never accurately capture what you find. It's rather like pointing your camera at some stunning scene, the resulting photo never quite matching what you see with the naked eye. You have to be here to see it, to touch it, to hear it, to smell it, to taste it, to experience Italy for yourself.

The next time you're in Italy, let me know. If you happen to be close by we could meet for a drink. If you've been to Italy and never explored Umbria, it really is something that you need to rectify. If you have been to Umbria and never visited Gubbio, well what possible reason could you have for making that mistake? In the future, don't let me know that you're in Umbria, once again missing out Gubbio, there is no justifiable excuse that I'll possibly accept. You can fall out with some people before you've even had a chance to meet them.

To be in Umbria, to be in Italy, at any time of the year is memorable. But an Italian summer is especially special. From June to September, to have the possibility of listening to live music each and every evening, much of it free, is simply unbelievable. Every village and every town has its own festival. Some in the mountains, others by a lake, some close to the sea. Hot days and warm evenings. Eating with friends, friendship shaded by olive trees. Tables and sparkling lights set between grape vines. Food that at times feels like a symphony in your mouth. A deep blue sky and a star-filled night. And if you live in the hills and mountains or you're just visiting, the possibility that a wolf, perhaps, will come calling, most often unseen.

People meet and chat, smile, laugh and joke. They dance and sing. They party on life, Italians having no need to drink to excess. 'Ciao, come stai?' 'Hi, how are you?' Come join us, eat with us, enjoy the night. Afterwards we'll slowly walk through the town. Through the streets of Rome, Florence, Palermo or Gubbio. Perhaps a cocktail in Martintempo. Italy holds you captive.

To be in Umbria, to be in Italy, is a chance for your body to breathe and your mind to relax. Allow Italy to absorb you, even with it's frustrating imperfections, accepting them and asking, what more could I want? But don't ever let me hear

you asking, why can't it be more like where I came from? You're here for the simple reason that it's not. Yes, there will be times when you will scream at her. And yes, there will be times when you will leave. But you know and Italy knows, you will return. You can't resist her charms, you can't say no. You will never be able to say, I've had enough.

There are so many ways to tell the story of life in Italy, this has been mine. That's it, you've almost reached the final page of the book. Just a few more pages to turn and you can put the book down. If you don't already live in Italy, go online, and book your tickets to travel here.

As I said at the very start of my ramblings, I hope I've enabled you to look at Italy with knowing eyes, asking questions that you may not have thought to ask before. If I have achieved that, then my job is done. One of the most rewarding compliments that I've had about my writing actually comes not from a foreigner, it came from an Italian neighbour and friend:

'Your words allow me to see things that I had stopped seeing. You make me ask questions that I'd stopped asking. I see Italy and Umbria through new eyes.'

And the politics, well everything that happens to us is shaped by political decisions. Without any doubt, over the past several years, the shape of politics has gone through incredible change, the impact on all of us difficult to ignore. Putin's invasion of the Ukraine is a prime example. And Covid-19, there is little more to say, its impact across the world immeasurable.

So, you have come to the end of my book. I certainly hope that you enjoyed the journey, you were entertained, at times you may have disagreed with what I had to say, that's fine. If we have the chance to meet we can debate and arm wrestle. Hopefully, you may have discovered something new, some snippet of knowledge that's fresh.

If you come to Italy in some expectation of finding perfection, the following quote comes to mind:

'If you look for perfection, you will always be disappointed.' Leo Tolstoy

Onwards to your next reading journey.

Hold on tight to your dream

Yea!!
Hold on tight to your dream

When you see your ship go sailing
When you feel your heart is breaking
Hold on tight to your dream

It's a long time to be gone
Oh!
Time just rolls on and on

When you need a shoulder to cry on
When you get so sick of trying
Just hold on tight to your dream

When you see the shadows falling
When you hear that cold wind calling
Hold on tight to your dream

. . . .

Electric Light Orchestra

OTHER STUFF

Acknowledgments

······································

Thank you to everyone, my Italian and foreign friends, without these very special people there would have been very few words to fill the pages of this book. Hopefully they will be happy with the way I have recorded my many experiences, especially if they recognise themselves in my jumble of words.

All books that eventually go to publication and then into the hands of readers, only get to that stage because of the support and advice of a whole group of people. Yes, the author feeds the words into a computer but without the endeavours of others, that's where those thousands of words would remain. So, many thanks to those who gave their time as first readers, giving valuable comment and feedback on the first completed draft before it went to proofreading and editing: Annette Wathen, Paul Wathen, Sally Stotton, Peter Jackson and Mike Bennett. Special thanks to Mark Stafford who has an ability that I simply do not possess, the ability to pick through each sentence and identify each clumsy mistake and unintended bug. Equally special are Lucy Hayward, Vian Andrews and Patricia Wordley for their critical and invaluable editing advice. Also, my thanks go to Karen Fox and Andrew Fox for their design work on the cover of the book and for gathering all of my rambling words into book format.

Finally, a big thank you to all who read Lorenzo's Vest, the comments and feedback received giving me the encouragement to write this second book.

OTHER STUFF

Bibliography

Andrews Geoff, *Not A Normal Country - Italy After Berlusconi*,
PLUTO PRESS LONDON, 2005

Gilmour David, *The Pursuit of Italy*,
PENGUIN BOOKS, LONDON 2012

Dickie John, *Mafia Brotherhoods*,
HODDER & STOUGHTON LTD, LONDON 2012

Dickie John, *Mafia Republic*,
HODDER & STOUGHTON LTD, LONDON 2013

Da Mosto Francesco, Francesco's Italy
BBC BOOKS, LONDON 2006

Barzini Luigi, *The Italians*,
PENGUIN BOOKS, LONDON 1964

Marshall Tim, *Prisoners of Geography - Ten maps that tell you everything you need to know about global politics*,
ELLIOT & THOMPSON, LONDON 2016

Umbria – Eyewitness Travel Guides,
PENGUIN, LONDON 2004

Marshall Tim, *Worth Dying For – The Power and Politics of Flags*,
ELLIOTT & THOMPSON, LONDON 2016

Journal of Natural Resources Policy Research,
VOLUME 2, 2010

Santini Loretta – Editor, *Guide to the Parks of Umbria*,
QUATTROEMME, PERUGIA 2003

Facaros Dana & Pauls Michael, *Umbria*,
CADOGAN GUIDES, LONDON 2002

Santini Loretta, *Guide to the Parks of Umbria*,
QUATTROEMME, PERUGIA 2003

Casa Editrice Perseus-Plurigraf, *Umbria Art & History*,
CENTRO STAMPA, SESTO FIORENTINE

Hatchwell Emily, *Umbria Eyewitness Travel Guides*,
DORLING KINDERSLEY LTD, LONDON 2003

The History and Civilization of China,
PUBLISHED IN CHINA 2003

Newell James, *The Politics of Italy*,
CAMBRIDGE UNIVERSITY PRESS, NEW YORK, 2010

The Rough Guide to Australia,
ROUGH GUIDES.COM, 2017

Obama Barack, *A Promised Land*,
PENGUIN BOOKS, RANDOM HOUSE, NEW YORK 2020

China,
LONELY PLANET GLOBAL LIMITED, 2017

McCarthy Donnachadh, *The Prostitute State: How Britain's Democracy Has Been Bought*,
3 ACORNS PUBLICATIONS, UK 2014

Montefiore Simon, *Speeches that changed the world*,
QUERCUS PUBLISHING, LONDON 2007

Marshall Tim, *The Power of Geography*,
ELLIOT AND THOMPSON LTD, LONDON 2021

Harrison Chris, *Head Over Heel*,
NICHOLAS BREALEY PUBLISHING, LONDON, 2009

Severgnini Beppe, *La Bella Figura – An Insider's Guide to the Italian Mind*,
HODDER & STOUGHTON, LONDON, 2007

A number of newspapers were consulted:

The Sunday Times

La Repubblica

Corriere Della Sera

The Independent

Corriere Dell' Umbria

New York Times

The Irish Times

The Financial Times

The Brussels Times

Washington Post

The Guardian

The Sun

Daily Mail

The Telegraph

Writing was also informed by:

www.statista.com

Eurostat Statistics

US Pew Research Centre

Lorenzo's Vest Notes from a house in Umbria

···

Why do people give 'Lorenzo's Vest' 5 stars?

···

Lorenzo's Vest is a book like no other I have ever read......and that, for me, a self-confessed book-alcoholic who reads 4-5 books most weeks is quite a statement. The characters drawn by Graham, the encounters, the detailed descriptions of the towns, large and small that he has visited, all paint a vivid picture of life in Italy's 'Green Heart' of Umbria. If you want one book to take you away from the humdrum and into a land of glorious welcomes, generous hospitality and an abiding wish to get to know it better, then I recommend Lorenzo's Vest to you! I know you will enjoy it!!!!

Lucy Haywood: GOODREADS

One of the best books I read in 2021. It brought me "back home" to Italy almost from the very first page. The writing is so realistic and true to life and the characters literally pop off of the page. Even though I live part time in Italy, I learned a lot from the book about country life, Italian history. Add this book to your reading list. I promise you won't be disappointed.

Joan Slavin: AMAZON

Graham does a fabulous job of bringing his characters to life. But not only that, he weaves in important details from Italian politics and history that illustrate the evolution of the country itself, as well as the strong cultural traditions of its people – information that really helps the reader understand Italian culture. Reading

Lorenzo's Vest has left me richer for the experience and has fuelled my desire to get back to Italy and make my plan a reality. I look forward to the day I can meet Graham and tell him I am now in his position – starting my own Italian journey. A truly enjoyable and inspiring read, I highly recommend it.

Linda Funay: GOODREADS

A brilliant read from start to finish. Full of humour, and a fantastic introduction to life and friendliness in Italy for someone who has never had the chance to visit the country and sadly will never be able to now age has crept up on me. I feel as if I have actually been there myself after reading this book.

Keith Pearce: GOODREADS

I enjoyed this book. The author draws in the reader to share his experience of buying a house and living among locals in Colpalombo, a small hamlet in the province of Perugia. Whether you are looking for a 'how to guide' to living in Italy or just a traveller seeking an authentic experience beyond the tourist track, this book makes sure you experience the real dolce vita in every way. It is more than just an account of life as an expat. It is a comprehensive and entertaining travel guide, it is a well-researched historical account of Italy, local areas as well as other regions. It delivers passion, enthusiasm, humour and ultimately acceptance.

Sunflower Publishing: AMAZON

This is a terrific book especially if you love Italy and a little history but most of all if you love a good personal yarn. It is a tale which is funny, charming, personal and yet educational, while told in a gentle, and at times, self-deprecating style which inevitably leaves you warming to the man, his neighbours and the beautiful Umbrian countryside in which he now lives.

Jim McGinley: GOODREADS

This book is so much more than the musings of someone lucky enough to have bought a house in Italy. It describes the challenges and delights of moving to a different country with humour and joy. It is a fabulous book for finding out about Umbria, with excellent pieces capturing the beauty of towns, villages and stunning landscapes. Graham's friendly writing style makes you really share in his delight at all he sees. By immersing himself in the life of his community, Graham comes over as someone who relishes and values all opportunities that come his way. He has a fantastic ability to combine his own personal growth in understanding of Italian customs and culture with an analysis of the history and political developments of the country alongside the nuances of developing relationships in his own little community. This is a sensitive, thoughtful and thoroughly delightful read. I cannot recommend it highly enough.

Janice Whelan: AMAZON

This book makes you feel like you are actually in Italy. I love the vivid descriptions of the people he meets and of all the beautiful places that he visits, it's laugh out loud throughout and at times, profound. The use of poetry is an added bonus. A thoroughly enjoyable read!

Gaynor Palfrey: AMAZON

A very enjoyable read. The author cleverly, sympathetically interweaves information into his own personal story with a rich dose of sunny humour. I shall be gifting copies to my friends who already know and love Italy, and also for those yet to visit.

Gretchen Traill: AMAZON

I'm planning a trip to Umbria in Italy and saw this book by Graham Hofmann after following a page - Mystical Umbria - on Facebook. It's a detailed read of living the dream - buying a second home in Italy! Graham paints a wonderful word portrait of small-town Italy - negotiating the purchase, fitting in with the neighbors, rambling the countryside and living la dolce vita. Highly recommended.

Tanya Bishop: AMAZON

Milton Keynes UK
Ingram Content Group UK Ltd.
UKHW010020070324
438984UK00004B/57

9 781803 022260